T0214277

Communications
in Computer and Information Science 1318

More information about this series at http://www.springer.com/series/7899

Luca Longo · Maria Chiara Leva (Eds.)

Human Mental Workload

Models and Applications

4th International Symposium, H-WORKLOAD 2020
Granada, Spain, December 3–5, 2020
Proceedings

 Springer

Editors
Luca Longo ⓘ
Technological University Dublin
Dublin, Ireland

Maria Chiara Leva ⓘ
Technological University Dublin
Dublin, Ireland

ISSN 1865-0929　　　　　　ISSN 1865-0937　(electronic)
Communications in Computer and Information Science
ISBN 978-3-030-62301-2　　　ISBN 978-3-030-62302-9　(eBook)
https://doi.org/10.1007/978-3-030-62302-9

This Springer imprint is published by the registered company Springer Nature Switzerland AG
The registered company address is: Gewerbestrasse 11, 6330 Cham, Switzerland

Preface

This year has been a very challenging one across the world due to the need to change and adapt in the context of a worldwide pandemic. The pandemic has affected many areas of our normal living, working environments and conditions including changing the landscape for many areas where mental workload can be experienced. We have seen a steep increase in remote working settings across various workforce and operational environments, and an increase in the weight of contextual conditions affecting it not just for remote working situations but also for frontline workers. These people have continued in their safety critical tasks with the extra weight of performance shaping factors such as fatigue from longer working hours to cover for the need of possible reduced staffing due to sick leave and/or the need to isolate. These factors have been witnessed in healthcare, in urban transports, in logistics, and in food manufacturing and distribution services, just to name a few. Similarly, external stressors have been observed, such as the fear of being at personal risk and/or with a changed family-related workload. In all of these situations, we have also recovered a sense of the role of human performance in an imperfect world not only as part of the imperfection but also as the one able to maintain continuity even in the face of adverse circumstances, with unexpected resilience. In this context, the requirement for cognitive resources has certainly seen an increase. Therefore, there is still a need to discuss the assessment of mental workload and its implications on human performance. The modeling of human mental workload can be used to inform the design of interfaces in this changing context, the technologies we are relying on more and more for remote working, monitoring of conditions, and our direct frontline activities, so as to ensure they can be better aligned to the human capabilities and limitations. There are many operational definitions and contexts to study mental workload in action in various fields, different ways to approach the problem, its dimensions, and the mechanism to aggregate these dimensions and the various contributing factors. This trend is also confirmed by the best papers selected in this book from the proceedings of the 4th International Symposium on Human Mental Workload, models, and applications (H-WORKLOAD 2020). The conference was held during December 3–5, 2020, in Granada, Spain; the conference was held virtually due to the COVID-19 pandemic. Selected papers have gone through a strict review process, with an average of four reviews for each paper. Some authors considered task-specific dimensions, while others chose a combination of task and user-specific dimensions. Primary researches have mainly employed self-reporting measurements or a combination of psychophysiological techniques. However, the development of a generally applicable model that manages to incorporate task, user, and context-specific dimensions is yet to be achieved.

As pointed out by an author in one of the chapters in this volume, the development of new methodologies should try and verify how subjective, task-objective, and physiological measures can work well together, so as to achieve cross validation and the convergence of various measurement techniques. Furthermore, other authors in the volume also highlight that it is useful to focus on complex safety-critical systems alongside manufacturing contexts where mental workload and fatigue may rather be induced by repetitive tasks, generating feasible ways to approach and assess the issue in the real contexts. We hope to continue as a community to provide steps in the right direction for progressing the field in terms of the fundamental problems and in terms of the usefulness and inclusiveness of their applications in various domains such as the models and measures adopted in rail, nuclear industry, aviation, manufacturing, and healthcare.

This book endeavors to stimulate and encourage further discussion on mental workload, its measures, dimensions, models, applications, and consequences. We believe this discussion should be multidisciplinary and not only confined to ergonomics. It should be at the intersection of human factors, computer science, psychology, neuroscience, and statistics. This book presents recent developments in the context of theoretical models of mental workload and practical applications aimed at task support and mental workload management in operations. This is why the contributions have been organized in two sections: models of mental workload and applications.

The idea for the H-WORKLOAD 2020 symposium is supported by the Irish Ergonomics Society, the conference Organizing Committee, and the reviewers without which neither the conference nor the book would have been realized. A special thanks goes to the University of Granada, Spain, Faculty of Psychology, for hosting the conference, even if in a virtual format, and the Technological University Dublin, Ireland, for all the support received.

September 2020   M. Chiara Leva
                                                                          Luca Longo

Organization

Organizing Committee

General Chairs, Editors, and Program Committee Chairs

Luca Longo	Technological University Dublin, Ireland
Maria Chiara Leva	Technological University Dublin, Ireland

Local Chairs

Enrique Muñoz De Escalona Fernandez	University of Granada, Spain
José J. Cañas Delgado	University of Granada, Spain

Finance Chair

Bridget Masterson	Irish Ergonomics Society, Ireland

Marketing, Graphics, and Publicity Chairs

Sagar Saxena	Technological University Dublin, Ireland

Program Committee

Julie Albentosa	French Armed Forces Biomedical Research Institute, France
Pietro Aricò	Neuroelectrical Imaging and BCI Lab, Fondazione Santa Lucia IRCCS, DIIAG, Sapienza University of Rome, Italy
Gianluca Borghini	Sapienza University of Rome, Italy
Bethany Bracken	Charles River Analytics, USA
Joan Cahill	Trinity College Dublin, Ireland
Giulia Cartocci	Sapienza University of Rome, Italy
Martin Castor	The Group for Effectiveness, Interaction, Simulation, Technology and Training, Sweden
Jose Cañas	University of Granada, Spain
C. Chauvin	Université Bretagne Sud, France
Dick De Waard	University of Groningen, The Netherlands
Micaela Demichela	Politecnico di Torino, Italy
Gianluca Di Flumeri	Sapienza University of Rome, Italy
Jialin Fan	Cardiff University, UK
Pedro Ferreira	Centre for Marine Technology and Ocean Engineering, Portugal
Matjaz Galicic	Mott MacDonald, Ireland

Glauco M. Genga	Società Amici del Pensiero Sigmund Freud, Italy
Bridget Kane	Karlstad University, Sweden, and Trinity College, St. James's Hospital, Ireland
Alison Kay	Centre for Innovative Human Systems, Trinity College Dublin, Ireland
Fiona Kenvyn	Metro Trains Melbourne, Australia
Florence Lespiau	CHROME, APSY-v, Lespiau Université de Nîmes, France
Patricia Lopez de Frutos	CRIDA, ATM R&D, Innovation Reference Centre, Spain
Anneloes Maij	Netherlands National Aerospace Laboratory (NLR), The Netherlands
Alice Marascu	Nokia Bell Labs, Ireland
Enrique Muñoz de Escalona Fernández	University of Granada, Cognitive Ergonomics Group, Spain
Fedja Netjasov	University of Belgrade, Serbia
Giuliano Orru	Technological University Dublin, Ireland
Maria Gabriella Pediconi	University of Urbino Carlo Bo, Italy
Sally Prescott	Milcot Engineering Services Ltd., UK
Melinda Ratkai	University of Malaga, Spain
Philippe Rauffet	Université Bretagne-Sud, France
Bujar Raufi	South East European University, North Macedonia
Audrey Reinert	The University of Oklahoma, USA
Lucas Rizzo	Universiade Federal de Minas Gerais, Brazil
Alfred Roelen	Netherlands National Aerospace Laboratory (NLR), The Netherlands
Vincenzo Ronca	BrainSigns, Italy
Alessandra Sala	Nokia Bell Labs, Ireland
Sagar Saxena	Machine Learning Labs, Technological University Dublin, Ireland
Andrew Smith	Cardiff University, UK
K. Tara Smith	Human Factors Engineering Solutions Ltd., UK
Giulia Vilone	Technological University Dublin, Ireland
Alessia Vozzi	BrainSigns, Italy
Mark Young	Loughborough University, UK
Rolf Zon	Netherlands National Aerospace Laboratory (NLR), The Netherlands

Contents

Models

An Objective Measure for Detecting Workload and Errors in Monotone, Repetitive or Fatigue-Causing Environments Using Pupil Variation

Oliver Straeter[✉]

Department of Human Engineering and Organizational Psychology, University of Kassel,
Heinrich-Plett-Strasse 40, 34132 Kassel, Germany
straeter@uni-kassel.de

Abstract. The measurement of workload in real working situations is a challenging issue. Subjective measures like questionnaires are often too intrusive because they disrupt the worker from the task and its workload, which then changes the assessment. Also, they are subjective measures always bringing up the argument whether it is a real impact or just a subjective opinion. Both issues diminish the validity of the questionnaire approach. Objective psychophysiological measures, on the other hand, are difficult to apply, as they are often confounded with physical load. As an example, heart rate variability is only a 'half-way valid' psychophysiological measure as physical load interplays with this measure; hence heart rate variability cannot be used in physically demanding situations. This deficiency excludes this parameter for almost all real working environments. The paper suggests using pupil-variation as a valid indicator for monotone or fatigue-causing work in real working conditions. The indicator was developed in different studies such as long-haul flights, manufacturing and computer-based training. This paper will outline the methodology and key results of the studies.

Keywords: Eye tracking · Objective workload measurement · Manufacturing · Fatigue · Monotony

1 Introduction

The measurement of workload is one of the challenging aspects in human factors design. In order to measure workload, subjective and objective measurements can be distinguished. Mental workload can be defined as a measure of human ability to retain focus and rational reasoning while processing multiple activities in a real work environment and facing external distractions [1]. Mental workload is a concept that is strongly correlated with task demand and performance in the literature, as both high level and low level of experienced mental workload affects negatively task performance and can be at the root of human errors [2, 3]. One of the main reasons to specify and evaluate the mental workload is to "quantify the mental cost involved during task performance in

© Springer Nature Switzerland AG 2020
L. Longo and M. C. Leva (Eds.): H-WORKLOAD 2020, CCIS 1318, pp. 3–12, 2020.
https://doi.org/10.1007/978-3-030-62302-9_1

order to predict operator and system performance" [4]. Hence in safety critical domain there is an increasing demand for assessing mental workload in real-time so as to identify a possible precursor of poor human performance. Unfortunately, one of the major difficulties encountered in studying mental load is its actual assessment. Traditionally, mental workload is evaluated through subjective and objective methods [5]. Subjective measures are obtained from individuals' subjective estimations of task difficulty and the overall person perceived experience of the task [5–7]. On the other hand, objective measures generally include metrics such as task score and accuracy. On the subjective side of measurement, one can distinguish questionnaires or thinking aloud methods for instance [8]. On the objective side, psychophysiological measurements come into play. They include physiological responses to mental activation and many studies have been able to highlight pros and cons and validation of physiological responses for quantifying the mental workload of individuals [9, 10]. Among them the most promising are neurophysiological measurements such as electroencephalography (EEG) signals that are directly correlated with mental demand experienced during the task [11] and the assessment of pupil diameter (pupillometry) [12] is also regarded as a useful non-intrusive way of collecting objective physiological data, which reacts to mental workload. While the first ones have the issue to interrupt workflow and hence influence the outcome of the measurement, the latter ones have been reported as having problems with interference of other physiological or environmental parameters that often requires them to be used mainly in laboratory environments. As an example, regarding the issue of questionnaires, if the questionnaire is to be answered every five minutes or so, the person that is measured has to interrupt his work, make up his mind on his workload and then make the rating. Therefore, this process works as a procedure that diminishes the validity of the rating and the realism of the workflow. As an example, regarding the issue of psychophysiological parameters, heart rate variability is an indicator for workload is certainly also confounded with the physical load of the person and hence can only be used in working situations, where there is minimal physical load. A further issue is the use of the results in the succeeding design process. Subjective measures are always questionable whether they are valid indicators. If for instance a new support system for air traffic management needs to be assessed using subjective measures of controllers, one always can argue, that the controllers voted on high workload because they do not like the support system for other reasons than workload issues. In order to express this, they then use high indications of workload as a vehicle to materialize their interests rather than it is a real issue of workload. In the final negotiation with decision-makers on the support system, it then comes to heavy discussions on the validity of the results and distrust between the users and designers. Generally, there is a trade-off between subjective versus objective measurement and issues of validity due to interests of measured persons when using subjective measures and multi-load situations of realistic working environments when using objective measures.

The present paper shows a way to overcome these general issues of workload-measurement in real settings using pupillometry as an objective measurement approach that is robust enough to deal with multi-load situations of real working conditions and simple enough to be implemented in a quite unobtrusive manner. This paper will describe how it was implemented using eye tracking measurement and pupil dilatation indicators.

1.1 The Approach of Pupil Dilatation

The approach of pupil dilatation is a well-known approach and developed into recognized standards like the pupilographic sleepiness test (PST), which was developed and used for the detection of sleepiness in monotonous environments [12]. It uses the psychophysiological property of the eye and in particular of the pupil's behavior as a reaction on monotonous environments. To understand how this indicator works, Fig. 1 shows anatomy the pupil and the basic properties of the sphincter and dilatator muscles, which determine the pupil dilatation and contraction.

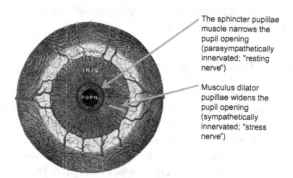

The sphincter pupillae muscle narrows the pupil opening (parasympathetically innervated; "resting nerve")

Musculus dilator pupillae widens the pupil opening (sympathetically innervated; "stress nerve")

Fig. 1. Anatomy of the pupil and muscular interventions.

Both are innervated by the parasympaticus and sympaticus of the vegetative system. As the parasympaticus and sympaticus of the vegetative system are the main physiological antagonists for steering sleepiness and fatigue, pupil dilatation is an interesting indicator for objective measurement of workload in monotone and fatigue causing environments. The result of this physiological antagonism is shown in Fig. 2. While a vivid eye has almost no variation in pupil diameter over time, because the negative system is in a balanced state. The tired eye has a high variance in diameter and in average the lower diameter of the pupil, what physiologically means that the parasympaticus and sympaticus are struggling with each other on the control of the body.

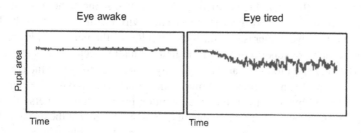

Fig. 2. distinction of vivid and tired persons using pupil diameter (figures taken from Brunner 2009) [13].

The PST procedure is optimized for a laboratory study with controlled experimental settings. The procedure prescribes that an overall measurement-period of 11 min needs to be conducted, where the pupil diameter is recorded. The 11 min trail is then subdivided into eight sections that are analyzed independently from each other using a Fourier-frequency-transformation and by building the difference between the pupil diameters in a section in relation to the overall average of the pupil diameter. Measurement problems due to eye-blinks need to be detected and corrected by pooling the data set. It is obvious, that such an approach is not suitable for real working environments. First, there is no standardized setting in real working environments and second, an 11 min trial with extensive measurement afterwards would be too intrusive. As an approach for solution, eye tracking generates the key parameter of the PST as a side product and can make use of the general approach of PST while making it available for real working environments. This will be shown in the following sections.

1.2   The Approach of Eye-Tracking

Eye movement analyzes have been used systematically used for decades to evaluate and design the ergonomics of cockpits or software interfaces. At the beginning, the technology was mainly reserved for the aviation sector, as extensive hardware was required and the effort involved in evaluating it was time-consuming and costly. Through the further development of the hardware and also of the software for evaluation, the technology found its way into other design areas, such as vehicle design and the evaluation of consumer goods. Nowadays, the technology is used in vehicle design to objectively evaluate the distraction effect of assistance systems in the context of autonomous driving. In the consumer goods sector, the technology is used to better evaluate the quality and attractiveness of the products or sales rooms for a user. Today the systems are inexpensive and miniaturized to such an extent that they can be used in almost all areas of life. For example, they are already installed as standard functions in data glasses for virtual reality (VR). The latest eye-tracking glasses hardly differ from classic glasses. The department of A&O developed the CeyeBERMANS system, which allows the analysis of body and eye movements to assess suitability for use, mental stress and fatigue [14]. The way eye movement measurement works has hardly changed in recent years. The principle is shown in Fig. 3.

At least two cameras are mounted on a pair of glasses and, with binocular detection (i.e. detection of both eyes), three cameras. The so-called scene camera is aligned with the main axis of the head and records the visual environment of the person. The eye camera (or the two eye cameras) captures the pupil(s) of the person. This creates two video films, which are superimposed in the first evaluation step. This is shown in the figure for a driving situation in a car. The anatomy of the eye shows that the center of the pupil (the black circle on the roadway) marks the human visual axis. The center of the pupil is determined by an optical image recognition process and the person's point of view is known on this (green cross). In the picture, you can see that the driver is looking at the middle of the road of the drawn right curve. In order to be able to interpret the focal point in terms of content, it must still be linked to the image content of the scene camera (blue diamond). This content-related environment recognition is done either with so-called markers that work like QRC codes (see an example in Fig. 4), or by using image recognition software that recognizes the lane, for example. Overall, this creates a gaze

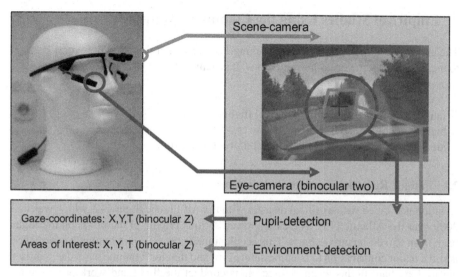

Fig. 3. General principle of eye-tracking (A&O 2020) [14].

film in which all geometrical and temporal data are available as to when the person was looking where.

The benefits of this technology can be seen directly in the example of driving a car: Were traffic signs looked at? How often did you look in the rearview mirror? How often was the vehicle interior looked at? How often was the car radio, cell phone or navigation display looked at? An evaluation therefore immediately yields important information for safe driving behavior and design tips.

1.3   Combining Eye Tracking with Measurement of Pupil Dilatation

Using the features of eye-tracking can make the PST approach suitable for real working environment as needed for human factors research. There are several issues that needs to be considered in the transformation of the approach. These are:

- Varying lighting situations
- Continuous measurement instead of a 11 min period
- No extensive measurements period
- No controlled conditions

The solution for a robust measurement in real work environments is to use a gliding average of the pupil diameter over the past 11 min in order to fulfil PST requirements, but to measure this in a continuous flow of the overall period, where the workload needs to be assessed. This equalizes variations in pupil diameter due to lighting variation and makes the deviations available for a fatigue or monotony assessment. In the empirical studies showed in the following section, could also demonstrate, that a complex Fourier transformation is not necessary to come to a conclusion on monotonous or fatigue situations.

2   Empirical Studies Using the Combined Approach

The algorithm of the combined eye-tracking/PST approach was used in several settings to measure monotone or fatigue situations. It is demonstrated by the use of the approach for:

– fatigue risk management in long haul flights
– highly repetitive manufacturing tasks
– identification of tasks and classification of human errors

2.1   Fatigue Risk Management in Aviation

Aviation was faced with a critical disaster with the Air France flight 447, which was lost 2009 over the Atlantic [15]. The case showed serious fatigue of the pilots on the flight back from Rio de Janeiro to Paris. This accident made obvious that human performance is still a major contribution to aviation safety [16] and that for it fatigue has a deep impact during long-haul flights, even if three pilots conduct the flight and work in a rotating shift-system. In the aftermath of this accident several airlines were working on the basis of the ICAO risk management approach on measurement as well as mitigations of fatigue during long-haul flights. Using subjective questionnaires for clarifying whether there is fatigue cause critical discussions between pilot associations and operators, whether the subjective measure is real fatigue or a more comfort driven issue of pilots or as a vehicle to have a better staffing during long flights. Such discussions led to the request to the department A&O by the German carrier Lufthansa to develop a method that is robust and objective enough to answer fatigue issues on an objective basis.

On a long-haul flight destination several measurements were taken in two phases of the approach. First, measurements of the status quo were conducted by overall 8 flights. Second, measurements with implemented mitigations on fatigue risk were conducted also overall in 8 flights. A typical example of using an eye-tracking based PST approach is shown in Fig. 4 [17]. One can see the fatigue profile of the typical long-haul flight based on pupil diameter variation measured in square pixel of the eye-camera of an eye-tracking system over the entire flight of about 13 h. The higher the values, the higher the monotony and fatigue effects. One can see right at the beginning of the flight already some fatigue issues that then stabilizes again after about hundred minutes and it then comes to the high peak in the middle of the flight, then stabilizes again and then raising at the end again. While the first peak is typically for the flight situation where pilots switch over to autopilot and then relax into auto-flight mode, the peak in the middle is proven to be an issue of fatigue. The last phase is an indicator of the busy and stressful landing phase.

The effects observed with the eye-tracking based PST measure were validated by several other indicators such as the Karolinska sleepiness scale, simple reaction time measurements and cognitive tests. As the flight is a night flight, lightning issues can be excluded.

Interestingly enough, the middle peak of fatigue is exactly in the time window where the Air France flight 447 was lost, hence in the peak period of the pilots' fatigue on the return flight to Europe. Because of their importance the data were analyzed in order

Pupil area / square-pixel

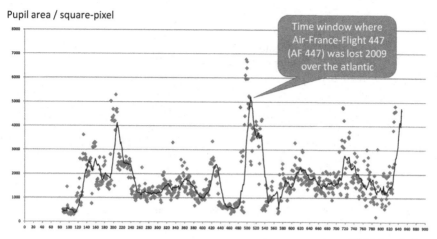

Flight time / minutes

Fig. 4. Typical average pupil dilatation on a long-haul intercontinental west-east flight (Color figure online)

to find a better shift-system to eliminate this fatigue peak during the flight. The shift-schedule was changed in such a way, that the change of pilots was planned shortly before the peak appears so that the tired pilot comes to a rest at the right time and a fresh pilot is in the pilot-flying mode. The new shift system was tried out and validation measures showed clearly that the peak disappears.

2.2 Workload Detection in U-Shaped Manufacturing Lines

As a second example, the eye-tracking PST approach was used to detect mental fatigue in monotone and repetitive manufacturing tasks. The same technology and the same algorithm as used for the pilots was applied to this setting. Manufacturing lines have issues with variation in lightening conditions and are physically stressful (whereas pilots sit on the fixed chair during night flight). Nevertheless, the algorithm was robust enough to measure mental fatigue.

Figure 5 shows the result of one U-shaped manufacturing line. At the beginning of the shift (yellow line) one can see that after about 17 min the pupil diameter gets lower than average. This is an indication for compensating the monotony effects by the worker. At the end of the shift (green line) one can see that the pupil diameter raises above average and almost stays there until end of the measurement after about 60 min [18].

The time where this gap occurs is a typical indicator for mental fatigue. Several U-shaped manufacturing lines were investigated using this approach and contrasted with subjective measures for mental fatigue and sleepiness. It could clearly be shown, that mental fatigue is higher, when the monotony effect comes earlier. In some manufacturing lines the gap in pupil diameter occurred already after five minutes, which indicates very high mental fatigue situation, whereas in some U-shaped manufacturing lines it came after 40 to 50 min, which is a less mental fatigue environment.

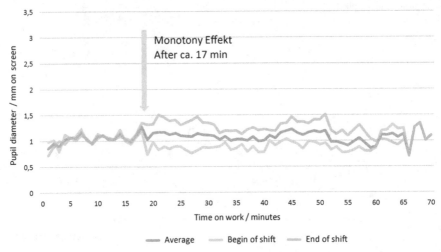

Fig. 5. Eye-tracking based investigation of mental fatigue in manufacturing. (Color figure online)

2.3 Error Detection While Performing Activities

Based on the promising results from aviation and manufacturing, Jennerich conducted a study of error detection while performing activities [19]. He investigated what else can be done with the eye-tracking PST approach for other psychologically interesting states and developed the combined eye-tracking PST approach into a general algorithm to identify psychologically interesting states. As empirical field he used the detection of tasks and errors in quality control. In order to do that, he complemented the measure of pupil diameter with other measures like fixation path, saccades etc. In particular he found that the following parameters are useful predictors:

– number of fixations
– average fixation duration
– standard deviation of pupil diameter
– average pupil diameter
– average of the amplitudes of the amplitude spectrum (FFT)
– standard deviation of the amplitudes

Using these parameters and classifying the task with an artificial intelligence/machine learning approach he could detect the actual task a person is doing as well as errors in conducting the tasks. Figure 6 shows one of the results.

In the state diagram, you can see in green color those tasks that the algorithm detected correctly based on the above-mentioned parameter and indicated in red the tasks that the algorithm did not detected correctly. Overall the algorithm was able to identify 93,8% of the tasks a person is performing. For those tasks not identified, the algorithm was in a second step able to decide whether it's an error conducted by the person or a misclassification of the algorithm (further details are reported in a study published by Jennerich in 2018) [19].

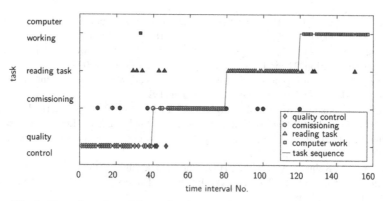

Fig. 6. Error detection while performing activities [19]. (Color figure online)

3 Discussion

The paper outlines a simple and feasible approach for the objective measurement of fatigue cause by a monotone working environment, such as manufacturing [20]. The practical use was demonstrated by examples from aviation and manufacturing. The general approach to use eye-tracking parameter for detecting psychologically interesting states that are potentially precursor to human errors was also demonstrated.

The approach enriches workload measurements in particular for situations where nonintrusive and objective measurements need to be undertaken. It allows, in conjunction with artificial intelligence and machine learning algorithms, to predict other psychological states that are precursor of human errors [21] but also for advancing the capacity to assess other aspects in human factors and ergonomics sectors related to human capabilities and limitations, both cognitive and physical, and what such knowledge can provide in assisting the design of technologies and work environments that can be more efficient, enjoyable and safer for people to interact with [22–24].

References

1. Recarte, M.A., Nunes, L.M.: Mental workload while driving: effects on visual search, discrimination, and decision making. J. Exper. Psychol. Appl. **9**(2), 119 (2003)
2. Gawron, V.J.: Human Performance Measures Handbook. Lawrence Erlbaum Associates Publishers, New Jersey (2000)
3. Paas, F.G., Van Merriënboer, J.J.: Variability of worked examples and transfer of geometrical problem-solving skills: a cognitive-load approach. J. Educ. Psychol. **86**(1), 122 (1994)
4. Cain, B.: A Review of the Mental Workload Literature, July 2007
5. Yeh, Y.Y., Wickens, C.D.: Dissociation of performance and subjective measures of workload. Hum. Factors **30**(1), 111–120 (1988)
6. Longo, L.: Subjective usability, mental workload assessments and their impact on objective human performance. In: Bernhaupt, R., Dalvi, G., Joshi, A., Balkrishan, D.K., O'Neill, J., Winckler, M. (eds.) INTERACT 2017. LNCS, vol. 10514, pp. 202–223. Springer, Cham (2017). https://doi.org/10.1007/978-3-319-67684-5_13
7. Longo, L.: Experienced mental workload, perception of usability, their interaction and impact on task performance. PLoS ONE **13**(8), e0199661 (2018)

8. Reid, G.B., Nygren, T.E.: The subjective workload assessment technique: a scaling procedure for measuring mental workload. Adv. Psychol. **52**, 185–218 (1988)
9. Gevins, A., Smith, M.E.: Neurophysiological measures of cognitive workload during human-computer interaction. Theor. Issues Ergon. Sci. **4**(1–2), 113–131 (2003)
10. Kramer, A.F.: Physiological metrics of mental workload: a review of recent progress. In: Multiple-task performance, pp. 279–328, London (1991)
11. Kartali, A., Janković, Milica M., Gligorijević, I., Mijović, P., Mijović, B., Leva, M.C.: Real-time mental workload estimation using EEG. In: Longo, L., Leva, M.C. (eds.) H-WORKLOAD 2019. CCIS, vol. 1107, pp. 20–34. Springer, Cham (2019). https://doi.org/10.1007/978-3-030-32423-0_2
12. Schwalm, M., Keinath, A., Zimmer, H.D.: Pupillometry as a method for measuring mental workload within a simulated driving task. In: Human Factors for assistance and automation, (1986), pp. 1–13 (2008)
13. Brunner, S.: Einfluss eines akustischen Vigilanztests auf den pupillographischen Schläfrigkeitstest. Inaugural-Dissertation an der Medizinischen Fakultät der Friedrich-Alexander-Universität. Erlangen-Nürnberg (2009)
14. AuO CeyebermanS - Ein Messsystem zur Analyse von Körper- und Blickbewegungen zur Einschätzung von Gebrauchstauglichkeit, mentaler Belastung und Ermüdung. https://www.uni-kassel.de/maschinenbau/institute/ifa/arbeits-und-organisationspsychologie/methoden.html. Accessed Sep 2020
15. Bureau d'Enquêtes et d'Analyses pour la sécurité de l'aviation civile. Final Report On the accident on 1st June 2009 to the Airbus A330-203 registered F-GZCP operated by Air France flight AF 447 Rio de Janeiro – Paris (2012). http://www.bea.aero/docspa/2009/f-cp090601.en/pdf/f-cp090601.en.pdf. Accessed Nov 2014
16. Trucco, P., Leva, M.C., Sträter, O.: Human error prediction in ATM via cognitive simulation: preliminary study. PSAM **8**, 1–8 (2006)
17. Sträter, O.: Bewertung des Gefährdungspotentials durch reduzierte Reaktionsfähigkeit bei Langstreckenflügen. Universität Kassel, Fachgebiet Arbeits- und Organisationspsychologie. Kassel
18. Sträter, O., Schmidt, S., Stache, S., Saki, M., Wakula, J., Bruder, R., Glitsch, U., Ditchen, D.: Forschungsvorhaben, U-Linien-Montagesysteme, Instrumente zur Gefährdungsbeurteilung und arbeitswissenschaftliche Gestaltungsempfehlungen zur Prävention. Abschlussbericht. BGHM. Düsseldorf (2018)
19. Jennerich, M. Proaktive Tätigkeitsunterstützung: Adaptive Tätigkeitserkennung in Abhängigkeit der Pupillendynamik und Entwicklung einer situativen Assistenz (Dissertation). Universität Kassel, Kassel (2018)
20. Comberti, L., Leva, M.C., Demichela, M., Desideri, S., Baldissone, G., Modaffari, F.: An empirical approach to workload and human capability assessment in a manufacturing plant. In: Longo, L., Leva, M.Chiara (eds.) H-WORKLOAD 2018. CCIS, vol. 1012, pp. 180–201. Springer, Cham (2019). https://doi.org/10.1007/978-3-030-14273-5_11
21. Sträter, O.: Hrsg. Risikofaktor Mensch? - Zuverlässiges Handeln gestalten. Beuth Verlag (2019)
22. Longo, L., Leva, M.C. (eds.): H-WORKLOAD 2017. CCIS, vol. 726. Springer, Cham (2017). https://doi.org/10.1007/978-3-319-61061-0
23. Longo, L., Leva, M.Chiara (eds.): H-WORKLOAD 2017. CCIS, vol. 726. Springer, Cham (2017). https://doi.org/10.1007/978-3-319-61061-0
24. Leva, M.C., Wilkins, M., Coster, F.: Human performance modelling for adaptive automation journal of physics: conference series. In: Journal of Physics: Conference Series, vol. 1065, no. 18 (2018)

Working Memory Resource Depletion Effect in Academic Learning: Steps to an Integrated Approach

André Tricot[1]([✉]), Sébastien Puma[2], Rémi Capa[3], Michel Audiffren[4], Nathalie André[4], Florence Lespiau[5], Stéphanie Roussel[6], Camille Jeunet[7], Emilie Massa[7], Dominique Bellec[8], Elisabeth Fonteneau[1], and Pom Charras[1]

[1] University Paul Valéry Montpellier, route de Mende, 34090 Montpellier, France
{andre.tricot,elisabeth.fonteneau}@univ-montp3.fr,
pomcharras@gmail.com
[2] Cergy Paris University, 2 rue de la Liberté, 93526 Saint-Denis, France
mr.aethis@gmail.com
[3] SCOTE, INU Champollion, Place de Verdun, 81012 Albi, France
remi.capa@univ-jfc.fr
[4] CeRCA, CNRS, Université Poitiers, 5, rue T. Lefebvre, 86073 Poitiers, France
{michel.audiffren,nathalie.andre}@univ-poitiers.fr
[5] Université Nîmes, rued du Docteur Georges Salan, 30021 Nîmes, France
florence.lespiau@gmail.com
[6] Université Bordeaux, 3 ter place de la Victoire, 33076 Bordeaux, France
stef.roussel@gmail.com
[7] CLLE, CNRS University, Toulouse 2, 5 allées Antonio Machado, 31058 Toulouse, France
{camille.jeunet,emilie.massa}@univ-tlse2.fr
[8] Lycée Nelson Mandela, 63 rue de la Bugellerie, 86022 Poitiers, France
dominique.bellec@ac-poitiers.fr

Abstract. Learning at school requires cognitive effort. Optimizing these efforts is one of the keys to academic learning achievement. Many controlled experiments, for example within the cognitive load theory framework, have identified the factors that impact this optimization. The temporal dimension of this optimization was evoked in 2018: certain academic learning tasks could exhaust students, resulting on learning impairing. The hypothesis of Sweller and other authors from cognitive load theory is that working memory resources would be depleted during a demanding learning task. The authors point out that this depletion of working memory resources could explain a famous effect in learning literature: the massed/spaced effect. But these authors do not say: What mechanisms govern this exhaustion? How can this depletion be measured? The working memory resource depletion effect project proposes to answer these questions. Our aim is to present this project, its objectives, method and the first results.

Keywords: Cognitive load · Cognitive load theory · Working memory resources · Resources depletion · Instructional design · Educational psychology

© Springer Nature Switzerland AG 2020
L. Longo and M. C. Leva (Eds.): H-WORKLOAD 2020, CCIS 1318, pp. 13–26, 2020.
https://doi.org/10.1007/978-3-030-62302-9_2

1 Introduction

In the last 30 years, many studies have shown that the optimization of working memory resources is a key factor in academic learning success. In educational psychology, cognitive load theory has shown (based on several thousand published experiments) that decreasing cognitive load in working memory could lead to a learning rise [1]. Recent works in this area have shown that working memory resources can be depleted during a learning task [2, 3]. Sweller and colleagues found that students performed better at a working memory test after a less demanding task than when the same test was completed immediately after a very demanding and time-consuming task. These authors thus introduce a new, dynamic variable in the field of working memory resource optimization for learning: The depletion of these resources. While they are insightful, these papers do not answer important questions: What is getting depleted? Due to what mechanisms? How is this depletion recovered? How long does it take?

The aim of the working memory resource depletion effect project (WM-RDE from now) is to investigate working memory resource depletion effect by considering Barrouillet's and Camos' Time-Based Resources Sharing model (TBRS [4]). The TBRS model allows simple and straightforward predictions about cognitive load in working memory, as well as about the solicited resource (controlled attention), and about the causes of this resource depletion (the temporal sharing of controlled attention between the processing devoted to refreshing memory traces and the processing devoted to new items). Therefore, the project's objectives are:

- to design, test and validate a new experimental paradigm, more rigorous than the one used by Sweller et al.'s, to obtain working memory resource depletion when performing an academic knowledge learning task;
- to propose an integrated approach based on multiple measures of working memory resource depletion, through four complementary standpoints: phenomenological (subjective measures), behavioral (task performance), physiological (cardiovascular reactivity) and neurophysiological (EEG measures);
- to study resource sharing over time as a critical factor responsible for resource depletion in working memory.

Once these objectives are achieved, and if the depletion effect is linear, then a secondary benefit will be obtained: we will be able to run objective cognitive load measures in instruction research. We make the following hypotheses:

1. The depleted resource is controlled attention (*i.e.* effortful control), as in the TBRS Model.
2. The TBRS model allows defining the consumption of attentional resources during the realization of a complex academic task.
3. When the task requirement is higher than the individuals' resources, the latter are gradually depleted and consequently task performance decreases, as in Sweller et al. results.
4. This depletion is measurable through a working memory test (behavioral performance) and physiological and neurophysiological techniques.

5. Increasing the time available to perform the task reduces or cancels the depletion effect, as predicted by the TBRS Model.
6. If resources are depleted, then the students will only be able to mobilize fewer resources and their performance at the task will decrease, as obtained by Puma et al. (2018).
7. The individuals can also disengage from the task (initially or throughout), thus preserving their resources at the expense of the learning task performance.

Our aim here is to present WM-RDE project, its theoretical background, its method and measures, and the results of a first pre-experiment.

2   State of the Art

2.1   The Depletion of Cognitive Resources: From Ego Depletion to WM Resources Depletion

Resource depletion has attracted considerable interest in psychology in recent years, since the first study on the ego depletion effect [5]. This effect is obtained when using the sequential-task protocol (see Fig. 1).

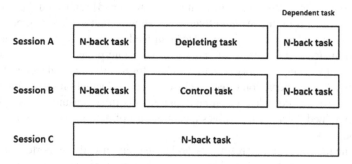

Fig. 1. The sequential-task protocol

This protocol encompasses two conditions: (A) a depleting condition, and (B) a control condition. In the depleting condition, the participants perform two consecutive tasks: a depleting task and a dependent task. These two tasks require a high level of self-control, i.e., the ability to inhibit embarrassing emotions, pressing urges, intrusive negative thoughts, behaviors repressed by social rules, habits and automated action patterns[1]. In the control condition, the participants also perform two consecutive tasks,

---

[1] The ego depletion effect has been much studied, often replicated [6], but the replication of the Sripada, Kessler and Jonides' experiment [7] by 23 labs (N = 2141) failed to obtain the ego depletion effect [8]. Another replication study by 12 labs (N = 1775) obtained a small but significant ego depletion effect [9]. A meta-analysis [10] shows that the ego-depletion is obtained under certain conditions (emotion videos) and not obtained under others conditions (attention videos). More recent meta-analyses also show a negative effect of ego depletion on subsequent physical endurance performance [11] [12].

the control task and the dependent task, with exactly the same time course than in the depleting condition. The control task, by definition, requires a low level of self-control by contrast to the depleting task. The ego depletion effect reflects a lower performance in the dependent task when it is carried out after the depleting task rather than after the control task. Within the framework of this resource approach, performance in the depleting condition drops and is assumed to be a direct consequence of a decrease in available resources induced by the depleting task. From that standpoint, cognitive fatigue is conceived as a state of depleted resources (and thus resource depletion can result in cognitive fatigue). This literature has led other researchers to question the depletion of resources of other cognitive processes. For instance, Sweller et al.'s studies have targeted working memory, considering its importance in academic learning.

Based on an ego depletion effect study, which used a working memory post-test as a measure of resource depletion due to a self-control task, Chen et al. [2] described a working memory resource depletion effect. These authors have compared the performance obtained by primary school students in massed vs. spaced learning conditions. In addition, the researchers asked the participants to perform a complex working memory test (involving processing and memorization) at the end of the learning sessions. The results confirmed the expected classic effect (spaced > massed). Chen et al. also observed that the participants who completed the massed condition obtained lower performances at the working memory test. The authors interpret this result as a working memory resource depletion effect. The following year, Leahy and Sweller [3] replicated the results in a series of experiments on the testing effect. They showed that the learning performance obtained in a delayed post-test (compared to an immediate post-test) was associated with better performance in the working memory test. They interpreted this dual performance as a recovery of working memory resources. Thus, for Sweller and colleagues, the working memory resource depletion effect is close to the ego depletion effect, but possibly more general: for any complex, resource-depleting and time-consuming task, the effect should be obtained, because it involves a central part of human cognitive architecture: working memory.

While the idea of cognitive resources depletion is empirically supported, the authors quoted above do not explain what is depleted or what mechanisms govern this depletion. Different researchers have proposed that brain glucose depletion could be a possible candidate of cognitive fatigue (e.g. [13]), but this hypothesis has been challenged and seriously criticized (e.g. [14]). Another plausible mechanism explaining cognitive fatigue has been recently proposed: a progressive deterioration of the connectivity within and between large-scale neuronal networks involved in effortful control. This phenomenon could be caused by an accumulation of adenosine in overloaded brain regions [15, 16]. In order to better understand the working memory resource depletion effect, our project uses the time-based resources sharing model of working memory [4]. These alternative theories will be taken into consideration in the present project by controlling different variables (e.g., motivation, cost/benefit of effortful control) and measuring other variables (e.g., prefrontal theta waves).

2.2 Contribution of the Time-Based Resources Sharing Model

The TBRS model [4] assumes that the resource used by working memory is controlled attention. The activation of information maintained in working memory when a task is performed decreases over time. Maintaining information in working memory requires refreshing, using attentional focus. During a complex task, the system quickly alternates the attentional focus between the new elements to be processed and the maintained information to be refreshed. The model proposes to define the cognitive load in working memory as a ratio. In a classic complex memory span protocol, the time spent processing distracting elements (Td) cannot be spent refreshing the information in working memory (Tr). As a matter of fact, the attention focus is being shared between the two activities. Thus, cognitive load can be defined as the ratio Td/(Td + Tr) or Td/T total. The more time spent on distracting elements increases, the more the ratio Td/(Td + Tr) increases and therefore the more the cognitive load increases. Similarly, reducing the time spent refreshing working memory information by keeping the time spent on distracting elements constant increases cognitive load. We have tested the robustness of this model in school learning situations and shown its compatibility with cognitive load theory [17, 18]. We have shown that the load predicted by the TBRS model was well observed at the physiological level [19] as well as neurophysiological level [20], particularly through the modulations of theta EEG activity [21]. One purpose of this project is to manipulate the different elements of the cognitive load during the depleting task and examine the residual depletion effect in the subsequent dependent task.

3 Method

The experiments conducted within the framework of this project will use the sequential-task protocol [5] described in Fig. 1. But, contrary to the depletion tasks used in this protocol, we will use a complex "processing and refreshing" task. This new protocol has already been tested (see bellow, Sect. 4).

3.1 Depleting Task

The depleting task included in session A must be a long and effortful task tapping working memory and inducing cognitive fatigue (*i.e.* a depletion of working memory resources). Several depleting tasks will be used throughout the project. However, a second language transcription task[2] will be used as main depleting task in several of our planned experiments.

In this task, the participants (French) have to write down an oral speech provided in English, i.e. a classical learning task for students in foreign language departments. It is a dual task: (1) listening comprehension of an oral speech and (2) transcription writing

---

[2] It is well known that simultaneous translation tasks are very demanding and exhausting [37], but we decided to begin our set of experiments with a second language transcription task because it is easier to objectively evaluate the performance. We previously developed methods and measure to evaluate performance and cognitive load in second language speech comprehension tasks [38].

task. But, during the second task, it demands the temporal sharing of controlled attention between refreshing memory traces (the sentences they just eared) and the processing devoted to new items (writing this sentence). It is therefore highly compatible with the TBRS model. This task is also demanding because it is in a second language. The task can be run over a long period of time (20 to 60 min): this is an experimental precaution to obtain a cognitive fatigue effect (e.g. [22]). The transcript of the speech is recorded in order to track accurately the words that have been correctly transcribed, the ones that have not. In this way, we are able to make a continuous measure of the performance during the task. The duration and frequency of pauses are empirically calibrated to make the task feasible but demanding.

3.2   Control Task

The control task included in session B must be as effortless and emotionally neutral as possible but with exactly the same duration than the depleting task. In addition, the control task must not be boring because boredom decreases arousal and requires compensatory effortful control. As for the depleting task, several control tasks will be used throughout the project. However, a simple listening task will be used as the main control task in several of our planned experiments. In the simple listening task, the participants do not have to transcript. A comprehension test is administered at the end of the session. Comprehension is evaluated with the Kintsch et al. protocol [22]: surface, text base and inference questions. Participants' resources are evaluated with standardized tests of English proficiency (Cambridge English Language Assessment) and typing speed (computerized test, words per minute, with French words and with English words). Other control tasks will be used in several of our planned experiments, such as watching an emotionally neutral movie that does not involve listening to a commentary. This type of control task is often used in studies examining the effects of cognitive fatigue on physical performance (e.g. [12]).

3.3   Dependent Task

The dependent task must be an effortful working memory task for the purpose of the project. One of the most popular measures of working memory is the n-back task (e.g. [23]). We chose a computerized visual version of the 2-back because it has been shown to be more sensitive to cognitive fatigue than the 3-back task [24]. In classical sequential-task protocols, the dependent task is performed immediately after the main task (i.e. depleting or control task). In order to have an additional reference performance in the beginning of each session, particularly for physiological measures, we add a 2-back task before the main task. To sum-up, participants will have to perform two blocks of 72 n-back trials before and after the main task. Finally, a session C will be added in several of our planned experiments to examine whether and how effortful control modulates physiological indexes over time spent on the n-back task.

3.4   Participants

Participants included in experiments throughout the project are French-speaking students studying English at university, typically year 3 and year 4. They are familiar with the task and enough fluent in English to perform it. English proficiency and typing speed are evaluated with standardized tests. Other asymptomatic or symptomatic populations will be selected in several of our planned experiments, as well as middle, high school and, more broadly, university students.

3.5 Procedure

Participants will achieve sessions A and B (plus session C in several experiments) in different days spaced by a minimum of 2 days. The orders of the sessions are counterbalanced across participants. Participants complete an n-back working memory test before and after performing the main task so that, unlike Sweller and colleagues' experiences cited above, we have two working memory measures per participant and per session. We will test the interaction Session (A vs B) x Moment (before vs after the main task) with the hypothesis that the n-back performance will not vary in control condition while it will degrade in the depleting condition. Experiments included in several of our planned experiments will evaluate the effect of changing the frequency and duration of breaks during the depleting task to increase or decrease the cognitive load in working memory in a way that is described by the TBRS model and that should be observable on measures of performance, resource depletion and task commitment.

3.6 Measures of Cognitive Resources Use and Depletion

As above mentioned, we assumed that performing a long and effortful task depletes intrinsic resources, i.e. weakens effortful control. Achievement of the WM-RDE project then requires different measures of resource depletion through the assessment of the capacity to exert effortful control. We will use three complementary approaches to assess effortful control: subjective, behavioral and physiological (cardiovascular and EEG) measures. Complementarity between these indexes is required to interpret the results. For example, a decrease of performance coupled with a higher feeling of fatigue and greater physiological activity could be interpreted as a compensatory effort mobilization, whereas an improvement of performance linked with a lower feeling of effort and less physiological activity could be interpreted as a learning effect. The different patterns of results are clearly identified and regularly discussed in the literature (*e.g.* [25–27]).

Subjective Measures. Subjective motivation, boredom, cognitive load and cognitive fatigue will be measured before and after each task with very simple visual-analogue scales. We will assess the costs and benefits of achieving the goal, task engagement and motivation, with a short version of the Motivated Strategies for Learning Questionnaire [28]. We will assess boredom and cognitive fatigue with a short version of the Fatigue Impact Scale [29], cognitive load and effort with Leppink et al. scale [30].

Behavioral Measures. The principal behavioral outcomes include percentage of correct and incorrect responses, percentage of omissions and reaction times recorded during the n-back task. We also operationalize accuracy by calculating the d prime index. Secondary behavioral outcomes include performance related to the depleting and control tasks.

Physiological Measures. Cardiovascular (electrocardiography -ECG-, impedance cardiography -ICG-) and EEG outcomes (spectral bands and ERPs) used in this project allow assessing effortful control but they differ in their temporality and capability to focus on specific cognitive processes. Cardiovascular indices will allow us to identify relatively slow effects (e.g. difference between blocks) and a general mobilization of resources, but without targeting specific brain areas. Spectral bands of brain activity allow identifying relatively slow effects (e.g. difference between blocks) and the approximate location of the brain regions involved in the generation of a specific rhythm (e.g. frontal-midline theta). ERPs provide a very fast temporal analysis during the time course of a trial and a way to determine the nature of cognitive processes impacted by a variation in effortful control according to the wave time-window.

Physiological signals (ECG, ICG, and EEG) will be recorded throughout the three two sessions A, B and C (see Fig. 1), but only in several of our planned experiments. Cardiovascular reactivity indexes and density of theta rhythm will be analyzed during the n-back, the depleting task and the control task as a function of time on task. ERP will be exclusively analyzed during the n-back tasks.

- *Cardiovascular reactivity.* Physiological indicators measure the level of activation of the sympathetic nervous system (SNS), which is responsible for mobilizing the resources the individual needs. One measure, the pre-ejection period (PEP), has been extensively used in recent years. This period represents the time between the contraction of the left ventricle of the heart and the first blood release. Unlike other physiological measures in the literature, PEP is the sole measure exclusively under the influence of beta-adrenergic SNS. Several studies have shown its sensitivity to resource mobilization [19, 31]. A decrease in PEP when performing a task can be interpreted as increased resource mobilization. Even if no study was published using the n-back task, a decrease in PEP was regularly obtained in working memory task (e.g. [31]).
- *Event-related potentials.* Several ERPs studies have obtained robust effects on the P300 amplitude with the n-back task (*e.g.* [32]). A time window of 250–500 ms was used after the onset of stimuli at frontal (F3, FZ and F4) and parietal (P3, PZ and P4) electrodes. The hypothesis is that P300 reflects available resources and a decrease of the P300 amplitude is associated with reduced attentional resources. ERP analyses are conducted only for correct responses to the target stimuli. The task is relatively easy to perform and generally leads to a low proportion of rejected trials (around 10%), even in the most difficult condition (4-back).
- *Spectral bands.* Brain oscillation frequencies are divided into the following spectral bands with distinct functional associations: delta (1–4 Hz), theta (4–8 Hz), alpha (8–14 Hz), beta (14–30 Hz), and gamma (>30 Hz). These oscillations cause fluctuations in cortical local field potentials that can be measured using EEG scalp detectors. Lakatos et al. [33] proposed that these oscillations are hierarchically organized as follows: brain regions that generate low-frequency oscillations (theta and alpha bands) modulate the activity of brain regions that generate higher frequency oscillations (beta and gamma bands). In that perspective, frontal-midline theta oscillations have been associated with effortful control exerted by anterior cingulate cortex over brain areas involved in the

ongoing task (*e.g.* [16]). A large number of studies showed an increase in the amount of frontal-midline theta with increasing working memory load, task difficulty, or mental effort during working memory tasks (see [34], for a review). More recently, Fairclough and Ewing [35] showed that frontal-midline theta was significantly higher during hard demand (4-back) compared to easy (1-back) and very hard demand (7-back) during a n-back task.

4 Preliminary Experiment

4.1 Participants

Eighteen university students in English language and civilization (year 4; average 22 years old) participated to the experiment. The results of only 12 participants were taken into account because 6 participants were either not expert enough to perform the main task, did not perform well enough at the n-back tasks, or encountered technical issues during the experiment (which were due to E-prime software). Their English proficiency was evaluated with the Cambridge test. The group average performance was 21.6 (max 25; *s.d.* = 1.8). Their typing speed was evaluated by the number of words typed per minute. The group average performance was 47 (*s.d.* = 15).

4.2 Materials

Participants had to transcript a 12 min sound file based on a TED conference in English language (Robert Waldinger "What make a good life. Lessons from the longest study on happiness"). Half the participants listened to the speech with normal pauses (control group) while the other half (test group), additional pauses (2.5 longer than natural pauses) were inserted in the speech, in order to transcript the discourse. The total time in the group was 35' (enough time to type but no other pauses were possible).

The transcription task was performed on a laptop and Open Office Writer software.

4.3 Procedure

1. Participants were trained at N-back tasks: 0-back (42 trials), 1-back (42 trials), 2-back (62 trials).
2. They performed the Cambridge level test.
3. They ran the Typing Speed test.
4. They ran the N-back pre-tests: Block 1 (42 trials), 5 s pause, followed by Block 2 (42 trials).
5. They ran the main task: transcription for the test group vs. listening task for the control group.
6. They ran, after a 5 s rest, the N-back post-test: Block 1 (42 trials) 5 s pause Block 2.
7. The participants' comprehension was evaluated: 8 literal and 8 inferential questions.
8. The participants answered 6 motivation, difficulty and fatigue questions: Before starting this study, did you feel motivated to participate? Was the letter memory task difficult for you? Was the transcription/listening task difficult for you? Was answering the questions difficult for you? Did you feel tired? Would you be willing to complete a new transcription/listening task?

4.4 Results

Both groups made fewer errors in the Post test than in the Pretest. The number of errors per block (and by splitting the blocks into sub-blocks of 21 trials), suggested irregular performances at the pre-test. We need to fix that point by training the participants before the pretest until their performance is stable and the training effect disappears. We report participants' individual measures to highlight the wide distribution of n-back performance, which is the main issue we need to address.

Comprehension. The control group responds better to inferential questions than the test group.

Transcription Task. No participant gave up the task. We analyzed the productions by counting the number of errors (including typos, rewording, spelling mistakes and untranscribed words). The transcription was split into seven consecutive 5 min parts to explore the evolution of the number of errors during the task: there is no general increase nor decrease of the performance during the task. This is a crucial aspect: no participant disengaged during the task and there was no learning effect (Table 1).

Table 1. Main performances of the 6 participants of the test group, mean performances of the test and control groups.

Participant	English proficiency	Typing speed	n-back pre	n-back post	Motivation new task	Literal questions	Inferences questions
1	21	43	6	5	60	5	5
2	22	45	11	10	65	6	7
3	20	32	6	6	73	7	8
4	23	43	32	23	98	6	7
5	23	43	11	13	89	7	6
6	25	77	11	8	21	7	7
Test (average)	22,3	47	12,8	10,8	68	6,3	6,7
Control (average)	21		9,8	7,2	87	6,3	7,5

In Fig. 2, each participant is represented by a colour line. It is remarkable to note that there is apparently no general increase nor decrease of the performance during the task, despite an important variation of the performances and important differences between participants. This is a crucial aspect because one possibility for the participants is to disengage from the task, increase the number of errors and save their cognitive resources. One variation during the task (see the 15-20' slot) is probably due to an easy part of the discourse to transcript, which can be explained by the fact that we used natural material for this experiment.

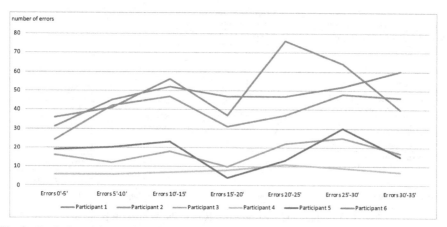

Fig. 2. Evolution of the number of errors according for each of the 6 participants of the test group

Perceived Difficulty/Fatigue. The test group found the n-back easier than the control group (perhaps they made a comparison with the transcription task). They also found the transcription task more difficult and were less motivated than the control group to do it again.

Performances of Each Participant. One of them is remarkable: he performed the best at the English test and, by far, at the typing speed; he is the one who makes the most mistakes at the transcription task, sometimes in huge proportion; his comprehension score is comparable to others; he makes few errors at n-back in pre-test and even less at n-back in post-test; he indicates the lowest motivation score for starting the task once again. In short, the amount of effort invested in the task depends on motivation. And the depletion of resources depends on the amount of effort invested. This participant had the means to do better than the others, but he decided to do not and saved his resources.

Participant Feedback. Participants reported that the task was stressful because they did not know how long it would last. They were relieved when the task ended and to move on to the n-back again.

5 Discussion

The WM-RDE project is summarized in Fig. 3. We aim at investigating the effect of the attentional demand of a task, according to time resources sharing, on resources depletion. We defined the variables involved, the relations between these variables, and how measuring these variables.

We believe that the aim is new: understanding the mechanisms that govern the working memory resources depletion. The involvement of academic tasks and knowledge (i.e. ecological validity) is a very important aspect of the project. We think that our protocol is a new experimental paradigm. We use physiological and neurophysiological measures that are not used in cognitive load theory experiments. Subjective motivation, cognitive

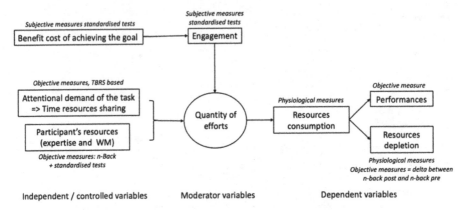

Fig. 3. Variables and measures involved in the WM-RDE project

load and fatigue are also assessed, making us able to perform a triangulation between resource depletion, task engagement and performance.

By submitting this paper to 4th International Symposium on Human Mental Workload, we hope to obtain feedback on this project, which is where it all started (Fig. 4).

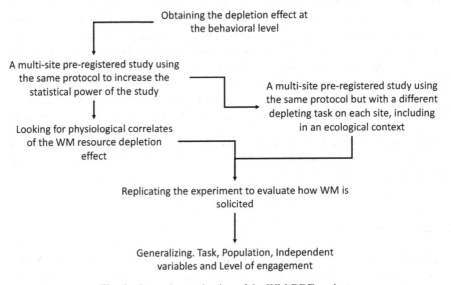

Fig. 4. General organization of the WM-RDE project

Acknowledgment. The WM-RDE project is funded by ANR, the French national agency for research.

References

1. Sweller, J., van Merriënboer, J. Paas, F.: Cognitive architecture and instructional design: 20 years later. Ed. Psy. Rev. 1–32 (2019)
2. Chen, O., Castro-Alonso, J.C., Paas, F., Sweller, J.: Extending cognitive load theory to incorporate working memory resource depletion: evidence from the spacing effect. Educ. Psychol. Rev. **30**, 483–501 (2018)
3. Leahy, W., Sweller, J.: Cognitive load theory, resource depletion and the delayed testing effect. Educ. Psychol. Rev. 1–22 (2019)
4. Barrouillet, P., Camos, V.: Working Memory: Loss and Reconstruction. Psychology Press (2015)
5. Baumeister, R.F., Bratslavsky, E., Muraven, M., Tice, D.M.: Ego depletion: Is the active self a limited resource? J. Pers. Soc. Psychol. **74**, 1252 (1998)
6. Baumeister, R.F., Tice, D.M., Vohs, K.D.: The strength model of self-regulation: conclusions from the second decade of willpower research. Perspect. Psychol. Sci. **13**, 141–145 (2018)
7. Sripada, C., Kessler, D., Jonides, J.: Methylphenidate blocks effort-induced depletion of regulatory control in healthy volunteers. Psychol. Sci. **25**(6), 1227–1234 (2014)
8. Hagger, M.S., et al.: A multilab preregistered replication of the ego-depletion effect. Perspect. Psychol. Sci. **11**(4), 546–573 (2016)
9. Dang, J., et al.: Multi-lab replication reveals a small but significant ego depletion effect (2019). https://psyarxiv.com/cjgru
10. Dang, J.: An updated meta-analysis of the ego depletion effect. Psychol. Res. **82**(4), 645–651 (2017). https://doi.org/10.1007/s00426-017-0862-x
11. Giboin, L.S., Wolff, W.: The effect of ego depletion or mental fatigue on subsequent physical endurance performance: a meta-analysis. Perf. Enh. Health **7**, 100150 (2019)
12. Brown, D.M.Y., Bray, S.R.: Effects of mental fatigue on physical endurance performance and muscle activation are attenuated by monetary incentives. J. Sport Exer. Psychol. **39**, 385–396 (2017)
13. Baumeister, R.F., Vohs, K.D., Tice, D.M.: The strength model of self-control. Curr. Direct. Psychol. Sci. **16**, 351–355 (2007)
14. Inzlicht, M., Berkman, E.: Six questions for the resource model of control (and some answers). Soc. Pers. Psychol. Compass **9**(10), 511–524 (2015)
15. Martin, K., Meeusen, R., Thompson, K.G., Keegan, R., Rattray, B.: Mental fatigue impairs endurance performance: a physiological explanation. Sports Med. **48**, 2041–2051 (2018)
16. André, N., Audiffren, M., Baumeister, R.: An integrative model of effortful control. Front. Syst. Neurosci. **13**, 79 (2019)
17. Puma, S., Matton, N., Paubel, P.-V., Tricot, A.: Cognitive Load theory and time variations: using the Time-Based Resource Sharing model. Ed. Psy. Rev. **30**, 1199–1214 (2018)
18. Puma, S., Tricot, A.: Cognitive load theory and working memory models. Comings and goings. In: Advances in Cognitive Load Theory, pp. 41–52. Routledge (2019)
19. Mallat, C., Cegarra, J. Calmettes, J.-C., Capa, R.: Curvilinear effect of mental workload on mental effort and behavioral adaptability: an approach with the pre-ejection period. Human Factors (2019)
20. Capa, R., Bouquet, C., Dreher, J., Dufour, A.: Long-lasting effects of performance-contingent unconscious and conscious reward incentives during cued task-switching. Cortex **49**, 1943–1954 (2013)
21. Puma, S., Matton, N., Paubel, P.-V., El-Yagoubi, R., Tricot, A.: Time Based Resource Sharing model as a mean to improve cognitive load measurement. In: 10th International Cognitive Load Theory Conference, 20–22, Wollongong, Australia (2017)

22. Kintsch, W., Welsch, D., Schmalhofer, F., Zimny, S.: Sentence memory: a theoretical analysis. J. Memory Lang. **29**, 133–159 (1990)
23. Massar, S.A.A., Wester, A.E., Volkerts, E.R., Kenemans, L.: Manipulation specific effects of mental fatigue: evidence from novelty processing and simulated driving. Psychophysiology **47**, 1119–1126 (2010)
24. Yaple, Z.A., Stevens, W.D., Arsalidou, M.: Meta-analyses of the n-back working memory task: fMRI evidence of age-related changes in prefrontal cortex involvement across the adult lifespan. NeuroImage **196**, 16–31 (2019)
25. Hopstaken, J., Linden, D., Bakker, A., Kompier, M.: A multifaceted investigation of the link between mental fatigue and task disengagement. Psychophysiology **52**, 305–315 (2015)
26. Capa, R., Audiffren, M.: How does achievement motivation influence mental effort mobilization? Int. J. Psychophysiol. **74**, 236–242 (2009)
27. Capa, R., Audiffren, M., Ragot, S.: The effects of achievement motivation, task difficulty, and goal difficulty on physiological, behavioral, and subjective effort. Psychophysiology **45**, 859–868 (2008)
28. Capa, R.L., Audiffren, M., Ragot, S.: The interactive effect of achievement motivation and task difficulty on mental effort. Int. J. Psychophysiol. **70**, 144–150 (2008)
29. Pintrich, P.R.: A manual for the use of the Motivated Strategies for Learning Questionnaire (MSLQ) (1991)
30. Fisk, J.D., Ritvo, P.G., Ross, L., Haase, D.A., Marrie, T.J., Schlech, W.F.: Measuring the functional impact of fatigue: initial validation of the fatigue impact scale. Clin. Infectious Diseases **18**(Supplement_1), S79–S83 (1994)
31. Leppink, J., Paas, F., Van der Vleuten, C.P.M., Van Gog, T., Van Merriënboer, J.J.G.: Development of an instrument for measuring different types of cognitive load. Behav. Res. Methods **45**(4), 1058–1072 (2013). https://doi.org/10.3758/s13428-013-0334-1
32. Richter, M., Gendolla, G.H., Wright, R.A.: Three decades of research on motivational intensity theory: what we have learned about effort and what we still don't know. In: Advances in Motivation Science, pp. 149–186. Elsevier
33. Wongupparaj, P., Sumich, A., Wickens, M., Kumari, V., Morris, R.G.: Individual differences in working memory and general intelligence indexed by P200 and P300: a latent variable model. Biol. Psychol. **139**, 96–105 (2018)
34. Lakatos, P., Shah, A.S., Knuth, K.H., Ulbert, I., Karmos, G., Schroeder, C.E.: An oscillatory hierarchy controlling neuronal excitability and stimulus processing in the auditory cortex. J. Neurophysiol. **94**, 1904–1911 (2005)
35. Mitchell, D.J., McNaughton, N., Flanagan, D., Kirk, I.J.: Frontal-midline theta from the perspective of hippocampal "theta". Prog. Neurobiol. **86**, 156–185 (2008)
36. Fairclough, S.H., Ewing, K.: The effect of task demand and incentive on neurophysiological and cardiovascular markers of effort. Int. J. Psychophy. **119**, 58–66 (2017)
37. Seeber, K.G., Kerzel, D.: Cognitive load in simultaneous interpreting: mmeets data. Int. J. Bilingualism **16**(2), 228–242 (2012)
38. Roussel, S.: A computer assisted method to track listening strategies in second language learning. ReCALL **23**(2), 98–116 (2011)

In the Sky Between Expertise and Unexpected Feelings and Resources of Pilots' Resilient Ego: A Psychoanalytic Point of View

Maria Gabriella Pediconi[1,4]([⊠]), Sarah Bigi[2], Michela Brunori[3], Glauco Maria Genga[4,5], and Sabrina Venzi[5]

[1] Urbino University, Urbino, Italy
maria.pediconi@uniurb.it

[2] Department of Linguistic Sciences and Foreign Literatures, Università Cattolica del Sacro Cuore, Milan, Italy
sarah.bigi@unicatt.it

[3] Department of Economics Society Politics, Urbino University, Urbino, Italy
michela.brunori@gmail.com

[4] Società Amici del Pensiero 'S. Freud' of Milan, Milan, Italy
glaucomaria.genga@fastwebnet.it

[5] Italian Air Force at Institute of Aerospace Medicine of Milan, Milan, Italy
sabrina.venzi@yahoo.it

Abstract. The psychoanalytic perspective of this paper suggests the notion of the Resilient Ego as an essential part of military pilots' job. In order to explore their subjective management of Human Mental Workload, we analysed their resilience based both on structural aspects of their job, and on practical factors of their daily performances and tasks. Moreover, our work presents a qualitative analysis of military pilots' testimonies about the most significant unexpected events of their career. We analysed their subjective perceptions as well as professional and interpersonal resources they used to face to unforeseen events. In order to describe the mental contents that make up the subjective factor that promotes success in managing the unexpected, we included the analysis of the textual component of pilots' interviews. We found that in mastering daily job as well as the unexpected, the Resilient Ego is based on realism and cooperative thoughts. On the one hand, technical and non-technical skills – expertise components – are specifically supported by Crew Resource Management (CRM), on the other hand military pilots' family relationships animate subjective perceptions during flight performances. The Resilient Ego in the sky feeds daily risky tasks with the affective relationships cared for on earth, even when pilots need to manage dangerous conditions. If unforeseen events are an integral part of military pilots' workload, the analysis of how pilots deal with the unexpected increases our knowledge of the Human Factor and provides information about the subjective factors of resilience.

Keywords: Mental workload · Unforeseen events · Resilience · Military pilots · Psychoanalysis

L. Longo and M. C. Leva (Eds.): H-WORKLOAD 2020, CCIS 1318, pp. 27–57, 2020.
https://doi.org/10.1007/978-3-030-62302-9_3

1 From the Unexpected to Expertise: Human Mental Workload and Resilience

"One must respect airline pilots for the amazing skill they have acquired. We all know how to drive a car and operate the steering wheel and pedals to manoeuvre a car at speed and sometimes within a few feet of other cars that are stationary or moving in the opposite direction. Some of us know how to sail boats using a tiller and a few ropes to tack upwind and come about with fickle wind gusts. But the airline pilot! To have acquired a mental model of how to operate multiple controls, some embodying a degree of automation, to regulate thrust, speed, attitude, altitude, and heading – all interacting in complex nonlinear ways in three dimensions of space plus time as governed by the physical constraints of aero dynamics and control – what is going on in the pilot's head?" (Sheridan 2016).

Thomas B. Sheridan, professor emeritus at MIT, in his review of the interesting book "Facing the Unexpected in Flight" by French engineer and pilot Jean Pinet (2015) – who first overcame the sound barrier aboard the Concorde –, asks: "What's going on in the pilot's head?". We would like to start from this question, which in a way is within the reach of anyone, although it has interested the science of psychology since its beginnings in the early twentieth century: "Aviation is one of the applied fields to which psychological science has most contributed." (Muñoz-Marrón 2018).

In different ways, the mental attitude of the pilot has been continuously explored, because of the strong impact that flying has really had and is having all over the world. What attitudes and skills support pilots in the exercise of their profession, ranked third among the most dangerous professions? What are the motivations at the origin of their career, and the risks they face? How to conceive an adequate preparation in the face of the continuous evolution of complex environments for the increasingly sophisticated man-machine interaction?

Adequate training for the unexpected became a front-page topic around the world on January 15, 2009, when Captain Chesley "Sully" Sullenberger, landing on the Hudson River, averted what would have been a huge disaster for NY. For the media, it was immediately the "Miracle on the Hudson". Well: Sully declared that in those three minutes after the double bird strike, he didn't think he could die at all: he knew he could make an emergency ditching that would save them all. We wonder: how did he do it? (Sullenberger and Zaslow 2009) Or, watching an Air Show, with applause and photos, many people don't even imagine that it is a 'Visual Flight', with the planes of the acrobatic patrol about five feet away from each other. Visual Flight – or VFR (Visual Flight Rules) Flight – means controlling the aircraft with the same mastery and competence with which one would put one's own car in the garage at home. In the Air Force pilots' experience, the "concept of expertise links closely to the concept of the four stages of competence, with novices moving from unconscious incompetence, conscious incompetence, conscious competence and finally unconscious competence." (Byrne 2017, pag. 193).

Our paper aims to show new connections among Human Factors, Mental Workload and Resilience. These factors have a common denominator, at least in part: the role of subjective contributions even in demanding situations, in which person-systems and technical-systems could be parallel. (Pediconi and Genga 2018) Mental workload

(MWL) has been described as "a fundamental design concept in Human-Computer Interaction (HCI) and Ergonomics (Human Factors) and it is sometimes referred to as Cognitive Load (CL), specifically in Cognitive Psychology. It is intrinsically complex and multifaceted. There is no widely accepted definition of MWL, however, it can be intuitively described as the total cognitive load needed to accomplish a specific task under a finite period of time." (Moustafa et al. 2017, p. 31). In general, MWL is a multidimensional construct involving interactions between task and system demands, the operator (including mental and emotional skills) and the environment. (Estes 2015, Longo and Leva 2018).

In his wide review of the literature, Cain (2007) resumes five different and formal definitions of MWL. Among them, we emphasize the following one and develop it in our research: "the relative capacity to respond, the emphasis is on predicting what the operator will be able to accomplish in the future." (Cain 2007, p. 27) Wickens (2017) suggests that MWL can be examined from three perspectives, those of measurement, of prediction and of consequences, even in a subjective way. Mental workload is not an inherent property of a pilot's brain, but emerges from the interaction between the requirements of tasks, the circumstances under which they are performed, and the technical/affective skills, behaviours, and perceptions of the pilot (Hart and Staveland 1988). To measure this construct the researchers have been proposed a variety of measures that include self-assessment measures – i.e. self-report and subjective rating scales – (Pickup et al. 2005; Rubio et al. 2004), performance measures and physiological measures (Charles and Nixon 2019; Lean and Shan 2012). In our research we used a self-assessment measures based on principles of qualitative research aiming to explore perceived MWL in subjective terms and its relations with resilience.

MWL has been examined in different areas: from the rail industry (Smith and Smith 2017; Fan and Smith 2018) to education (Byrne 2018; Omosehin and Smith 2019), medical field (Carswell et al. 2005; Smith 2019; Di Flumeri et al. 2019) and risky professions (Bargiotas et al. 2018; Borghini et al. 2014; Cahill et al. 2018; 2019; Orlandi and Brooks 2018). Pilots as well as all human beings do not seem weak against adverse effects of stressful situations and we can monitor the "brain at work" in complex real-life situations such as while operating aircraft. (Dehais et al. 2019). Also what psychologists have called the cognitive unconscious is actually the part of our brain that is responsible for storing information from our previous experiences. (Riili and Falcone 2019).

If stressful situation can disrupt MWL, also MWL can modulate anxious response (Schmeichel et al. 2008). The maintenance of an optimal performance is a challenge especially in complex working environments where individuals have to cope with a high mental workload (Borghini et al. 2014) and stressful (Causse et al. 2011) or unexpected situations (Causse et al. 2013). Indeed, "sometimes we do gain intrinsic pleasure and value by investing more effort: the feeling of "flow" in working hard at an engaging interesting task". (Wickens 2017, p. 26) The link between MWL and stress has also been widely studied, and it has been seen that MWL can be good or bad, and that stress and anxiety are different concepts. (Alsuraykh et al. 2019).

In general, we can assume that "even if the relationships between workload, performance, satisfaction, stress and health are not well understood, there is a high level of evidence that factors such as job security, level of control and various other sources of satisfaction are also important influences. It is a common belief that people who enjoy their work – for a range of possible reasons – are to some degree protected from what might otherwise be the ill effects of excessively high workloads". (MacDonald 2003) The contribution of psychoanalysis can be useful to specify the subjective components of mental workload. According to Hancock (2017), in our work, we ask whether satisfaction is a governor of perceived workload.

The other important concept needed to study such demanding work as piloting is Resilience, of which there is no univocal definition (Bhamra et al. 2011; Lisnyak 2015; Weidlich and Ugarriza 2015). According to Rutter (2006), it is prudent to assume that resilience does not indicate a precise and limited concept: either because it is purely descriptive (avoiding negative behaviors and adopting the positive ones in terms of survival and success), or because the term is adopted by different disciplines and therefore crosses very different factors and parameters. As we know, it has been taken as a characteristic of the individual or the environment, of a group, of a social system. (Kendra and Wachtendorf 2003). Recent researches (Cantoni 2014, Fornette et al 2015) include, among the psychological constituents of resilience, determination, challenge desire, obstinacy, auto-efficacy. In sociology and psychology, as well as in systemic psychiatry, this notion began to spread in the 1980s. In the US, "the army began to explore the concept of deep resilience after the terrorist attacks of 11 September 2001". (Weidlich and Ugarriza 2015).

Among psychologists, resilience refers to three general meanings: good developmental outcomes despite high risk status; sustained competence under stress; recovery from trauma. (Fleming and Ledogar 2008). Luthar and colleagues (2000 2006) called resilience a construct with two distinct dimensions: significant adversity and positive adaptation despite adversity. Regarding the possibility of measuring resilience, qualitative methods seem to be especially relevant (Ungar et al. 2006). In any case, resilience shows in quite an impressive way the role of the Ego as an adaptive resource, dealing with the possibility of overcoming stressful situations with the least damage possible, not merely aiming to limit damage, but also obtaining new opportunities.

Our psychological approach, based on psychoanalytic discoveries, suggests a more proactive analysis of the development of resilience skills, in order to discover how individuals prepare themselves to resist the strong and negative effects of stressful events and situations, and in this way support their overall personal wellbeing (Deppa et al. 2016; Grant 2014; Malaguti 2015; Rozenfeld 2014).

Recent studies on the resilience characteristics in pilots show an increasing importance given to the inclusion of the 'surprise' factor in their training. Landman et al. (2017) claim that pilots have more difficulty in managing an adverse situation (i.e., an aerodynamic stall) when this situation is presented unexpectedly, and they experience a startle reflex. (Martin et al. 2016) If we consider that the loss of control in flight is the most important cause of serious flight accidents, we understand how ñch attention must be given to the study of reactions in the face of surprise. "Aviate, Navigate, Communicate" is what is repeated to military pilots during training, as if it were a mantra: and they actually learn this trio by heart and hold it like a precious compass in the sky. Hence the importance of perfecting "individual and team capabilities during critical events", as we will point out in the following paragraph about Crew Resource Management (CRM), where crucial skills are "situational awareness, decision-making, leadership, teamwork, workload management, stress management, and fatigue management." (Martin 2019, pag. 207) CRM consists of five fundamental components that influence each other and can determine the success or failure of a flight: communication, stress management, situational awareness, decision making and effective leadership. (Cooper 1980; Helmreich et al. 1999; Helmreich and Merritt 2000; Kanki et al. 2010). It is the CRM's task, especially in conditions of high operating pressure and attention channeling, to make pilots able to mitigate the consequences of errors. (Di Trani 2018).

In our research, we consider the role of the Ego as an adaptive resource. In this regard, our paper could strengthen the concept of individual resilience thanks to the Freudian doctrine. Freud's approach gives us the possibility of comparing resilience with the process managed by the subject to overcome the mourning event. The work *Mourning and Melancholia* (Freud 1915) describes the subjective faculty to start investing thoughts and affections in external reality again after having experienced mourning. This kind of work does not merely aim to limit damage, but also to obtain new opportunities and creative performances. Resilience resembles what Freud called "working through": when the Ego comes to light after mourning, it is a resilient Ego.

On the one hand the level of automation achieved by flight means that the on-board system is in a sense like a third crew member on the cockpit. And this is where new problems arise, because human-machine interaction is a very sensitive and even UASs factor. On the other hand any enterprise is possible if conducted in partnership with a someone else, that is the core of team orientation of pilots' work. (Ohlander et al. 2019) It recalls the structural question of *Civilization and its Discontents* (Freud 1929) where Freud emphasizes the opportunities and the difficulties to work with others.

The question of how to measure subjective resilience is still open: "The specific resilient skills and behaviors for flight crews are more difficult to pin down but could be observed via archival analyses of incident and accident reports and simulator training scenarios". (Pruchnicki et al. 2019) "The importance of using and recognizing coping strategies for individuals that work in extremely stressful conditions, such as the emergency context, as to avoid the development of burnout or even of a post-traumatic stress disorder (PTSD)" was detected in a study on Aviation and Emergency Personnel. (Ceschi et al. 2019) In Italy, the Air Force has taken on and promoted this same value with growing conviction and good results since the 1990s. This commitment has meant that pilots were encouraged to report, rather than hide, the flight incidents that had happened to them. The result has been an increase in the recorded incidence of flight incidents, but also a reduction in flight accidents.

2 The Resilient Ego at Work: An Empirical Study About Military Pilots in Their Managing Workload and Unexpected

From the theoretical background to the research questions. Despite the fact that the concept of resilience is rather complicated and deep in content as well as quite complex for an assessment and measurement, increasing research on resilience in extended contexts and dimensions is being carried out. (Bahmra et al. 2011; Lisnyak 2015) We consider resilience as the subjective mental resource in facing workload and unforeseen events.

Although the quantitative methods remain privileged in the field (Bakker et al. 2007; Estes 2015, Herbst et al. 2014;), a qualitative data collection involving field operators could help to elicit workload aspects related to the subjective side, both in positive and problematic terms. Among researchers, not only psychologists, attention to foundational knowledge of qualitative research methods in social sciences is increasing in order to gain clearer access to human experience, attitudes and resources; (Cahill et al. 2018; Wertz et al. 2011). The concept of workload emerged in aviation industry, where the need to evaluate the performance of pilots and air traffic controllers was increasingly necessary.

Our research aims to measure the resilience of military pilots in terms of the subjective perception of the job and its expected tasks. Military pilots' job is strongly characterized by a demand for highly specialized operations that often are related to the personal safety of workers and/or others. Military operations need high mental workload: focusing on the mental content that fosters the development of increased self-efficacy, increased social support and flexible and accurate thinking habits allow us to discover which subjective factors promote success in the management of workload and unforeseen events.

The sample of our research was composed of a group of 40 military pilots. They are people typically engaged in delicate operations in which individual skills and team-work coordination are decisive in order to obtain maximum efficiency. Their personal perception of profession is composed of cognition and feelings related to the structural aspects of their jobs and the performative aspects of their specific tasks and operations. In doing their jobs, pilots experience very intense situations, both related to emotions and feelings and also to professional and specific tasks. On the one hand, the difficult situations met in their jobs challenge their behavioural and mental health, but on the other hand, their behavioural and mental health can be seen as a favourable condition and even as a resource during specific operations.

Our exploration aims to lead a qualitative analysis of professional experience in terms of subjective perceptions. The strength of the Ego is very important for the success of operations and for the personal safety of the single worker. In particular, we will explore which kinds of mental contents accompany specialized performances. According to Freudian discoveries, our path suggests an analysis of connections among human factors, mental workload and resilience inspired by the psychoanalytic point of view. In particular, it has helped us to focalize the importance of contributions of single individuals even in the hardest conditions.

The Resilient Ego at Work in Mastering the Unforeseen Situations. It has been found that at least 70% of all air accidents involve human error. Causes of error include fatigue, workload size, and fear as well as cognitive overload, poor interpersonal communication, imperfect processing of information, and flawed decision making. (Ciniglio Appiani 2010; Weidlich and Ugarriza 2015) Recent works take into account the relationship between the concepts of MW, situation awareness and operative performance that can support the success of operations. (Borghini et al 2014)

We will analyze resilience as the subjective mental resource in facing unexpected events and Mental Workload from a qualitative research perspective. Focusing on the mental content allows us to discover which subjective factors promote success in the management of unforeseen situations. The pilot remains the undisputed protagonist of the analysis, evaluation and management of risks, both in the case of single operations, complex activities and interactions. The resilient Ego needs to manage interactions with: (a) machinery and equipment, (b) context and (c) social group (O'Connor et al. 2002).

In order to read the subjective experience in facing unforeseen events we find useful the concept of insight. Psychology uses this concept both to indicate the output of cognitive processes regarding data and information – problem solving – and for the elaboration of affective materials based on self-observation (Hatcher 1973). The APA Dictionary gives this definition: insight is "a cognitive form of learning involving the mental *rearrangement* or restructuring of the elements in a problem to achieve a *sudden understanding* of the problem and arrive at a solution". More specifically, insight can be defined as the sudden and often novel realization of the solution to a problem. This is the opposite type of solution to trial-and-error solutions. In 1926 Graham Wallas, co-founder of the London School of Economics, published the four stages of the creative process: (1) preparation; (2) incubation; (3) illumination; and (4) verification. Gary Klein (2014) extends Wallas' analysis. The impasse paradigm fits the Wallas model and is the most common method for studying insights. Humans use insights in facing impasses or detecting flawed assumptions: this is the first way of insight. The second variety of insight hinges on spotting a contradiction – something that doesn't make sense. The third variety of insight involves a connection, among different fields, as we found in many scientific discoveries.

Among the mental contents of our pilots, we can recognize elements regarding: 1) the 'working-through' of an actual situation, 2) a sudden comprehension of involved factors, 3) looking for a possible solution to manage the emergency.

Our research develops in two specific directions. On the one hand, we explore mental contents that accompany specialized performance of military pilots. On the other hand, we lead a qualitative analysis of subjective testimonies about the most representative, unforeseen events met during pilots' military careers. Subjective self-report measures concern perceived level of task demand. Actually "no one else is more prepared to provide an accurate judgment on workload experience than oneself" (Da Silva 2014, p. 314), even if it becomes difficult to discriminate between physical workload and mental workload, and the person may consider that the external task demands and the mental effort experiences as only one perception, and quantify jointly the mental effort invested.

According to scientific literature about pilots' strength of the Ego as a very impor-tant factor for the success of operations and for their personal safety, especially during unforeseen situations, we analyze:

- some common structural aspects of both jobs in terms of subjective perceptions: risks, team work, workload, belonging to a special department;
- some common performative aspects of expected performance of both jobs during their specific operations (hours of flight for military pilots), in terms of subjective percep-tions: instructions, team-colleagues, members of family, personal safety, passengers involved.
- subjective testimonies about the most representative unforeseen events met during pilots' military career.

We will take into account some aspects of the relational and educational background of our sample: age, training, composition of their original family and current family, the family reaction to their choice of job and how the decision for their job came about.

We will answer two research questions:

- **RQ1**. *The subjective network of resilience as a factor of aviation job*. How the perceptions of risk and workload are linked with other aspects of the job and performance, and what kind of personal resources are called into play, based also on the relational background of the subjects.
- **RQ2**. *Pilots' specific resilience in mastering the unforeseen events*. What kind of mental contents compose the subjective factor that promotes the success in the management of unforeseen situations, and how the Ego masters external and interpersonal conditions involved in the accident.

3   Methods and Materials

Sample. In our research we interviewed 40 Italian military pilots (aged between 28 and 60 years; mean age 43,60; sd 7,67). Specifically, the 40 pilots interviewed came from: The Air Force (17), the Land Army (10), the Carabinieri (3), the Navy (5), the Financial Guard (3), the Firefighters (2).

The aircrafts on which they operate (generally for several years, since they are officers in SPE (Permanent Effective Service) are fixed-wing (10) or rotating-wing (30). Both planes and helicopters are used for different purposes: from transport to reconnaissance, training, rescue or combat. It is not possible for us to specifically refer here to the aircraft models, because they are currently in use by the Italian Armed Forces, which treat this information as confidential.

Materials Collecting Data. Pilots were interviewed during the periodical check-up visits they must undergo at the Institute of Aerospace Medicine *Angelo Mosso* in Milan.[1] More precisely, our sample was composed of Official Pilots intercepted during their "ordinary visits", or "routine visits", i.e. without the object of the visit being the emergency of a symptomatology or anything else that could affect suitability. Each of them was asked to consent to the collection of data, specifying that their anonymity would be preserved. In all cases, they gladly accepted the invitation to talk about the most significant unexpected event that they had to face during their career and what resources they activated in order to overcome the dangerous situation.

1. Pilots answered a survey with 9 items based on a Likert scale from 1 to 10:

- 4 items refer to subjective perceptions of the "setting" of their job: they are *risk, teamwork, workload, sense of belonging* to a special service. I.e. "I ask you to quantify the workload from 1 to 10 in the ordinary tasks of your work."

---

[1] We would like to thank the Chief of Institute of Aerospace Medicine of Milan Dr. Gen. Giuseppe Ciniglio Appiani and Dr. Col. Alessandro Randolfi, Chief of Psychiatric Section, for having hosted this research from the beginning. Furthermore, our thanks go to Col. Riccardo Ferraresi for the precise explanations and kind constant advice on this paper. .

- 5 items refer to subjective perceptions of the "values" that affect daily performances and tasks: they are *instructions, teammates, personal safety, family, passengers*. I.e. "How much do you think about the *instructions manual* during daily operations?"

2. We also asked each pilot a subjective testimony about the most representative, unforeseen events met during military career.

Based on the survey we obtained 9 qualitative evaluations we called indicators: *risk, teamwork, workload, sense of belonging, instructions, teammates, personal safety, family, passengers*. The matching of the observed indicators gives us the *subjective network of resilience* composed on the one hand by the perception of structural factors of one's own job and, on the other hand, by the individual perception of expected performance even when they manage the risks. We matched defined indicators with other variables: age, compositions of their original and current families, the family reaction to their choice of job.

We applied some statistical operations (correlations, contingency tables, averages comparison with t-student or ANOVA). In contingency tables, where applicable, we have considered the significance of the Fisher test. T-test was considered based on Levene test.

We have summarized the descriptive data extracted from the testimonies of the 40 pilots we met. The data provide an overview of the main factors that can be detected in the management of unforeseen events in terms of *conditions* and *reactions* and how contribute to creating resilience.

Among *conditions* of unforeseen events we find:

- the aircraft
- the role of the pilot involved
- the event as incident or accident
- the specific task of flight
- the cause of emergency related to: 1) the machine; 2) the weather conditions or external conditions of the aircraft (birds, lack of visibility, high voltage wires, brown out): 3) human error (HE), their own or those of others (such as: wrong manoeuvre, uncoordinated manoeuvre, physical indisposition; forgetfulness of a passage of the procedure, avalanche induced by the blades, bang to the trolley, sheared cable, etc.)

Among *reactions* of unforeseen events we find:

- the perceived *Extra-workload* in terms of operative pressure;
- the *First Insight*, as referring to the *perceived surprise* experienced by the pilot the first moment after the unexpected event; we can refer here to first thoughts when the unexpected event was detected by pilots; it is the subjective condition of situational awareness recorded by the pilot, the first name that the pilot gives to the shock he is experiencing at moment of event. We labeled the *First Insight* with A if the shock perceived is immediately attributed to a mechanical cause or in any case to the machine (« Oh, God! the engine went out! » , or « Oh, s…t, the engine went out! »). We labeled

the *First Insight* with B, when the shock perceived is immediately attributed to a human error (« Oh, God, what have I done! »). A + B collects the cases in which the pilot perceives a shock that first seems attributable to a breakdown of the machine, and immediately later to an error of the pilot or flight partner. *First Insight* includes three main affections: 1) a feeling of *impotence* due to an emergency resulting from technical failure or external conditions of the aircraft; 2) *remorse or guilt* in the case of unforeseen events caused by human error; 3) *anger* if the perceived danger seems due to mechanical damage but it is caused by a human error.

- the *Other's Presence* is the perceived feeling of pilots about the contribution of others in managing the unforeseen event. It can be 1) *favourable* when others of the crew or on the ground have supported and favoured positive resolution of the critical event; 2) an obstacle (*adverse*) if others are perceived as a problem, a factor that contributed to produce or aggravate the critical event: 3) even the *Hierarchy* comes into play when the presence of the other, known for his institutional role, has helped to make the critical event more complex; 4) *neutral* when pilot doesn't mention other's contribution;
- *The professional resource* used to deal with the unexpected. We indicated with *expertise* the technical and procedural competence that pilots have learned and internalized through training and experience. This concept is linked to the concept of the four stages of competence, studied by authors in several fields, "with novices moving from unconscious incompetence, conscious incompetence, conscious competence and finally unconscious competence". (Byrne 2017, p. 193). We called *CRM* the resolution procedure in which the contribution of crew cooperation has assumed a predominant importance with respect to the inevitable technical competence.

In coherence with the research questions and, in particular, in the effort to describe the mental contents that compose the subjective factor that can promote the success of management of unforeseen situations, we included in our study the analysis of the textual component of our interviews. Only the final part of the interviews has been selected for this kind of analysis, i.e. the part in which the pilots were asked to briefly describe an unexpected event, occurred while the pilots were on duty. They were asked to describe an event in which they had to come up with a solution. The focus was explicitly not on a sensational episode, but on something that had left an impression on them.

One peculiarity of our corpus, which should be kept in mind, is that the texts we have are not verbatim transcripts of the pilots' original words, but notes taken by the interviewers. Therefore, we cannot provide in-depth linguistic analysis of lexicon and information structure, as we cannot be sure which were the words actually used by the interviewees and which were additions and/or rephrasing of the interviewers. For this reason, we chose to analyze this part of the interviews using the method of content analysis, and in particular a directed approach to content analysis (Hsieh and Shannon 2005). Content analysis is a method to approach the study of discourse that can be developed quantitavely or qualitatively (Franzosi 2007; Zaidman-Zait 2014). Given the dimension of our sample we chose the latter. In content analysis, patterns or structures of meaning are looked for in stretches of discourse by following a variety of methodologies. In general, any approach is characterized by the definition of a series of coding categories that are then used to classify and describe the content in the analysed sample of discourse.

In the directed approach to content analysis, coding categories are defined previously, based on theory or on a hypothesis.

In our case, the source of the coding categories was the claim described in the previous sections according to which resilience can be defined as the subjective mental resource in facing workload and unforeseen events. The categories reflect some of the factors extracted from the analysis of the previous parts of the interviews. They also reflect the typical structure of narratives, which usually report the development of action through time, through the particular point of view of the narrator.

As initial coding categories, we identified the following:

- the type of reported event
- the reported cause of the event
- the participants in the event
- the roles of the participants (both professional and in relation to the event)
- the first impressions regarding the event, if reported
- the described reaction of the narrator and/or of the other participants to the event
- the epilogue
- final considerations, if reported

4 Data and Findings

Also as an invitation to keep the focus on the subjectivity of pilots, we present how the pilots reported what was the occasion and at what time of their lives they chose the profession of flight.

- Only the 15% of our airmen undertook the pilot profession at random or taking an opportunity as adults.
- Instead, the clear majority of 85% cultivated the idea of becoming a 'man of the sky' since childhood.

The sentence *"When I grow up I want to become..."* has taken shape over time and gives us the image of a kind of vocation that continues to guide the inclinations of our pilots in undertaking and conducting with satisfaction the profession of military pilot.

We now begin the presentation of the results with Fig. 1 in which we see the composition of the current family of our sample. We are prone to thinking about the figure of the pilot as a technician of the highest level, a professional focused on a very risky job, always away from home, in flight, away from his loved ones and with the need to privilege the technical-professional precision neutralizing emotional involvement. This position is required by professions that can be very different from each other, especially those with very specific and technically sophisticated tasks including military pilots and certain health professions.

A position also highlighted by Freud in this comparison: "I cannot advise my colleagues too urgently to model themselves during psycho-analytic treatment on the surgeon, who puts aside all his feelings, even his human sympathy, and concentrates his mental forces on the single aim of performing the operation as skillfully as possible."

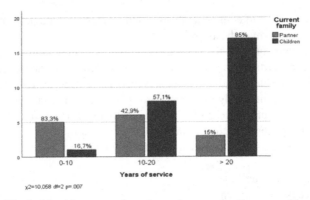

Fig. 1. Matching years of service and current family composition

(Freud 1912, p. 115) What have in common a surgeon, a pilot and an analyst? Their jobs are all three very delicate and very important for involved others, are based on a strict technique and require a talented Ego. From a dynamic point of view, in these jobs the affections are not really excluded but is the affective regulation that allows a full subjective participation for the success of tasks.

In fact, we hardly ever imagine the pilot involved with his family relationships in his private life, when we do not even think of him as single, without family. Instead, here we find pilots all engaged in stable family relationships, with or without children. In particular, pilots with more years of service have a family with children, while the youngest in service live with their partners. Therefore, the professional career not only does not prevent the establishment of family relationships but is accompanied by the possibility of caring for the offspring as the years of service progress. The link with the "earthly affections" therefore supports the feat of flying. It looks like it is he who is well bound to the earth, who knows best how to stay in sky.

These data give us a good introduction to the results that we present and in which we see the 'family factor' emerge several times.

We can observe Pearson's correlations in Table 1 to describe the significant connections among indicators. The table presents only the significant correlations omitting the coefficients for the sake of brevity and leaving only the asterisks relating to significance. When we see * the correlation is significant at level 0.05 (two-sided); when ** the significance is at level 0.001 (two-sided). The sign - before * indicates the negative correlation.

Observing correlation presented in Table 1 we can see that all indicators are linked with one or more of the others except the indicator called *Instructions*. We can consider these conjunctions as a confirmation of resilience as a complex and many-sided subjective dimension.

If correlation is positive and significant it means that correspondent indicators support each other. If correlation is negative and significant it means that correspondent indicators are linked but inversely: when one of them increases the other decreases. Indeed, we can see that the age and the years of service are inversely linked with the perception of workload: we can say that experience remains the first way to learn to manage the

Table 1. The network of resilience

	Risk	Team Work	Workload	Belonging	Instructions	Team-mates	Personal Safety	Family	Passengers
Years of service	-*		-**						
Age			-**			*			
Risk							**	**	
Team Work						**		*	*
Belonging								*	
Teammates		**							**
Safety	**							**	
Family	**	*		*			**		**
Passengers		*				**		**	

*p < 0.05, **p < 0.001

workload also in order to contain its pressure. Years of service are inversely linked with the perception of risk as a second acquisition due to job experience.

a) *Results about RQ1. The network of resilience.*

Observing these correlations is useful to remember that *Risk, Teamwork, Workload* and *Belonging* are indicators of how military pilots perceive fundamental factors of their professional status through the very constitutive aspects of their ordinary job. Other indicators – *Instructions, Teammates, Safety, Family* and *Passengers* – are referred to thoughts that military pilots perceive as connected with their daily performances and tasks, as mental contents that keep them company during their daily missions. Resilience keeps connected feelings towards the profession with feelings towards daily tasks, as a subjective network that is affectively connoted.

On the one hand, the *perception of risk* is conditioned by *years of service*, on the other hand it is linked with apprehension for *family relationships* and the sense of *personal safety*. The experience helps to mitigate the *risk perception* but it remains sensitive to a sense of *self safety* and the primal affects of individual existence.

The perception of *teamwork* is connected with the importance reserved to *teammates, family members* and *passengers*, revealing the interpersonal thinking of pilots.

Also, the sense of *belonging* that indicates the military pilots' attachment to their Army, supports thoughts about *family* members during daily tasks, revealing a sort of interchangeability between primal affects and job affects.

The feelings towards *teammates* during operations, supported by the importance of *teamwork*, are linked with the *passengers* and increases with *age*, confirming the job of military pilot is founded on a sense of sharing.

The sense of *personal safety* changes based on the *perception of risk*, but is supported by *family* relationships. Military pilots link the subjective attention for themselves with the care for the others involved in the job.

The attention for *passengers*, supported by *teamwork* as an important factor of the pilot job, is supported by *interpersonal and collaborative thoughts* about *teammates*-on-board and *family*-at-home during daily missions.

The indicator which is more closely connected with many others is the *family*: it is significantly connected with the *perception of risk* and supports the *teamwork* and the *sense of belonging* to an institutional organization. Moreover, the sense of *personal safety* and the attention reserved to *passengers* are very influenced by it. We can synthetize that the resilience of military pilots is supported in a special way by *family* relationships that maintain a considerable importance during daily performances. Military pilots in this way manage to keep the sky tied to their home on the ground.

What can we say about the only indicator that is not linked with others, i.e. *Instructions*? It remains independent from other aspects of military pilots' job: it could confirm a sort of first independent place grounding all other aspects of this complex job that is to drive an aircraft in the sky for very delicate missions. Without awareness about *Instructions* during daily operations the military pilots' job itself would be impossible.

By comparing the averages, we can observe which independent variables, taken from the personal and relational background of our workers, influence the indicators of resilience (Table 2).

Table 2. The relevance of family relations for military pilots

Family	Indicators averages	T test	P
Parents and relatives reactions	Teamwork	−3,65	.001
Positive	9,56		
Worried	10		
Current family reactions	Teamwork	−3,21	.003
Positive	9,63		
Worried	10		
Current family composition	Risk perception	2,05	.04
With children	6,12		
No children	7,21		
Family of origin composition	Passengers	3,34	.01
Brothers/sisters	8,41		
Only son	3,38		

The analysis of averages also documents the importance of family relationships for military pilots, both with the family of origin and with the current family. In particular, it is the perception of teamwork that is influenced by the reactions that pilots collect in the family. Particularly, if the family of origin supports their professional choice, the perception of the team is slightly tempered. The same effect of mitigation is produced by the positive consideration received by the current family. On the other hand, those who collect worried reactions both from the family of origin and the current family give greater importance to teamwork.

In both cases, the family of origin and the current family play similar roles and produce comparable effects. The impact of family on the importance of teamwork could be interpreted as a kind of affective interchangeability between family on the ground and the flying team. The teamwork can be confirmed as a characterizing factor in the military pilot's profession, not only from a professional technical point of view, but also from the point of view of the affections.

b) *Results to RQ2. Resilient mastering of unforeseen events.*

Analyzing the narratives of the military pilots, we have identified the situational factors inherent in the unforeseen events that each of them reported and the reactions that each of them had, both in terms of perceptions and in terms of resources. If the first ones are descriptive of the conditions that the pilots have had to manage, the second ones are subordinate to the individual and professional dispositions that the pilots have invested in the unexpected situation in terms of resilience. Each one told the most difficult unforeseen event of his career, from which he came out unscathed, having saved his own life and that of any others involved, thanks to specific resilient skills according to Pruchnicki et al. (2019).

Following is a description of each of the factors presented in Table 3.

Table 3. Factorization of unforeseen event based on pilots' testimonies

	FACTORS	Specific indicators	%
Conditions	Aircraft	FWA	25%
		RWA	75%
	Role	**Pilot**	77,5%
		Copilot	22,5%
	Event	Incident	17,5%
		Accident	82,5%
	Task	**Mission**	52,5%
		Training	35%
		Rescue	12,5%
	Cause	**Aicraft failure**	47,5%
		Human error	35%
		Weather conditions	17,5%
Reactions	Extra-Workload	**Yes**	85%
		No	15%
	First Insight	**A**	57,5%
		B	25%
		A + B	17,5%

(continued)

Table 3. (*continued*)

FACTORS	Specific indicators	%
Other's Presence	**Favourable**	32,5%
	Obstacle	27,5%
	Hierarchy	22,5%
	Neutral	17,5%
Resources	**Expertise**	52,5%
	CRM	47,5%

- *Aircraft*: FWA = Fixed Wing Aircraft (Combat Aircraft or Transport/Cargo/Multiengine Aircraft) or RWA = Rotary Wing Aircraft (Helicopter)
- *Role*, or position. The specific role of the pilot during the mission in which the unexpected occurred: pilot or co-pilot.
- Kind of unforeseen *Event*: Flight Incident or Flight Accident.
- *Task* in term of Flight Type: Mission, including Combat Flight and Transport Flight; Training; Rescue (SAR) Flight.
- *Cause*. the reason of unforeseen event due to: Aircraft malfunctioning; Weather conditions; Human Error
- *Extra-workload*: perceived Operative Pressure during the unforeseen event.
- *First Insight* in terms of kind of surprise or recognition if what has occurred (as attributable to a mechanical cause (A) or to a Human error (B), or both (A + B)).
- *Other's Presence*: it can be perceived as favourable or adverse (obstacle); we describe it as 'neutral' when the subject does not make any reference to it and 'hierarchy' when the pilot referred to any influence of hierarchical positions during the event.
- Professional *Resources* in terms of the *Expertise* due to training and experience or the contribution of Crew Resource Managment (CRM).

To analyze the development of the resilient conduct of military pilots in mastering an unforeseen event we observe how their perception of workload changes when they are involved in inconveniences or accidents during their careers (Fig. 2).

As the service years grow, the perception of operative pressure increases considerably, a perception that goes from 50% in the first 10 years, to 95% after 20 years of service. A datum that could be interpreted as follows: the knowledge acquired about the conditions and consequences of accidents and also human causes that produce them also result into a greater awareness of the additional workload that unforeseen events entail. It is also important to note how those who feel a greater workload during the unforeseen event and those who do not register it are distributed during the first 10 years of service: Operative pressure is explicitly perceived by 50% of pilots while the other 50% does not note this reaction. This data could be read as a stronger confidence in one's own expertise and abilities in the first years of service: Self-confidence that gives way to the learning experience with the progress of the military career, which seems to support the perception of an Extra-workload following an unforeseen event. This finding is consistent with other research about connections between high mental workload and

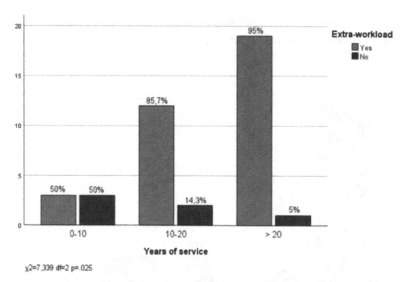

χ2=7,339 df=2 p=.025

Fig. 2. Matching years of service and perceived extra-workload during unforseen event

resilience (Righi et al. 2015; Wohleber et al. 2015). The increasing importance of learned experiences based on years of service can confirm MWL as a multidimensional construct involving interactions between task and system demands, the operator (including mental and emotional skills) and the environment. (Longo and Leva 2018) Individual factors in particular can be influenced both by positive feelings in working hard at an engaging, interesting task (Wickens 2017), or by stress and anxiety (Alsuraykh, et al. 2019). "The self-regulatory system and the coping strategies are aimed at stabilizing the emotional-mental-motor systems and allow decisions and motor actions to be balanced within the optimal emotions-related performance zone" (Tenenbaum et al. 2008, p. 21). The perception of increased operative pressure by the more experienced pilots could be due both to a greater awareness of the difficulties that may occur during the unforeseen events, and to the increased responsibilities that their learned experience and degree of seniority in the military corp involve, as compared to the younger colleagues. We can hypothesize that, in the same way as professional athletes, the most experienced pilots' mental representations associate emotions with adequate motor performance, and that these specific knowledge structures learned and stored in long-term memory enable them to cope efficiently with stress.

Figure 3 shows the distribution of perceived Extra-workload based on driven aircraft. 93.3% of helicopter pilots perceive the increase in operative pressure in the case of unforeseen events unlike FWA pilots who tell it in only 60% of cases. A first reading of this significant difference could be given taking into account the composition of our sample. Recall that the pilots interviewed came from: The Air Force (17), the Land Army (10), the Carabinieri (3), the Navy (5), the Financial Guard (3), the Firefighters (2). The aircraft on board which they operate are fixed-wing (10) or rotating-wing (30). Both planes and helicopters are used for different purposes: from transport to reconnaissance, training, rescue or combat. Our FWA pilots mostly belong to AM, while the RWA pilots also come from the other Armed Forces corps.

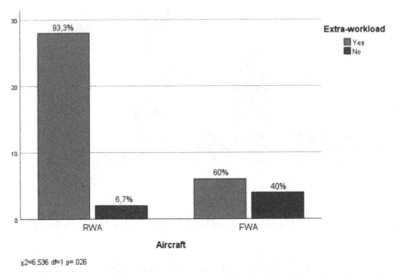

$\chi2=6,536$ df=1 p=.026

Fig. 3. Matching perceived Extra-workload and driven aircraft during the unforseen event

Taking into account this composition that includes military pilots of various Corps and Armed Forces we must take into consideration the following elements: a) the role played by flight in each of these Forces is very different; b) there is a marked difference about tasks and missions; c) the training of airmen and the general flying culture will also be very different. The primary tasks of an Army such as the Finance Guard, for example, involve limited and ancillary use of helicopters, which are therefore used in "simpler" routine operations compared to the missions of other AM rotary-wing machines engaged in out-of-area operations and operational theaters. The latter involves increased and continuous training. Taking these differences into account, we can assume that FWA pilots – mostly members of the AM – during the training are better prepared to face the unforeseen than helicopter pilots, in our case belonging to mostly other bodies of the Armed Forces. This reading argues that mastery of the medium and of the situation in the face of an unforeseen event would be directly proportional to training (Fig. 4).

In the face of the unforeseen event, helicopter pilots put in place their expertise made up of technical skills and accumulated experience in significantly greater way. On the other hand, fixed-wing aircraft pilots rely significantly more on CRM, consisting of teamwork and crew collaboration. An analysis of serious incidents or accidents has shown that, beyond individual competence, collective competence was a key factor in the "quality" of the management of such situations. Studies in collective work also illuminated the fact that individual competence of team members does not ensure team competence to collectively tackle a new, difficult, or critical situation. Rogalski and colleagues (2002) showed that simulation situations appear to be unavoidable resources for operators, both from the point of view of experiencing incidental situations, and

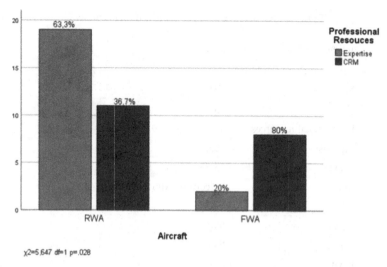

χ2=5.647 df=1 p=.028

Fig. 4. Matching professional Resources and driven aircraft during the unforseen event

from those of being trained to cope with such incidents. Specific simulation and training situations are then required not only for foreseen incidental or unavoidable situations but also for the purpose of developing competence for unforeseen situations. Echoing the words of one of our AM pilots: "It was a rescue op in the mountains, there was a degradation of the power of the engines during the rescue. [...] *Thanks to the teamwork* I re-evaluated the reconnaissance and we evaluated the escape route." Here the success of the operation is clearly attributable to the CRM, which the training of AM privileges compared to the training of other Army Forces Corps that consider it like other aspects. Nullmeyer and Spiker (2003), evaluating training situations, showed the importance of the quality of crew interactions for the mission performance. Consistently with other researches, (Dekker and Lundström 2006; Di Trani 2018; Thomas 2004) our results show on the one hand that CRM problems arise mainly from decision making and communication within crews, on the other hand that the most effective crews showed strong situational awareness and time management skills, in terms of correct analysis of the situation.

Even the comparison between the averages presented in Table 4 shows us that with years of service the perception of operative pressure increases in the face of unforeseen events. The unforeseen event involves an overloading of the professional task that becomes more difficult to manage. Up to 13 years of service the pressure does not seem to be so high – this is the average of the years of service of those who have not detected an increase in operative pressure in the narrative of the unforeseen event –, at 22 years of service the perception of operative pressure in case of unforeseen events becomes clearly perceived. With the years of service also the professional resources put in place in the management of unforeseen events change. Until 18 years of service, individual technical skills in terms of expertise win, after 23 years of service the value of teamwork in terms of CRM increases. A fact that could be interpreted as an enrichment of the expertise that the military pilot gains as his career progresses. Along with the years of

Table 4. Job factors and experience of military pilots

Job factors	Experience	T-test	P
Perceived Extra-workload	Years of service	2,61	.01
Yes	22		
No	13		
Professional resources	Years of service	-2,17	.03
expertise	18,05		
CRM	23,53		
Role	Perceived Extra-workload	-2,23	.03
Pilot	7,52		
Co-pilot	6,67		
Aircraft	Passengers	2,55	.02
RWA	8,40		
FWA	4,40		

service also grows resorting to sharing their professional resources, both as a sharing of responsibilities and resolutions. The perception of an increased workload that the unforeseen event entails is also influenced by the role played in the missions in which thay had to cope with the accident: the pilot felt more the weight of responsibility than the co-pilot. A data that confirms our expectations. In a different way from expectations instead we can read the interaction that the table shows between the aircraft piloted during the unforeseen event and the average of the scores that the pilots had attributed to the importance of passengers during the ordinary performance of their work. Here we find a connection between two different sources of information. On the one hand the pilot/co-pilot told us which vehicle he was driving when he found himself involved in the most significant unforeseen event of his career. The same pilot/co-pilot had already told us in the first part of the interview, not knowing that he would be asked to tell the most significant unforeseen event of his career, what importance he gave to some aspects of his performance including "how much he thinks of passengers during the flight". Pilots who were in the helicopter during the accident/incident had already stated that during ordinary flights they typically think more about passengers than their fixed wing colleagues. On the one hand, we could assume that helicopter pilots are typically engaged in missions with the helicopter and that pilots of fixed wing aircraft are regularly piloting this type of medium. In this case, we could generalize our result by saying that helicopter pilots seem to give much more importance to passengers than to fixed wing colleagues, who might be engaged in missions that do not require this specific attention. We could also hypothesize that the interpersonal availability of these helicopter pilots, revealed by the attention they would regularly reserve to passengers, has positively contributed to the management and resolution of the serious unforeseen situation they have faced, enabling them to overcome it.

In this direction, we could recognize in the attention paid to the passengers a factor of resilience of the military pilots. On the other hand, we could read this predisposition of RWA pilots to pay attention to passengers as greater receptivity to the presence of others during the flight: a predisposition that would favor them in any rescue missions. Often it is the helicopter pilots who conduct complex missions that tend to worsen during the course of action, with frequent unforeseen events and in which the weight of others is more felt. An example of this are the Alpine rescue missions, the search for people and the search at sea, situations in which the levels of stress are very high, the outcome uncertain and the resources of resilience demands very expensive.

Speaking of interpersonal thinking of military pilots, we can read the data presented by Fig. 5 that shows how the resources used by our sample in the management of the unforeseen event are distributed based on the composition of their family, with or without children.

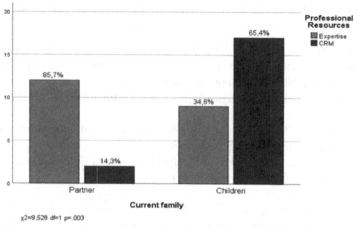

$\chi^2 = 9,528$ df$=1$ p$=.003$

Fig. 5. Matching the current family composition and professional Resources in mastering the unforseen event

Pilots without children that live with the partner typically trust their own technical expertise in mastering the unexpected; they use a strategy that is more based on individual skills.

On the contrary, pilots with a family including children typically choose collaborative ways in mastering imponderable situations. We can interpret their attitude as a shared resilience: a sort of extension of parental experience that is based on a family that is not only more numerous, but more complex interpersonally.

The next tables allow us to see in depth the individual psychological factor: it has drawn and supported the mastering of unexpected events in terms of resilience orienting their positive outcome.

Figure 6 presents the contingency table that matches pilots' First Insight, as the first mental contents pilots noticed at the moment of impact, and the real cause of correspondent accident/incident that was verified only post hoc.

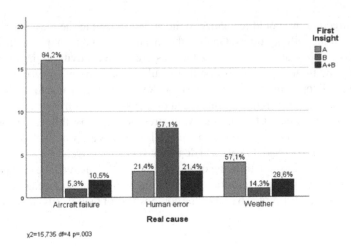

χ2=15,735 df=4 p=.003

Fig. 6. Matching First Insight about unforeseen event and real cause of incident/accident

With the term *First Insight* we labeled the mental contents that pilots focused on in their testimonies about the moment of impact with the unexpected event, i.e. the moment in which they realized that something unexpected was happening with a surprise effect. Between these first contents as insights is possible to distinguish a double direction:

– "What is happening?": we called *First Insight* A the first intuition about something related to the airplane or the flight conditions
– "What did I do? What did you do?": we called *First Insight* B the first intuition about something that was generated by a human error.

The third option is represented by the double attribution, both the human error and aircraft failure or weather conditions. It is the *First Insight* we called A + B. The case of keeping together both mental contents can be interpreted as impossibility to decide for one or another attribution; it could be due to a sort of suspension or inhibition of subjective judgement because of stressor effect of the unforeseen event.

According to O'Hare (2001) "there has been considerable progress in the past decade in the field of human error, particularly in terms of conceptualizing the broader constraints that shape individual behaviours. It is now commonly recognized that there is much more to accident investigation than describing the actions of the nearest individuals in the *last moments before* the event." (p. 2016; our emphasis). This paper adds the possibility to explore the *first moment after* the event, in which the individual thinking formulates the first insight that is at the same time an attribution to understand what is happening and the first comprehension based on subjective feelings. Indeed, the first insight is the strong possibility to address specific individual actions towards the resolution of accident/incident.

In Fig. 6 we see that the surprise related to situational factors (*First Insight* A) is significantly associated to the aircraft failure (84,2%) or to bad weather conditions (57,1%) that are the real causes of the unexpected event.

First Insight B related to human errors is significantly associated with the unexpected event actually being caused by the human factor (51,7%).

We see that the first insight interprets with a precision very close to the reality the real cause of the unexpected event before the investigation that will confirm all aspects of the incident/accident.

The *First Insight* shows the pilots' psychological competence in analysing and interpreting step by step, even in the very stressing moment, what is happening during the flights.

We observe the cases of unexpected events caused by human errors in Fig. 6. The correspondent *First Insight* B is 57,1%, but *First Insight* A and *First Insight* A + B are both present both and are around 20%. How can we read this result? We can interpret it as a higher difficulty to admit the human factor compared with the easier recognition of mechanical failures.

It is interesting to observe the *First Insight* A + B in case of unexpected events caused by bad weather conditions, which corresponds to 28,6%. It can be interpreted as a pilots' tendency to a self-attribution of a part of responsibility even in cases in which human errors are not present.

In general, Fig. 6 shows us the strict correspondence between the perceived surprise at the moment of impact (*First Insight*) and the real cause of the unexpected event. It is a demonstration of pilots' brilliant skills in managing the unexpected and understand its real causes. This finding is consistent with recent studies on the characteristics of resilience in pilots, which show an increasing importance given to the inclusion of the "surprise" factor in their training. On the one hand, we know that Landman et al. (2017) claim that pilots have more difficulty in managing an upset situation (i.e., an aerodynamic stall) when this situation is presented unexpectedly, and they experience a startle reflex. (Martin et al. 2016). On the other hand, our findings are consistent with what Chittaro (2014) shows, i.e. that even the simulation of emergency conditions through persuasive technology can increase the fundamental safety actions especially in terms of internal locus of control. Similarly, a study of airline pilots by You et al. (2013) showed that locus of control influences safe operation behavior. Hunter (2002) analysed safety locus of control in pilots and reinforced these results, finding that civil aviation pilots with a more internal orientation were involved in fewer hazardous events. Hunter and Stewart (2009; 2012) extended the investigation of locus of control to U.S. Army aviators, developing the Army Locus of Control Scale and finding significant associations which are consistent with research conducted on civil aviation pilots. In particular, aviators with a more internal control orientation experienced fewer accidents than aviators who were low on that construct.

Results of the Content Analysis. We included in our study the analysis of the textual component of our interviews. It is based on coded categories according to which resilience can be defined as the subjective mental resource in facing workload and unforeseen events. The categories reflect some of the factors extracted from the analysis of the previous parts of the interviews. They also reflect the typical structure of narratives, which usually report the development of action through time, through the particular point of view of the narrator. We identified the following: the type of reported event; the reported cause of the event; the participants in the event; the roles of the participants (both professional and in relation to the event); the first impressions regarding the event, if reported; the described reaction of the narrator and/or of the other participants to the event; the epilogue; final considerations.

Main Findings of the Content Analysis. The types of reported events refer mostly to difficulties during flight or landing. Of those who responded, about one third reported events caused by human error, but of these, only 3 cases referred to errors made by the narrator himself. Another group of answers (also about one third of the respondents) were about events caused by mechanical issues.

Except for the case in which the pilot reports an event occurred to others, the narrators are always directly involved in the incidents they describe. In a minority of cases, a higher-ranking officer is present during the event; this hierarchical asymmetry is usually reported as problematic, either because it is the cause of the incident itself, or because it hinders its solution.

In most cases, the pilots depict themselves as the ones who found the solution that averted tragedy. Some of them acknowledge the importance of teamwork, only 4 cases explicitly refer to luck as having had a crucial 'role' in the happy ending of the event.

Discussion of Results of the Content Analysis. Based on the results of the analysis, a few considerations can be made. Among the interviewed pilots, the majority of those who accepted to report an incident chose to tell a story in which they are the main 'character': they find the solution to a situation that in a few cases could have ended tragically and that only in very few cases had been caused by the narrator himself.

The role of 'hero' the narrators choose for themselves comes across also in relation to the other participants' actions: as reported in the results, only a very small number of pilots acknowledge the importance of the crew's participation in the solution of the situation. In general, the pilots describe their own reaction to the sudden problem as almost automatic, as though they had first reacted and only later reflected and realized what had really happened; they often explain this kind of behavior as an effect of the training they received. Following are some examples from the interviews: "a cell in my memory snapped open; I remembered what I had to do from the manual and I did it"; "I did everything automatically, I was not hearing anything else"; "when I landed, personally I felt nothing, I did everything automatically".

There is also an additional element, which was not included in our coding categories, but which stands out in the final considerations or comments that conclude the pilots' narratives, i.e. the role of emotions. In the majority of cases, emotions are not mentioned. When they are, the pilots tend to deny having experienced any (in only one case, the pilot acknowledges having had a sort of emotional breakdown when all was over). There is also a small number among those who did not mention any emotions, who feel the need to report that they went back to flying almost immediately after the incident ("after four hours I was back in the air"; "there were no consequences"; "after 3 days I was back in the air").

In general, although they were not asked to report of dangerous episodes, the pilots chose to tell stories that in most cases involved a risk to their life or to the life of others. The representation these pilots choose to give of themselves is that of persons who are able to react immediately to a sudden dangerous situation. Most of them seem to have always been in control, even when they were not the first pilot or were in training.

The narratives about human errors are particularly interesting in this respect: "the pilot's excessive trust in his own skills was the cause of the disaster"; "we were flying too high, but the instructor said everything was ok"; "the pilot was in training, he was supposed to perform a certain maneuver for landing but he got scared and he froze. So I took command from behind him".

5 Conclusions and Limitations

"The point, however, is to understand that we pilots must never forget to fly the airplane first, to make our decisions based on the safety of the airplane and not the pressure brought to bear by outside forces. Taking care of the crew and passengers begins with taking care of the airplane" (Albright 2017, P.34).

About RQ1 The network of resilience – our findings show the configuration of resilience as a subjective network, composed by many aspects related both to the structure of the job and to the nature of performance. We can confirm that the resilient Ego at work manages both job and performance in order to face the adversity in a positive way. Among the indicators we explored, two emerge for their relevance: the first is the place reserved to family relationships during operations; the second place is taken by the importance of teamwork, the teammates and the passengers, as confirmation of the cooperative nature of professional resilience, supported by relational competence and tied to an affective background (Jex et al. 2003; Meyer and Allen 1997). Our research confirms the Multilevel Resilience Framework (Turan et al. 2016). Resilience is the ability to adjust both behaviour and thinking during or following changes and disturbances.

In a resilience process, failures do not stand for a breakdown or malfunctioning, but rather represent the converse of the adaptations necessary to cope with the real world complexity, especially when resources and time are finite, as when unexpected events occurs. In order to be able to manage the operational procedures on board and to deal successfully with safety critical operations and harsh environments, multilevel system resilience is required. It is what we called *resilience as a trait*.

About RQ2. Resilient mastering of unforeseen events – We found that in mastering the unexpected, the Resilient Ego is based on realism and cooperative thoughts. On the one hand, technical and non-technical skills – expertise components – are specifically supported by Crew Resource Management (CRM). On the other hand, military pilots' family relationships animate subjective perceptions during flight performances. The Resilient Ego in the sky feeds daily risky tasks with the affective relationships cared for on earth, even when pilots need to manage dangerous conditions.

Here we suggest a *Resilient Subjective Factor* (RSF) as a subjective dimension that allows pilots to develop both a *resilience as a trait* in leading their ordinary job – daily tasks and performances – and a *shared resilience* in facing the unexpected.

RSF is a dimension composed by some structural factors:

– the attachment to family relationships
– peculiar interpersonal skills: favoring teamwork and teammates within resilience as a trait; favoring CRM and the importance reserved to passengers within the shared resilience in mastering the unforeseen event

– specific self-efficacy based on realistic knowledge, supported by expertise, activated by creative First Insights.

About *First Insight*, already Hurtes&Allen (2001) had considered insight as one of the seven dimensions of resilience. Santo Di Nuovo (2017) analyzes resilience as the ability to master strong emotions thanks to the self-efficacy that favors the internal locus of control and avoids passivation. Among the main protective and predictive factors are the request for help and social support. Our findings confirm the same main components of this first brilliant work of individual thinking – the *First Insight* – at the moment of impact of unexpected.

The perception of increased operative pressure by the more experienced pilots could be due both to a greater awareness of the difficulties that may occur during the unforeseen events, and to the increased responsibilities that their training and degree involve. We observe here a process of internalization similar to that of professional athletes: pilots' mental representations associate emotions with adequate motor performance and these specific knowledge structures learned and stored in long-term memory enable them to cope efficiently with stress (Tenenbaum et al. 2008). On the one hand this self-regulatory system keeps available all the learned materials during the experience, an internalization that has the appearance of an automatism. On the other hand, the unexpected calls into play the subjective resources of a kind of creative thinking we saw in action in terms of *First Insight*.

Self-efficacy processes we observed can play a decisive role in efficiently coping with emotional pressure and task demands. Perceived self-efficacy helps to account for many elements in coping behavior produced by different influences, i.e. the level of physiological stress reactions, the self-regulation of refractory behavior, the achievement strivings, the resignation and despondency to failure experiences (Bandura 1997). As a result, the individual who perceives high levels of confidence is likely to expend greater effort and persist longer in the face of adversity in terms of resilience and performance accomplishments (Tenenbaum et al. 2008). When the pilots feel competent and confident in executing the complex task, even these feelings are used to self-regulate subjective states and manage shocking stressor events.

Based on our findings, compared to the research literature about subjective features of pilots' resilience, we see that interpersonal skills, first insight and shared resilience can be explored in depth in future researches, especially in their relations with MWL management in demanding situations.

A limitation of this study concerns the limited size of the sample. In future research, it would be interesting to have the opportunity to record interviews so as to be able to carry out a more in-depth discourse analysis. If in our research we have tried to define the qualitative and affective aspects of the unforeseen events and of resilience network, in a future research it could be interesting to explore also the combination and the comparison between quantitative and qualitative methods applied to the same goals.

References

Albright, J.: When Pilots Become Passengers. Bus. Commer. Aviat. 33 (2017)

Alsuraykh, N.H., Wilson, M.L., Tennent, P., Sharples, S.: How stress and mental workload are connected. In: PervasiveHealth 2019: Proceedings of the 13th EAI International Conference on Pervasive Computing Technologies for Healthcare, pp. 371–376 (2019)

Bakker, A., Hakanen, Y., Demerouti, E., Xanthopoulou, D.: Job resources boost work engagement, particularly, when job demands are high. J. Educ. Psychol. **99**(2), 274–284 (2007)

Bandura, A.: Self-efficacy: The exercise of control. Freeman, New York (1997)

Bargiotas, I., Nicolaï, A., Vidal, P.-P., Labourdette, C., Vayatis, N., Buffat, S.: The complementary role of activity context in the mental workload evaluation of helicopter pilots: a multi-tasking learning approach. In: Longo, L., Leva, M.Chiara (eds.) H-WORKLOAD 2018. CCIS, vol. 1012, pp. 222–238. Springer, Cham (2019). https://doi.org/10.1007/978-3-030-14273-5_13

Bhamra, R., Dani, S., Burnard, K.: Resilience: the concept, a literature review and future directions. Int. J. Prod. Res. **49**(18), 5375–5393 (2011)

Borghini, G., Astolfi, L., Vecchiato, G., Mattia, D., Babiloni, F.: Measuring neurophysiological signals in aircraft pilots and car drivers for the assessment of mental workload, fatigue and drowsiness. Neurosci. Biobehav. Rev. **44**, 58–75 (2014)

Byrne, A.: Mental workload as an outcome in medical education. In: Longo, L., Leva, M.C. (eds.) H-WORKLOAD 2017. CCIS, vol. 726, pp. 187–197. Springer, Cham (2017). https://doi.org/10.1007/978-3-319-61061-0_12

Byrne, A.: The effect of education and training on mental workload in medical education. In: Longo, L., Leva, M.Chiara (eds.) H-WORKLOAD 2018. CCIS, vol. 1012, pp. 258–266. Springer, Cham (2019). https://doi.org/10.1007/978-3-030-14273-5_15

Cahill, J., Cullen, P., Gaynor, K.: Estimating the impact of work related stress on pilot wellbeing and flight safety. In: Longo, L., Leva, M.C. (eds.) Human Mental Workload. Models and Applications, pp. 7–32. Springer, Cham (2018)

Cahill, J., Cullen, P., Gaynor, K.: Pilot wellbeing & work related stress (Wrs). In: 20th International Symposium on Aviation Psychology, pp. 43–48 (2019)

Cain, B.: A review of the mental workload literature. Report No. RTO-TR-HFM-121-Part-II. Toronto, Canada: Defence Research and Development Canada Toronto Human System Integration Section (2007)

Cantoni, F.: La resilienza come competenza dinamica e volitiva. G Giappichelli Editore (2014)

Carswell, C.M., Clarke, D., Seales, W.B.: Assessing mental workload during laparoscopic surgery. Surgical innovation **12**(1), 80–90 (2005)

Causse, M., Dehais, F., Pastor, J.: Executive functions and pilot characteristics predict flight simulator performance in general aviation pilots. Int. J. Aviat. Psychol. **21**(3), 217–234 (2011)

Causse, M., et al.: Affective decision making under uncertainty during a plausible aviation task: an fMRI study. NeuroImage **71**, 19–29 (2013)

Ceschi, A., Costantini, A., Zagarese, V., Avi, E., Sartori, R.: The NOTECHS + : a short scale designed for assessing the non-technical skills (and more) in the aviation and the emergency personnel. Front. Psychol. **10**, 902 (2019)

Charles, R.L., Nixon, J.: Measuring mental workload using physiological measures: a systematic review. Appl. Ergon. **74**, 221–232 (2019)

Chittaro, L.: Changing user's safety locus of control through persuasive play: an application to aviation safety. In: Spagnolli, A., Chittaro, L., Gamberini, L. (eds.) PERSUASIVE 2014. LNCS, vol. 8462, pp. 31–42. Springer, Cham (2014). https://doi.org/10.1007/978-3-319-07127-5_4

Ciniglio Appiani, G.: Argomenti di medicina aeronautica, (ed). Rivista Aeronautica, Roma (2010)

Cooper, G.E. (Ed.): Resource Management on the Flight Deck, Proceedings of a NASA/Industry Workshop, San Francisco, California June 26–28 1979, NASA (1980)

Da Silva, F.P.: Mental workload, task demand and driving performance: what relation? Procedia-Soc. Behav. Sci. **162**, 310–319 (2014)

Dehais, F., et al.: Monitoring Pilot's mental workload using ERPs and spectral power with a six-dry-electrode EEG system in real flight conditions. Sensors **19**, 1324 (2019)

Dekker, S.W., Lundstrom, J.: From threat and error management (TEM) to resilience. Hum. Fact. Aerospace Saf. **6**(3), 261 (2006)

Deppa, K.F., Saltzberg, J.: Resilience Training for Firefighters: An Approach to Prevent Behavioral Health Problems. SF. Springer, Cham (2016). https://doi.org/10.1007/978-3-319-38779-6

Di Nuovo, S.: Trauma e resilienza tra neuroscienze e aspetti psico-sociali. J. Appl. Ceremonial Commun. Manage. anno II numero 1, pp. 24–43 (2017)

Di Flumeri, G., et al.: EEG-based workload index as a taxonomic tool to evaluate the similarity of different robot-assisted surgery systems. In: Longo, L., Leva, M.C. (eds.) H-WORKLOAD 2019. CCIS, vol. 1107, pp. 105–117. Springer, Cham (2019). https://doi.org/10.1007/978-3-030-32423-0_7

Di Trani, M.: Non sottovalutare mai il briefing pre-volo, Anatomia di un inconveniente di volo HH212-ICO. Rivista Sicurezza Volo **325**(2018), 28 (2018)

Estes, S.: The workload curve: subjective mental workload. Hum. Factors **57**(7), 1174–1187 (2015)

Fan, J., Smith, A.P.: Mental workload and other causes of different types of fatigue in rail staff. In: Longo, L., Leva, M.C. (eds.) H-WORKLOAD 2018. CCIS, vol. 1012, pp. 147–159. Springer, Cham (2019). https://doi.org/10.1007/978-3-030-14273-5_9

Fleming, J., Ledogar, R.J.: Resilience, an evolving concept: a review of literature relevant to aboriginal research. Pimatisiwin **6**(2), 7–23 (2008)

Fornette, M.P., Darses, F., Bourgy, M.: How to improve training programs for the management of complex and unforeseen situations? In: de Waard, D., Sauer, J., Röttger, S., Kluge, A., Manzey, D., Weikert, C., Toffetti, A. R (2015)

Franzosi, R.: Content Analysis: Objective. Systematic, and Quantitative Description of. Springer, Dordrecht (2007). doi:10.1007/978-94-007-0753-5_552

Freud, S.: The Dynamics of Transference. SE, vol. 12, p. 115 (1912)

Freud, S.: Mourning and Melancholia, SE, vol. 14 (1915)

Freud, S.: Civilization and its Discontents. SE, vol. 21 (1929)

Grant, LK.G.: Developing Resilience for Social Work Practice, Palgrave Macmillan (2014)

Hancock, P.A.: Whither workload? mapping a path for its future development. In: Longo, L., Leva, M.C. (eds.) Human Mental Workload. Models and Applications, pp. 3–17. Springer, Cham (2017). https://doi.org/10.1007/978-3-319-61061-0_1

Hart, S.G., Staveland, L.E.: Development of NASA-TLX (Task Load Index): results of empirical and theoretical research. Adv. Psychol. **52**, 139–183 (1988)

Hatcher, R.L.: Insight and self-observation. J. Am. Psychoanal. Assoc. **21**(2), 377–398 (1973)

Helmreich, R.L., Merritt, A.C., Wilhelm, J.A.: The evolution of Crew Resource Management training in commercial aviation. Int. J. Aviat. Psychol. **9**(1), 19–32 (1999)

Helmreich, R.L., Merritt, A.C.: Safety and error management: the role of crew resource management. In: Hayward, B.J., Lowe, A.R. (eds.) Aviation Resource Management, pp. 107–119. Ashgate, Aldershot (2000)

Herbst, N.R., Huber, N., Kounev, S., Amrehn, E.: Self-adaptive workload classification and forecasting for proactive resource provisioning. Concurr. Comput. Pract. Exper. **26**, 2053–2078 (2014)

Hsieh, H.F., Shannon, S.E.: Three approaches to qualitative content analysis. Qual. Health Res. **15**(9), 1277–1288 (2005)

Hunter, D.R.: Development of an aviation safety locus of control scale. Aviat. Space Environ. Med. **73**, 1184–1188 (2002)

Hunter, D.R., Stewart, J.E.: Locus of Control, Risk Orientation, and Decision Making Among U.S. Army Aviators. Technical Report 1260, U.S. Army Research Institute for the Behavioral and Social Sciences, Fort Rucker, AL (2009)

Hunter, D.R., Stewart, J.E.: Safety locus of control and accident involvement among army aviators. Int. J. Aviat. Psychol. **22**, 144–163 (2012)

Hurtes, K.P., Allen, L.R.: Measuring resiliency in youth: the resiliency attitudes in skills profile. Therapeutic Recreat. J. **35**, 333–347 (2001)

Jex, S.M., Adams, G.A., Bachrach, D.G., Sorenson, S.: The impact of situational constraints, role stressors, and commitment on employee altruism. J. Occup. Health Psychol. **8**(3), 171 (2003)

Kanki, B., Anca, J., Helmreich, R.: Crew Resource Management. Academic Press in an Imprint of Elsevier, 2nd edn. (2010)

Kendra, J.M., Wachtendorf, T.: Elements of resilience after the world trade center disaster: reconstituting New York city's emergency operations center. Disasters **27**(1), 37–53 (2003)

Klein, G.: Seeing What Others Don't. the Remarkable Ways We Gain Insights. Nicholas Brealey Publishing, London (2014)

Landman, A., Groen, E.L., van Paassen, M.M., Bronkhorst, A., Mulder, M.: The influence of surprise on upset recovery performance in airline pilots. Int. J. Aerospace Psychol. **27**(1–2), 2–14 (2017)

Lean, Y., Shan, F.: Brief review on physiological and biochemical evaluations of human mental workload. Hum. Fact. Ergon. Manuf. Serv. Ind. **22**(3), 177–187 (2012)

Lisnyak, S.: Literature review regarding the concept of resilience and its assessment in the context of the economic dimension. CES Working Papers **7**(2A), 511–518 (2015)

Longo, L., Leva, M.C. (eds.): Human Mental Workload. Models and Applications. Springer, Cham (2018)

Luthar, S.S., Cicchetti, D.: The construct of resilience: implications for interventions and social policies. Dev. Psychopathol. **12**, 857–885 (2000)

Luthar, S.S., Cicchetti, D., Cohen, D.J.: Resilience in development: a synthesis of research across five decades. Dev. Psychopathol.: Risk Disorder Adaptation **3**, 739–795 (2006)

MacDonald, W.: The impact of job demands and workload on stress and fatigue. Aust. Psychologist. **2**, 102–117 (2003)

Malaguti, E.: Educarsi alla resilienza: come affrontare crisi e difficoltà e migliorarsi. Edizioni Erickson (2005)

Martin, W.L., Murray, P.S., Bates, P.R., Lee, P.S.Y.: A flight simulator study of the impairment effects of startle on pilots during unexpected critical events. Aviation Psychol. Appl. Hum. Fact. **6**(1), 24–32 (2016). Hogrefe Publishing

Martin, W.L.: Crew Resource management and individual resilience. In: Crew Resource Management, pp. 207–226. Academic Press (2019)

Masys, A.J.: Complexity and the Social Sciences: Insights from complementary theoretical perspectives. In: Minai, A.A., Braha, D., Bar-Yam, Y. (eds.) Unifying Themes in Complex Systems VII, pp. 195–204. Springer, Heidelberg (2012). https://doi.org/10.1007/978-3-642-18003-3_19

Meyer, J.P., Allen, N.J.: Commitment in the Workplace: Theory, research, and Application. Sage, Thousand Oaks (1997)

Moustafa, K., Luz, S., Longo, L.: Assessment of mental workload: a comparison of machine learning methods and subjective assessment techniques. In: Longo, L., Leva, M.C. (eds.) H-WORKLOAD 2017. CCIS, vol. 726, pp. 30–50. Springer, Cham (2017). https://doi.org/10.1007/978-3-319-61061-0_3

Muñoz-Marrón, D.: Human factors in aviation: CRM (Crew Resource Management). Papeles del Psicólogo/Psychologist Papers **39**(3), 191–199 (2018)

Nullmeyer, R.T., Spiker, V.A.: The importance of crew resource management behaviors in mission performance: implications for training evaluation. Mil. Psychol. **15**(1), 77–96 (2003)

O'Connor, P., Flin, R., Fletcher, G.: Methods used to evaluate the effectiveness of flighterew CRM training in the UK aviation industry. Hum. Fact. Aerospace Saf. **2**, 235–255 (2002)

O'Hare, D.: The 'Wheel of Misfortune': a taxonomic approach to human factors in accident investigation and analysis in aviation and other complex systems. Ergonomics **43**(12), 2001–2019 (2000)

Ohlander, U., Alfredson, J., Riveiro, M., Falkman, G.: Fighter pilots' teamwork: a descriptive study. Ergonomics **62**(7), 880–890 (2019)

Omosehin, O., Smith, A.P.: Do cultural differences play a role in the relationship between time pressure, workload and student well-being? In: Longo, L., Leva, M.C. (eds.) H-WORKLOAD 2019. CCIS, vol. 1107, pp. 186–204. Springer, Cham (2019). https://doi.org/10.1007/978-3-030-32423-0_12

Orlandi, L., Brooks, B.: Measuring mental workload and physiological reactions in marine pilots: building bridges towards redlines of performance. Appl. Ergon. **69**, 74–92 (2018)

Pediconi, M.G., Genga, G.M.: On the earth as well as in the sky. Facing the risks between workload and resilience: a psychoanalytic point of view. In: Longo, L., Leva, C. (eds.) H-Workload 2018 the 2nd International Symposium on Human Mental Workload. Netherlands Aerospace Centre, Amsterdam, 20–21 (2018)

Pickup, L., Wilson, J.R., Norris, B.J., Mitchell, L., Morrisroe, G.: The Integrated Workload Scale (IWS): a new self-report tool to assess railway signaller workload. Appl. Ergon. **36**(6), 681–693 (2005)

Pinet, J.: Facing the Unexpected in Flight: Human Limitations and Interaction with Technology in the Cockpit. CRC Press, USA (2015)

Pruchnicki, S., Key, K., Rao, A.: Problem Solving/Decision Making and Procedures for Unexpected Events: A Literature Review. Office of Aerospace Medicine Federal Aviation Administration 800 Independence Ave., S.W. Washington, DC (2019)

Righi, A.W., Saurin, T.A., Wachs, P'.: A systematic literature review of resilience engineering: research areas and a research agenda proposal. Reliab. Eng. Syst. Saf. **141**, 142–152 (2015)

Riili, A.D., Falcone, A.E.: "Vi ho mai raccontato di quella volta che…?", Anatomia Inconveniente di Volo SH3D, 12–19 (2019)

Rogalski, J., Plat, M., Antolin-Glenn, P.: Training for collective competence in rare and unpredictable situations. In: Boreham, N., Samurçay, R., Fischer, M. (eds.) Work Process Knowledge, pp. 134–147. Routledge, London (2002)

Rozenfeld, A.: La resilienza, una posizione soggettiva di fronte alle avversità. Fratelli Frilli Editore (2014)

Rubio, S., Díaz, E., Martín, J., Puente, J.M.: Evaluation of subjective mental workload: a comparison of SWAT, NASA-TLX, and workload profile methods. Appl. Psychol. **53**(1), 61–86 (2004)

Rutter, M.: Implications of resilience concepts for scientific understanding. Ann. N. Y. Acad. Sci. **1094**(1), 1–12 (2006)

Schmeichel, B.J., Volokhov, R.N., Demaree, H.A.: Working memory capacity and the self-regulation of emotional expression and experience. J. Pers. Soc. Psychol. **95**(6), 1526 (2008)

Sheridan, T.B.: Book review facing the unexpected in flight. IEEE Aerospace Electr. Syst. Mag. **31**(8), 46–46 (2016)

Smith, Andrew P.: Student workload, wellbeing and academic attainment. In: Longo, L., Leva, M.C. (eds.) H-WORKLOAD 2019. CCIS, vol. 1107, pp. 35–47. Springer, Cham (2019). https://doi.org/10.1007/978-3-030-32423-0_3

Smith, Andrew P., Smith, Hugo N.: Workload, fatigue and performance in the rail industry. In: Longo, L., Leva, M.Chiara (eds.) H-WORKLOAD 2017. CCIS, vol. 726, pp. 251–263. Springer, Cham (2017). https://doi.org/10.1007/978-3-319-61061-0_17

Sullenberger, C.B., Zaslow, J.: Highest duty: my search for what really matters. Harper Collins (2009)

Tenenbaum, G., Edmonds, W.A., Eccles, D.W.: Emotions, coping strategies, and performance: a conceptual framework for defining affect-related performance zones. Mil. Psychol. (2008)

Thomas, M.J.W.: Predictors of threat and error management: identification of core nontechnical skills and implications for training systems design. Int. J. Aviat. Psychol. **14**(2), 207–231 (2004)

Turan, O., et al.: Can we learn from aviation: safety enhancements in transport by achieving human orientated resilient shipping environment. Transp. Res. Procedia **14**, 1669–1678 (2016)

Ungar, M., Clark, S.E., Kwong, W.M., Makhnach, A., Cameron, C.A.: Studying resilience across cultures. J. Ethnic Cult. Diversity Soc. Work **14**(3–4), 1–19 (2006)

Wallas, G.: The Art of Thought. Watts&Co, New York (1926)

Weidlich, C.P., Ugarriza, D.N.: A pilot study examining the impact of care provider support program on resiliency, coping, and compassion fatigue in military health care providers. Mil. Med. **180**(3), 290 (2015)

Wertz, F.J., Charmaz, K., McMullen, L., Josselson, R., Anderson, R., McSpadden, E.: Five Ways of Doing Qualitative Analysis Phenomenological Psychology, Grounded Theory, Discourse Analysis, Narrative Research, and Intuitive Inquiry. Routledge (2011)

Wickens, C.D.: Mental workload: assessment, prediction and consequences. In: Longo, L., Leva, M.C. (eds.) H-WORKLOAD 2017. CCIS, vol. 726, pp. 18–29. Springer, Cham (2017). https://doi.org/10.1007/978-3-319-61061-0_2

Wohleber, R.W., Matthews, G., Reinerman-Jones, L.E., Panganiban, A.R., Scribner, D.: Individual differences in resilience and affective response during simulated UAV operations. In: Proceedings of the Human Factors and Ergonomics Society Annual Meeting, vol. 59, no. 1, pp. 751–755. Sage CA: Los Angeles, CA: SAGE Publications (2015)

You, X., Ji, M., Han, H.: The effects of risk perception and flight experience on airline pilots' locus of control with regard to safety operation behaviors. Accid. Anal. Prev. **57**, 131–139 (2013)

Zaidman-Zait, A.: Content analysis. In: Michalos, A.C. (ed.) Encyclopedia of Quality of Life and Well-Being Research. Springer, Dordrecht (2014). https://doi.org/10.1007/978-1-4614-5690-2_100099

Fundamental Frequency as an Alternative Method for Assessing Mental Fatigue

Enrique Muñoz-de-Escalona(✉), José Juan Cañas, and Jessica F. Morales-Guaman

Mind, Brain and Behaviour Research Centre, University of Granada, Granada, Spain
{enriquemef,delagado}@ugr.es, jessicamorales@correo.ugr.es

Abstract. The development of methods for measuring mental workload and fatigue is still a central issue in the research agenda of Human Factors and Ergonomics researchers. There exist several different methodologies which offers indexes which are sensitive to mental workload and fatigue changes. One of these methodologies, the physiological measures offers many advantages, but comes with the main disadvantages of being very intrusive and require expensive and specialized equipment. To overcome thes disadvantages, we propose the use of voice parameters, particularly the fundamental frequency, as an alternative valid method for assessing mental fatigue in complex and dynamic situations. In this study we tested our proposal. We manipulated the time during which participants performed the MATB-II task battery with high and constant task demands in order to induce mental fatigue over time; while subjective reports of fatigue, performance, pupil size and voice speech were collected as our dependent variables. Results showed that all of these measures, including the fundamental frequency obtained from participants' voice, were sensitive to the emergence of mental fatigue. High correlations among all measurements also confirmed the appropriate use of fundamental frequency as an alternative sensitive measure for assessing mental fatigue.

Keywords: Mental fatigue · Mental workload · Fatigue measures · Fundamental frequency

1 Introduction

Research over the past 50 years has clearly shown that performance on complex tasks depends, among many other factors, on the mental resources that are demanded by tasks, but also on the operators' available mental resources to cope with those demands. The relation between demanded and available resources is what we call mental workload [1–4]. This relationship can be expressed as a fraction where the numerator is the amount of demanded resources and the denominator is the amount of available resources. When this fraction is greater than one, we say that we are in an overload condition, in which demanded resources are higher than available resources. If, on the contrary, the result of the fraction is less than one we have an underload condition, in which available resources are higher than task demands. The conditions of extreme overload and extreme underload negatively affect the performance of the task and the operator's welfare [1–4].

© Springer Nature Switzerland AG 2020
L. Longo and M. C. Leva (Eds.): H-WORKLOAD 2020, CCIS 1318, pp. 58–75, 2020.
https://doi.org/10.1007/978-3-030-62302-9_4

For this reason, human work is designed to avoid these situations. It should be noted that performance would not be impaired with intermediate levels of mental workload [5]. An overload condition is mainly caused by an excessive demand on resources when, for example, the task is very complex. However, overloading can also occur when there is a decrease in available resources as a result of the emergence of mental fatigue (during long periods performing the tasks) or when the tasks do not change the objectives for a long time [6, 7]. For this reason, estimating the amount of available resources at any given time has been and continues to be a very important research topic in the area of Human Factors and Ergonomics. Therefore, in the agenda of researchers who study the variables that affect performance in a complex task, there is one main objective which is to develop methods that would allow us to measure the mental resources that a person has at a given time. However, all the methods that have been proposed have advantages but also have disadvantages and more research is still needed to find methods to measure available resources that would avoid them.

In this paper we will describe an experimental study carried out to explore the possibility of estimating the available resources from an acoustic parameter of the voice, its fundamental frequency (F0). Previous research has shown that the fundamental frequency of operators' voice increases as mental workload gets higher [8]. We hypothesize that this increase in fundamental frequency that occurs with time on task may be due to a decrease in available resources because of the gradual emergence of mental fatigue. In the experiment we manipulated the time spent performing the task while keeping high constant task demands. We measured the participants' performance, their subjective estimation of fatigue, their pupil diameter and the fundamental frequency of their voice. We expected to find that as participants spent more time performing the task, their execution would worsen, their subjective perceptions of fatigue would increase, their pupil would shrink reflecting less physiological activation, and especially the fundamental frequency would increase. In Sect. 2 we will review the different methodologies for measuring mental fatigue to focus, afterwards, in the acoustic parameters, particularly in the fundamental frequency. Section 3 describes the design and methodology used in our study. In Sect. 4 we describe the obtained results and in Sect. 5 the discussion about our findings and future possible research in this line. Finally, in Sect. 6 we conclude the study and provide implications about using fundamental frequency as a mental fatigue index.

2 Related Work

2.1 Methods for Measuring Available Resources

Over the past few decades, researchers have designed several methods to measure the mental resources a person has while performing a task. All these methods can be classified in various ways according to various criteria, but a first criterion that is often used is the temporary moment at which the amount of resources is measured. According to this criterion we can distinguish between "offline methods" and "online methods".

Offline methods basically consist of estimating the amount of mental resources once the task has been completed. These methods have the advantage that they normally do not interfere with the performance of the task because they are collected at the end of the task but have the disadvantage that they do not allow an estimation during the performance of the task. Sometimes, what we are interested in, is how many mental resources a person has left after the task is completed. For example, we would be in that situation when we want to know how tired a person is at the end of his or her working day and not how the mental resources have been managed during the performance of his tasks at work. In these situations, offline methods would be appropriate for our purposes. However, if our objectives were to estimate mental resources during task performance, we would need to use the so-called online methods.

Regardless of whether the evaluation is offline or online, the methods can be classified into three big categories. The first category of methods is the so-called "concurrent task performance-based methods" which consist of asking the person to perform a task that is called the secondary task while he or she performs his or her primary task, which is the one he or she has to perform at work. Basically, these methods measure the performance of the secondary task and apply the following logic: since both the primary task and the secondary task have to share the same resources, the performance of the secondary task is a reflection of how many resources are "left over" after performing the primary task [4]. If we observe that the secondary task is performed very well, we can interpret that the primary task requires few resources. Conversely, if the secondary task is poorly performed, it will mean that the primary task is consuming most of the resources. These performance-based methods are good online methods for diagnosing the causes of overload or underload. However, these methods have two fundamental drawbacks. First, in real situations (not in the laboratory or in a simulator) sometimes we cannot afford to have a secondary task drawing resources that may be needed to perform well the primary task (which is the main task the person has to perform). Secondly, it is often difficult to ask the person whose mental resources we are estimating to understand that he or she has to "prioritize" the primary task over the secondary task.

The second category of methods is made up of subjective methods that consist of asking the operators themselves to give a subjective estimation of their current available mental resources, normally using a numerical interval scale where the available mental resources can be expressed from less to more during the performance of the task. The main disadvantage of these methods is that they can interfere with the completion of the task when performed online. Although most of these methods only require operators to verbally give their estimation of the amount of mental resources, doing so may distract their attention from the task and impair their performance. Therefore, they are usually used offline at the end of the task or working day.

Finally, the third category of methods, which are known as psychophysiological methods, are based on our knowledge about the relationship between mental resources and certain psychophysiological parameters. There are currently several psychophysiological methods, all of these with advantages and disadvantages. Most of these psychophysiological recording methods that are currently being proposed (records of ocular parameters such as blink rate, pupil diameter, records of the electrical activity of the cerebral cortex, etc.) require high technical expertise and the use of some particular recording equipment, which is expensive and needs the operator to be equipped with it so that the physiological parameters can be properly recorded. For example, records of ocular parameters require the operator to be equipped with special eye-trackers, and the records of cortical electrical activity have to be done by equipping the operator with a set of electrodes on the head that can be annoying and interfere with the task. Therefore, there is currently a great need to explore other psychophysiological methods for the estimation of mental resources, especially online, which meet two main requirements: they should not require expensive recording equipment and they do not need to ask the operator to be equipped with it during the performance of his task. The methods that we should explore must record psychophysiological parameters in a natural way from some aspect of the operators' open behavior while she or he is performing the task. One of these methods may be the estimation of mental resource states from acoustic parameters of the voice. In many situations where it is necessary to estimate the amount of mental resources that a person has, verbal communications are (or can be) recorded automatically, often for security reasons. One of these situations is the one we have at Air Traffic Management (ATM) [9].

2.2 Effects of Mental Workload on the Acoustic Parameters of the Voice

In the communication between two people it is very important that both are able to perceive the emotional state of the other. For this perception of the emotional state of the person we are communicating with, we can use several signals, the most important of which is the gesture of the face [10]. We humans manifest our internal psychological states very well through gestures of the face. However, another characteristic of human communication that also shows the internal psychological state is the voice. In the field of ATM, the relationship between mental states and communications has been known for a long time. For example, Bailey, Willems and Peterson [11] found that the number of communications between route controllers and pilots increased in high mental load conditions. However, the current interest in this area is primarily to explore the relationship between the acoustic characteristics of verbal communications and the mental states. In this line, many of the first studies that were carried out on the acoustic parameters of the voice were aimed at exploring the relationship between these parameters and stress. In an internal EUROCONTROL report, Hagmüller, Kubin and Rank [12] reviewed the empirical evidence on the influence of stress caused by mental workload on the acoustic parameters of the voice. The authors argue that since voice is a common communication tool of Air Traffic Controllers (ATCOs), the analysis of its acoustic characteristics can be very useful to identify its psychological states during the performance of the control task. The authors considered mental workload as a "psychological" stress-causing factor that is different from other physical (e.g., vibrations produced by machines), physiological (e.g., illness, lack of sleep), or perceptual (e.g., noise) factors. One of the most important conclusions of the review conducted by these researchers was that the Fundamental Frequency is sensitive to changes in stress caused by mental workload.

The fundamental frequency is the lowest frequency of a periodic waveform. In the case of the human voice, when a person produces a sound, the vocal cords vibrate at a certain speed by rapidly opening and closing with small bursts of air. In this way the sound produced is composed of a spectrum of frequencies that we can break down to obtain the lowest frequency of the spectrum. That lower frequency of the produced sound is what we call the fundamental frequency. We should not confuse the fundamental frequency with the tone of a sound even though they are related. Tone is a unit of measurement for "perception". We could say that fundamental frequency is a "physical" measure of sound that can be obtained by placing a wide-range microphone directly in the throat, above the vocal cords, but below the resonant structures of the vocal tract. While pitch is a "psychological" measure that reflects how frequencies are perceived in the human nervous system and is measured by the Mel Scale. The name Mel comes from the word melody to indicate that it is based on human perception of tone. The relationship between fundamental frequency and tone would be similar to the relationship between physical sound intensity and the decibel scale which is a perceptual psychological measure of intensity. In any case, since the relationship between frequency and tone is a complex relationship that leads us to the field of Psychophysics, researchers have preferred to measure fundamental frequency directly in their research on the relationship between mental states and the physical parameters of the voice.

Effects on fundamental frequency have been consistently found in studies where participants were asked to identify whether or not a person was stressed by hearing what this person said. In these studies, researchers have found that the characteristic that listeners use to make a meaningful classification is Fundamental Frequency [13, 14]. These studies soon distinguished between the different causes of stress. Although, in a general way we can say that stress is a psychological and physiological response of the organism to a danger, we can distinguish between the different types of dangers, called stressors, to which the organism responds. In this line, Scherer, Grandjean, Johnstone, Klasmeyer, and Bänziger pointed out that one thing is the stress produced by mental overload and another is the stress produced by other situations of danger [15]. Consider two examples: the stress of an ATCo may be caused by a high taskload, but it is also possible that the stress we observe in an ATCo is due to a situation of danger from an imminent conflict. In the latter case the observed stress has a causal component with an emotional component due to the perceived risk of collision. In the experiment carried out by these authors, the participants had to perform a logical reasoning task in one of two conditions (1) focusing on this task without any distraction; (2) performing the task while simultaneously attending to an auditory monitoring task. In the logical reasoning task, they had to make deductions based on premises that appeared on a screen. In the auditory monitoring task, they had to respond to one sound while ignoring another sound, both appearing randomly. The authors hypothesized that in the condition of the logical reasoning task there would only be a mental workload effect, while in the dual task, in addition to increasing this mental workload by having to perform two tasks simultaneously, there would be an effect of emotional stress due to time pressure and the same stressful noise defect. In this study, the participants were asked to say a few sentences appearing on the screen at intervals while they were performing the tasks. The duration of the intervals was random. These sentences were of the type "This is task number 345629". In the sentence, only the number changed from one time to the next. In this way, there was one part that was always fixed and another part that was changing, the number.

The results of the experiment showed a clear statistical independence of the effects of stress and workload on F0. The two effects did not interact, allowing the researchers to conclude that they can be considered independent effects. However, although the effect of stress was statistically significant, the effect of workload was only marginally so. The authors argued that this lack of significance was due to the large individual differences they found in the sample of participants. Based on the results of questionnaires that the participants had to fill out, the authors suggested that the participants with higher levels of anxiety caused by the desire to perform the task well were those who showed the most significant results on the effect of F0. Huttunen, Keränen, Väyrynen, Pääkkönen, and Leino have conducted a study with military pilots in a flight simulator piloting task [16]. The three mental load conditions in which the pilots performed their task were (1) mental workload due to the complexity of Situation Awareness; (2) mental workload due to the complexity and critical value of information; and (3) mental workload due to the difficulty of the decision making processes. Taking as a baseline the recordings collected in a period of time before the simulation, the authors calculated the differences in F0 as a function of mental workload in these three conditions. The results showed that F0 increased as a function of mental workload in all three conditions.

In a word recall task under controlled laboratory conditions, Boyer, Paubel, Ruiz, El Yagoubi and Daurat found that the F0 increased with the number of words participants had to remember [17]. The authors interpreted that the number of words can be considered a factor that increases cognitive demand and, therefore, its effect on the F0 can be interpreted as evidence of the relationship between mental workload and this acoustic parameter of the voice. Therefore, we can say that there is experimental evidence of the effect of mental workload on an acoustic parameter of the voice, the fundamental frequency of people who are performing complex tasks. The fundamental frequency increases when the mental workload increases. However, it would be interesting to know if this effect of mental workload can be due to an increase on mental demands or a decrease in available resources. We believe that a decrease in the available resources due, for example, to the time spent performing the task may be also a factor affecting the observed increase in the Fundamental Frequency due to the emergence of mental fatigue.

2.3 Effects of Fatigue on Fundamental Frequency

Fatigue research has found results that show how acoustic parameters of the voice, such as fundamental frequency, can be sensitive to fatigue. For example, research in recent years has shown that fatigue can affect different phases of speech production. According to the review by Krajewski, Batliner, and Golz these phases would be as follows [18]:

1. Cognitive speech planning has been found to result in a slowdown in cognitive processing, impaired speech planning, impaired neuromuscular motor coordination processes, impaired fine motor control and slow movement of the articulator, and sluggish articulation and slower speech.
2. There are effects on breathing that manifest themselves in decreased muscle tension, flat and slow breathing, reduced subglottal pressure, and lower fundamental frequency, intensity, articulatory accuracy and joint rate.
3. The effects on phonation that have been found are as follows: decreased muscle tension, increased vocal cord elasticity and decreased vocal cord tension, decreased body temperature, change in vocal cord viscoelasticity, change in spectral energy distribution, breathable and lax voice, non-lifting larynx, decreased resonant (formant) frequency positions and increased formant bandwidth.

4. The effects on the articulation/resonance are decreased muscle tension, unrestricted pharynx and softening of the vocal tract walls, loss of speech signal energy, wider formant bandwidth; postural changes, lowering of the torso and head, change in the shape of the vocal tract, change in the position of the formant, increased salivation, loss of energy, decreased body temperature, reduced heat conduction, change in friction between the walls of the vocal tract and the air, changes in laminar flows, jet streams and turbulence, change in spectral energy distribution, increased formant bandwidth, increased formant frequencies especially in lower formants.

5. As for the radiation the effects are a decrease of the orofacial movement, facial expression and lip extension (visualization of open and relaxed mouth), lengthening of the vocal tract, lower positions of the first and second formant, reduction of the articulation effort, lower degree of openness, relaxed articulation, decrease of the first formant, oropharyngeal relaxation, decrease of the veil, coupling of the nasal cavity, increase of the nasality, band width of the extended Formant 1, lower amplitude of Formant 1.

Based on these known effects of mental fatigue on speech production, research has been aimed at identifying which acoustic parameters best reflect the effects of mental fatigue. In a study by Cho, Yin, Park, and Park, the authors found that when participants were divided into two groups according to a subjective fatigue scale, some acoustic parameters such as fundamental frequency shaking, brightness, HNR (the ratio of harmony to noise), SNR (the signal-to-noise ratio), and shaking amplitude were predictors of mental fatigue [19]. These results suggest that it would be possible to use some of these parameters to assess mental fatigue. Whitmore and Fisher conducted a study in which a group of American bomber pilots, divided into groups of four, participated in a pilot task for periods of 36 h in a flight simulator [20]. The piloting periods were interspersed with rest periods of 36 h. Approximately every 3 h the participants had to perform cognitive tasks, subjective fatigue assessments and repeat the sentence:

"Futility Magellan, this is xxx yyy. The time is zz:zz Zulu".

where:
XX was the participant's rank
YY was the Participant's Name
ZZ:ZZ was the time when you say the phrases

The results showed that the fundamental frequency and duration of words were good indices of subjective fatigue and performance in the cognitive tasks. Other researchers have conducted research using methodologies based on voice data recorded during conversations in a natural context. This is what Krajewski, Batliner, and Golz did, who conducted a validation experiment to examine whether automatically trained voice database models can be used to recognize subject drowsiness [21]. Their methodological approach can be summarized in four steps:

– They collected individual speech data as well as associated sleepiness scores for each subject.
– Then, they extracted relevant acoustic characteristics from the speech data.

– With that data, they constructed statistical models of sleepiness scores based on the acoustic characteristics.
– Finally, they tested learned models on new speech data.

   With this methodological procedure the researchers did not need to conduct a study in which, in a controlled manner, a group of people were required to verbally express a certain text every certain period of time, as has been done in other empirical studies designed to study this same topic. In contrast, with the procedure used by these authors, the voice data were collected in the natural context in which the people performed their tasks. Pattern recognition algorithms were applied to the data collected with this procedure. These algorithms were trained to recognize basic acoustic characteristics according to the acoustic-preceptual concepts of (1) Prosody (tone, intensity, rhythm, pause pattern and speed of speech); (2) Articulation (speech difficulty, reduction and elision); and (3) Speech quality (breathable, tense, high-pitched, hoarse or modal voice). The algorithms were also trained according to signal processing categories (time domain and frequency domain) and state space characteristics. With this procedure, the classification algorithms, working with an unusually large set of data, were able to determine whether a subject's sleep was beyond a critical threshold. Subsequently, the authors conducted a validation study with new data in which they achieved an accuracy rate of over 86% in unseen data, but from known speakers, with an SVM (artificial intelligence algorithm) classifier.

   As this review showed, there is enough empirical evidence about the effect of mental fatigue on some acoustic parameters of the human voice. Empirical evidence on the effect of fatigue on the acoustic parameters of the voice supports the hypothesis that the effect of mental workload on these parameters may be reflecting a decrease in available resources. According to the definition of mental workload as a relationship that can be expressed as a division between demanded and available resources, a decrease in available resources due to factors such as fatigue may be the cause of the effect of the observed mental workload.

   The aim of the experiment described below has been to test this hypothesis. In the experiment a group of participants performed a set of tasks in which their performance was measured at the same time as their pupil diameter, the subjective estimation of their fatigue and the fundamental frequency of their voice. The pupil diameter measurement was measured because it has proven to be a good index of the level of activation [22]. Task demands remained constant throughout the task. The variable that was manipulated was the time spent performing the task. We expected to find that the longer time performing the task, the greater the fatigue, causing a decrease in performance, a smaller pupil diameter, a greater subjective feeling of fatigue and, most importantly according to our hypothesis, an increase in the fundamental frequency of participant's voice.

3   Design and Methodology

3.1   Materials and Instruments

MATB-II Software. The participants of the experiment had to perform the Multiple Attribute Task Battery (MATB-II) [23]. This task battery is designed to assess the performance and workload of operators by means of different tasks similar to those performed by flight crews. The software used to perform the tasks has a user-friendly interface that allows non-pilot participants to use it. MATB-II comes with default event files that can be easily modified to suit the needs or objectives of an experiment. The program records the events presented to the participants, as well as their responses. MATB-II contains the following four tasks: the System Monitoring Task (SYSMON), the Tracking Task (TRACK), the Communications Task (COMM), and the Resource Management Task (RESMAN) (see Fig. 1).

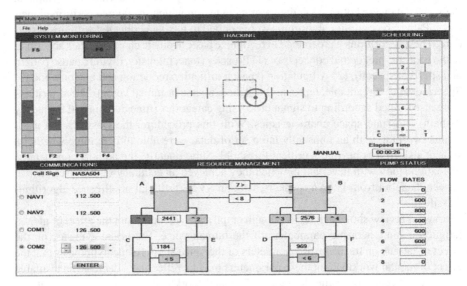

Fig. 1. MATB-II task display. Taken from https://matb.larc.nasa.gov/

- The task of SYSMON is divided into two sub-tasks: the lights task and the scales task. For the sub-task of lights, participants are required to respond as quickly as possible to a green light turning off and a red light turning on, and to turn the lights back on and off, respectively. For the scale sub-task, participants are asked to detect when the lights on four moving scales deviate from their normal position and respond accordingly by clicking on the deviated scale.
- In the TRACK task, there are two modes. Participants can work only in a manual mode. During this manual mode, participants have to keep a circular target in the centre of an inner box using a joystick with their left hand (the dominant hand was necessary for the use of the mouse). During the automatic mode of the task, the circular target will remain in the inner box by itself.
- In the COM task, an audio message with a specific callsign is displayed and the participant is asked to respond by selecting the appropriate radio channel and by setting the correct frequency, but only if the callsign matches his or her own (callsign: "NASA504"). The participant is not required to respond to messages in other callsigns.
- In the RESMAN task, participants have to maintain the fuel level in tanks A and B, within ± 500 units of the initial condition of 2500 units each. To maintain this

objective, participants must transfer the fuel from the supply tanks to A and B or transfer the fuel between the two tanks.

Praat Software. "Praat" is a scientific license free tool for analyzing spectrograms of audio records. It was developed at the University of Amsterdam by Paul Boersma and David Weenink in 1992 and it is constantly being updated with improvements implemented by authors, some of them suggested by users [24]. Once the audio file is loaded you can obtain multiple audio parameters such as fundamental frequency, intensity, volume, formants, etc. In this study we used Praat software for obtaining the fundamental frequency intervals average.

Tobii T120 Eyetracker. Pupil diameter measurements were obtained using an infrared eye tracking system with a sampling frequency of 120 Hz, the model Tobii T120 marketed by Tobii Video System. This equipment is completely non-intrusive, does not have a visible eye movement tracking system and provides high accuracy and an excellent compensating head movement mechanism, ensuring high quality data collection.

Instantaneous Self-assessment Scale. We employed an easy and intuitive instantaneous subjective fatigue scale called Instantaneous Self-assessment, which provides momentary subjective ratings of perceived mental fatigue during task performance. Participants evaluated the mental fatigue they experienced at any given time on a scale ranging from 1 (no mental fatigue) to 9 (maximum mental fatigue). Participants were taught to use the scale just before starting the experimental stage.

3.2 Participants

17 students from the University of Granada participated in the study. Participants' ages ranged from 18 to 32, with an average of 23.6 and a standard deviation of 2.25. A total of 13 women and 4 men participated. It should be noted that there is a greater number of female participants due to the fact that psychology students at the University of Granada are mostly women. Recruitment was achieved through the dispersion of posters and flyers around the university, as well as an advertisement for the study on the university's online platform for experiments (http://experimentos.psiexpugr.es/). The requirements for participation included (1) not being familiar with the MATB-II program, (2) Spanish as a native language, and (3) visual acuity or correction of visual impairment with contact lenses, as glasses impair the utilized eye-tracking device from collecting data. Participants' participation was rewarded with extra credit.

3.3 Procedure

The participants went through an experimental session consisting of two phases:

1. **Training stage:** training took place for no longer than 30 min. The objective of this stage was for participants to familiarize themselves with the program so that they could carry out the tasks securely during the data collection stage. The procedure

was conducted as follows: upon entering the lab and after filling out the informed consent form, the participant was instructed to read the MATB-II instruction manual and inform the researcher once they had finished. The researcher then sat down with the participant to allow for questions and resolve any doubts on how to use the program. Afterward, on a computer monitor, participants were presented with each MATB-II task separately and were first given a demonstration as to how to execute the task and after what they were given time (3 min or more if needed) to perform the task themselves. The participants were always free to consult the manual and ask the researcher questions during the training stage in case of doubts or uncertainties. Once the participants had completed all four tasks and resolved all doubts, they were ready for the data collection stage, which followed immediately afterwards. During the training stage, participants could work in one room equipped for training with the MATB-II software, and no special attention to room conditions was needed.

2. **Data collection stage:** the data collection stage lasted a period of 60 min that was divided into thirty intervals of 2 min. The first interval was left as a training interval in order to focus the attention of participants into the task. During this first 2 min interval only the tracking task was activated. Then, during the second interval and until the end of the experiment, the three tasks of the MATB-II software were activated (TRACK, SYSMON and RESMAN), thus mental workload level was high and constant throughout the experimental session in order to facilitate the emergence of mental fatigue. The participants were instructed to verbalize the ISA (Instantaneous Self-Assessment) scale every 2 min when a scheduled alarm sounded. They were also instructed to verbalize every action they were performing in the SYSMON (e.g. "I press F3 button") and the RESMON (e.g. "I activate fuel pump n°1") tasks in order to collect our F0 variable through audio recordings. Prior to the start of the task-battery, the eye-tracker system was calibrated, and the participants were told to keep head and body movements to a minimum. During the data collection stage, standardizing room conditions was essential. Thus, the testing rooms were temperature controlled to 21 °C, and lighting conditions (the main extraneous variable in pupil diameter measurement) were kept constant with artificial lighting; there was no natural light in the rooms. Moreover, participants always sat in the same place, a comfortable chair spaced 60 cm from the eye-tracker system.

This study was carried out in accordance with the recommendations of the local ethical guidelines of the committee of the University of Granada institution: "Comité de Ética de Investigación Humana". The protocol was approved by the "Comité de Ética de Investigación Humana" under the code: 779/CEIH/2019. All subjects gave written informed consent in accordance with the Declaration of Helsinki.

3.4 Variables

Independent Variable

The only independent variable was the time spent performing the task. The period of one hour performing the task was divided into 2-min intervals resulting in 30 intervals. The first period of 2 min was taken as a baseline to calculate the pupil diameter so it will not be analyzed and we are left with only 29 intervals that constitute the 29 levels of our independent variable "intervals" during the time performing the task.

Dependent Variables

Performance. MATB-II provides us with many indicators of participants' performance: e.g. root mean square deviation (RMSD) for the TRACK task, number of correct and incorrect responses for the SYSMON and COMM tasks, and the arithmetic mean of tanks "A-2500" and "B-2500" in absolute values for the RESMAN task. However, for the purposes of this experiment we will only consider the RMSD performance indicator. The RMSD performance indicator reflects the distance of the circle to the target point, in such a way that, performance impairment is reflected by a higher score on this variable.

Pupil Size. Fatigue can be estimated by several physiological indexes such as EEG, HVR, and several ocular metrics. We decided to use pupil diameter as our physiological fatigue indicator, as it effectively reflects mental fatigue [19] and minimize intrusiveness. While our eye-tracking system allows continuous sampling rate recording at 120 Hz, we set a total of 30 intervals lasting 2 min each. Since expressing pupil size in absolute values has the disadvantage of being affected by slow random fluctuations in pupil size (source of noise), we followed a procedure for standardizing the values of pupil size for each participant.. To do this, for every participant, we took his/her pupil size value during the first interval of 2 min, and then subtracted it from the obtained value in each of the rest of 29 intervals, thereby giving a differential standardized value allowing us to reduce noise in our data. Analyses were carried out for the average of both the left and right pupils. A negative value meant that the pupil was contracting while a positive value meant that it was dilating.

Subjective Fatigue. We used an online subjective fatigue scale created for this purpose, the "Instantaneous Self-Assessment Scale". Ratings were obtained at 2 min intervals throughout the 60 min of the experimental stage, obtaining a total of 30 subjective mental fatigue ratings. The rating from the first 2 min interval was discarded for the analysis.

Fundamental Frequency (F0). We recorded the verbalizations of participants through the microphone integrated in our eye-tracker system during the data collection stage. The 60 min obtained audio file was divided into 30 intervals which were analyzed with the "Praat" software in order to obtain the average F0 of each interval.

Synchronization of Measures. Performance, pupil size, subjective, and fundamental frequency measures were obtained continuously throughout the experimental session. Synchronization between measures was simple, as the eyetracker (pupil and F0) and MATB-II performance log files began to record data simultaneously at the start of the experimental session. The scheduled alarm (every 2 min) was also synchronized by the experimenter, as it was simultaneously activated with the MATB-II software. This would also allow the ISA scale to be synchronized with the performance, F0 and pupil size measures.

3.5 Experimental Design

The experimental design was One-Way with Intervals as the only within-subject variable with 29 experimental levels.

4 Results

We performed four one-way within-subject ANOVA to analyze collected results, one for each different measure. Firstly, the ANOVA for our performance variable revealed a significant effect of intervals $F(28,448) = 2.27$, $MSe = 52.71$, $p < .01$. As we can see in the graph, performance worsened considerably during the first intervals (2 to 4), and then, it stabilized. However, we can appreciate that it continued worsening through intervals until the end of the experiment. Trend analysis confirmed this statements, as linear trend found to be significant, $F(1,16) = 5.02$, $MSe = 330.21$, $p < .05$ (see Fig. 2).

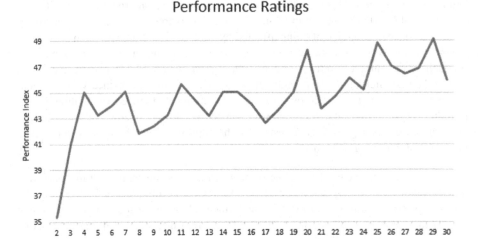

Fig. 2. Participants' performance during task development.

Regarding subjective mental fatigue scores, we found a linear increase through intervals. The ANOVA for this variable revealed a significant main effect of intervals $F(28,448) = 66.14$, $MSe = .79$, $p < .01$. Trend analysis supports the linear increase of mental fatigue through intervals, $F(1,16) = 189.87$, $MSe = 7.34$, $p < .01$ (see Fig. 3).

With respect to our first psychophysiological variable, pupil size, the ANOVA showed a significant effect of intervals $F(28,448) = 20.63$, $MSe = .01$, $p < .01$. The graph revealed a sudden dilation in pupil size from interval 2 to 3 and then, we can appreciate a linear decrease through intervals which tends to stabilize during the last 6 intervals. Trend analysis also revealed a linear trend for this variable, $F(1,16) = 33.0$, $MSe = .1$, $p < .01$ (see Fig. 4).

The ANOVA analysis for our second psychophysiological variable, F0, revealed again a significant main effect of intervals $F(28,448) = 2.04$, $MSe = 91.33$, $p < .01$.

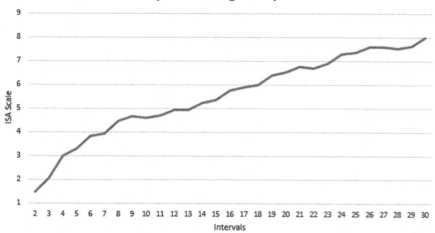

Fig. 3. Participants' subjective mental fatigue ratings during task development.

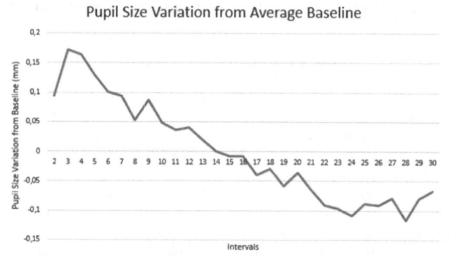

Fig. 4. Participants' pupil size variation ratings from the average baseline during task development.

We can see in the graph that F0 increased linearly through intervals, as trend analysis revealed, $F(1,16) = 6.35$, MSe $= 540.69$, $p < .05$ (see Fig. 5).

Finally, the correlation chart in Table 1 revealed significant very high correlations among measurements: we found a positive correlation between subjective fatigue and performance .73, $p < .01$; a negative correlation between subjective fatigue and pupil $-.94$, $p < .01$; a positive correlation between subjective fatigue and F0 .83, $p < .01$; a negative correlation between performance and pupil size $-.65$, $p < .01$; a positive

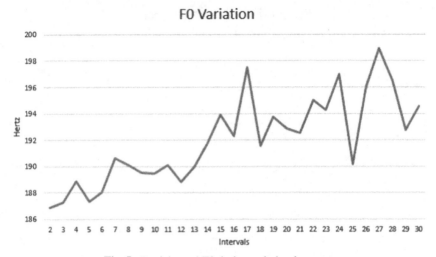

Fig. 5. Participants' F0 during task development.

correlation between performance and F0 .56, p < .01 and a negative correlation between pupil and F0 −.86, p < .01.

Table 1. Correlation chart between measures.

		Performance	Sub. fatigue	Pupil	F0
Performance	Spearman correlation	1	.725**	−.652**	.564**
	Sig. (bilateral)		,000	,000	,001
	N	29	29	29	29
Sub. Fatigue	Spearman correlation	.725**	1	−.938**	.834**
	Sig. (bilateral)	,000		,000	,000
	N	29	29	29	29
Pupil	Spearman correlation	−.652**	−.938**	1	−.856**
	Sig. (bilateral)	,000	,000		,000
	N	29	29	29	29
F0	Spearman correlation	.564**	.834**	−.856**	1
	Sig. (bilateral)	,001	,000	,000	
	N	29	29	29	29

*. The correlation is significant at the level .05 (bilateral).
**. The correlation is significant at the level .01 (bilateral).

5   Discussion

The results show a clear effect of time performing the tasks on every dependent variables: subjective fatigue, task performance, pupil diameter and the fundamental frequency of participants' voice. Particularly, the more time participants spent performing the tasks the worse their performance got, the greater their reports of subjective mental fatigue were, the more contracted their pupil got (indicating that their activation level was decreasing) and the higher the fundamental frequency in their voice got as well. Therefore, considering the above mentioned results we can say that our hypothesis was fulfilled, and the results significantly showed that the fundamental frequency can also be considered an appropriate alternative index to other measures of mental fatigue such as EEG [25, 26], HRV [27, 28], blink rate [29]. The emergence of mental fatigue would be caused by a decrease in available resources (as our pupil size variable reflected) resulting from resources' depletion caused by time on task. These results were in line with literature research and proved that the fundamental frequency can be used as an appropriate index of mental fatigue. It is especially important to note that all measures of mental fatigue correlated significantly in the appropriate direction indicating that participants showed the effects of mental fatigue throughout the task on the one hand, and that every mental fatigue measure in this study was found to be sensitive to mental fatigue as well. However, we must consider that these results should be viewed under certain methodological limitations. First, our sample was small and only composed of young university students, so we believe that these findings should also be tested under working situations in real contexts in order to verify that the fundamental frequency can be used out of the laboratory with satisfactory results, also we must take into account that the number of levels of our independent variable is higher than the number of participants and it might affect to the statistical power of the ANOVA, so our findings must be taken cautiously. Finally, it would also have been interesting to consider different time periods, some of them longer and shorter than 60 min and also under different task demand levels. Further research should consider this methodological modifications in order to analyse the sensitivity of the fundamental frequency to the emergence of mental fatigue to different degrees.

6   Conclusions

The aim of this research was to provide empirical evidence in favour of the hypothesis on the effect that mental fatigue has on an important parameter of the human voice such as the fundamental frequency. The results obtained showed that indeed, the fundamental frequency increases with fatigue. These results allow us to propose the fundamental frequency as an appropriate psychophysiological index of fatigue that may be a viable alternative to other psychophysiological indices that have been proposed. The advantage of fundamental frequency over the other psychophysiological indices is that it does not require expensive and intrusive equipment to record it. The human voice can be recorded in a natural and easy way in many tasks where operators have to communicate to perform their tasks. A direct implication would be that mental fatigue could be predicted at certain works (such as ATM) directly from human voice records, in an automated, economic and reliable way. Also, historical voice records could be used to analyse the mental fatigue that operators were experiencing at a given time or period to, for example, analyse work-related accidents or productivity at work.

Acknowledgement. This research has been supported by contract between CRIDA (https://crida. es/webcrida/) and the University of Granada to the first two authors and by the master thesis research grant from CRIDA to the third author.

References

1. Longo, L., Leva, M.C. (eds.): H-WORKLOAD 2017. CCIS, vol. 726. Springer, Cham (2017). https://doi.org/10.1007/978-3-319-61061-0
2. Longo, L., Leva, M.C. (eds.): H-WORKLOAD 2018. CCIS, vol. 1012. Springer, Cham (2019). https://doi.org/10.1007/978-3-030-14273-5
3. Longo, L., Leva, M.C. (eds.): H-WORKLOAD 2019. CCIS, vol. 1107. Springer, Cham (2019). https://doi.org/10.1007/978-3-030-32423-0
4. Wickens, C.D.: Mental workload: assessment, prediction and consequences. In: Longo, L., Leva, M.Chiara (eds.) H-WORKLOAD 2017. CCIS, vol. 726, pp. 18–29. Springer, Cham (2017). https://doi.org/10.1007/978-3-319-61061-0_2
5. Hancock, P.A.: Whither workload? Mapping a path for its future development. In: Longo, L., Leva, M.C. (eds.) H-WORKLOAD 2017. CCIS, vol. 726, pp. 3–17. Springer, Cham (2017). https://doi.org/10.1007/978-3-319-61061-0_1
6. Desmond, P.A., Neubauer, M.C., Matthews, G., Hancock, P.A. (eds.): The Handbook of Operator Fatigue. Ashgate Publishing, Ltd, Farnham (2012)
7. Hockey, B., Hockey, R.: The Psychology of Fatigue: Work Effort and Control. Cambridge University Press, New York (2013)
8. Hagmüller, M., Kubin, G., Rank, E.: Evaluation of the human voice for indications of workload induced stress in the aviation environment. Eurocontrol (2005)
9. Luig, J., Sontacchi, A.: Workload monitoring through speech analysis: towards a system for air traffic control. In: 27th Congress of The International Council of Aeronautical Sciences, pp. 1–10 (September 2010)
10. X Belin, P., Campanella, S., Ethofer, T. (eds.). Integrating face and voice in person perception. Springer, New York (2012)
11. Bailey, L.L., Willems, B.F., Peterson, L.M.: The effects of workload and decision support automation on enroute r-side and d-side communication exchanges. Federal Aviation Administration Oklahoma City Ok Civil Aeromedical Inst (2001)
12. Hagmüller, M., Kubin, G., Rank, E.: Evaluation of the human voice for indications of workload induced stress in the aviation environment. Eurocontrol (2005)
13. Protopapas, A., Lieberman, P.: Fundamental frequency of phonation and perceived emotional stress. J. Acoust. Soc. Am. **101**(4), 2267–2277 (1997)
14. Zhou, G., Hansen, J., Kaiser, J.: Nonlinear feature based classification of speech under stress. IEEE Trans. Speech Audio Process. **9**(3), 201–216 (2001)
15. Scherer, K.R., Grandjean, D., Johnstone, T., Klasmeyer, G., B¨anziger, T.: Acoustic correlates of task load and stress. In: Proceedings of the International Conference on Spoken Language Processing, pp 2017–2020, Denver, Col- orado, USA (2002)
16. Huttunen, K., Keränen, H., Väyrynen, E., Pääkkönen, R., Leino, T.: Effect of cognitive load on speech prosody in aviation: Evidence from military simulator flights. Appl. Ergon. **42**(2), 348–357 (2011)

17. Boyer, S., Paubel, P.V., Ruiz, R., El Yagoubi, R., Daurat, A.: Human voice as a measure of mental load level. J. Speech Lang. Hear. Res. **61**(11), 2722–2734 (2018)
18. Krajewski, J., Batliner, A., Golz, M.: Acoustic sleepiness detection: Framework and validation of a speech-adapted pattern recognition approach. Behav. Res. Methods **41**(3), 795–804 (2009). https://doi.org/10.3758/BRM.41.3.795
19. Cho, S., Yin, C.S., Park, Y., Park, Y.: Differences in self-rated, perceived, and acoustic voice qualities between high- and low-fatigue groups. J. Voice **25**(5), 544–552 (2011). https://doi.org/10.1016/j.jvoice.2010.07.006
20. Whitmore, J., Fisher, S.: Speech during sustained operations. Speech Commun. **20**(1–2), 55–70 (1996)
21. Krajewski, J., Batliner, A., Golz, M.: Acoustic sleepiness detection: framework and validation of a speech-adapted pattern recognition approach. Behav. Res. Methods **41**(3), 795–804 (2009). https://doi.org/10.3758/BRM.41.3.795
22. Muñoz-de-Escalona, E., Cañas, J.J., Noriega, P.: Inconsistencies between mental fatigue measures under compensatory control theories. Psicológica J. **41**, 103–106 (2020). https://doi.org/10.2478/psicolj-2020-0006
23. Santiago-Espada, Y., Myer, R. R., Latorella, K.A., & Comstock Jr, J.R.: The multi-attribute task battery ii (matb-ii) software for human performance and workload research: A user's guide (2011)
24. Boersma, P., Van Heuven, V.: Speak and unSpeak with PRAAT. Glot Int. **5**(9/10), 341–347 (2001)
25. Shen, K.Q., Li, X.P., Ong, C.J., Shao, S.Y., Wilder-Smith, E.P.: EEG-based mental fatigue measurement using multi-class support vector machines with confidence estimate. Clin. Neurophysiol. **119**(7), 1524–1533 (2008)
26. Borghini, G., et al.: Assessment of mental fatigue during car driving by using high resolution EEG activity and neurophysiologic indices. In: 2012 Annual International Conference of the IEEE Engineering in Medicine and Biology Society, pp. 6442–6445. IEEE (August 2012)
27. Hong, L.Y.J.Y., Zheng, Y.X.L. W.: Study of Mental Fatigue Based on Heart Rate Variability. Chinese J. Biomed. Eng. **29**, 1 (2010)
28. Melo, H.M., Nascimento, L.M., Takase, E.: Mental fatigue and heart rate variability (HRV): the time-on-task effect. Psychol. Neurosci. **10**(4), 428 (2017)
29. Stern, J.A., Boyer, D., Schroeder, D.: Blink rate: a possible measure of fatigue. Hum. Factors **36**(2), 285–297 (1994)

Contactless Physiological Assessment of Mental Workload During Teleworking-like Task

Vincenzo Ronca[1,2]([✉]), Dario Rossi[3], Antonello Di Florio[2], Gianluca Di Flumeri[1,4,5], Pietro Aricò[1,4,5], Nicolina Sciaraffa[1,4,5], Alessia Vozzi[1,2], Fabio Babiloni[1,4,6], and Gianluca Borghini[1,4,5]

[1] Department of Anatomical, Histological, Forensic and Orthopaedic Sciences, Sapienza, University of Rome, Rome, Italy
vincenzo.ronca@uniroma1.it
[2] BrainSigns srl, Rome, Italy
[3] Department of Business and Management, LUISS University, Rome, Italy
[4] Department of Molecular Medicine, Sapienza University of Rome, Rome, Italy
[5] IRCCS Fondazione Santa Lucia, Rome, Italy
[6] Department of Computer Science, Hangzhou Dianzi University, Hangzhou, China

Abstract. Human physiological parameters have been proven as reliable and objective indicators of user's mental states, such as the Mental Workload. However, standard methodologies for evaluating physiological parameters generally imply a certain grade of invasiveness. It is largely demonstrated the relevance of monitoring workers to improve their working conditions. A contactless approach to estimate workers' physiological parameters would be highly suitable because it would not interfere with the working activities and comfort of the workers. Additionally, it would be very appropriate for teleworking settings. In this paper, participants' facial videos were recorded while dealing with arithmetic tasks with the aims to 1) evaluate the possibility to estimate their Heart Rate (HR) through facial video analysis, and 2) assess their mental workload under the different experimental conditions. The HR was also estimated through last-generation smartwatches. The results demonstrated that there was no difference between the HR estimated via the contactless technique and smartwatches, and how it was possible to discriminate the two mental workload levels by employing the proposed methodology.

Keywords: Contactless · Physiological signals · Autonomic parameters · Teleworking · Mental workload · Heart rate

1 Introduction

According to the Eurofund report, in 2018 approximately 3.2 million non-fatal and 3.793 fatal work-related accidents occurred in Europe [1], and the 7.4% of the EU population suffered from one or more work-related health problems [1]. Among the principal causes of work-related accidents there is the Human Factor (HF) [2, 3]. In fact, it has been demonstrated that human errors are the main causes of work-related accidents [4–6]. Workers' common errors are largely correlated with the condition of

© Springer Nature Switzerland AG 2020
L. Longo and M. C. Leva (Eds.): H-WORKLOAD 2020, CCIS 1318, pp. 76–86, 2020.
https://doi.org/10.1007/978-3-030-62302-9_5

high mental workload, tiredness and distractions [7, 8]. These findings clearly indicate the relevance of being able to monitor in real time worker's psychophysical state, such as mental workload and tiredness, in working operational environments [9]. In this context, scientific literature largely highlighted the limit of using subjective methodologies to evaluate such HFs [10–12]. As a potential countermeasure, in the last decades neuroscientific disciplines have been dedicating a great effort in investigating human physiological correlates of user's mental states in order to develop monitoring tools able to detect incoming cognitive impairments (e.g. mental overload) on the basis of specific biomarkers (e.g. skin sweating increasing, heart rate variability, brain electrical activity increasing in specific rhythms over particular cortical sites) [13–15]. Nevertheless, it is evident the need of reducing at minimum the invasiveness related to monitoring methodologies during the working tasks to do not negatively interfere with the workers' activities and comfort [16]. This last consideration is very consistent with the concept of remote and contactless monitoring.

The remote monitoring of workers in coping with variable complexity tasks could play a significant role in workers' wellbeing and safety improvements. Nowadays, the relevance and interest in such a methods have grown consistently in parallel to the huge increase of the teleworking adoptions by several companies all around the world, especially following the pandemic COVID-19 [17]. The remote monitoring methodology is also compatible with the recent World Health Organization provisions related to the physical distancing practices to cope with the health emergency [18, 19]. From a pure physiological perspective, several human biomarkers have been correlated with mental workload dynamics [13, 20]. One of the most relevant autonomic parameters involved in the mental workload evaluation is the *Heart Rate* (HR) [21–23]. The HR is a physiological measure derived by the Electrocardiographic signal (ECG). The HR is modulated by the sympathetic and parasympathetic systems: the sympathetic activation increase the HR and the parasympathetic activation decrease the HR [24]. It has been largely demonstrated that the HR increases when the mental workload increases [22, 25]. The present study is based on an innovative technique that aims to estimate the HR through the analysis of the user's face video recorded by mean of the PC webcam. Such a contactless methodology has been already explored in prior works [26, 27], and its principle concept is based on the modulation of the reflected ambient light from the skin by the absorption spectrum of haemoglobin in the blood [26]. In other words, the analysis is based on the extraction and processing of the Red component of the facial video. The minute colour variations on the skin are created by the blood circulation and they module the Red component of the video signal along the time. In this article, the physiological parameter of HR was extracted during teleworking-like activities. This proposed study is part of the European project named "WorkingAge: Smart Working for All Ages" (GA: 826232). Therefore, the present study is based on the experimental hypothesis that HR is a physiological feature sensitive to human mental workload fluctuations accordingly to scientific literature above introduced. Thus, it aimed at addressing two main objectives:

- Comparing the HR estimation of the contactless method (i.e. via webcam) with the one provided by last-generation smartwatch equipped with three photoplethysmographic (PPG) sensors to assess its reliability.

- Employ the proposed contactless method to assess the user's mental workload while performing an arithmetic task under different difficulty conditions.

2 Materials and Methods

2.1 The Experimental Protocol

Eight participants, six male and two females (31.1 ± 3.9 years old), from the Sapienza University of Rome were recruited and involved on a voluntary basis in this study. The experiment was conducted following the principles outlined in the Declaration of Helsinki of 1975, as revised in 2000. Informed consent and authorization to use the video graphical material were obtained from each subject on paper, after the explanation of the study. The embedded PC webcam was used for the experimental protocol. The RGB camera was set with a resolution of 640×480 pixels at 30 frame per second. The last-generation smartwatches were considered as the *gold standard* and their HR values were recorded at the beginning and at the end of each experimental condition. The experimental protocol consisted initially in a baseline phase where the participants were asked to look at a black cross on white background picture, and then a white cross on black background picture for 30 s each. Finally, the participants performed an arithmetic task under two different conditions: the easy ("Easy Math task") was characterized by single and double-digits sums and one-carry, while the hard ("Hard Math task") was characterized by triple-digits sums with two-carry (Fig. 1, please refer to Subsect. 2.2). The participants had 15 s to answer each mathematical computation by the PC keyboard. During the whole protocol the facial video has been recorded through the software Free2X Webcam Recorder. Finally, the Reaction Time (RT) and the Correct Response Rate (CRR) have been collected during the two mathematical tasks. These parameters were combined to compute an Inverse Efficiency Score (IES) [28] for each participant in each mathematical task to assess both the accuracy and the speed of the user within one synthetic index. The IES has been computed using the formula provided below:

$$IES = \frac{RT}{1 - PE} = \frac{RT}{CRR}.$$

Where RT is the reaction time corresponding to the correct answers, PE is the error rate and CRR is the correct response rate.

2.2 The Arithmetic Task

The two arithmetic tasks have been chosen in order to elicit two different levels of mental workload. In particular, the mathematical task consisted in solving repeated additions proposed to the subjects through a desktop computer: each subject was asked to solve the additions trying to achieve his/her best performance (i.e. to provide the correct answer within the least time possible). The two levels of task difficulty (to elicit two different levels of mental workload) were designed accordingly to the principles adopted by Zarjam and colleagues [29]. More in detail, the 3-min-long EASY task consisted in a *1- and 2-digits numbers with one carry* sum (e.g. $5 + 54$, *Very low* level in [29]), while the

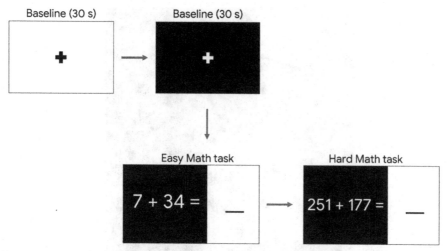

Fig. 1. The three different phases of the experimental protocol: i) during the baseline the participants were asked to look at a white-screen video and then at a black-screen video; during the ii) easy and iii) hard arithmetic tasks the participants were asked to perform, respectively, double-digits and triple-digits sums.

3-min-long HARD task consisted in a *2- and 3-digits numbers with 1 carry* sum (e.g. 31 + 477, *High* level in [29]). This task was chosen because there is a rich literature on the concepts and procedure of mental arithmetic operations [30, 31], while in [32] it is shown that the manipulation of the number of carry operations and the value of the carry is an important variable in varying the difficulty of arithmetic sums. Each subject took confidence with the mathematical task [33, 34], while the order of the two tasks has been randomized among subjects, in order to avoid any habituation effect.

2.3 Data Collection and Data Processing

The image frame is the fundamental part of the video, and two regions of interest (ROI) were selected on each image frame within the participant's face area (Fig. 2).

Thereafter, the Fast Fourier Transform (FFT) and Principal Component Analysis (PCA) were applied to extract the Red component from the raw video signal. The PCA algorithm was used also to remove the Red component fluctuations due to the motion artefacts, while the FFT was applied to extract the frequency corresponding to the HR. Such a frequency corresponds to the highest power spectrum within a specific operational frequency band (Fig. 3).

A specific Python library named Dlib [35] coupled with an adaBoost classifier was used to select a certain number of visual feature on the participant's face. Two ROIs were selected on both the participant's cheeks (green rectangles in Fig. 2). The ROIs were selected taking as references the participant's eyes and nose [27]. The Python library allowed us to automatically detect the participant's face and follow the head movements during the experiments, as long as they were included in the field of view (FOV) of the webcam. The Red (R), Green (G), Blue (B) colour values are the fundamental

Fig. 2. Two regions of interest automatically identified on the participant's face. Informed consent and authorization to use the video graphical material were obtained from each subject on paper, after the explanation of the study. The use of facial pictures is here necessary to illustrate the employed methodology: for this purpose, explicit consent was provided by the subject. (Color figure online)

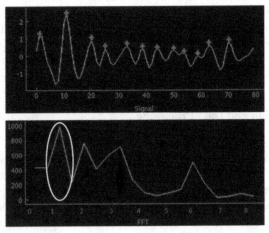

Fig. 3. The image shows the highest frequency band selected to extract the HR from the signal. (Color figure online)

components of the RGB video. These elements were extracted from the two ROIs as a 3 × 1 matrix, where in each raw the RGB component were stored (Fig. 3). Finally, only the Red component was selected and extracted as a bidimensional signal in time domain. The three RGB components were extracted by using the PCA methodology, fully implemented in the *sklearn.decomposition. PCA* Python library related to the larger Scikit-Learn Python library [36].

The signal detrend was applied to remove unwanted trending from the time series. In this case, the potential unwanted trends were represented by the effect of the illumination variations during the experiments, mainly due to PC's display contents variation which were partially reflected on the participant's skin. This kind of trend could generate drifting and noising on the signal of interest. Therefore, the R-component was detrended using the methods proposed by [37] based on smoothness priors approach using a smoothing parameter $\lambda = 10$ and a cut-off frequency $= 0.060$ Hz. After the signal detrending, the Red component extracted in each image frame was filtered by Hamming window characterized by 128 points, between 0.6 and 2.2 Hz, such a frequency range corresponds to a normal HR value interval between 36 and 132 beats per minute (BPM). The filtered signal was normalized using z-score by the formula provided below (Fig. 4):

Fig. 4. The three video components (Red, Green and Blue) automatically identified for each image frame. The use of facial pictures is here necessary to illustrate the employed methodology: for this purpose, explicit consent was provided by the subject. (Color figure online)

$$X_i = \frac{Y_i(t) - \mu_i(t)}{\delta_i}.$$

To extract the HR value a sliding time window corresponding to 100 image frames was considered. HR values were extracted for each experimental phase ("Baseline", "Easy Math task" and "Hard Math task"), and for each condition the HR values estimated by the facial video (*HR_RGB*) and the smartwatches (*HR_Smart*) were reported.

3   Results

3.1   Behavioural Data

The Wilcoxon signed rank tests performed on the IES parameter showed a significant increase of the IES during the Hard Math task (Z = 9.52; p = 0.0078) (Fig. 5).

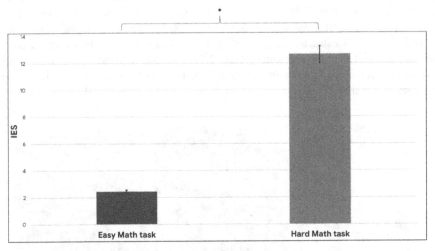

Fig. 5. The IES score significantly increase (p = 0.0078) during the Hard Math task.

3.2   Heart Rate

The Wilcoxon signed rank test performed on the HR values obtained for each subject for each task with respectively the camera-based algorithm and the smartwatch sensors (Fig. 6) revealed a non-significant effect of the used methodology (Z = −3.12; p = 0.2969). In other words, the HR values estimated through the contactless approach (HR_RGB) were not statistically different from the ones estimated through the smartwatches (HR_Smart).

On the contrary, the Wilcoxon signed rank tests revealed a significant difference of both the HR_RGB and HR_Smart between the easy and hard conditions of the arithmetic task (HR_RGB: Z = 4.27; p = 0.0069; HR_Smart: Z = 4.18; p = 0.0078) (Fig. 7).

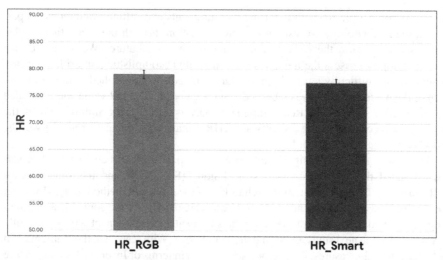

Fig. 6. The HR value evaluated through the contactless methodology was not significantly different (p > 0.05) to the HR values evaluated through the smartwatches.

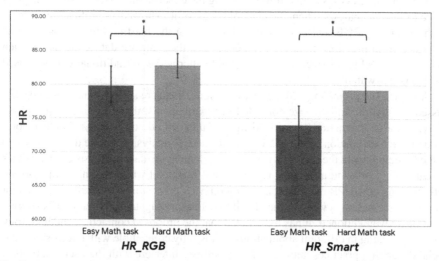

Fig. 7. Both the HR_RGB and HR_Smart significantly increased (p = 0.0069; p = 0.0078, respectively) during the Hard Math task.

4 Discussion and Conclusions

The present study aimed to evaluate the capability and reliability of a contactless methodology for the estimation of the Heart Rate (HR), and for developing a remote monitoring technology able to assess user's mental workload. The methodology considered is relatively easy to implement and implies low cost as it requires a standard PC webcam.

Also, it is compatible for both real time measurements and offline evaluations. In particular, the methodology consists in the HR estimation through the user's facial video analysis and extracting the Red component among the video features. We employed such a methodology to assess the mental workload while accomplishing an arithmetic task under different difficulty levels. In particular, 8 subjects were enrolled in the study: for each of them a facial video was recorded using a webcam. The HR value was estimated from the video, through the Red component analysis (HR_RGB). Simultaneously, the HR value was collected using a smartwatch (HR_Smart) to evaluate the reliability of the proposed contactless methodology.

The results showed no significant differences (p = 0.2969) between the HR values evaluated through the contactless technique (HR_RGB) and the smartwatches (HR_Smart) as demonstration of the reliability of the proposed methodology. However, the results showed a slight tendency to overestimate the HR by the contactless methodology compared to the HR estimated by the smartwatches: this aspect will be carefully investigated in the next study, enlarging the sample size. With respect to the mathematical task, behavioural measures, i.e. performance results in terms of Inverse Efficiency Score (IES), demonstrated that the two mathematical tasks were actually different in terms of difficulty demand, since performance during the Hard task were significantly worse than those during the Easy task, therefore validating the experimental hypothesis at the basis of the following analysis. Then, the physiological results showed a significant increment of the both HR_RGB and HR_Smart values during the hard arithmetic condition as described from previous literature evidences [22], therefore validating the use of such a contactless technique (webcam) as a reliable alternative to traditional contact-based sensors (smartwatch).

Although the promising and interesting results, there are some limitations to be discussed. Firstly, the sample size consisted in 8 participants, therefore in the next phase we will enlarge it to better support and validate the methodology proposed in this work. Secondly, the estimation of the HR was performed by analysing offline the facial video of the participants. In the next study we will implement the data processing and analysis in real time in order to assess the user's mental workload while dealing with working activities and be GDPR compliant avoiding relevant privacy issues. Moreover, different illumination conditions will be considered to better investigate the potential HR overestimation abovementioned. It has to be noted that the proposed contactless methodology is very promising in different applications as it is fully compatible with teleworking and social distancing practices, and does not negatively interfere with the user's activities, therefore paving the way for future safety-oriented applications [21, 38–40], other mental states assessment like stress [41], vigilance [42], and cognitive control behaviour [43], as well as employment despite of social restrictions [17].

References

1. Quality of Life Quality of life, quality of public services, and quality of society (2016)
2. Hansen, F.D.: Human Error: a Concept Analysis, January 2006
3. Wirth, Tanja., Wendeler, Dana., Dulon, Madeleine, Nienhaus, Albert: Sick leave and work-related accidents of social workers in Germany: an analysis of routine data. Int. Arch. Occup. Environ. Health **92**(2), 175–184 (2018). https://doi.org/10.1007/s00420-018-1370-z

4. Melchior, C., Zanini, R.R.: Mortality per work accident: a literature mapping. Safety Science **114**, 72–78 (2019)
5. Roets, B., Christiaens, J.: Shift work fatigue and human error: an empirical analysis of railway traffic control. J. Transp. Saf. Secur. **11**(2), 207–224 (2019)
6. Jahangiri, M., Hoboubi, N., Rostamabadi, A., Keshavarzi, S., Hosseini, A.A.: Human error analysis in a permit to work system: a case study in a chemical plant. Saf. Health Work **7**(1), 6–11 (2016)
7. Filho, Anastacio., Berlink, Thais, Vasconcelos, Tales: Analysis of accidents involving machines and equipment using the human factor analysis and classification system method (HFACS). In: Arezes, Pedro Miguel Ferreira Martins (ed.) AHFE 2018. AISC, vol. 791, pp. 438–444. Springer, Cham (2019). https://doi.org/10.1007/978-3-319-94589-7_43
8. Bevilacqua, M., Ciarapica, F.E.: Human factor risk management in the process industry: a case study. Reliab. Eng. Syst. Saf. **169**, 149–159 (2018)
9. Parasuraman, R., Rizzo, M.: Neuroergonomics: The Brain at Work. Oxford University Press, New York (2009)
10. Wall, T.D., et al.: On the validity of subjective measures of company performance. Pers. Psychol. **57**(1), 95–118 (2004)
11. Aricò, P., et al.: Human factors and neurophysiological metrics in air traffic control: a critical review. IEEE Rev. Biomed. Eng. **10**, 250–263 (2017)
12. Babiloni, Fabio: Mental workload monitoring: new perspectives from neuroscience. In: Longo, Luca, Leva, Maria Chiara (eds.) H-WORKLOAD 2019. CCIS, vol. 1107, pp. 3–19. Springer, Cham (2019). https://doi.org/10.1007/978-3-030-32423-0_1
13. Borghini, G., Astolfi, L., Vecchiato, G, Mattia, D., Babiloni, F.: Measuring neurophysiological signals in aircraft pilots and car drivers for the assessment of mental workload, fatigue and drowsiness. Neurosci. Biobehav. Rev. **44**, 58–75 (2014)
14. Aricó, P., Borghini, G., Di Flumeri, G., Sciaraffa, N., Colosimo, A., Babiloni, F.: Passive BCI in operational environments: Insights, recent advances, and future trends. IEEE Trans. Biomed. Eng. **64**(7), 1431–1436 (2017)
15. Fairclough, S.H.: Fundamentals of physiological computing. Interact. Comput. **21**(1–2), 133–145 (2009)
16. Maggi, Piero., Ricciardi, Orlando, Di Nocera, Francesco: Ocular indicators of mental workload: a comparison of scanpath entropy and fixations clustering. In: Longo, Luca, Leva, Maria Chiara (eds.) H-WORKLOAD 2019. CCIS, vol. 1107, pp. 205–212. Springer, Cham (2019). https://doi.org/10.1007/978-3-030-32423-0_13
17. Belzunegui-Eraso, A., Erro-Garcés, A.: Teleworking in the Context of the Covid-19 Crisis. Sustainability **12**(9), 3662 (2020)
18. Fong, M.W., et al.: Nonpharmaceutical measures for pandemic influenza in nonhealthcare settings-social distancing measures. Emerg. Infect. Dis. **26**(5), 976–984 (2020)
19. Coronavirus. https://www.who.int/health-topics/coronavirus#tab=tab_2. Accessed 03 Jun 2020
20. Charles, R.L., Nixon, J.: Measuring mental workload using physiological measures: a systematic review. Appl. Ergon. **74**, 221–232 (2019)
21. Borghini, G., Ronca, V., Vozzi, A., Aricò, P., Di Flumeri, G., Babiloni, F.: Monitoring performance of professional and occupational operators. Handb. Clin. Neurol. **168**, 199–205 (2020)
22. Borghini, Gianluca., et al.: Quantitative assessment of the training improvement in a motor-cognitive task by using EEG, ECG and EOG signals. Brain Topogr. **29**(1), 149–161 (2015). https://doi.org/10.1007/s10548-015-0425-7
23. Cartocci, G., et al., Mental workload estimations in unilateral deafened children. In: Proceedings of the Annual International Conference of the IEEE Engineering in Medicine and Biology Society, EMBS 2015, vol. 2015-November, pp. 1654–1657 (2015)

24. Backs, R.W.: Going beyond heart rate: autonomic space and cardiovascular assessment of mental workload. Int. J. Aviat. Psychol. **5**(1), 25–48 (1995)
25. Delliaux, S., Delaforge, A., Deharo, J.-C., Chaumet, G.: Mental workload alters heart rate variability, lowering non-linear dynamics. Front. Physiol. **10**, 565 (2019)
26. Rahman, H., Ahmed, M.U., Begum, S.: Non-contact physiological parameters extraction using facial video considering illumination, motion, movement and vibration. IEEE Trans. Biomed. Eng. **67**(1), 88–98 (2020)
27. Rahman, H., Uddin Ahmed, M., Begum, S., Funk, P.: Real Time Heart Rate Monitoring From Facial RGB Color Video Using Webcam (2016)
28. Bruyer, R., Brysbaert, M.: Combining speed and accuracy in cognitive psychology: is the inverse efficiency score (IES) a better dependent variable than the mean reaction time (RT) and the percentage of errors (PE)? (2011)
29. Zarjam, P., Epps, J., Chen, F., Lovell, N.H.: Estimating cognitive workload using wavelet entropy-based features during an arithmetic task. Comput. Biol. Med. **43**(12), 2186–2195 (2013)
30. Logie, R.H., Gilhooly, K.J., Wynn, V.: Counting on working memory in arithmetic problem solving. Mem. Cognit. **22**(4), 395–410 (1994)
31. Di Flumeri, G., Aricò, P., Borghini, G., Sciaraffa, N., Di Florio, A., Babiloni, F.: The dry revolution: evaluation of three different EEG Dry electrode types in terms of signal spectral features, mental states classification and usability. Sensors **19**(6), 1365 (2019)
32. Imbo, I., Vandierendonck, A., De Rammelaere, S.: The role of working memory in the carry operation of mental arithmetic: Number and value of the carry. Q. J. Exp. Psychol. **60**(5), 708–731 (2007)
33. Borghini, G., et al.: Neurophysiological measures for users' training objective assessment during simulated robot-assisted laparoscopic surgery. In: Proceedings of the Annual International Conference of the IEEE Engineering in Medicine and Biology Society, EMBS 2016, vol. 2016-October, pp. 981–984 (2016)
34. Borghini, G., et al.: A new perspective for the training assessment: machine learning-based neurometric for augmented user's evaluation. Front. Neurosci **11**, 325 (2017)
35. King, D.E., Dlib-ml: A Machine Learning Toolkit (2009)
36. Sklearn.decomposition.PCA — scikit-learn 0.23.1 documentation. https://scikit-learn.org/stable/modules/generated/sklearn.decomposition.PCA.html. Accessed 10 Jun 2020
37. Tarvainen, M.P., Ranta-aho, P.O., Karjalainen, P.A.: An advanced detrending method with application to HRV analysis. IEEE Trans. Biomed. Eng. **49**(2), 172–175 (2002)
38. Di Flumeri, G., et al.: EEG-based mental workload neurometric to evaluate the impact of different traffic and road conditions in real driving settings. Front. Hum. Neurosci. **12**, 509 (2018)
39. Di Flumeri, G., et al.: Brain–computer interface-based adaptive automation to prevent out-of-the-loop phenomenon in air traffic controllers dealing with highly automated systems. Front. Hum. Neurosci. **13**, 296 (2019)
40. Di Flumeri, Gianluca., et al.: EEG-based workload index as a taxonomic tool to evaluate the similarity of different robot-assisted surgery systems. In: Longo, Luca, Leva, Maria Chiara (eds.) H-WORKLOAD 2019. CCIS, vol. 1107, pp. 105–117. Springer, Cham (2019). https://doi.org/10.1007/978-3-030-32423-0_7
41. Borghini, G., et al.: A multimodal and signals fusion approach for assessing the impact of stressful events on air traffic controllers. Sci. Rep. **10**(1), 1–18 (2020)
42. Sebastiani, M., Di Flumeri, G., Aricò, P., Sciaraffa, N., Babiloni, F., Borghini, G.: Neurophysiological vigilance characterisation and assessment: laboratory and realistic validations involving professional air traffic controllers. Brain Sci. **10**(1), 48 (2020)
43. Borghini, G., et al.: EEG-based cognitive control behaviour assessment: an ecological study with professional air traffic controllers. Sci. Rep. **7**(1), 1–16 (2017)

Effects of Perceptions of Information Overload, Noise and Environmental Demands on Wellbeing and Academic Attainment

Hasah Alhenieidi and Andrew P. Smith[⊠]

Centre for Occupational and Health Psychology, School of Psychology, Cardiff University, 63 Park Place, Cardiff CF10 3AS, UK
smithap@cardiff.ac.uk

Abstract. The present research considers components of information overload, which may have a negative impact on wellbeing and academic attainment. 179 university students completed a survey consisting of an information overload scale (IOS) and the wellbeing process questionnaire. Their academic attainment scores were also added to the database. The IOS scale also included questions relating to noise exposure. Both the noise scores and non-noise IOS scores were associated with greater negative wellbeing and lower positive wellbeing. There were no significant effects of noise or IOS scores on academic attainment. Wellbeing is predicted by a number of factors such as exposure to stressors, negative coping, social support and psychological capital. When these established factors were included in the analyses, the effects of noise and other aspects of IOS could be accounted for by exposure to other stressors and were no longer significant predictors of negative or positive wellbeing.

Keywords: Information overload · Noise · Environmental demands · Wellbeing · Attainment

1 Introduction

1.1 Mental Workload

There has been considerable recent interest in models and applications of mental workload research [1–3]. Mental workload has been examined using a variety of different methodologies [4, 5], and it has a long history in Psychology and related disciplines [6, 7]. It has been studied in both laboratory settings [8, 9] and the occupational context [10, 11], and a variety of measures of mental workload have been developed [12–17]. These include physiological measures, task measures and self-assessment. Subjective report measures include the Subjective Workload Assessment Technique [4], the NASA Task Load Index [18], and the Workload Profile [19]. Recent research has shown that even single items measuring perceptions of workload are often highly correlated with longer scales and can predict the wellbeing of workers. Other approaches have examined specific aspects of workload, such as time pressure. This is a major component of the Karasek Job Demands scale, which has been shown to predict health and safety outcomes of workers [20].

© Springer Nature Switzerland AG 2020
L. Longo and M. C. Leva (Eds.): H-WORKLOAD 2020, CCIS 1318, pp. 87–96, 2020.
https://doi.org/10.1007/978-3-030-62302-9_6

1.2   Effects of Noise

One explanation of the negative effects of noise on performance is that the noise acts as an extra source of information that requires extra resources. These resources are then no longer available for the task being performed and performance is impaired [21, 22]. Results from a number of studies [23–27] show that noise increases mental workload. Information overload has been studied extensively, and the aim of the present research was to examine the effects of information overload on the wellbeing and academic attainment of university students. Another specific aim, which forms the basis of the present paper, was to compare information overload due to noise with information overload from other sources.

1.3   Information Overload

The term "information overload" was mentioned by Toffler [28] in his book "Future Shock". Toffler described information overload as the difficulty a person may have in understanding an issue and making decisions because of the high presence of information. Information overload (IO) is the state of stress experienced when the amount of information given exceeds the limit of information user processing capacity [29]. This results in an impaired decision-making process, which can confuse the user and affect their overall work quality [30]. Several concepts, synonyms and related terms of information overload have been provided. These include cognitive overload, information fatigue syndrome, communication overload, sensory overload, knowledge overload, information anxiety, infobesity, information avoidance and social overload due to social networks services. Numerous psychological and economic consequences of information overload result in severe implications at an individual and organizational level. Information overload is a form of cognitive barrier, whereby it blocks, limits or hampers the information-seeking process and causes frustration to the information user [31]. Research has revealed that information overload costs the US economy US$900 billion annually [32], with resulting work stress triggering depression, anxiety, heart disease and high blood pressure [33]. However, more recent information overload implications are attributed to the evolving use of, and emerging reliability on, different internet activities, resulting in more distraction and excessive information flow. A heavy load of information confuses the user, affects their ability to set priorities, or makes prior information harder to recall [34]. Although the user can select where to focus their attention, paying attention is a cognitive limited resource that can be defective in overload situations [35]. Miller [36] hypothesized that processing performance of information is positively correlated with the received amount of information. When the information flow rises to the threshold, it leads to a cognitive decline in the ability to process the information.

Information overload in the workplace has been widely investigated, and its negative consequences on employees and companies have been documented. However, there is a lack of research about information overload on students and its association with wellbeing. There is also insufficient research on whether the large amount of information students receive from academic/scholarly activities, as well as non-scholarly/non-academic sources influence their wellbeing and academic performance.

1.4 The Perceive Information Overload Scale

There are many causes of information overload, and a questionnaire has been developed to measure exposure to these. The Perceived Information Overload Scale was developed by Misra and Stokols [37] and has good internal consistency ($\alpha = .86$), and validity. The scale consists of 16-items that measures two subscales of information overload, environment-based and cyber-based information overload. The first part consists of nine items that explore the user's experience of information overload from cyber-based sources in the previous month, through a Likert scale of 5-points ($0 =$ never and $4 =$ very often). Information users are asked about how often they felt overwhelmed to answer emails/instant messages quickly; how often they felt that they had too many messages/emails or any social network notifications. The second part of the scale consists of seven items measuring participants' experience of the environment or place based on information overload in the last month. The questions explored include the workplace demands exceeding the user's ability to work, as well as a noisy and distracting work and the home environment. The items are summed to produce a total cyber-based information overload score and place-based information overload score. Although information overload is an indicator of stress, the findings of Misra and Stokols [37] indicate that the Perceived Information Overload Scale score and the Perceived Stress Scale score are not overlapping, which suggests that cyber-based and place-based information overload scales measure different concepts from perceived stress. Information overload and wellbeing have been investigated in five studies [38–42]. All the findings confirm the negative effect of information overload on wellbeing, although two studies demonstrated a positive effect if the internet connection is controlled.

1.5 The Wellbeing Process

Wellbeing is difficult to define and involves many different factors. The "wellbeing process model" we use is a holistic approach to wellbeing and attempts to provide a theoretical framework that could lead to the development of a questionnaire that could be useful in practice and policy. The initial research was based on the Demands-Resources-Individual Effects (DRIVE) model, which was developed to conduct research in occupational stress [43–47]. This model included job characteristics, perceived stress, personal characteristics such as coping styles and negative outcomes (e.g. anxiety and depression). The next version of the model [48–51] included positive characteristics such as self-esteem, self-efficacy and optimism, and positive appraisals (e.g. job satisfaction) and outcomes (e.g. positive affect and happiness). Positive outcomes form the basis of a wide number of approaches to subjective wellbeing. However, it is important to include both positive and negative aspects of wellbeing as they involve different CNS mechanisms. One initial problem was that the wellbeing process model required measurement of many variables and that use of long scales which led to a questionnaire that was very lengthy and not very acceptable to the respondents. In order to remove this problem, short scales were developed, and these were found to be significantly correlated with the longer scales from which they were derived [52–55, 57]. The questionnaire has been modified to use in research with students [57]. The outcome measures have also been increased to include academic attainment and perceptions of workload, work efficiency and course stress [58, 59]. The established predictors of student wellbeing are student stressors (e.g. too much academic work), social support, psychological capital (self-esteem, self-efficacy and optimism) and negative coping strategies (e.g. avoidance, wishful thinking and self-blame). The initial aim of the present study was to examine whether noise-overload, information and overload from IT and media sources were associated with reduced wellbeing and poorer academic attainment. If these univariate analyses were significant, multi-variate analyses including the established predictors of wellbeing and attainment would be carried out, to determine whether noise and information overload had independent effects or whether they could be accounted for by other factors.

2 Method

2.1 Participants

One hundred and seventy-nine first-year psychology undergraduate students participated in the study as part of their course requirements. The majority of the sample population (91%) were females. The age range was 18–50 years; 89.9% were 18–21 years old. Course and exam scores were collected at the end of the semester using students' ID numbers.

2.2 The Survey

Questionnaires were completed electronically in a computer laboratory at the beginning of the academic year. Consent with the key features of voluntary participation, freedom to withdraw, anonymous databases, instructions, and debrief forms were provided at the start and the end of the study. The ethics committee at Cardiff University's School of Psychology approved the study. Data collection occurred in 2015.

2.3 Measuring Instruments

The survey included the Perceived Information Overload Scale (IOS) and the Student Wellbeing Process Questionnaire (WPQ). Attainment scores (examination and coursework marks) were obtained at the end of the first semester.

3 Results

3.1 Analysis Strategy

Initial analyses examined the bivariate correlations between the IOS scores and the WPQ predictors and outcomes. Following this, regressions were carried out with the positive and negative wellbeing scores as dependent variables and the IOS scores and established predictors as independent variables.

3.2 Correlations

The three information overload scores were significantly correlated (IO due to noise/IO due to environment: $r = 0.55$, $p < 0.001$; IO due to noise/IO due to media: $r = 0.30$, $p < 0.001$; IO due to environment/IO due to media: $r = 0.34$, $p < 0.001$). IO due to noise was negatively correlated with positive wellbeing ($r = -0.20$, $p = 0.008$) and positively correlated with negative wellbeing ($r = 0.26$, $p < 0.001$). IO due to environmental factors was negatively correlated with positive wellbeing ($r = -0.21$, $p = 0.004$) and positively correlated with negative wellbeing ($r = 0.25$, $p = 0.001$). IO due to media was not significantly correlated with positive wellbeing but was correlated significantly with negative wellbeing ($r = 0.17$, $p = 0.02$). The three IO measures were also positively correlated with exposure to stressors (IO noise: $r = 0.25$, $p = 0.001$; IO environment: $r = 0.30$, $p < 0.001$; IO media: $r = 0.25$, $p = 0.001$) and negative coping (IO noise: $r = 0.23$, $p = 0.002$; IO environment: $r = 0.21$, $p = 0.004$; IO media: $r = 0.23$, $p = 0.002$). There were no significant correlations between the IO measures and the academic attainment scores (Exams and IO noise: $r = -0.08$, $p = 0.32$; Exams and IO due to media: $r = 0.00$, $p = 0.97$; Exams and IO environment: $r = -0.02$, $p = 0.77$; Coursework and IO Noise: $r = -0.08$, $p = 0.26$; Coursework and IO media: $r = 0.00$, $p = 0.97$; Coursework and IO environment: $r = -0.04$, $p = 0.58$).

3.3 Regressions

Regressions were conducted with positive outcomes and negative outcomes as the dependent variables. The three IO scores and the established predictors from the WPQ (exposure to stressors, negative coping, positive personality and social support) were the independent variables. Negative outcomes were predicted by positive personality, exposure to stressors and negative coping but not by any of the information overload scores. These results are shown in Table 1. High stressor and negative coping scores were positively associated with negative wellbeing. In contrast, high positive personality (psychological capital) scores were negatively associated with negative wellbeing.

Table 1. Predictors of negative outcomes

Model	B	SE	Beta	t	p
Constant	37.288	4.952		7.530	.000
IO noise	.379	.328	.072	1.155	.250
IO environment	.109	.140	.050	.780	.437
IO media	.020	.094	.012	.216	.830
Stressors	.257	.056	.281	4.558	.000
Social support	−.197	.129	−.083	−1.533	.127
Negative coping	.310	.123	.148	2.530	.012
Positive personality	−.690	.086	−.461	−7.981	.000

Positive outcomes were predicted by positive personality and social support but not by any of the IO measures. This is shown in Table 2.

Table 2. Predictors of positive outcomes

Model	B	S.E.	Beta	t	p
Constant	2.955	1.704		1.734	.085
IO noise	−.055	.113	−.030	−.487	.627
IO environment	−.090	.048	−.116	−1.873	.063
IO media	.028	.032	.048	.879	.381
Stressors	−.023	.019	−.071	−1.179	.240
Social support	.164	.044	.195	3.696	.000
Negative coping	−.020	.042	−.026	−.465	.642
Positive personality	.331	.030	.626	11.138	.000

4 Discussion

The aim of the present study was to examine whether information overload was related to wellbeing and academic attainment. Information overload from noise was compared with information overload from media, such as the internet, and other demands due to work or leisure time activities. The three types of overload were correlated with each other and also with predictors of wellbeing such as stressors and negative coping. When established predictors of wellbeing were included in the regressions, there were no significant effects of any of the information overload variables for either negative or positive wellbeing. The established predictors of wellbeing had their usual associations with wellbeing, which gives one confidence in the information overload results.

4.1 Effects of Noise

Information overload due to noise was correlated positively with negative wellbeing and negatively with positive wellbeing. There were no significant correlations between information overload from noise and attainment measures. Other recent results [60] suggest that it is possible to demonstrate associations between noise exposure and wellbeing in a sample of office workers. This effect of noise remained significant when established predictors of wellbeing and environmental satisfaction were co-varied. The exposure of the office workers may be much higher than that of students, which could plausibly explain the different pattern of results. Further research investigating information overload in workers is now required to address this possibility.

4.2 Information Overload and Wellbeing

The pattern of results obtained here is similar to other findings that show that initial effects attributed to perceptions of information overload reflect associated factors. Alternatively, the negative results may reflect the fact that the students were only just starting at university when they completed the survey. Other results with student samples [61] shows that information overload from the internet is associated with poorer academic attainment, and it is possible that this effect takes time to develop.

4.3 Limitations

The present study has a number of limitations. The first reflects the characteristics of the sample which consisted largely of female psychology students just starting university. A more representative sample of students would have been better, and it might have been wise to test them either before arriving at university or after they had been there for some time. It was not possible to remove these limitations in the present study due to logistic issues relating to who could be tested and when data collection could occur. Future research on this topic should also use other measures of noise, information overload, workload and wellbeing. The present research was restricted to an online survey which reduced the feasibility of objective measurement. Finally, it is difficult to identify causal mechanisms with a cross-sectional design, and future research should be longitudinal, preferably involving interventions.

5 Conclusion

The present research investigated whether components of information overload have a negative impact on wellbeing and academic attainment. A sample of first-year university students completed a survey consisting of an information overload scale (IOS) and the wellbeing process questionnaire. Their academic attainment scores were also available. The IOS scale included questions relating to the media, noise exposure and environmental demands. Both the noise scores and non-noise IOS scores were associated with greater negative wellbeing and lower positive wellbeing. There were no significant effects of noise or IOS scores on academic attainment. When the established predictors of wellbeing were included in the analyses, the effects of noise and other aspects of IOS could be accounted for by exposure to other stressors and were no longer significant predictors of negative or positive wellbeing. Further research with other samples, objective measurement and longitudinal designs is required to help explain such results and determine the impact on policy and practice.

References

1. Longo, L., Leva, M.C. (eds.): H-WORKLOAD 2017. CCIS, vol. 726. Springer, Cham (2017). https://doi.org/10.1007/978-3-319-61061-0
2. Longo, L., Leva, M.C. (eds.): H-WORKLOAD 2018. CCIS, vol. 1012. Springer, Cham (2019). https://doi.org/10.1007/978-3-030-14273-5

3. Longo, L., Leva, M.C. (eds.): H-WORKLOAD 2019. CCIS, vol. 1107. Springer, Cham (2019). https://doi.org/10.1007/978-3-030-32423-0
4. Reid, G.B., Nygren, T.E.: The subjective workload assessment technique: a scaling procedure for measuring mental workload, vol. 52, North-Holland (1988)
5. Stassen, H.G., Johannsen, G., Moray, N.: Internal representation, internal model, human performance model and mental workload. Automatica 26(4), 811–820 (1990)
6. De Waard, D.: The measurement of drivers' mental workload. The Traffic Research Centre VSC. University of Groningen (1996)
7. Hart, S.G.: Nasa-task load index (nasa-tlx); 20 years later. In: Human Factors and Ergonomics Society Annual Meeting, vol. 50. Sage Journals (2006)
8. Smith, A.P., Smith, K.: Effects of workload and time of day on performance and mood. In: Megaw, E.D. (ed.) Contemporary Ergonomics, pp. 497–502. Taylor & Francis, London (1988)
9. Evans, M.S., Harborne, D., Smith, A.P.: Developing an objective indicator of fatigue: an alternative mobile version of the psychomotor vigilance task (m-PVT). In: Longo, L., Leva, M.Chiara (eds.) H-WORKLOAD 2018. CCIS, vol. 1012, pp. 49–71. Springer, Cham (2019). https://doi.org/10.1007/978-3-030-14273-5_4
10. Smith, A.P., Smith, H.N.: Workload, fatigue and performance in the rail industry. In: Longo, L., Leva, M.C. (eds.) H-WORKLOAD 2017. CCIS, vol. 726, pp. 251–263. Springer, Cham (2017). https://doi.org/10.1007/978-3-319-61061-0_17
11. Fan, J., Smith, A.P.: Mental workload and other causes of different types of fatigue in rail staff. In: Longo, L., Leva, M.C. (eds.) H-WORKLOAD 2018. CCIS, vol. 1012, pp. 147–159. Springer, Cham (2019). https://doi.org/10.1007/978-3-030-14273-5_9
12. Cortes Torres, C.C., Sampei, K., Sato, M., Raskar, R., Miki, N.: Workload assessment with eye movement monitoring aided by non-invasive and unobtrusive micro-fabricated optical sensors. In: Adjunct Proceedings of the 28th Annual ACM Symposium on User Interface Software & Technology, pp. 53–54 (2015)
13. Yoshida, Y., Ohwada, H., Mizoguchi, F., Iwasaki, H.: Classifying cognitive load and driving situation with machine learning. Int. J. Mach. Learn. Comput. 4(3), 210–215 (2014)
14. Wilson, G.F., Eggemeier, T.F.: Mental workload measurement. In: Karwowski, W. (ed.) International Encyclopedia of Ergonomics and Human Factors, 2nd edn., vol. 1, chap. 167. Taylor & Francis (2006)
15. Young, M.S., Stanton, N.A.: Mental workload. In: Stanton, N.A., Hedge, A., Brookhuis, K., Salas, E., Hendrick, H.W. (eds.) Handbook of Human Factors and Ergonomics Methods, chap. 39, pp. 1–9. CRC Press (2004)
16. Young, M.S., Stanton, N.A.: Mental workload: theory, measurement, and application. In: Karwowski, W. (ed.) International Encyclopedia of Ergonomics and Human Factors, 2nd edn., vol. 1, pp. 818–821. Taylor & Francis (2006)
17. Moustafa, K., Luz, S., Longo, L.: Assessment of mental workload: a comparison of machine learning methods and subjective assessment techniques. In: Longo, L., Leva, M.C. (eds.) H-WORKLOAD 2017. CCIS, vol. 726, pp. 30–50. Springer, Cham (2017). https://doi.org/10.1007/978-3-319-61061-0_3
18. Hart, S.G., Staveland, L.E.: Development of NASA-TLX (task load index): results of empirical and theoretical research. Adv. Psychol. 52(C), 139–183 (1988)
19. Tsang, P.S., Velazquez, V.L.: Diagnosticity and multidimensional subjective workload ratings. Ergonomics 39(3), 358–381 (1996)
20. Karasek Jr., R.A.: Job demands, job decision latitude, and mental strain: implications for job redesign. Adm. Sci. Q. 24, 285–308 (1979)
21. Smith, A.P.: A review of the effects of noise on human performance. Scand. J. Psychol. 30, 185–206 (1989)

22. Smith, A.P., Jones, D.M.: Noise and performance. In: Smith, A.P., Jones, D.M. (eds.) Handbook of Human Performance. The Physical Environment, pp. 1–28. Academic Press, London (1992)

23. McNeer, R., Bennett, C., Dudaryk, R.: Intraoperative noise increases perceived task load and fatigue in anesthesiology residents: a simulation based study. Anesth. Analg. **122**(2), 512–525 (2016)

24. Rosen, M., Dietz, A., Lee, N., Wang, I.-J., Markowitz, J., Wyskiel, M., et al.: Sensor-based measurement of critical care nursing workload: unobtrusive measures of nursing activity complement traditional task and patient level indicators of workload to predict perceived exertion. PLoS ONE **13**(10), e0204819 (2018)

25. Jahncke, H., Bjorkeholm, P., Marsh, J., Odelius, J., Sorqvist, P.: Office noise: can headphones and masking sound attenuate distraction by background speech? Work **55**(3), 505–513 (2016)

26. Gao, J., Liu, S., Feng, Q., Zhang, X., Zhang, J., Jiang, M., et al.: Quantitative evaluations of the effects of noise on mental workloads based on pupil dilation during laparoscopic surgery. Am. Surg. **84**(12), 1951–1956 (2018)

27. Becker, A., Warm, J., Dember, W., Hancock, P.: Effects of jet engine noise and performance feedback on perceived workload in a monitoring task. Int. J. Aviat. Psychol. **5**(1), 49–62 (1995)

28. Toffler, A.: Future Shock. Bantam Books, New York (1970)

29. Eppler, M.J., Mengis, J.: The concept of information overload: a review of literature from organization science, accounting, marketing, and related disciplines. Inf. Soc. **20**(5), 325–344 (2004)

30. Chewning Jr., E.G., Harrell, A.M.: The effect of information load on decision makers' cue utilization levels and decision quality in a financial distress decision task. Account. Organ. Soc. **15**(6), 527–542 (2009)

31. Savolainen, I., Kaakinen, M., Sirola, A., Oksanen, A.: Addictive behaviors and psychological distress among adolescents and emerging adults: a mediating role of peer group identification. Addict. Behav. Rep. **7**, 75–81 (2018)

32. Spira, J., Burke, C.: Intel's war on information overload: case study. Basex (2009). http://iorgforum.org/wp-content/uploads/2011/06/IntelWarIO.BasexReport1.pdf

33. Guarinoni, M., et al.: Occupational Health Concerns: Stress-Related and Psychological Problems Associated with Work. European Parliament's Committee on Employment and Social Affairs, Brussels (2013)

34. Schick, A.G., Gorden, L.A., Haka, S.: Information overload: a temporal approach. Account. Organ. Soc. **15**(3), 199–220 (1990)

35. McLeod, S.A.: Selective attention (2008). http://www.simplypsychology.org/attention-models.html

36. Miller, G.A.: The magical number seven, plus or minus two: some limits on our capacity for processing information. Psychol. Rev. **63**(2), 81–97 (1956)

37. Misra, S., Stokols, D.: Psychological and health outcomes of perceived information overload. Environ. Behav. **44**(6), 737–759 (2011)

38. LaRose, R., Connolly, R., Lee, H., Li, K., Hales, K.D.: Connection overload? A cross cultural study of the consequences of social media connection. Inf. Syst. Manag. **31**(1), 59–73 (2014)

39. Lee, H., Connolly, R., Li, K., Hales, K., LaRose, R.: Impacts of social media connection demands: a study of Irish college students (2013). https://aisel.aisnet.org/amcis2013/SocialTechnicalIssues/GeneralPresentations/6/

40. Saunders, C., Wiener, M., Klett, S., Sprenger, S.: The impact of mental representations on ICT-related overload in the use of mobile phones. J. Manag. Inf. Syst. **34**(3), 803–825 (2017)

41. Sonnentag, S.: Being permanently online and being permanently connected at work: a demands–resources perspective. In: Permanently Online, Permanently Connected, pp. 258–267. Routledge (2017)

42. Swar, B., Hameed, T., Reychav, I.: Information overload, psychological ill-being, and behavioral intention to continue online healthcare information search. Comput. Hum. Behav. **70**, 416–425 (2017)
43. Mark, G.M., Smith, A.P.: Stress models: a review and suggested new direction. In: Houdmont, J., Leka, S. (eds.) Occupational Health Psychology: European Perspectives on Research, Education and Practice, pp. 111–144. Nottingham University Press, Nottingham (2008)
44. Mark, G., Smith, A.P.: Effects of occupational stress, job characteristics, coping and attributional style on the mental health and job satisfaction of university employees. Anxiety Stress Coping **25**, 63–78 (2011)
45. Mark, G., Smith, A.P.: Occupational stress, job characteristics, coping and mental health of nurses. Br. J. Health. Psychol. **17**, 505–521 (2012)
46. Mark, G., Smith, A.P.: A qualitative study of stress in university staff. Adv. Soc. Sci. Res. J. **5**(2), 238–247 (2018)
47. Mark, G., Smith, A.P.: Coping and its relation to gender, anxiety, depression, fatigue, cognitive difficulties and somatic symptoms. J. Educ. Soc. Behav. Sci. **25**(4), 1–22 (2018)
48. Smith, A.P.: A holistic approach to stress and wellbeing. Occup. Health (At Work) **7**(4), 34–35 (2011)
49. Smith, A.P., Wadsworth, E.: A holistic approach to stress and wellbeing. Part 5: what is a good job? Occup. Health (At Work) **8**(4), 25–27 (2011)
50. Smith, A.P., Wadsworth, E.J.K., Chaplin, K., Allen, P.H., Mark, G.: The Relationship Between Work/Wellbeing and Improved Health and Wellbeing. IOSH, Leicester (2011)
51. Wadsworth, E.J.K., Chaplin, K., Allen, P.H., Smith, A.P.: What is a good job? Current perspectives on work and improved health and wellbeing. Open Health Saf. J. **2**, 9–15 (2010)
52. Williams, G.M., Smith, A.P.: Using single-item measures to examine the relationships between work, personality, and wellbeing in the workplace. Psychol.: Spec. Ed. Posit. Psychol. **7**, 753–767 (2016)
53. Williams, G.M., Smith, A.P.: A holistic approach to stress and wellbeing. Part 6: the wellbeing process questionnaire (WPQ short form). Occup. Health (At Work) **9**(1), 29–31 (2012)
54. Williams, G.M., Smith, A.P.: Diagnostic validity of the anxiety and depression questions from the wellbeing process questionnaire. J. Clin. Transl. Res. **10**, 101 (2018)
55. Williams, G.M., Pendlebury, H., Smith, A.P.: Stress and wellbeing of nurses: an investigation using the demands-resources- individual effects (DRIVE) model and wellbeing process questionnaire (WPQ). Jacobs J. Depress. Anxiety **1**, 1–8 (2017)
56. Williams, G., Thomas, K., Smith, A.P.: Stress and wellbeing of university staff: an investigation using the demands-resources- individual effects (DRIVE) model and wellbeing process questionnaire (WPQ). Psychology **8**, 1919–1940 (2017)
57. Williams, G.M., Pendlebury, H., Thomas, K., Smith, A.P.: The student wellbeing process questionnaire (student WPQ). Psychology **8**, 1748–1761 (2017)
58. Smith, A.P., Firman, K.L.: Associations between the wellbeing process and academic outcomes. J. Educ. Soc. Behav. Sci. **32**(4), 1–10 (2019)
59. Smith, A.P.: Student workload, wellbeing and academic attainment. In: Longo, L., Leva, M.C. (eds.) H-WORKLOAD 2019. CCIS, vol. 1107, pp. 35–47. Springer, Cham (2019). https://doi.org/10.1007/978-3-030-32423-0_3
60. Langer, J., Taylour, J., Smith, A.P.: Noise exposure, satisfaction with the working environment, and the wellbeing process. ICBEN 2020. (in Press)
61. Smith, A.P., Izadvar, S.: Effects of the internet, other media and study time on wellbeing and academic attainment of university students. Int. J. Educ. Humanit. Soc. Sci. **3**(02), 1–13 (2020)

Applications

Direct and Constructivist Instructional Design: A Comparison of Efficiency Using Mental Workload and Task Performance

Giuliano Orru and Luca Longo[✉]

School of Computer Science, College of Health and Sciences, Technological University Dublin, Dublin, Republic of Ireland
Luca.Longo@tudublin.ie

Abstract. Cognitive Load Theory is based upon the assumption that working memory can process only explicit and direct instructions. Therefore, it is believed that inquiries techniques, not employing explicit instructional methods for teaching, are set to fail. This paper aims to fill this gap by extending the traditional direct instruction teaching method, with a highly guided inquiry activity and comparing their efficiency. In detail, the efficiency of the former is expected to be lower than the efficiency of the latter hybrid method. The likelihood model of efficiency, originally based upon a unidimensional subjective measure of effort and an objective measure of performance, was originally applied and extended with a multidimensional measure of cognitive load. Empirical evidence partially supports the above hypothesis but reveals some limitations of the traditional statistical tools applied to group comparisons of small sample size, often the case in higher educational settings. This suggests that future scholars should dedicate effort on the identification and application of statistical methods for the analysis of the efficiency of instructional conditions in small sample-size groups.

Keywords: Cognitive load theory · Mental workload · Efficiency · Direct instruction methods · Inquiry methods

1 Introduction

Cognitive Load Theory (CLT), a well-known theory in educational psychology, is structured on the premise that working memory can process explicit and direct instructions only [1]. Kirschner and colleagues (2006) criticized experiments based on unguided collaborative methodologies because they tend to ignore the role of working memory in the process of learning. Consequently, teaching approaches that do not explicitly consider the importance of direct instructions are set to fail [1]. In CLT, the acquisition of knowledge is supposed to take place within human cognitive architecture whose core system is working memory. If explicit instructions are not considered, working memory cannot process the information related to any underlying learning task. This is the gap emerged from the literature review connected to CLT and the constructivists techniques usually used in collaborative learning. Jonassen (2009), replying to Kirchner et al.

© Springer Nature Switzerland AG 2020
L. Longo and M. C. Leva (Eds.): H-WORKLOAD 2020, CCIS 1318, pp. 99–123, 2020.
https://doi.org/10.1007/978-3-030-62302-9_7

(2006) affirms that, in the field of educational psychology, a comparison between the effectiveness of inquiry methods and direct instruction is not possible [2] because the two approaches come from different theory assumptions and they use different research methods. Constructivists methods usually employ qualitative analysis. On the contrary, direct instructions methods, as per those used in CLT, usually employ quantitative analysis [2]. Quantity and quality cannot be compared as they are different in their nature, consequently Jonassen (2009) states that the assumption of Kirchner and colleagues (2006) is not supported by any empirical comparison or evidence. Besides that, another problem is the lack of a shared learning outcome. The two methodologies must share the same dependent variable to be compared. In the case of the current set of experiments, the achievement of factual, conceptual and procedural knowledge is the shared dependent variable, evaluated by multiple choices questionnaire (MCQ) as performance test. The current research is motivated by the aforementioned gap between explicit instructional designs characteristic of CLT, and the features of the community of inquiry approach that focus on the learning connection between cognitive abilities and knowledge construction. The proposed solution is to extend the approach of direct instructions connected to a learning task with highly guided inquiries activities, the purpose is to establish whether this extension improves the efficiency of learners compared with learners who receive direct instructions only. Empirically evaluating instructional approaches is not a trivial task in Pedagogy. The likelihood efficiency measure, proposed by Hoffman and Schraw (2010), has been employed to tackle this problem on. The related formula is based upon two other measures: the cognitive load, namely the cognitive cost of learning task on working memory, and performance score [3]. The research question being proposed in this study is:

to what extent can an inquiry activity based upon cognitive trigger questions, when added to a direct instruction conventional teaching method, improve its efficiency, impact the effort and mental workload experienced by learners and improve their learning performance?

The current research proposes a requalified teaching methodology that is aimed at combining the cognitive approach of CLT focused on explicit instruction and the community of inquiry approach based on cognitive questions by extending the first with the second and comparing its efficiency with that associated to explicit instructions only. Explicit instructions are direct, precise, specific and clear teaching explanations aimed at facilitating how to deal with a learning task or problem solving. The proposed inquiry activity is aimed at engaging learners in the learning process by the use of dialogue focused on cognitive trigger questions.

The reminder of this paper is structured as it follows. Section 2 informs the reader on the related background and the literature review that originated the current research. Section 3 describes the design of the empirical comparative experiment and the methodology employed while Sect. 4 outlines the analysis of the results of such comparison, the related effect sizes and proposes an interpretation of data. Section 5 summarizes the paper highlighting its contribution and delineating future work.

2 Literature Review and Background

The aim of this section is to inform the reader with the basic notions and background on cognitive load theory, mental workload and its measurement, collaborative learning and instructional efficiency, theoretical contents that are critical to give an account of the layout of the proposed experiment described in Sect. 3.

2.1 Cognitive Load Theory

Cognitive Load Theory is widely known in educational psychology as a reference to improve the learning process by developing new instructional techniques aligned with the limitations of the human cognitive architecture [4]. This happens by optimizing the cognitive load imposed on working memories while carrying on a task. Cognitive load is, in fact, the cognitive cost, in terms of memory resources, experienced by learners when performing a learning task [5]. Working memory and long term-memory are the two dimensions of human cognitive architecture that stores information, retrieving and processing it for reasoning and decision making [6–8]. The premise for acquiring knowledge in CLT is that learners have to be instructed by means of direct instructional designs [4, 9]. Studies in CLT are based on the comparison between a control and experimental group of learners, the former is taught according to a conventional instructional procedure, the latter according to a new instructional procedure [10]. A test phase follows to see if there are any differences in learning outcomes. If statistical analyses on the test results demonstrate that learning improves by the new instructional procedure, then a new cognitive load effect is demonstrated and a superior instructional procedure generated as summarized by Sweller in his recent review of CLT [4]. Among others, the Collective Working Memory effect is particularly relevant to give an account of collaborative techniques that enable learners to share working memories while attending the same task. The assumption is that the use of working memory of many people can reduce the overall cognitive cost of that task. Collaborative techniques are supposed to engage students in higher order skills [11] and in activities valuable to the enhancement of learning such as self-directed learning, negotiating, meaning, verbalizing, explaining, justifying and reflecting, as well as giving each other mutual support [12]. Along with these positive findings, however, there is also a body of research showing mixed and negative benefits regarding both the learning process itself [13, 14] and the dynamics of group formation [15]. The main negative effect is the cognitive cost of information transfer: the transactive interaction, could generate too much cognitive load hampering the learning phase instead of facilitating it [16]. This depends on the complexity of the task. In tasks with high level of complexity, in fact, the cognitive cost of transfer is compensated by the advantage of using working memories of multiple people. In contrast, in tasks with low level of complexity, the working memory of one person is supposed to be sufficient and the transfer costs of communication might hamper the learning phase.

2.2 Mental Workload

According to Wickens (1979) '… the concept of operator workload is defined in terms of the human's limited processing resources'. His Multiple Resource Theory (MRT) states that humans have a limited set of resources available for mental processes [17]. Mental Workload can be defined as 'the volume of cognitive work necessary for an individual to accomplish a task over time' [18, 19]. It is not 'an elementary property, rather it emerges from the interaction between the requirements of a task, the circumstances under which it is performed and the skills, behaviors and perceptions of the operator' [20–22]. However, these are only practical definitions, as many other factors influence mental workload [23–26]. The concept of cognitive load is mainly employed within Education whereas the concept of Mental Workload mainly in Ergonomics [27–30]. The former relates to working memory resources only, whereas latter takes into account other factors as the level of motivation, stress and the physical demand experienced by participants as a consequence of the task. Despite of their different fields of research, CLT and MRT share a common assumption: the limits of working memory must be considered to predict humans' performance while accomplishing an underlying task. A well-known multi-dimensional self-reporting measures of mental workload is the NASA-task Load Index (NASA-TLX) [31–33]. In contrast to unidimensional scales of overall cognitive load, such as effort and task difficulty proposed by Paas and Van Merriënboer (1993, 1994) [34, 35], Paas et al. (2003) [36] and Zijistra [37], NASA-TLX focuses on different components of load as per mental, physical, and temporal demands, frustration, effort, and performance. In education it is not widely employed, however, a number of studies have confirmed its validity and sensitivity [38–40]. A lighter version of the NASA-TLX exists. This is the RAW-NASA-TLX, in which the weighting process employed in the original questionnaire is eliminated.

2.3 Genealogy of Community of Inquiry

On the relation between instructional technique and its capacity to have an impact on learning outcomes, John Dewey suggests to re-think the semantic distinction between 'Technique' as practice and 'Knowledge' as pure theory. Practice, in fact, is not foundationalist in its epistemology anymore, in other words it does not require a first principle as its theoretical foundation. In the philosophy of Dewey, 'Technique' means an active procedure aimed at developing new skills starting from the redefinition of the old as resumed in the 'Theory of Inquiry' of Dewey [41]. Therefore, the configuration of epistemic theoretical knowledge is a specific case of technical production and 'Knowledge' as a theory is the result of 'Technique' as practice. Both are deeply interconnected and they share the resolution of practical problems as starting point for expanding knowledge [41]. The aim of this pragmatist approaches to learn is improving the techniques of humans by a process of autocorrective feedback within inquiring environments [41]. Inquiry is proposed as teaching and learning technique that is deeply linked with a continuous autocorrective process of knowledge's development: this is the reason why Dewey identifies technology, the discipline whose focus is the study of techniques, with education. Through the process of inquiry an unsatisfactory situation can be converted into satisfactory by connecting all of its constituent into a coherent and unified whole [41]. This is the reason why, in educational contexts, inquiry techniques are proposed to improve the comprehension of complex learning tasks [42]. The research of Garrison (2007) conducted on the community of inquiry online was influenced by the philosophy of education of Dewey and by its notion of inquiry. Garrison provided a clear exemplification of the social and cognitive structure a community of inquiry consists of [42]. The social context is based on democratic features as free risk expression, encouragement and collaboration. The cognitive dimensions, instead, consist in exploring a problem by exchanging information on its constituent parts, integrating that information by connecting related ideas and solving it suggesting alternatives and new ideas. The core ability in solving a problem consists in connecting the right tool to reach a specific aim. The community of inquiry may be defined as 'a teaching and learning technique, an instructional technique of a group of learners who, through the use of dialogue, examine the conceptual boundary of a problematic concept proceeding all the parts this problem is composed of in order to solve it' [30]. Inquiring may be defined, in a nutshell, as critical and creative thinking. The former consists in connecting tools with aims consistently, in order to solve problems and expanding human knowledge, the latter consists in coherently connecting the constituents parts of a problem with its whole [43]. Dewey and after him Lipman who extended the community of inquiry with a philosophical model of reasoning, connected the meaning of inquiry with the meaning of community, the individual and the community can only exists in relation to each other along a continuous process of adaptation that ends up with their reciprocal, critical and creative improvement [41–43]. In line with the definition of inquiry, a pedagogical framework grounded in the 'Philosophy for Children' proposed by Mathew Lipman exists (the project NORIA) [44]. It proposes a set of cognitive questions aimed to exercise the cognitive abilities of a learner and to develop a higher level of thinking. The goal of the trigger questions is to support the development of the cognitive skills of learners [44]. Among others, they are aimed at developing cognitive skills of conceptualization by comparing and contrasting, defining, classifying, and reasoning by relating cause and effect, tools and aims, parts and whole and by establishing criteria [44].

2.4 Taxonomy of Anderson and Models of Instructional Efficiency

The taxonomy of educational objectives proposed by Anderson distinguishes between dimensions of knowledge (factual, conceptual, procedural and metacognitive knowledge) and dimension of cognitive process (remember, understand, apply, analyze evaluate and create) [45]. These dimensions of educational objectives assume a critical importance in the design of the experiment proposed in Sect. 3. If a performance test, as per Multiple Choice Questions, is aligned with the aforementioned dimensions of knowledge, then it can be employed to compare the performance of students who receive different teaching methods based on the same contents. In problem solving, learning and instruction, efficiency is generally defined in terms of ability to reach established goals by minimal expenditure of time, effort or cognitive resources [3]. The Likelihood model computes a measure of efficiency based on the ratio of work output to work input. Output can be identified with learning, input with work, time or effort [46]. The likelihood model has been widely used in educational psychology to analyze relative gain between two variables as a consequence of a methodological intervention [47, 48]. It is based on the ratio between performance and effort, a raw score for test performance or a learning outcome denoted as P divided by a raw score for time or effort denoted as R:

$$Efficiency = P / R$$

R can be any self-report or an objective measure based on time or cognitive resources employed [3]. An estimation of the rate of change of performance is calculated by dividing P per R. This ratio diverges from zero to extensive positive values, it goes towards zero when performance is low and effort is high (low efficiency), it goes towards extensive positive values when performance is high, and effort is low (high efficiency). The result represents the individual efficiency based on individual scores [3].

2.5 Summary

The gap emerged from the literature review points to the relationship between working memory and constructivists techniques: inquiry techniques are believed to fail in educational contexts because of their lack of direct and explicit instructions that are instead required by working memory to process information as proposed within Cognitive Load Theory [49]. However, this claim is not backed up by empirical tests and a lack of comparison of their effectiveness exists. This is justified by the fact that, on one hand, constructivists techniques usually employ qualitative research methods, while, on the other hand, those employed within cognitive load theory are quantitative. This, make such a comparison non-trivial. However, multiple choice questionnaires, as extensively used within education [50], is a potential tool for supporting such a comparison and allowing the evaluation of factual, conceptual and procedural knowledge as well as the assessment of learning produced with different instructional approaches. Formulas of efficiency for the evaluation of instructional conditions exist, such as the likelihood model, based upon the combination of test performance scores and a measure of effort or cognitive load. The likelihood model seems to be effective in detecting changes within experimental studies.

3 Design, Material and Methodology

Given the research question of Sect. 1, a primary research experiment has been designed and the following research hypothesis was set:

> H1: if an explicit instructional design method is extended with an inquiry activity focused on cognitive trigger questions, then, its efficiency is improved, the experienced effort and mental workload of learners is impacted, and their learning performance is positively enhanced.

The approach employed in CLT and the collective working memories principles recently summarized by Kirschner and colleagues [51], have been taken in consideration in the design of the experiment. In the current research, in fact, two instructional design conditions were compared: one following the direct instruction approach to learning (instructional condition 1), and one that extends this with a collaborative activity inspired by the community of inquiry approach to learning (instructional condition 2). In detail, the former involved a theoretical explanation of an underlying topic, whereby an instructor presented information through direct instructions along a set of slides. The latter involved the extension of the former with a highly guided inquiry activity based upon cognitive trigger questions. These questions, aligned to the Anderson's taxonomy, are supposed to develop cognitive skills in conceptualizing and reasoning that stimulate knowledge construction in working memory [52]. All lecturers at Technological University Dublin, School of Computer Science were contacted by email and invited to take part in the experiment. Only a number of them accepted and among these, only those using the traditional direct instruction approach to learning were selected. Each of these lecturers identified one or two suitable topics, already part of their modules, for experimental purposes. The material required by each selected lecturer was: 1) a set of slides on the selected topic. 2) A computer connected to a projector to display these slides in the classroom. 3) MCQ as originally proposed by Haladyna (2002) [50] designed on the contents of the slides to evaluate factual, conceptual and procedural knowledge. 4) a set of trigger questions designed for the selected topics as part of the inquiry activity of instructional condition 2. An example of guidelines for the inquiry activity (instructional condition 2) and examples of trigger cognitive questions on the topic 'Semantic Web' are depicted in Table 1.

Table 1. Community of Inquiry guidelines and examples of trigger questions employed during the inquiry activity in the topic 'Semantic Web'.

Section 1: Take part in a group dialog considering the following democratic habits: free-risk expression, encouragement, collaboration and gentle manners.

Section 2: Answer the questions below and follow these instructions:
- Exchange information related to the underlying topic
- Connect ideas in relation to this information
- FIRST find an agreement about each answer collaboratively, THEN write the answer by each group member individually

Trigger questions (examples below with meta-cognitive function elicited):
- What does a Triple define? (Conceptualizing)
- How a Triple is composed of? (Reasoning)
- What is Linked Data? (Conceptualizing)
- What does a RDF File contain? (Reasoning)
- What does RDF identify by using XML namespace? (Reasoning)

The first section explains the social nature of the inquiry activity while the second outlines the cognitive process involved in answering the trigger questions. Trigger questions are adapted from the work of Satiro (2006) [44]. As shown in Table 2, they are aimed at developing cognitive skills of conceptualization by comparing and contrasting, defining, classifying, and reasoning by relating cause and effect, tools and aims, parts and whole and by establishing criteria [44].

MCQs and trigger questions were ratified by lecturers to guarantee the preservation of the semantic behind each question and answer. All selected topics were supposed to be of high difficulty to justify the need of the collaborative activity. The students associated to the classes of selected lecturers were informed on the criteria of voluntary acceptance of the experiment and anonymity of any published data. In detail, to guarantee good standards of ethical research and scholarly practice, study information and consent

Table 2. Examples of trigger cognitive questions employed during the inquiry activity for the topics "Research Hypothesis", 'Problem Solving' and 'Operating System'.

Topic	Trigger question	Goal
Research hypothesis	What is a 'research hypothesis?	Conceptualizing
Research hypothesis	Which are the criteria you must consider in order to test a research hypothesis?	Reasoning
Problem solving	What is the 'lateral thinking'?	Conceptualizing
Problem solving	Which is the right set of actions to analyze 'facts and logic'?	Reasoning
Operating systems	Can you define the name of each section of the following full filename?	Conceptualizing
Operating systems	What is the function of the forc() command in Linux?	Reasoning

form were distributed at the beginning of each class and these were previously approved by the Ethical Committee of Technological University Dublin under the criteria of the European Code of Conduct for Research Integrity and the IUA Policy Statement on Ensuring Research Integrity in Ireland. Fidelity to this ethical protocol was ensured by the first author of this paper who gathered data. After signing study information and consent forms, the students who accepted to participate in the study were randomly divided in two groups: control and experimental groups. Both received direct instructions (instructional condition 1) while only the experimental group subsequently participated in the inquiry activity (instructional condition 2). The control group received the Rating Scale of Mental Effort and the NASA Task Load aimed at quantifying their self-reported effort and overall cognitive load respectively, as well as a multiple-choice questionnaire (MCQ) associated to the topic they were taught. The experimental group was in turn split in teams of three or four students for performing the inquiry activity. Subsequently, guidelines instructed each member of each team to write down the shared answer individually. This is a strategy designed to elicit metacognition and facilitate the process and transfer of information in working memory. After that, each student in the experimental group received the questionnaire aimed at quantifying their self- reported effort and mental workload, similarly to the students in the control group. Moreover, in order to make the relation between the outcomes of the inquiring process (the written answers to the trigger questions) and the achievement of knowledge as explicit as possible, the students in each team were allowed to use the answers, agreed during the inquiry activity, while answering the MCQ. This was assumed to be an advantage if the inquiring activity would have produced the right answer. However, if the shared answers were wrong, the extra-support provided by the inquiry activity was assumed to be a disadvantage. The contents under evaluation were exactly the same for both groups, consequently, the inquiring trigger questions were identical to those provided in the MCQ. The aim was to evaluate the impact of the inquiry technique on the achievement of knowledge and comparing it with the impact of direct instructions only. However, the way answers were required was different. The MCQ showed the right answer that was selectable out of four options. On the contrary, during the inquiry activity, the answers to the trigger questions were supposed to be elaborated, constructed among the member of each team by reaching an agreement. Eventually, two slightly different designs of the described experimental study were planned, and these differ in the length of each questionnaire and in the type of measure of efficiency: training efficiency in the first was extended with learning efficiency in the second. These two experimental designs are detailed in the following sections as 'tuning' and 'experimental' phase respectively.

3.1 Tuning Phase: Participants and Procedures

Four lecturers and four different topics were selected in the first semester of the academic year 2018/19 involving a total of 122 students aged between 20 and 25 for bachelor and between 25 to 60 for masters. Table 3 provides details on these topics, academic stage, participants, number of slides and delivery length for the instructional condition 1 and 2.

Table 3. Description of each taught topic and associated information for the tuning phase.

Topic	Level	# participants	Control group	Experimental group	# slides	Length (mins)
Advanced database	B.Sc. (4th year)	25	13	12	28	50
Research Methods	M.Sc.	26	12	14	20	35
Amazon Cloud Watch	B.Sc. (3th year)	29	15	14	25	25
Semantic Web	B.Sc. (1th year)	42	26	16	55	75

The first design involved the use of the Rating Scale Mental Effort (RSME) and the original Nasa Task Load Index (NASA-TLX) respectively as measures of self-reported effort and cognitive load. The likelihood model of efficiency, as described in Sect. 2, was used with these two measures and the performance scores from the MCQs.

As shown in Fig. 1, students in the experimental group took part in a collaborative and inquiry activity. With a measure of performance (the multiple-choice score in percentage) and the overall cognitive load scores computed with the RSME and NASA-TLX (answered by students before the performance test) instruments, a measure of *training efficiency*, where the overall cognitive load was measured before the MCQ [53], was calculated using the likelihood model described in Sect. 2.

3.2 Experimental Phase: Participants and Procedures

Six lecturers and six different topics were delivered during the second semester of the academic year 2018/2019 involving a total of 160 students aged between 20 and 25 for

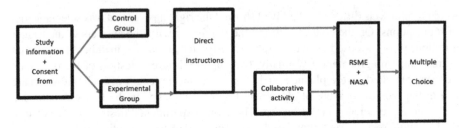

Fig. 1. The layout of the first set of experiment aimed at comparing the efficiency of two instructional conditions, one employing a direct instructional approach, and one extending this with a collaborative activity.

bachelor and between 25 to 60 for masters. Table 4 provides details on these topics: academic stage, participants, number of slides and delivery length for the instructional conditions 1 and 2. As depicted in Fig. 2, the Experimental phase was slightly different from the Tuning phase.

Table 4. Description of each taught topic and associated information for the experimental phase (C = control group, E = experimental group).

Topic	Level	# students	C	E	# slides	Length (mins)
Research Methods	M.Sc.	29	14	15	30	27
Research Hypothesis	M.Sc.	36	20	16	21	25
Geo Spatial Data	M.Sc.	12	5	7	60	40
Operating System	B.Sc. (4th Year)	39	20	19	142	60
Problem Solving	M.S.C	25	14	11	70	90
Data Mining	B.Sc. (4th Year)	19	10	9	62	60

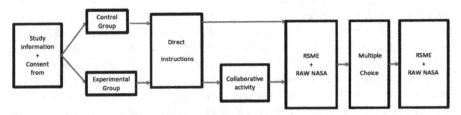

Fig. 2. A refined layout of the second set of experiments aimed at comparing the efficiency of two instructional conditions, one employing a direct instructional approach, and one extending this with a collaborative activity.

In detail, the pair comparison of the NASA-TLX instrument (15 questions) was eliminated in favor of the RAW-NASA-TLX. This was possible because it has been empirically demonstrated that even by removing this pairwise comparison, the computation of the subjective mental workload experienced by students can be still considered valid [54]. A further difference showed in Fig. 2, is that students were asked to fill the questionnaire associated to the self-reported overall effort and cognitive load not only before the MCQ but also after. This change was introduced to verify the impact of the compared instructional conditions along different stages of the learning process. As suggested by Van Gogh and Paas (2008), in fact, filling questionnaires on cognitive load before and after the performance test corresponds to two different measures: training efficiency the former and learning efficiency the latter [53].

4   Results and Discussion

The scatterplots depicted in Fig. 3 show the overall relations between test performance (MCQ), the overall cognitive load (Nasa Task Load Index) and mental effort (RSME) respectively pre and post MCQ. The line in blue represents the linear regression of these two measures. As noticeable, in most of the cases, the overall increment of mental workload and effort does not affect the performance test as measured by multiple choice questionnaires. The latter seems to be independent from the amount of mental workload and effort experienced during the deliveries of instructional materials. This suggests these measures of load and performance are independent and their combination might deliver more insight. Consequently, this fully justifies the use of the selected model of efficiency. Table 5 shows means and standard deviations of RSME, NASA-TLX and MCQ associated to each topic and related group. All the experimental groups experienced, on average, more overall effort (RSME) and more overall cognitive load (NASA) than the control group. Intuitively, this can be attributed to the extra mental cost required by collaboration. As noticeable in Table 5, the collaborative activity increased also the overall level of performance of learners belonging to the experimental group across all experiments. To verify the normality of the distribution of the data a Shapiro Wilk test was computed followed by a T-Test for normal distributions (p-values > 0.05) and a Mann Whitney U Test (M.W.T) for not normal distributions (p-values < 0.05) to compare the means of control and experimental groups. Outliers were computed and eliminated. Table 6 shows the results of the related T-Test and Mann Whitney U Test.

Higher values of T-Value, in connection to the number of participants in each group, indicate that a large difference exists between data related to control and experimental groups. Higher values of M-Value, instead, indicate that the difference between groups is due to the experimental intervention rather than to chance. However, any statistical difference between groups is given by the P-Value.

Despite all experimental groups performed higher than the control groups (Table 5), the P-Value of T-Test shown in Table 6 is statistically relevant in the MCQ of Semantic Web only. This finding confirms the research hypothesis proposed: the inquiry activity statistically increases the performance of related group in Semantic Web. Unfortunately, in relation to the others MCQ, the research hypothesis is not supported by the same evidence, the related T-Test and Mann Whitney U Test, in fact, are all above the significance level. Given the dynamics of third-level classes and the heterogeneity of students having different characteristics such as prior knowledge and learning strategy, this was

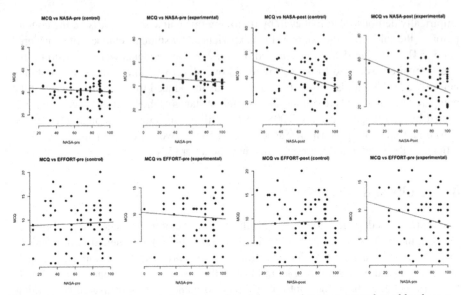

Fig. 3. Overall relations in control and experimental groups between mental workload, mental effort (measured before and after the MCQ) and test performance. The linear regression is represented by the line in blue (Color figure online).

Table 5. Means and standard deviations of the RSME, NASA-TLX and MCQ grouped by control and experimental groups (C = control group, E = experimental group)

Topic	RSME mean (SD)		NASA mean (SD)		MCQ mean (SD)	
	C	E	C	E	C	E
Advanced Database	36.00 (12.83)	47.91 (13.72)	43.61 (15.39)	47.80 (9.91)	42.92 (21.26)	54.91 (14.27)
Amazon Cloud Watch	56.00 (25.64)	68.57 (32.07)	50.00 (8.19)	54.45 (16.12)	61.33 (15.52)	66.42 (13.36)
Research Methods	47.08 (8.38)	67.85 (23.67)	49.38 (9.37)	49.85 (8.96)	68.41 (15.72)	69.57 (18.88)
Semantic Web	61.92 (29.19)	66.31 (32.08)	47.74 (10.98)	50.62 (9.43)	34.42 (18.10)	47.12 (18.77)

not a surprising outcome. Moreover, all experiments were conducted in real educational environments, consequently the collection of related data might have been affected by the 'noise' that characterizes the composition of a group of learners. In other words, external factors as the 'background noise', might have partially influenced the results. As per Table 6, the perceived effort of the experimental group in Research Methods statistically increases. Probably, the experimental group experienced more effort than the control group as a consequence of the inquiry activity whose impact presumably

Table 6. Values (V) of T-Test (T) or Mann Whitney U Test (M) and related P-values (P-V) (at significance level < 0.05) of the multiple choice percentage scores (MCQ), perceived effort scores (RSME) and the overall cognitive load scores (NASA-TLX).

Topic	MCQ		RSME		NASA	
	V	P-V	V	P-V	V	P-V
Advanced Dataset	53.5 (M)	0.18 (M)	42.5 (M)	0.52 (M)	−4.38 (T)	0.39 (T)
Amaz. Cloud Watch	85 (M)	0.4 (M)	−12.5 (T)	0.25 (T)	−4.58 (T)	0.15 (T)
Research Methods	−1.15 (T)	0.86 (T)	38 (M)	**0.01** (M)	−2.25 (T)	0.5 (T)
Semantic Web	−12.7 (T)	**0.03** (T)	203 (M)	0.9 (M)	−2.88 (T)	0.39 (T)

augmented the transactive cost of communication [51]. Unfortunately, in regard to the related measure of efficiency depicted in Table 7, this extra cost of communication (measured as higher effort) did not have a positive effect: the experimental group in Research Methods class, in fact, performed lower than the control group. Table 7 lists the efficiency scores across groups and topics computed with RSME and with NASA TLX employing the likelihood formula. The efficiency computed with the RSME is higher in the experimental group of Semantic Web only, whereas the efficiencies of the experimental groups in Advanced Database, Amazon Cloud Watch and Research Methods are lower than the control groups. A more coherent picture emerges when, as represented in Table 7, the efficiency is computed with the NASA-TLX. In fact, the efficiency scores are, on average, always slightly higher in the experimental group.

Table 7. Means and standard deviations of the efficiencies scores computed with the likelihood formula by using the Rating Scale Mental Effort (RSME) and the Nasa Task Load Index (NASA TLX) (C = control group, E = experimental group).

Topic	RSME mean (SD)		NASA-TLX mean (SD)	
	C	E	C	E
Advanced Database	1.3 (0.77)	1.23 (0.51)	1.15 (0.79)	1.24 (0.65)
Amazon Cloud Watch	1.4 (0.98)	1.33 (1.01)	1.24 (0.29)	1.34 (0.98)
Research Methods	1.50 (0.45)	1.15 (0.52)	1.42 (0.38)	1.44 (0.48)
Semantic Web	0.65 (0.41)	0.92 (0.6)	0.7 (0.38)	0.96 (0.44)

Again, a Shapiro Wilk test was computed to verify the normality of the distribution of the data followed by a T-Test for normal distributions and a Mann Whitney U Test (M.W.T) for not normal distributions. Despite of the average increment of the efficiency scores summarized in Table 7, these, as noticeable in Table 8, are not statistically different across design conditions with the NASA-TLX. All p-values, in fact, are greater than the significance level (0.05).

Table 8. Values (V) of T-Test (T) or Mann Whitney U Test (M) and related P-values (P-V) of the analysis of variance of the efficiency scores with the NASA Task Load Index (NASA-TLX) and the Rating Scale Mental Effort (RSME).

Topic	NASA-TLX		RSME	
	V	P-V	V	P-V
Advanced Database	68	0.61 (M)	0.06	0.8 (T)
Amazon Cloud Watch	96	0.71 (M)	86	0.42 (M)
Research Methods	−0.015	0.93 (T)	0.35	0.08 (T)
Semantic Web	−0.21	0.1 (T)	−0.31	**0.042** (T)

The evidence of the positive impact of the collaborative inquiry activity is limited to Semantic Web class. Here, higher efficiency of experimental group is statistically supported by the P-Value of T-Test. Table 7 shows that measuring the cognitive load by unidimensional or multidimensional instruments have an impact regardless of the model of efficiency employed. In fact, with the unidimensional RSME, the experimental group, on average, had a lower efficiency than the control group across topics (this is not true for Semantic Web). On the other hand, with the multidimensional NASA-TLX, the efficiency of the control group was always somewhat better than the experimental across topics. In contrast, the efficiency of the experimental group computed with the RSME in Semantic Web was higher than the control group and the difference was statistically significant as showed by T-Test in Table 8. Moreover, the layout of the inquiry activity boosted the related performance (MCQ) in all classes (Table 5). According to collaborative cognitive load theory, nine principles, can be used to predict the impact of collaborative activities on related performance and cognitive load of learners [51]. Among these, task complexity is particularly relevant to justify or not the implementation of collaborative activities. In relation to the current set of experiments, three factors were observed to infer task complexity: amount of content delivered, time employed for its delivery and level of prior knowledge of learners. Indeed, where the level of complexity overcomes working memories limits, collaboration is critical to share information and to free memory resources up [55]. According to this, Advanced Database was delivered in 50 min by 28 slides, Amazon Cloud Watch for 25 min and 25 slides were employed, Research Methods in 35 min by 20 slides, Semantic Web in 75 min by 55 slides. Prior knowledge could be inferred from the year the topic was delivered: Semantic Web first year BSc in Computer Science; Amazon Cloud Watching third year, Advanced Database fourth year, and Research Methods post-graduate level. Semantic Web was the learning task with the higher level of complexity in terms of number of slides (55), delivery time (75 min) and prior knowledge (first year). Results are in line with the assumption of collaborative cognitive load theory: collaborative learning is more effective when the level of the complexity of an instructional design is high [56]. In fact, on one hand Advanced Database, Amazon Cloud Watching, and Research Methods are of lower complexity to justify the utility of a collaborative activity that involves sharing working memory resources among different learners. On the other, the higher complexity of

Semantic Web justifies the utility of collaborative activities and the exploitation of extra memory resources among different learners in processing information and enhancing the learning outcomes [57]. In relation to the second set of the implemented experiments along the second semester 2018/19, Table 9 shows means and standards deviations of MCQ scores for each associated group and topic.

Table 9. Means and standard deviations of the multiple-choice percentage scores grouped by taught topic (C = control group, E = experimental group)

Topic	C mean (SD)	E mean (SD)
Research Methods	71.50 (22.12)	75.33 (14.36)
Research Hypothesis	82.35 (17.37)	89.00 (13.91)
Geo Spatial Data	45.40 (20.88)	44.94 (25.78)
Operating System	65.50 (22.04)	84.36 (11.77)
Problem Solving	76.21 (24.17)	54.81 (25.26)
Data Mining	37.80 (14.43)	32.22 (11.04)

As observable in Table 9, the performance in the MCQ of the experimental group in Research Methods, Research Hypothesis, and Operating System is, on average, higher than the control group but lower in Problem Solving, Visualizing Geospatial Data and Data Mining. Table 10 displays means and standard deviations of the perceived mental effort pre and post MCQ associated to each group and topic. The experimental group in Research Methods, Visualizing Geo Spatial Data and Problem Solving experienced, on average, more effort than the control group when the effort was measured before of the MCQ. Intuitively this can be attributed to the extra mental cost required by the communication developed within the collaborative activity. This is not true for Research Hypothesis, Operating System and Data Mining where the effort of the experimental groups is lower. Moreover, in Research Methods, Research Hypothesis and Problem Solving the effort post MCQ of the control groups is higher than the experimental but lower in Visualizing Geo Spatial Data Operating system and Data Mining.

The assumption of sharing working memories is valid for the analysis of the mental workload also. As displayed in Table 11, the experimental groups experienced higher overall cognitive load (measured before the MCQ) than the control groups in all classes except of Research Hypothesis. The perceived overall cognitive load of the control groups (measured after the MCQ) is higher in Research Methods, Research Hypothesis and Operating System but lower in Visualizing Geo Spatial Data, Problem Solving and Data Mining. In Research Hypothesis only, the experimental groups experienced, over all variables, less effort and cognitive load than the control groups (Table 10 and Table 11). Results in Research Hypothesis may be interpreted as a consequence of the inquiry activity that freed working memories up and optimized cognitive load by sharing mental resources among multiple working memories. To test the statistical relevance of results depicted in Tables 9, 10 and 11, a Shapiro Wilk test was performed to verify the

Table 10. Means and standard deviations of the Rating Scale Mental Effort (RSME) scores PRE and POST execution of the multiple-choice questionnaire (C = control group, E = experimental group)

Topic	Pre mean (SD)		Post mean (SD)	
	C	E	C	E
Research Methods	49.35 (29.13)	56.53 (35.31)	51.21 (26.38)	50.13 (26.61)
Research Hypothesis	55.00 (26.73)	37.20 (22.30)	60.60 (28.91)	41.69 (25.99)
Geo Spatial Data	39.80 (35.95)	47.85 (22.51)	53.80 (37.69)	79.57 (24.69)
Operating System	45.90 (32.38)	36.16 (26.27)	31.50 (20.65)	37.42 (34.33)
Problem Solving	39.35 (22.75)	48.72 (25.90)	50.92 (27.39)	47.18 (22.55)
Data Mining	54.10 (30.07)	38.55 (23.59)	56.30 (34.39)	82.55 (26.81)

normality of the distribution of the data followed by a T-Test for normal distributions and a Mann Whitney U Test (M.W.T) for not normal distributions to compare the means of control and experimental groups. Outliers were spotted and eliminated

Table 12 shows P-Values statistically relevant in the RSME pre-MCQ and post-MCQ of Research Hypothesis and in the RSME post-MCQ of Data Mining. As shown in Table 10, the control group in Research Hypothesis experienced, on average, more effort than the experimental that, instead, perceived less effort, likely because of sharing working memory [58]. In Data Mining instead, the experimental group perceived more effort likely as a consequence of the collaboration activity that increased the communicative costs on the working memories of multiple learners [51]. Table 12 depicts also two statistically significant P-Values in the MCQ of Operating System and Problem Solving.

Table 11. Means and standard deviations of the mental workload scores computed with the RAW Nasa Task Load Index (C = control group, E = experimental group)

Topic	PRE mean (SD)		POST mean(SD)	
	C	E	C	E
Research Methods	43.86 (11.66)	47.50 (17.73)	41.36 (20.68)	41.00 (19.07)
Research Hypothesis	44.66 (13.24)	41.45 (08.9)	40.25 (15.39)	37.05 (16.28)
Geo Spatial Data	35.5 (19.50)	46.19 (09.29)	42.00 (11.17)	47.85 (05.94)
Operating System	36.7 (13.62)	42.98 (15.24)	32.29 (16.52)	29.29 (14.88)
Problem Solving	42.2 (15.07)	43.86 (06.54)	40.00 (17.65)	42.65 (12.38)
Data Mining	42.66 (7.56)	46.38 (18.00)	50.58 (16.46)	58.14 (15.60)

Table 12. Values (V) of T-Test (T) or Mann Whitney U Test (M) and related P-values (P-V) of the multiple choice percentage scores (MCQ), the Rating Scale Mental Effort scores (RSME) and the mental workload scores computed with the Raw Nasa Task Load Index (RAW NASA-TLX) using a two tails distribution and two-sample equal variance

Topic	RSME				MCQ		RAW NASA-TLX			
	Pre		Post				Pre		Post	
	V	P-V	V	P-V	V	P-V	V	P-V	V	P-V
Research Methods	−0.5 (T)	0.961 (T)	1 (M)	0.91 (T)	104 (M)	1 (M)	−3.6 (T)	0.52 (T)	98 (M)	0.78 (M)
Research Hypothesis	21.2 (T)	**0.017** (T)	18.9 (T)	0.04 (T)	120 (M)	0.21 (M)	154 (M)	0.86 (M)	158 (M)	0.96 (M)
G. Spatial Data	9.5 (M)	0.2 (M)	-25 (T)	0.18 (T)	0.45 (T)	0.97 (T)	−10 (T)	0.23 (T)	−5 (T)	0.26 (T)
Operating System	155 (M)	0.47 (M)	175 (M)	0.89(M)	87 (M)	**0.005** (M)	−6.2 (T)	0.18 (T)	161 (M)	0.59 (M)
Problem Solving	−9.3 (T)	0.346 (T)	3.7 (T)	0.71 (T)	40 (M)	**0.04** (M)	−4.2 (T)	0.3 (T)	−2 (T)	0.67 (T)
Data Mining	26.5 (M)	0.133 (M)	−33 (T)	**0.02** (T)	5.5 (T)	0.362 (T)	42 (M)	0.84 (M)	−7 (T)	0.32 (T)

In Operating System the experimental group, as per Table 9, performed higher than the control group. In contrast, in Problem Solving the experimental group performed lower. To give a more precise account of these opposite results, a qualitative interpretation of the inquiry activity is proposed as following: the design of the trigger questions related to Operating System might have implied a technical discussion on how to use the commands functions in Linux. In contrast, the design of the questions related to Problem Solving might have generated a dialogue more complex whose abstract and theoretical nature, based on the six different way of thinking proposed by De Bono 2017 [59], might have hampered the comprehension of the delivery. Table 13 and Table 14 show that the efficiencies scores of the experimental groups, computed pre and post MCQ with RSME and RAW NASA, are always higher in Research Hypothesis and Operating System. On the contrary, the control groups in Visualizing Geo Spatial Data, Problem Solving and Data Mining performed always better. This is valid for Research Methods too, a part of the efficiency pre-MCQ computed with the RAW NASA that is equal for both groups.

Again, a Shapiro Wilk test was computed to test the normality of the distribution of the data followed by a T-Test for normal distributions and a Mann Whitney U Test for not normal distributions to compare the means of control and experimental groups. Outliers were spotted and eliminated. Table 15 points out P-Values statistically significant in the efficiency of Research Hypothesis class considering the RSME before and after the MCQ. Here, the distribution of the efficiency in the experimental groups, shown in Table 13, is higher than the control groups. Unfortunately, despite all members of

Table 13. Means and standard deviations of the efficiency scores computed with the likelihood model using the Rating Scale Mental Effort (RSME) grouped by taught topics, control and experimental groups, pre and post multiple choice (C = control group, E = experimental group)

Topic	PRE mean (SD)		POST mean (SD)	
	C	E	C	E
Research Methods	6.84 (19.0)	2.24 (2.19)	7.96 (23.91	5.91 (16.1)
Research Hypothesis	2.20 (1.96)	14.5 (33.3)	2.34 (2.56)	12.44 (28.4)
Geo Spatial Data	1.55 (1.02)	1.13 (0.82)	1.09 (0.82)	0.68 (0.53)
Operating System	2.54 (2.24)	10.7 (19.5)	7.87 (16.8)	10.8 (21.3)
Problem Solving	7.57 (0.92)	1.54 (1.05)	2.10 (1.60)	1.36 (0.78)
Data Mining	1.09 (1.05)	1.04 (0.64)	1.22 (1.11)	0.44 (0.23)

Table 14. Means and standard deviations of the efficiency scores computed with the likelihood model using the Raw Nasa Task Load Index (NASA-TLX), grouped by taught topics, control and experimental groups, pre/post multiple choice (C = control group, E = experimental group)

Topic	PRE mean (SD)		POST mean (SD)	
	C	E	C	E
Research Methods	1.86 (1.11)	1.86 (1.05)	3.35 (4.66)	2.31 (1.39)
Research Hypothesis	1.96 (0.67)	2.28 (0.77)	2.58 (1.87)	3.13 (2.26)
Geo Spatial Data	1.70 (1.69)	0.95 (0.54)	1.06 (0.50)	0.98 (0.60)
Operating System	2.08 (1.04)	2.40 (1.71)	2.53 (1.52)	3.92 (2.51)
Problem Solving	2.04 (0.91)	1.25 (0.64)	2.51 (1.66)	1.33 (0.67)
Data Mining	0.92 (0.41)	0.80 (0.39)	0.86 (0.44)	0.59 (0.24)

experimental groups knew what they had to do (take part in a dialogue), how (democratically social setting structured by cognitive phases), with whom they had to work with and what they had to communicate about (answering cognitive trigger questions), these findings are the only evidences emerged within this set of studies in favor of the proposed research hypothesis.

Table 15 represents statistically significant P-Values in the efficiency of Problem Solving either computed before and after the MCQ with RAW-NASA-TLX. Here, the average mean in the efficiency of the control group, is higher than the experimental (Table 14). Consequently, it can be deducted that the impact of the experimental design on the efficiencies of learners was negative. The direct instructions whereby the topic was delivered, indeed, were supposed to be enough to inform the students. In contrast, the design of the inquiry activity might have created a redundant effect on the comprehension of the delivery, decreasing the efficiency in experimental group instead of

Table 15. Values (V) of T-Test (T) or Mann Whitney U Test (M) and related P-values (P-V) of the efficiency scores computed with the likelihood model grouped by pre and post multiple choice questionnaire, the mental workload instruments (Rating Scale Mental Effort or Raw Nasa Task Load Index) with 2 tailed distribution and two sample equal variance.

Topic	RSME				RAW-NASA-TLX			
	PRE	PRE	POST	POST	PRE	PRE	POST	POST
	V	P-V	V	P-V	V	P-V	V	P-V
Research Methods	97.5 (M)	0.74 (M)	90.5 (M)	0.53 (M)	92.5 (M)	0.591 (M)	98 (M)	0.78 (M)
Research Hypothesis	97 (M)	**0.04** (M)	89.5 (M)	**0.02** (M)	138.5 (M)	0.49 (M)	142 (M)	0.58 (M)
G. Spatial Data	0.41 (T)	0.45 (T)	0.48 (T)	0.24 (T)	14 (M)	0.63 (M)	−0.11 (T)	0.77 (T)
Operating System	138 (M)	0.22 (M)	143 (M)	0.29 (M)	177 (M)	0.94 (M)	122 (M)	0.09 (M)
Problem Solving	52 (M)	0.18 (M)	54 (M)	0.22 (M)	0.93 (T)	**0.02** (T)	1.17 (T)	**0.03** (T)
Data Mining	40 (M)	0.72 (M)	22 (M)	0.06 (M)	0.11 (T)	0.53 (T)	0.26 (T)	0.13 (T)

improving it. Considering the cost of communication experienced answering the trigger questions, the inquiry activity does have an influence on the efficiency of learners. In order to better define the relation between 'communicative cost' of inquiring and complexity of the delivery, it is worthy accounting for the design of the inquiring activity in Research Hypothesis and Problem Solving, whose respective trigger questions were more technical in the former and more theoretical in the latter. To sum up, the cost of communication in the experimental design of Problem Solving probably increased the element interactivity of the learning task (its difficulty), generating extraneous instead of germane load. In other words, the extra cost of communication experienced during the inquiring activity of Problem Solving might have confused the experimental group instead of benefiting it as for the Research Hypothesis topic. Table 16 shows that the effect sizes computed on T-Test of the efficiency and MCQ scores in Semantic Web topic are medium under the criteria proposed by Cohen (2013) but in the zone of desired effects as per the barometer of effect sizes proposed in Fig. 4 [60].

Based on the criteria proposed by Cohen (2013), Table 16 shows large and medium effect sizes computed for Mann Whitney U Tests [61]. As observable per Table 16, the evidence against the hypothesis are confirmed by the large effect size found in the MCQ of Problem Solving and in its efficiency pre and post MCQ with RAW-NASA-TLX. Nonetheless, the evidences in favor of the hypothesis are strongly confirmed as well because the effect size for efficiency and MCQ in Semantic Web is medium under the Cohen's criteria but within the zone of desired effects as per Hattie's barometer. Moreover, Table 16 shows that the effect size of efficiency pre and post MCQ in Research

Table 16. Effect sizes grouped by taught topic, instrument and statistical T-test (T) or Mann Whitney U Test (M) and their sizes (medium ≥ 0.5 and <0.8; large ≥ 0.8 for T-test) (large ≥ 0.5 for Mahan Whitney U Test) [61].

Topic	Instrument (details)	Test	Effect	Size
Res. Methods	RSME	M	Large	0.718
Semantic Web	Efficiency Likelihood Model	T	Medium	0.542
Semantic Web	MCQ	T	Medium	0.691
Data Mining	RSME (post MCQ)	T	Large	0.845
Problem Solving	Efficiency Likelihood Model (RAW NASA pre-MCQ)	T	Large	0.982
Problem Solving	Efficiency Likelihood Model (RAW NASA post-MCQ)	T	Large	0.891
Research Hypothesis	Effort (pre MCQ)	T	Medium	0.712
Research Hypothesis	Effort (post MCQ)	T	Medium	0.618
Problem Solving	MCQ	M	Large	0.71
Operating System	MCQ	M	Large	0.73
Research Hypothesis	Efficiency Likelihood Model (RSME Pre-MCQ)	M	Large	0.72
Research Hypothesis	Efficiency Likelihood Model (RSME Post-MCQ)	M	Large	0.721

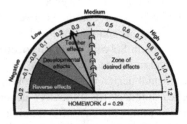

Fig. 4. A typical barometer of influence. This aims to judge the success of educational innovations relative to a hinge point, a zone of desired effects empirically found at $d = 0.4$ from which influences start to have the greatest impact on student achievement outcomes [60].

Hypothesis is large: here the statistical results confirmed that the experimental design increased the efficiencies of learners. This tendency is further supported by the large effect size found in the MCQ of Operating System and by the medium effect size found in the perceived effort pre and post MCQ in Research Hypothesis where the inquiry activity statistically decreased the perceived effort optimizing the efficiencies of learners.

Very often, the constructivist community of inquiry method was employed in contexts of learning where the process for forming knowledge is ill structured, as for instance in topics whose goal is to reach an agreement on ethical issues by learners and construct knowledge collaboratively. On the contrary, direct instruction methods were employed in context of learning where the process for forming knowledge is well structured. Their respective research approaches to evaluate learning outcomes, in fact, are different: mainly quantitative the former and mainly qualitative the latter. Their respective learning outcomes are different too. Consequently, it was critical to establish shared learning outcomes that have been identified in factual, conceptual and procedural knowledge for both approaches. The main limitation of the studies under examination was that the design of the deliveries and the related element interactivity, were not under the direct control of the researchers. However, the conditions of the delivery were identical for both the control and experimental groups, with the only difference that the latter performed a subsequent inquiry activity. The comparison of efficiency, in fact, occurred within members of groups of the same class who received the same instructions in a number of controlled experiments. Results showed that changes in the independent variable (the instructional design) partially affected the effort and cognitive load experienced by students, their performance and the related efficiency of learners. The analysis of variance computed on the average of these variables per groups was not statistical different either. By a deeper analysis of data, it emerged that the trigger questions are the core structure of the experimental design and are supposed to generate a dialogue whose transactive cost of communication can increase or decrease the efficiency of learners.

5 Conclusion

A literature review revealed a lack of comparison of the efficiency of direct instruction and inquiry teaching methods. Motivated by the statement provided by Kirshner and colleagues (2006) whereby inquiries techniques are believed to be ineffective in the absence of explicit direct instructions, an empirical experimental study has been designed. In detail, a comparison of the efficiency of the traditional instructional design, based upon explicit direct instructions, and its extension with a highly guided inquiry activity, was proposed. The research hypothesis was that if the traditional explicit instructional method is extended with an inquiry technique, then, its efficiency is higher than by employing the former method alone. Efficiency was measured by employing the likelihood model of efficiency [3]. The original models are based upon a unidimensional measure of subjective perceived human effort and objective performance. In this study, these were extended with a multidimensional measure of cognitive load. In detail, the Rating Scale Mental Effort [37] has been selected as the unidimensional measure while the Nasa Task Load Index and its shorter version, the RAW Nasa [20], have been chosen as multi-dimensional measures of cognitive load. In relation to objective performance, multiple choice questionnaires were employed, tailored to each experimental study and the taught content to learners. A number of lecturers were involved in this study and their classes were split in control and experimental groups. The former received direct instructions, while the latter also participated in an inquiry activity based on trigger questions to support the development of cognitive skills of conceptualization and reasoning. Results showed partial evidence in favour of the hypothesis, supported by good effect sizes. However, a clear separation and a statistical significant difference of the efficiency between the groups of students who have received direct instructional method alone, and those who have received its extended version with the inquiry technique, is hard to be achieved because of the small sample sizes of these groups in typical higher-education classes, usually in the order of ten/twenty students per group. Therefore, further statistical tests for small sample-size groups comparison should be explored such as cluster analysis and shift functions. Future work will focus on the design of a lighter collaborative inquiry activity to mitigate the extra-cost of communication among students and thus supporting a measurement of their cognitive load that better reflect their experience within this activity itself. The aim is to promote a dialogical environment, increase the germane load of students and minimize their extraneous load with expected positive consequences on instructional efficiency. This research contributes to the existent body of knowledge by demonstrating how the impact of the community of inquiry method can be empirically tested using existing measures of efficiency, cognitive load and performance. In doing so, it requalifies the constructivist approach of the community of inquiry technique by creating a replicable experiment for enhancing learning that extends the traditional method for teaching, based upon direct instructional designs only.

References

1. Kirschner, P.A., Sweller, J., Clark, R.E.: Why minimal guidance during instruction does not work: an analysis of the failure of constructivist, discovery, problem-based, experiential, and inquiry-based teaching. Educ. Psychol. 41(2), 75–86 (2006)
2. Jonassen, D.: Reconciling a human cognitive architecture. In: Constructivist Instruction, pp. 25–45. Routledge (2009)
3. Hoffman, B., Schraw, G.: Conceptions of efficiency: applications in learning and problem solving. Educ. Psychol. 45(1), 1–14 (2010)
4. Sweller, J., van Merriënboer, J.J., Paas, F.: Cognitive architecture and instructional design: 20 years later. Educ. Psychol. Rev. 31, 1–32 (2019)
5. Orru, G., Longo, L.: The evolution of cognitive load theory and the measurement of its intrinsic, extraneous and germane loads: a review. In: Longo, L., Leva, M.C. (eds.) H-WORKLOAD 2018. CCIS, vol. 1012, pp. 23–48. Springer, Cham (2019). https://doi.org/10.1007/978-3-030-14273-5_3
6. Miller, G.A.: The magical number seven, plus or minus two: some limits on our capacity for processing information. Psychol. Rev. 63(2), 81 (1956)
7. Atkinson, R.C., Shiffrin, R.M.: The Control Processes of Short-Term Memory. Stanford University, Stanford (1971)
8. Sweller, J.: Working memory, long-term memory, and instructional design. J. Appl. Res. Mem. Cogn. 5(4), 360–367 (2016)
9. Sweller, J.: Cognitive Load Theory, Evolutionary Educational Psychology, and Instructional Design. In: Geary, D.C.C., Berch, D.B.B. (eds.) Evolutionary Perspectives on Child Development and Education. EP, pp. 291–306. Springer, Cham (2016). https://doi.org/10.1007/978-3-319-29986-0_12
10. Orru, G., Longo, L.: Direct instruction and its extension with a community of inquiry: a comparison of mental workload, performance and efficiency. In: CSEDU (1), pp. 436–444 (2019)
11. Sloffer, S., Dueber, B., Duffy, T.M.: Using asynchronous conferencing to promote critical thinking: two implementations in higher education. In: HICSS, p. 1083. IEEE (1999)
12. Van Boxtel, C., Van der Linden, J., Kanselaar, G.: Collaborative learning tasks and the elaboration of conceptual knowledge. Learn. Instr. 10(4), 311–330 (2000)

13. Gregor, S.D., Cuskelly, E.: Computer mediated communication in distance education. J. Comput. Assist. Learn. **10**(3), 168–181 (1994)
14. Heath, E.: Two cheers and a pint of worry: an on-line course in political and social philosophy. Teach. Philos. **20**(3), 277–300 (1997)
15. Paas, F., Sweller, J.: An evolutionary upgrade of cognitive load theory: Using the human motor system and collaboration to support the learning of complex cognitive tasks. Educ. Psychol. Rev. **24**(1), 27–45 (2012)
16. Kirschner, F., Paas, F., Kirschner, P.A.: Individual and group-based learning from complex cognitive tasks: effects on retention and transfer efficiency. Comput. Hum. Behav. **25**(2), 306–314 (2009)
17. Wickens, C.D.: Measures of workload, stress and secondary tasks. In: Moray, N. (ed.) Mental Workload. NATO Conference Series, vol. 8. Springer, Boston (1979). https://doi.org/10.1007/978-1-4757-0884-4_6
18. Longo, L.: A defeasible reasoning framework for human mental workload representation and assessment. Behav. Inf. Technol. **34**(8), 758–786 (2015)
19. Rizzo, L., Dondio, P., Delany, S.J., Longo, L.: Modeling mental workload via rule-based expert system: a comparison with NASA-TLX and workload profile. In: Iliadis, L., Maglogiannis, I. (eds.) AIAI 2016. IAICT, vol. 475, pp. 215–229. Springer, Cham (2016). https://doi.org/10.1007/978-3-319-44944-9_19
20. Hart, S.G.: NASA-task load index (NASA-TLX); 20 years later. In: Proceedings of the Human Factors and Ergonomics Society Annual Meeting, pp. 904–908. Sage Publications, Sage (2006)
21. Longo, L., Orru, G.: An evaluation of the reliability, validity and sensitivity of three human mental workload measures under different instructional conditions in third-level education. In: McLaren, B.M., Reilly, R., Zvacek, S., Uhomoibhi, J. (eds.) CSEDU 2018. CCIS, vol. 1022, pp. 384–413. Springer, Cham (2019). https://doi.org/10.1007/978-3-030-21151-6_19
22. Longo, L.: Designing medical interactive systems via assessment of human mental workload. In: International Symposium on Computer-Based Medical Systems, pp. 364–365 (2015)
23. Longo, L., Barrett, S.: Cognitive effort for multi-agent systems. In: Yao, Y., Sun, R., Poggio, T., Liu, J., Zhong, N., Huang, J. (eds.) BI 2010. LNCS (LNAI), vol. 6334, pp. 55–66. Springer, Heidelberg (2010). https://doi.org/10.1007/978-3-642-15314-3_6
24. Longo, L.: Formalising human mental workload as a defeasible computational concept. Ph.D. thesis, Trinity College Dublin (2014)
25. Longo, L.: Experienced mental workload, perception of usability, their interaction and impact on task performance. PLoS ONE **13**(8), e0199661 (2018)
26. Longo, L., Leva, M.C. (eds.): H-WORKLOAD 2018. CCIS, vol. 1012. Springer, Cham (2019). https://doi.org/10.1007/978-3-030-14273-5
27. Longo, L.: Human-computer interaction and human mental workload: assessing cognitive engagement in the world wide web. In: Campos, P., Graham, N., Jorge, J., Nunes, N., Palanque, P., Winckler, M. (eds.) INTERACT 2011. LNCS, vol. 6949, pp. 402–405. Springer, Heidelberg (2011). https://doi.org/10.1007/978-3-642-23768-3_43
28. Longo, L.: Subjective usability, mental workload assessments and their impact on objective human performance. In: Bernhaupt, R., Dalvi, G., Joshi, A., Balkrishan, D.K., O'Neill, J., Winckler, M. (eds.) INTERACT 2017. LNCS, vol. 10514, pp. 202–223. Springer, Cham (2017). https://doi.org/10.1007/978-3-319-67684-5_13
29. Rizzo, L., Longo, L.: Inferential models of mental workload with defeasible argumentation and non-monotonic fuzzy reasoning: a comparative study. In: AI^3 @ AI*IA, pp. 11–26 (2018)
30. Orru, G., Gobbo, F., O'Sullivan, D., Longo, L.: An investigation of the impact of a social constructivist teaching approach, based on trigger questions, through measures of mental workload and efficiency. In: 10th International Conference on Computer Supported Education (CSEDU 2018), pp. 292–302 (2018)

31. Hart, S.G., Staveland, L.E.: Development of NASA-TLX (task load index): results of empirical and theoretical research. Adv. Psychol. **52**, 139–183 (1988)
32. Rizzo, L.M., Longo, L.: Representing and inferring mental workload via defeasible reasoning: a comparison with the NASA task load index and the workload profile (2017)
33. Longo, L.: On the reliability, validity and sensitivity of three mental workload assessment techniques for the evaluation of instructional designs: a case study in a third-level course. In: 10th International Conference on Computer Supported Education (CSEDU 2018), pp. 166–178 (2018)
34. Paas, F.G., Van Merriënboer, J.J.: The efficiency of instructional conditions: an approach to combine mental effort and performance measures. Hum. Factors J. Hum. Factors Ergon. Soc. **35**(4), 737–743 (1993)
35. Paas, F.G., Van Merriënboer, J., Adam, J.J.: Measurement of cognitive load in instructional research. Percept. Mot. Skills **79**(1), 419–430 (1994)
36. Paas, F., Tuovinen, J.E., Tabbers, H., Van Gerven, P.W.: Cognitive load measurement as a means to advance cognitive load theory. Educ. Psychol. **38**(1), 63–71 (2003)
37. Zijlstra, F.R.H.: Efficiency in work behavior: a design approach for modern tools. Doctoral thesis. Delft University Press (1993)
38. Gerjets, P., Scheiter, K., Catrambone, R.: Can learning from molar and modular worked examples be enhanced by providing instructional explanations and prompting self-explanations? Learn. Instr. **16**(2), 104–121 (2006)
39. Kester, L., Lehnen, C., Van Gerven, P.W., Kirschner, P.A.: Just-in-time, schematic supportive information presentation during cognitive skill acquisition. Comput. Hum. Behav. **22**(1), 93–112 (2006)
40. Gerjets, P., Scheiter, K., Catrambone, R.: Designing instructional examples to reduce intrinsic cognitive load: molar versus modular presentation of solution procedures. Instr. Sci. **32**(1/2), 33–58 (2004)
41. Dewey, J.: Logic-The Theory of Inquiry. Read Books Ltd., Redditch (2018)
42. Garrison, D.R.: Online community of inquiry review: social, cognitive, and teaching presence issues. J. Asynchronous Learn. Netw. **11**(1), 61–72 (2007)
43. Lipman, M.: Thinking in Education. Cambridge University Press, Cambridge (2003)
44. Sátiro, A.: Jugar a pensar con mitos: este libro forma parte dle Proyecto Noria y acompña al libro para niños de 8-9 años: Juanita y los mitos. Octaedro (2006)
45. Krathwohl, D.R.: A revision of bloom's taxonomy: an overview. Theory Pract. **41**(4), 212–218 (2002)
46. Smith, P.C., Street, A.: Measuring the efficiency of public services: the limits of analysis. J. R. Stat. Soc. Ser. A Stat. Soc. **168**(2), 401–417 (2005)
47. Kalyuga, S., Sweller, J.: Rapid dynamic assessment of expertise to improve the efficiency of adaptive e-learning. Educ. Technol. Res. Dev. **53**(3), 83–93 (2005)
48. Warnick, E.M., Bracken, M.B., Kasl, S.: Screening efficiency of the child behavior checklist and strengths and difficulties questionnaire: a systematic review. Child Adolesc. Ment. Health **13**(3), 140–147 (2008)
49. Plass, J.L., Moreno, R., Brünken, R.: Cognitive Load Theory. Cambridge University Press, Cambridge (2010)
50. Haladyna, T.M., Downing, S.M., Rodriguez, M.C.: A review of multiple-choice item-writing guidelines for classroom assessment. Appl. Meas. Educ. **15**(3), 309–333 (2002)
51. Kirschner, P.A., Sweller, J., Kirschner, F., Zambrano R., J.: From cognitive load theory to collaborative cognitive load theory. Int. J. Comput.-Support. Collab. Learn. **13**(2), 213–233 (2018). https://doi.org/10.1007/s11412-018-9277-y
52. Popov, V., van Leeuwen, A., Buis, S.: Are you with me or not? Temporal synchronicity and transactivity during CSCL. J. Comput. Assist. Learn. **33**(5), 424–442 (2017)

53. Van Gog, T., Paas, F.: Instructional efficiency: revisiting the original construct in educational research. Educ. Psychol. **43**(1), 16–26 (2008)
54. Bittner Jr, A.C., Byers, J.C., Hill, S.G., Zaklad, A.L., Christ, R.E.: Generic workload ratings of a mobile air defense system (LOS-FH). In: Proceedings of the Human Factors Society Annual Meeting, pp. 1476–1480. SAGE Publications, Sage (1989)
55. Kirschner, F., Paas, F., Kirschner, P.A.: Task complexity as a driver for collaborative learning efficiency: the collective working-memory effect. Appl. Cogn. Psychol. **25**(4), 615–624 (2011)
56. Kirschner, P., Kirschner, F., Janssen, J.: The collaboration principle in multimedia learning. Camb. Handb. Multimed. Learn. **2**, 547–575 (2014)
57. Kirschner, F., Paas, F., Kirschner, P.A.: A cognitive load approach to collaborative learning: united brains for complex tasks. Educ. Psychol. Rev. **21**(1), 31–42 (2009)
58. Kirschner, F., Paas, F., Kirschner, P.A.: Superiority of collaborative learning with complex tasks: a research note on an alternative affective explanation. Comput. Hum. Behav. **27**(1), 53–57 (2011)
59. De Bono, E.: Six thinking hats. Penguin UK (2017)
60. Hattie, J.: Visible Learning: A Synthesis of Over 800 Meta-Analyses Relating to Achievement, p. 378. Routledge, London (2010)
61. Cohen, J.: Statistical Power Analysis for the Behavioral Sciences. Routledge, Abingdon (2013)

The Effects of Chewing Gum on Perceived Stress and Wellbeing in Students Under a High and Low Workload

Andrew P. Smith[✉] and Hope Clayton

Centre for Occupational and Health Psychology, School of Psychology, Cardiff University, 63 Park Place, Cardiff CF10 3AS, UK
smithap@cardiff.ac.uk

Abstract. Research has suggested that chewing gum relieves perceptions of stress in stressed and non- stressed individuals but is most beneficial for those experiencing a greater amount of negative work characteristics. To determine if this was true in a student sample, the present study assigned 36 students to four one-day intervention conditions in which participants either chewed or refrained from gum and experienced a high or low workload. The results showed that an individual's perceptions of stress and mental fatigue decreased as a result of chewing gum. Depression and cognitive failures decreased as a result of experiencing a high workload. Perceptions of physical fatigue decreased when chewing gum under a high workload. The findings suggested that gum may be an effective way to reduce certain stress characteristics, and also reassuring students that a high workload is not necessarily detrimental to their wellbeing.

Keywords: Workload · Chewing gum · Wellbeing

1 Introduction

1.1 Mental Workload

Mental workload has been widely studied [1, 2] over a long period of time [3, 4]. The research has been carried out in both laboratory [5, 6] and occupational settings [7, 8], and a variety of measures of workload have been developed [9–14]. Workload measures include self-assessment, task measures and physiological measures. Self-assessment measures have taken several forms such as the NASA Task Load Index [15], the Workload Profile [16] and the Subjective Workload Assessment Technique [1]. Recent research has confirmed that even single items about perceptions of workload can predict the well-being of workers and students. Other approaches have examined specific components of workload, such as time pressure, and one example of this is the Karasek Job Demands scale, which predicts health and safety outcomes of workers [17]. Overall, there has been increased recent interest in both models and applications on research on mental workload [18–20].

L. Longo and M. C. Leva (Eds.): H-WORKLOAD 2020, CCIS 1318, pp. 124–137, 2020.
https://doi.org/10.1007/978-3-030-62302-9_8

University life can induce a prolonged period of stress as students face academic demands to succeed, competition with peers, financial strain, the social pressures and the usual daily issues that occur as a by-product of independence [21]. Studies have shown that acute, time-limited stress serves an adaptive function [22–24], whereas chronic ongoing stress is often detrimental to an individual's psychological and physical wellbeing [25]. For example, research using student samples has detected significant correlations between illness and stress, anxiety and depression [26]. The student population has risen by 44% in recent years [27], and despite increases in tuition fees, the number of university applicants and places is not expected to decline. The historically large numbers of individuals attending universities suggests that poor psychological and physical health in students is potentially more prevalent and of more concern than ever.

1.2 Chewing Gum and Stress

Research has shown that interventions designed to target stress in students can impact positively on their perceived stress levels, depressive symptoms, coping [28], self-esteem [29], academic success [30] and health [31]; however, the majority of these interventions are costly and time-consuming. According to the Association for University and College Counselling, universities are insufficiently equipped to provide services that facilitate these interventions [32], and due to government cuts in university funding, this problem is only going to increase. Chewing gum may be a relatively inexpensive and effortless way to reduce stress. In a survey involving 8,930 university students, 41% claimed to chew gum to relieve stress and tension [33], suggesting chewing gum may aid stress relief. As research has shown that students may engage in negative behaviors to relieve stress such as consuming alcohol [34], smoking [35] and illicit drug use [36], chewing gum also appears to be a healthier alternative. The beneficial effects of chewing gum were first documented when Hollingworth [37] demonstrated that collateral motor automatisms involving masticatory muscles can reduce self-reported and direct muscular tension, suggesting that chewing gum can operate as a form of relaxation. However, Freeman [38] consequently showed that foot-tapping was as effective as chewing gum in reducing tension, suggesting that the relaxing effects elicited by motor automatisms are not limited to chewing gum.

Research has also examined whether chewing gum can reduce naturally occurring stress [39]. A web-based survey of 2,248 full-time workers found that despite reporting a higher prevalence of negative occupational demands, gum chewers demonstrated lower levels of perceived stress and depression and were less likely to have seen their doctor for high blood pressure or cholesterol compared to non-gum chewers [40]. These results remained after controlling for health-related behaviors, personality, negative job characteristics and a range of demographics; however, due to the cross-sectional nature of the study it was not possible to establish whether gum does indeed reduce stress or if those who are less stressed have chosen to chew gum.

Intervention studies have helped to clarify the matter, suggesting that chewing gum exerts a positive effect on perceived stress. Zibell and Madansky [41] used a cross-over design to examine whether those who did and did not regularly chew gum would perceive themselves as less or more stressed after abstaining or chewing gum for a period of time and then subsequently switching to the opposite chewing behavior. The results demonstrated that during periods of abstinence, perceived stress levels increased significantly in those who did and did not regularly chew gum. During periods of chewing, the opposite pattern was observed; perceived stress was significantly reduced in both groups. These findings suggest that chewing gum aids stress reduction regardless of individuals' regular gum-chewing habit. However, the study was based on self-perception and asking participants to directly assess whether gum had reduced their levels of stress implies that demand characteristics were present [42]. It is therefore likely that the results, while interesting, cannot be considered conclusive and should be subject to intervention studies involving a more reliable methodology.

To address this, Smith, Chaplin and Wadsworth [43] used a cross over design to determine whether chewing gum for at least 20 min a day for two weeks would reduce work and life stress, fatigue, depression and cognitive failures and improve mood and work performance in university employees. The results demonstrated that chewing gum was associated with reduced stress, greater wellbeing and enhanced performance at work, suggesting that chewing gum over a relatively long time has beneficial effects. In another study involving university staff, participants were required to either abstain or chew gum for one workday [44]. Questionnaire measures completed at the beginning and end of the day demonstrated that chewing gum was associated with fewer cognitive problems, but had no significant effect on fatigue, occupational stress, anxiety, depression or being behind at work. Allen and Smith [44] suggest that the discrepancies between these two studies involving university employees may be due to the short nature of the intervention in their study; it is possible that in order to see beneficial effects of chewing gum on mental health and wellbeing, the gum must be chewed for an extended time period. A longer intervention was undertaken to investigate whether the findings of Smith et al. [40] could be replicated in a student sample. Smith and Woods [45] instructed participants to either partake or refrain from chewing gum for a period of two weeks. Their analysis demonstrated that those who had chewed gum considered themselves significantly less stressed post-treatment compared to those who had refrained from chewing gum. This effect occurred in a dose-response fashion so that those who chewed the most gum perceived themselves as the least stressed.

1.3 The Present Study

Research examining the effects of chewing gum on naturally occurring stress in students has so far failed to address whether it exerts beneficial effects on all levels of stress. Chewing gum has been shown to exert positive effects on stressed and non-stressed individuals [46], and it appears that chewing gum is most beneficial to those experiencing a greater degree of negative work characteristics [40]. The present study aimed to determine causality by investigating whether the proposed benefits of chewing gum under a high workload would apply to a student sample. Although research has shown that chewing gum does enhance wellbeing in students, it has not examined the effects of workload on perceived stress. It is therefore, possible that all participants were experiencing a high degree of stress due to a heavy workload, accounting for the beneficial effects of chewing gum. To address these issues, a within-subjects intervention design was used here. Research has shown that chewing gum for 20 min a day is sufficient to exert beneficial effects on an individual's perceived stress and wellbeing [43, 45]. Participants were, therefore, instructed to do so under a high and low workload. A control condition was also included; participants refrained from chewing gum under a high and low workload. As previous research has suggested that a one-day intervention is sufficient to exert beneficial effects on characteristics of perceived stress and wellbeing [44], the four conditions each lasted a day. Given that chewing gum has been associated with a vast range of stress and wellbeing phenomena including stress, anxiety, depression, fatigue, cognitive failures, and the ability to get work done, this study assessed these variables.

Participants reported their self-perceptions via an online questionnaire at the beginning of each day and at the end of each day. Given that the study was investigating perceived stress, instructing participants to complete several questions, each measuring a single construct may itself have affected stress levels. Single-item measures of wellbeing are highly correlated with their full-scale counterparts [47]. For example, single item questions relating to work characteristics, appraisals and outcomes were found to be an adequate replacement for the demands-control-support questionnaire, the revised ways of coping checklist, the hospital anxiety and depression scale, and the patient health questionnaire using a university employee sample [48]. As a significant effect of chewing gum on perceived stress has been demonstrated using these single-item questions with an occupational sample [44], the present study employed single-item measures to assess participants' self-reported perceptions of stress and wellbeing in the student sample.

2 Method

Two hypotheses were explored:

(1) Chewing gum has been shown to exert positive effects on a number of variables in both stressed and non-stressed individuals. The first hypothesis predicted a main effect of chewing gum; under both high and low workload, chewing gum would reduce stress, anxiety, depression, mental and physical fatigue, problems with memory, attention or action, and being behind at work compared to the no gum control conditions.

(2) Research has also demonstrated that chewing gum is most beneficial to those experiencing a high degree of negative work characteristics. The second hypothesis predicted an interaction between chewing gum and the severity of workload - participants would experience a greater reduction in the variables listed in hypothesis 1 when experiencing a high workload and chewing gum.

This study was carried out with the approval of the ethics committee, School of Psychology, Cardiff University and the informed consent of the volunteers.

2.1 Design

The experiment had two independent variables: degree of workload, and gum chewing. These were both within-subject variables. Each IV had two levels: high and low workload and chewing or refraining from gum. The dependent variables were the difference scores (end of working day – beginning of working day) for the measures of stress, depression, anxiety, mental and physical fatigue, problems with memory, attention or action and getting behind with work. The orders of gum conditions were counterbalanced, and high and low workload conditions were counterbalanced within the gum conditions. Participants were randomly allocated to a particular order in which to complete the conditions.

2.2 Materials: Instruction Sheets

Participants received one of eight instruction sheets, identical but for the heading at the top of the sheet, stipulating the order that the conditions were to be completed. The aim of the experiment was briefly described, and the subsequent task outlined in numbered bullet points. Participants were to select two periods of six days within the next two weeks, and within each period were to choose one high workload day and one low workload day. On one of the high and low workload days they were to chew at least two pieces of gum for at least 20 min; on the other two days, they were to refrain from chewing gum. For undergraduate students, a high workload day was defined as a day in which participants had two or more lectures and were working on an assignment and/or in paid or voluntary work whilst a low workload day was defined as one during which participants had one or fewer lectures and/or were not working on an assignment or in paid or voluntary work. PhD students were able to replace the lecture criteria with research, so that one lecture corresponded to one hour of research work. The final point stated that participants would be e-mailed the link to the online survey, which they were to complete at the beginning and end of each of their four chosen days (see Appendix A for an example instruction sheet).

2.3 Gum

Participants were given two packets of chewing gum. To promote chewing, they were allowed free choice from a range of flavors from the Wrigley's sugar-free Extra and Extra Ice range (spearmint, peppermint, cool breeze). Participants recorded how much gum they had consumed at the end of each of the four days.

2.4 Online Questionnaire

The questionnaire was written and accessed via Survey Tracker. Participants firstly indicated how many pieces of chewing gum they had consumed so far that day, how many hours of lectures they had attended and how many hours they had spent studying and/or in paid or voluntary work before completing questions taken from Allen and Smith's [41] one-day intervention study. Using a 7-point Likert scale, participants were asked to indicate how stressed, anxious, depressed and mentally and physically fatigued they felt at that time, and whether they were experiencing problems of memory, attention or action, or getting behind with work (Appendix B).

2.5 Procedure

At recruitment participants were invited into the lab, two at a time. Each participant sat at a desk at opposite ends of the room so that they could not communicate. They were instructed to read and sign the consent form, advising that the study was investigating the effects of chewing gum on perceived stress. Participants were handed the instruction sheet and were asked to read it. The experimenter also read them aloud to each participant before asking if they had any questions regarding their subsequent task. It was explained that the instructions, survey link and their participant number would be e-mailed to them as soon as they left the lab. Participants were informed that they would be e-mailed the debrief form and granted their course credit when they had completed the study. Before leaving the lab participants were invited to take two packets of chewing gum. Throughout the task the experimenter kept in regular contact with the participants to avoid attrition; when participants had completed their first questionnaire of the day, a reminder e-mail was sent to remind them to complete the second questionnaire. Participants also received an e-mail one week after commencing the task, prompting them to continue participating and thanking them for their efforts. When participants had completed all their questionnaires, they were e-mailed a debrief form.

2.6 Analysis

To control for individual differences, statistical tests were carried out on the difference scores of each DV. Difference scores were calculated by subtracting the beginning of the day score from the end of the day score for each variable in each condition for each participant. Therefore, a minus score reflected that participants were less stressed at the end of the day. To examine any main effects or interactions between the IVs, thereby investigating hypothesis 1 and 2, a two-way repeated- measures ANOVA was conducted for each DV.

3 Results

The descriptive statistics for all variables are shown in Table 1.

3.1 Main Effects of Chewing Gum

There was a significant main effect of chewing gum on stress, $F(1, 35) = 4.73, p < .05$, $MSE = 14.69$. The effect was in the expected direction, so that a significant reduction in stress occurred when chewing gum under both high and low workload, compared to refraining from chewing gum under a high and low workload. There was also a significant main effect of mental fatigue, $F(1, 35) = 6.52, p < .05, MSE = 12.25$. Participants reported significantly reduced mental fatigue when chewing gum under both high and low workload compared to refraining from gum under a high and low workload.

Table 1. Mean difference scores in the workload and gum conditions

	High Workload and Gum	High Workload No Gum	Low Workload Gum	Low Workload No Gum
Stress	−0.60	0.08	−0.42	1.8
Mental fatigue	−0.24	0.83	0.50	0.71
Depression	−0.24	−0.31	0.06	1.40
Problems of memory, attention and action	−0.47	0.05	0.43	0.31
Physical fatigue	−0.45	0.90	0.25	0.52
Getting behind with work	−0.05	0.20	0.12	0.23
Anxiety	−0.60	−0.48	−0.53	−0.18

3.2 Main Effects of Workload

There was a significant main effect of workload on depression, $F(1,35) = 4.58$, $p < .05$, $MSE = 5.062$. This occurred in the expected direction, so that participants considered themselves as significantly less depressed under a high workload compared to the low workload condition when chewing or refraining from gum. A significant main effect of workload on problems with memory, attention or action was also detected, $F(1, 35) = 5.46$, $p < .05$, $MSE = 8.03$. Problems with memory, attention or action were significantly reduced when experiencing a high workload when chewing or refraining from gum compared to the low workload conditions.

3.3 Interaction Between Workload and Gum Conditions

The interaction between gum condition and workload for reported physical fatigue difference scores was significant, $F(1, 35) = 4.81$, $p < .05$, $MSE = 9.51$. A significant reduction in physical fatigue was found when participants chewed gum under a high workload compared to chewing gum under a low workload and refraining from gum under a high and low workload.

3.4 Non-significant Effects

There were no significant effects of gum or workload, either as main effects or interactions, for the anxiety or getting behind with work variables.

4 Discussion

4.1 Effects of Chewing Gum

The study set out to address whether chewing gum under a high and low workload would affect participant's perceptions of stress and wellbeing. The results from the present study partly supported the hypotheses. There was a main effect of gum on stress and mental fatigue so that those who chewed gum experienced the most beneficial effects; furthermore, this effect was enhanced under a high workload. Taken together, these results support hypotheses 1 and 2. A significant interaction was also detected for measures of physical fatigue so that participants experienced the greatest benefit when chewing gum under a high workload. The means demonstrated that perceptions of stress were lower in the gum conditions. Together, these findings also support hypotheses 1 and 2. The workload manipulation was also somewhat successful; under a high workload participant experienced a greater reduction in depression and problems with cognition, but contrary to hypothesis 1, this occurred in both gum conditions. With respect to stress and mental fatigue, the findings corroborated results from previous research [37, 40], demonstrating that gum had a significant beneficial effect on stress and mental fatigue in stressed and non-stressed students. Several studies suggest there are plausible biological mechanisms underlying these effects [34], although this type of research is still in its infancy. Chewing gum exerted main effects on stress and mental fatigue, but several stress variables previously shown to be reduced after chewing gum [43, 45] did not appear to be affected. As Allen and Smith [44] suggest, this may have been because previous research used a longer intervention period. Chewing a minimum of two pieces of gum in a one-day intervention may not have been enough to find significant main effects of chewing gum on these variables.

4.2 Effects of Workload

A main effect of workload on some of these variables was detected instead; self- reported perceptions of depression and problems with memory, attention and action were significantly reduced in high workload conditions. While this does not completely corroborate previous research that found a greater association between chewing gum and negative work characteristics, finding an effect of workload with or without gum is interesting in itself. It may indicate that individuals are distracted from feelings of depression or problems with cognition. Indeed, research has demonstrated that distraction reduces the intensity of negative mood, which may exert a knock-on effect on an individual's perception of their cognitive abilities. Additionally, or alternatively, the reductions in these perceived stress scores by the end of the day might signify feelings of relief, or satisfaction, having anticipated a stressful experience at the beginning of the day. It is feasible that this expectation may have arisen from labelling the days as 'high' or 'low' workload days, consequently engendering expectations about participant's imminent experiences. However, as an effect of workload was not found for all variables, this possibility is unlikely. Failing to find an effect of workload on mental fatigue and stress is probably due to the mentally demanding nature of the workload manipulation. As research has shown physical activity to override the negative effects of psychological stress and mental fatigue, future research should examine whether differences in a physical workload affect these variables when chewing or refraining from gum.

4.3 Interactions Between Workload and Chewing Gum

A significant interaction was also detected for measures of physical fatigue; participants experienced the greatest benefit when chewing gum under a high workload. The means fell in the expected direction; fatigue scores were lower in the gum conditions than the control conditions, corroborating previous research. There were no significant main effects or interactions found for being behind at work. Although the research with an occupational sample has found effects of chewing gum on this variable [40], getting-behind with work may arguably be perceived as more severe within a student sample given that the present sample were attending university, presumably with the main intention of studying. According to previous research, more severe types of stress are unaffected by chewing gum [41], which may account for the non-significant effects of gum on getting behind with work with this student sample. Alternatively, it may be that this variable is unlikely to be affected by a one-day intervention; getting-behind with work is often not apparent for several weeks.

4.4 No Effect of Workload or Chewing Gum

Additionally, the analysis failed to find any main effects or interactions with respect to anxiety. Somewhat surprisingly, the average difference scores for the four conditions demonstrated that participants were considerably less anxious at the end of the day in all four conditions. Given that this trend was not found in any other variables, it is likely that this finding owes itself to the considerable variation in participant's responses. Future research should replicate the experiment, taking note of the suggestions for a tighter methodology, as mentioned in the discussion, to determine whether these individual differences can be reduced.

4.5 Limitations and Future Research

The present study had several limitations that may facilitate an understanding of why the experiment failed to fully support the hypotheses. Firstly, the dependent variables relied on a participant's accurate and consistent recognition of perceived stress. Although the questionnaires were designed with convenience in mind, it is likely that over the course of completing eight surveys, participants became accustomed to highlighting an answer without careful and precise consideration. Furthermore, research shows that psychological stress measures do not necessarily equate with their physiological correlates, suggesting that questionnaire measures may not represent an accurate depiction of an individual's internal state. Future research should also examine physiological measures, such as heart rate and cortisol variability, in addition to psychological measures to detect whether discrepancies exist or whether the data complement each other. This may help obtain a more objective portrayal of stress and wellbeing levels and filter out possible practice effects.

Secondly, the precise time of day at which participants completed the questionnaires was not specified. Consequently, there was considerable variability in the time that participants chose to do so, which may have affected their responses. Furthermore, participants were not instructed to chew gum at particular times of the day. As the questionnaire asked participants to rate how they were currently feeling, their responses may not have been related to chewing gum or workload if, for example, they had chewed gum during their lecture at 8am but completed the second questionnaire much later in the day. Future research should measure participant's stress levels, and the amount of gum chewed at specific times throughout the day, via an electronic diary, in order to ensure that workload and gum are related to participants' perceptions of stress and wellbeing, and determine whether variations in their responses can be attributed to chewing or working at certain times [44].

Thirdly, the extent to which participants experienced a high and low workload was not sufficiently controlled. Whilst some participants had no work on a low workload day, and ten hours of work on a high workload day, the reality of the criteria meant that another participant had one lecture on a low workload day and two lectures in addition to half-an-hours written work on a high workload day. Similarly, this variation also occurred within participants, so that the number of lectures an individual attended on their high workload days was significantly different from one another. Unfortunately, due to resource limitations, the only participants available were psychology students who attended a limited number of lectures per week. Also, the lectures that students were assigned to tended to be consistently spread out across the days of the week so that it was difficult to select days in which participants would have had a considerably higher workload than another. Future research should recruit students from different academic backgrounds, in which the difference between participants' workload is significantly large. Additionally, the study should involve some form of fixed criteria to satisfy a high and a low workload day.

Finally, limited measurement of workload was conducted. Future research should use the well-established measures of subjective workload. In addition, more attention should be paid to both short- and longer-term effects of the workload and the chewing gum intervention. Again, these are well established and could include physiological recording, measurement of cognitive performance, and electrophysiological measurement of brain function.

5 Conclusion

In conclusion, the present study showed that chewing a minimum of two pieces of gum for 20 min a day exerts beneficial effects on certain characteristics of perceived stress in students. This finding has promising implications; compared with some current forms of stress relief in students and chewing gum may act as a cheaper and healthier alternative. Additionally, identifying that some qualities of perceived stress and wellbeing were reduced under a high workload, with or without chewing gum, may reassure students that a high workload is not necessarily detrimental to their wellbeing. This is likely to be of particular importance when approaching a deadline or during examination periods. Future research should now use a similar design over a longer intervention period to determine whether greater support could be obtained for the hypotheses. A thorough investigation into the physiological and psychological mechanisms responsible for the effects of chewing gum and workload on perceived stress and wellbeing will increase understanding of the processes involved in reducing stress and help to maximize the benefits of chewing.

Appendix a

Instructions

GUM: HIGH, LOW. NO GUM: LOW, HIGH
Thank you for agreeing to participate in this project.
The aim of the experiment is to see whether chewing gum has an effect upon stress levels in students under a high and low workload.

Now for your part:

1. Please select 2 periods of 6 days within the next 2 weeks.
2. In the first 6 day period please select 1 day in which you have a high workload and another day in which you have a low workload, in that order. Please chew at least 2 pieces of gum on these 2 days for at least 20 min in total.
3. In the second 6 day period please select 1 day in which you have a low workload and another day in which you have a high workload, in that order. Please refrain from chewing gum on these 2 days.
4. High workload is defined as: a day in which you have two or more lectures and are working on an assignment and/or in paid/voluntary work. Low workload is defined as a day where you have one or less lectures and/or are not working on an assignment or in paid/voluntary work.
5. You need to complete this twice on each day: both at the beginning of each of the 4 days that you have chosen, and at the end of each day

Appendix B

Gum survey

Below is a list of descriptions that may or may not apply to you. For each description, please say to what extent you are experiencing this as you complete the questionnaire. Do not think for too long before answering but give your immediate reaction. Please be careful not to miss out any of the items. Give your answer by circling any number from 1 to 7 below the item, where appropriate.

   $1 = $ not at all, $4 = $ moderately and $7 = $ extremely

Feeling anxious	1	2	3	4	5	6	7
Feeling depressed	1	2	3	4	5	6	7
Feeling stressed	1	2	3	4	5	6	7

(*continued*)

(*continued*)

Feeling mentally fatigued	1	2	3	4	5	6	7
Feeling physically fatigued	1	2	3	4	5	6	7
Having problems of memory, attention or action	1	2	3	4	5	6	7
Not getting as much work done as you would like.	1	2	3	4	5	6	7
How many pieces of gum have you chewed today? Number of pieces:							
How many hours of lectures have you attended today? Number of hours:							
How many hours have you spent studying and/or in paid or voluntary work? Number of hours:							

References

1. Reid, G.B., Nygren, T.E.: The subjective workload assessment technique: a scaling procedure for measuring mental workload. In: Advances in Psychology, vol. 52. North-Holland (1988)
2. Stassen, H.G., Johannsen, G., Moray, N.: Internal representation, internal model, human performance model and mental workload. Automatica **26**(4), 811–820 (1990)
3. De Waard, D.: The Measurement of Drivers' Mental Workload. The Traffic Research Centre VSC, University of Groningen, The Netherlands (1996)
4. Hart, S.G.: Nasa-task load index (NASA-TLX); 20 years later. In: Human Factors and Ergonomics Society Annual Meeting, vol. 50. Sage Journals (2006)
5. Smith, A.P., Smith, K.: Effects of workload and time of day on performance and mood. In: Megaw, E.D. (ed.) Contemporary Ergonomics, pp. 497–502. Taylor and Francis, London (1988)
6. Evans, M.S., Harborne, D., Smith, A.P.: Developing an objective indicator of fatigue: an alternative mobile version of the psychomotor vigilance task (m-PVT). In: Longo, L., Leva, M.Chiara (eds.) H-WORKLOAD 2018. CCIS, vol. 1012, pp. 49–71. Springer, Cham (2019). https://doi.org/10.1007/978-3-030-14273-5_4
7. Smith, A.P., Smith, H.N.: Workload, fatigue and performance in the rail industry. In: Longo, L., Leva, M.C. (eds.) H-WORKLOAD 2017. CCIS, vol. 726, pp. 251–263. Springer, Cham (2017). https://doi.org/10.1007/978-3-319-61061-0_17
8. Fan, J., Smith, A.P.: Mental workload and other causes of different types of fatigue in rail staff. In: Longo, L., Leva, M.C. (eds.) H-WORKLOAD 2018. CCIS, vol. 1012, pp. 147–159. Springer, Cham (2019). https://doi.org/10.1007/978-3-030-14273-5_9
9. Cortes Torres, C.C., Sampei, K., Sato, M., Raskar, R., Miki, N.: Workload assessment with eye movement monitoring aided by non-invasive and unobtrusive micro-fabricated optical sensors. In: Adjunct Proceedings of the 28th Annual ACM Symposium on User Interface Software and Technology, pp. 53–54 (2015)
10. Yoshida, Y., Ohwada, H., Mizoguchi, F., Iwasaki, H.: Classifying cognitive load and driving situation with machine learning. Int. J. Mach. Learn. Comput. **4**(3), 210–215 (2014)

11. Wilson, G.F., Eggemeier, T.F.: Mental workload measurement. In: Karwowski, W. (ed.) International Encyclopedia of Ergonomics and Human Factors, 2nd edn., vol. 1, chap. 167. Taylor and Francis (2006)

12. Young, M.S., Stanton, N.A.: Mental workload. In: Stanton, N.A., Hedge, A., Brookhuis, K., Salas, E., Hendrick, H.W. (eds.) Handbook of Human Factors and Ergonomics Methods, chap. 39, pp. 1–9. CRC Press (2004)

13. Young, M.S., Stanton, N.A.: Mental workload: theory, measurement, and application. In: Karwowski, W. (ed.) International Encyclopedia of Ergonomics and Human Factors, 2nd edn, vol. 1, pp. 818–821. Taylor and Francis (2006)

14. Moustafa, K., Luz, S., Longo, L.: Assessment of mental workload: a comparison of machine learning methods and subjective assessment techniques. In: Longo, L., Leva, M.C. (eds.) H-WORKLOAD 2017. CCIS, vol. 726, pp. 30–50. Springer, Cham (2017). https://doi.org/10.1007/978-3-319-61061-0_3

15. Hart, S.G., Staveland, L.E.: Development of NASA-TLX (Task Load Index): results of empirical and theoretical research. In: Advances in Psychology, vol. 52(C), pp. 139–183 (1988)

16. Tsang, P.S., Velazquez, V.L.: Diagnosticity and multidimensional subjective work- load ratings. Ergonomics 39(3), 358–381 (1996)

17. Karasek Jr, R.A.: Job demands, job decision latitude, and mental strain: Implications for job redesign. Adm. Sci. Q. 24, 285—308 (1979)

18. Longo, L., Leva, M.C. (eds.): H-WORKLOAD 2017. CCIS, vol. 726. Springer, Cham (2017). https://doi.org/10.1007/978-3-319-61061-0

19. Longo, L., Leva, M.C. (eds.): H-WORKLOAD 2018. CCIS, vol. 1012. Springer, Cham (2019). https://doi.org/10.1007/978-3-030-14273-5

20. Longo, L., Leva, M.C. (eds.): H-WORKLOAD 2019. CCIS, vol. 1107. Springer, Cham (2019). https://doi.org/10.1007/978-3-030-32423-0

21. Tosevski, D.L., Milovancevic, M.P., Gajic, S.: Personality and psychopathology of university students. Curr. Opin. Psychiatry 23(1), 48–52 (2010)

22. Dhabhar, F.S.: Acute stress enhances while chronic stress suppresses skin immunity: the role of stress hormones and leukocyte trafficking. Ann. N. Y. Acad. Sci. 917, 876–893 (2000)

23. Atanackovic, D., et al.: Acute psychological stress alerts the adaptive immune response: stress-induced mobilization of effector T cells. J. Neuroimmunol. 176, 141–152 (2006)

24. McEwan, B.S.: The neurobiology of stress: from serendipity to clinical relevance. Brain Res. 886, 172–189 (2010)

25. Juster, R.P., McEwan, B.S., Lupien, S.J.: Allostatic load biomarkers of chronic stress and impact on health and cognition. Neurosci. Biobehav. Rev. 35, 2–16 (2009)

26. Rawson, H.E., Bloomer, K., Kendall, A.: Stress, anxiety, depression, and physical illness in college students. J. Genet. Psychol. Res. Theor. Hum. Dev. 155(3), 321–333 (1994)

27. Davis, C.: Decade ends with record student numbers. Organization for Economic Co-operation and Development (2010). https://community.oecd.org/docs/DOC-4271

28. Hamden-Mansour, A., Bandak, A., Puskar, K.: Effectiveness of cognitive- behavioural intervention on depressive symptomatology, stress and coping strategies among university students in Jordan. Issues Ment. Health Nurs. 30, 188–196 (2009)

29. Godbey, K.L., Courage, M.M.: Stress-management program: intervention in nursing student performance anxiety. Arch. Psychiatr. Nurs. 8(3), 190–199 (1994)

30. Saklofske, D.H., Austin, E.J., Mastoras, S.M., Beaton, L., Osborne, S.E.: Relationships of personality, affect, emotional intelligence and coping with student stress and academic success: different patterns of association for stress and success. Learn. Individ. Differ. 22(2), 251–257 (2011)

31. Grossman, P., Niemann, L., Schmidt, S., Walach, H.: Mindfulness-based stress reduction and health benefits: a meta-analysis. J. Psychosom. Res. 57(1), 35–43 (2004)

32. Morris, S., Ford, L.: Universities 'can't cope with depressed students' (2004). http://www.guardian.co.uk/society/2004/jun/18/mentalhealth.studenthealth

33. Princeton Review and Wrigley: Study Habits Survey. Princeton Review, New York (2005)

34. Ham, L.S., Hope, D.A.: College students and problematic drinking: a review of the literature. Clin. Psychol. Rev. 23(5), 719–759 (2003)

35. Magid, V., Colder, C.R., Stroud, L.R., Nichter, M.: Negative affect, stress, and smoking in college students: unique associations independent of alcohol and marijuana use. Addict. Behav. 34(11), 973–975 (2009)

36. University of Michigan Health System: Stress may lead students to use stimulants (2008). http://www.sciencedaily.com/releases/2008/04/080407195349.htm

37. Hollingworth, H.L.: Chewing as a technique of relaxation. Science 90, 385–387 (1939)

38. Freeman, G. L.: Dr. Hollingworth on chewing as a technique of relaxation. Psycholo. Rev. 47(6), 491–493 (1940)

39. Allen, A.P., Smith, A.P.: A review of the evidence that chewing gum affects stress, alertness and cognition. J. Behav. Neurosci. Res. 9, 7–23 (2011)

40. Smith, A.P.: Chewing gum, stress and health. Stress and Health 25, 445–451 (2009)

41. Zibell, S., Madansky, E.: Impact of gum chewing on stress levels. online self- perception research study. Curr. Med. Res. Opin. 25(6), 1491–1500 (2009)

42. Allen, A.P., Smith, A.P.: Demand characteristics, pre-test attitudes and time-on-task trends in the effects of chewing gum on attention and reported mood in healthy volunteers. Appetite 59, 349–356 (2011)

43. Smith, A.P., Chaplin, K., Wadsworth, E.: Chewing gum, occupational stress, work performance and wellbeing. an intervention study. Appetite 58(3), 1083–1086 (2012)

44. Allen, A.P., Smith, A.P.: A brief intervention method for investigating the effects of chewing gum on occupational wellbeing. In: Anderson, M. (ed.) Contemporary Ergonomics and Human Factors. Taylor and Francis, Oxford (2012)

45. Smith, A.P., Woods, M.: Effects of chewing gum on stress and work of university students. Appetite 58, 1037–1040 (2012)

46. Smith, A.P.: Effects of chewing gum on cognition function, mood and physiology in stressed and non-stressed volunteers. Nutr. Neurosci. 13(1), 7–16 (2010)

47. Williams, G., Smith. A. P.: A holistic approach to stress and wellbeing. Part 6: The Wellbeing Process Questionnaire (WPQ short-form). Occupational Health (at Work) (2012)

48. Williams, G.: Developing short, practical measures of wellbeing. In: Anderson, M. (ed.), Contemporary Ergonomics and Human Factors. Oxford, UK: Taylor and Francis (2012)

Associations Between Job Demands, Perceptions of Noise at Work and the Psychological Contract

Mohamad Irwan Ahmad and Andrew P. Smith[✉]

Centre for Occupational and Health Psychology, School of Psychology, Cardiff University,
63 Park Place, Cardiff CF10 3AS, UK
smithap@cardiff.ac.uk

Abstract. Despite the widespread interest in the effects of workload on behaviour, there has been little research on the effects of it on attitudes and values in the workplace and life generally. The aim of the present research was to examine associations between noise exposure (which increases workload) and components of the psychological contract (fairness; trust; organisational commitment; work satisfaction; motivation; organisational citizenship; and intention to stay/quit). 166 workers completed a survey measuring components of the psychological contract, perceptions of noise exposure and other job characteristics. Univariate analyses showed that higher noise exposure was associated with a more negative psychological contract. However, adjustment for other job characteristics, both negative (e.g. job demands) and positive (e.g. control and support), removed the significant effects of noise. These results confirm previous research suggesting that psychosocial stressors have greater behavioural effects than components of the physical working environment such as noise.

Keywords: Psychological contract · Noise · Job demands · Wellbeing

1 Introduction

1.1 Mental Workload

There has recently been renewed interest in models and applications of mental workload [1–3]. Mental workload has been investigated in many different ways [4, 5], and it has a long history in Experimental and Applied Psychology [6, 7]. It has been examined in laboratory studies [8, 9] and in the workplace [1, 10], and a variety of measures of workload have been put forward [11–16]. These include subjective reports, measures of task parameters and physiological function. Self-assessment or subjective reports such as the NASA Task Load Index [17], the Workload Profile [18] and the Subjective Workload Assessment Technique [4] have been widely used. Even single items about perceptions of mental workload are now used, and these are often highly correlated with longer scales and can predict wellbeing and other outcomes. Other research has examined specific aspects of workload, such as time pressure, and this approach formed the basis of the Karasek Job Demands scale, which has been found to predict safety and health outcomes of workers [19].

L. Longo and M. C. Leva (Eds.): H-WORKLOAD 2020, CCIS 1318, pp. 138–146, 2020.
https://doi.org/10.1007/978-3-030-62302-9_9

1.2   Effects of Noise on Performance

One explanation of the negative effects of noise on performance is that the noise acts as an extra source of information that requires extra resources. These resources are then no longer available for the task being performed and performance is impaired [20, 21]. This view is supported by studies which have measured workload and shown that it is increased in noise [22–26]. In addition, the extra workload may lead to increased stress and, in the long term, chronic health problems. There has been little research on the effects of noise on attitudes and values in the workplace and life generally. The present study examined the Psychological Contract which is the exchange relationship between the organization and employee.

1.3   The Psychological Contract

In the Psychological Contract the employee gives an obligation to the organization, and, in return, the organization will respond with some terms and agreement [27]. The Psychological Contract is seen as playing an important role in explaining changes in relationships between employees and their organization [28–30]. A 'Psychological Contract Breach' happens when employees feel that the organization does not support their well-being but is only safeguarding the interests of the organization. The employee might not be prepared to face change but may be required to deliver their best without rewards that are commensurate with the difficulties caused by the change. As a result, their well-being at the work place is disturbed and eventually could lead to various performance-related effects such as low work performance [31, 32], low engagement [33] and weak organizational citizenship behavior [34–36]. Both parties may suffer negative consequences with the organization no longer operating effectively and employees no longer having an interest in their work. When a breach of the Psychological Contract occurs, employees may exhibit negative emotional stress like anger, disappointment and betrayal and, finally, they may cease to work efficiently and may intend to quit the organization [37]. The model proposed by Guest [38] showed the attitudinal and behavioral effects related to changes in the Psychological Contract. In this model the background factors were both individual and organizational characteristics. When the Psychological Contract was working well this led to a state of "Fairness", "Trust" and "The delivery of the deal". Attitudinal consequences of the Psychological Contract include: organizational commitment, work satisfaction, good employment relations, good work-life balance and job security. The behavioral consequences include: high motivation/effort, organizational citizenship and intention to stay in the job rather than quit. Work effort can be defined as the amount of energy employees put in to work successfully [39]. Work effort is different from motivation and there is always some confusion between both of these definitions. In this case, motivation comes first and is the psychological state that pushes the employees to make an effort of any required behaviors [40].

1.4   Aims and Objectives

The aim of the present study was to examine whether the perception of noise at work (a risk factor for increased workload) influenced Psychological Contract Fulfilment (perceptions of fairness, trust and fair treatment). Organizational commitment was the key attitudinal consequence measured. Affective commitment was another variable measured here and it refers to the emotional attachment between the employee and the organization. Effort and intention to quit were the behavioral consequences investigated. One could suggest that wellbeing outcomes should also have been examined. Recent research [41–43] has shown that changes in wellbeing attributed to the Psychological Contract can be better explained by other job characteristics or individual characteristics. Indeed, this is a common issue in occupational workload research, where effects attributed to workload turn out to be due to correlated attributes. For example, some of the effects of noise on accidents reflect the fact that job with high noise levels also involved dangerous machinery [44]. Negative job characteristics were, therefore, also measured, as were positive job characteristics which could plausibly account for high Psychological Contract Scores.

2 Method

This study was carried out with the approval of the ethics committee, School of Psychology, Cardiff University and the informed consent of the volunteers.

2.1 The Survey

An online survey was carried out using Qualtrics software.

2.2 Measuring Instruments

In the present study fairness, trust, delivery of deals and overall Psychological Contract Fulfilment were measured using The Psychological Contract Fulfilment Scale developed by Guest and Conway [27]. The measurement assessed the extent to which the respondent felt the organization had kept its promises (7 items), treated them fairly (2 items) and how much they trusted the organization (4 items). Example items include "Has the organization fulfilled its promise or commitment to.... provide you with a reasonably secure job", "Overall, do you feel you are fairly rewarded for the amount of effort you put into your job." and "To what extent do you trust your immediate manager to look after your best interests." A main focus of the study was on the attitudinal and behavioural consequences of Psychological Contract Fulfilment. Affective organizational commitment was measured using the Affective, Normative and Continuance Commitment Scale [45]. In the present study, the Work Effort Scale developed by De Cooman et al. [46] was used. This scale consists of 10-items which measure three dimensions of work effort, namely intensity, direction and persistence. These dimensions were summed to give an overall work effort score. In this study, intention to quit/leave was measured using the scale developed by Kuvaas [47]. This scale contains 5-items and asks general questions about intention to leave the current job.

2.3 Participants

The participants were 166 workers from the USA recruited using Mechanical Turk. Details of their demographics characteristics are shown in Table 1.

Table 1. Respondents' demographic profile

Variable	Response category	Frequency	Percentage (%)
Age	20–30 years	54	32.5
	31–40 years	68	41.0
	41–50 years	21	12.7
	51–60 years	11	6.6
	61–70 years	12	7.2
Sex	Male	96	57.8
	Female	70	42.2
Marital status	Single	59	35.5
	Living with partner	29	17.5
	Married	67	40.4
	Separated	3	1.8
	Divorced	7	4.3
	Widowed	1	0.6
Education	Undergraduate	108	65.1
	Post-Graduate	51	30.7
	Doctorate	4	2.4
	Other	3	1.8
Work sector	Public	68	41.0
	Private	98	59.0
Full or part-time work	Full time	151	91.0
	Part-time	15	9.0
Work pattern	Fixed hours	116	69.9
	Flexi hours	37	22.3
	Shift work	13	7.8

3 Results

Perceived noise exposure was dichotomised into those who were never exposed to noise at work and those who were. The descriptive statistics for the dependent variables are shown for these groups in Table 2.

The group means show that those exposed to noise reported lower scores for promises, fairness, trust and the global Psychological Contract measure. In addition, they reported lower affective commitment, lower effort and a greater intention to quit the job. A MANOVA showed that the overall effect of noise was statistically significant (Wilks Lambda = 0.909 $p < 0.05$) and individual ANOVAs showed that this was true for all the individual variables. The next analysis examined whether this effect of noise

Table 2. Descriptive statistics for the psychological contract measures

Variable	Noise group	Mean	Std. deviation	N
Promises	No Noise	20.83	5.41	103
	Noise	17.56	5.44	63
Fairness	No Noise	13.56	3.10	103
	Noise	12.46	3.06	63
Trust	No Noise	20.94	4.47	103
	Noise	18.86	4.86	63
Psychological contract global	No Noise	55.33	11.47	103
	Noise	48.87	11.97	63
Affective commitment	No Noise	27.73	5.68	103
	Noise	25.92	5.71	63
Work effort	No Noise	59.81	7.40	103
	Noise	57.40	10.03	63
Intention to quit	No Noise	11.36	5.30	103
	Noise	14.22	6.00	63

remained significant when positive and negative job characteristics were included as covariates in the analyses. The factor scores for positive and negative job characteristics were included in these analyses. Positive job characteristics had an overall significant effect (Wilks Lambda = 0.605 $p < 0.001$) and also a significant effect for all the individual variables. The same was true for negative job characteristics (Wilks Lambda = 0.713 $p < 0.001$). The overall effect of perceived noise exposure was no longer significant in this analysis (Wilks Lambda = 0.976 $p = 0.70$). There were no significant effects of noise in the analysis of the individual variables.

4   Discussion

The aim of this research was to examine the association between perceived exposure to noise at work, which may represent increased mental workload, and values, attitudes and behaviors that are part of the Psychological Contract. Perceived noise was assessed by a single question that examined the frequency of exposure to background noise at work that interferes with concentration on the job. Aspects of the Psychological Contract were measured using well established scales. An important feature of the research was the measurement of other job characteristics that have been shown to be associated with Psychological Contract measures [41–43] and with reported noise exposure [48].

4.1   Effects of Noise

The initial analyses suggested that exposure to noise at work led to a more negative attitude that influenced promises, perceived fairness and trust. Attitudinal consequences of this weaker Psychological Contract were also apparent as shown by the lower affective commitment scores. Behavioral consequences, as shown by reduced effort and a greater intention to quit, were also significant.

4.2   Controlling for Job Characteristics

The second set of analyses included positive and negative job characteristics. These had significant effects on the Psychological Contract variables, both overall and at the individual variable level. In addition, the effects of noise were no longer significant when these other job characteristics were included in the analyses. Overall, the results of the present study show that initial consideration of noise in isolation suggests a negative impact on all parts of the Psychological Contract. However, adjustment for other job characteristics shows that it is these, not noise, that influence the strength of the Psychological Contract. In this respect, this is another study showing that it is the nature of the work carried out in noise, rather than noise per se, that influences attitudes and behavior. Mental workload, in the form of job demands, had a negative effect on the Psychological Contract and this effect accounted for the smaller effects of another source of mental workload, namely exposure to background noise.

4.3   Limitations

There are clear limitations associated with the present study. First, noise exposure would ideally be objectively measured. Secondly, workload should also be measured, preferably objectively but at the very least with subjective scales. It should be noted, however, that objective measures are difficult with online survey methodology. Thirdly, it is important to know the tasks that are carried out in noise as this often determines whether impairments are observed or not. Finally, a longitudinal design, preferably with an intervention, would be much better than the cross-sectional analyses presented here.

5   Conclusion

There has been little previous research on the effects of mental workload on attitudes and values. The Psychological Contract is the exchange relationship between the organization and employee where the employee offers an obligation to the organization and the organization in return will appreciate this with positive terms and agreements. The objective of the present research was to examine associations between noise exposure (which increases workload) and aspects of the Psychological Contract: trust; fairness; organizational commitment; job satisfaction; organizational citizenship; motivation and effort; and intention to stay/quit. Workers from a variety of jobs completed a survey measuring components of the psychological contract, perceptions of noise exposure and other job characteristics (e.g. job demands, control and support). Univariate analyses showed that higher noise exposure was associated with a more negative psychological contract. However, adjustment for other job characteristics, both positive and negative, removed the significant effects of noise. These results confirm previous research suggesting that psychosocial stressors have greater behavioral effects than components of the physical stressors such as noise.

References

1. Smith, A.P., Smith, H.N.: Workload, fatigue and performance in the rail industry. In: Longo, L., Leva, M. (eds.) H-WORKLOAD 2017. CCIS, vol. 726, pp. 251–263. Springer, Cham (2017). https://doi.org/10.1007/978-3-319-61061-0_17
2. Longo, L., Leva, M.C. (eds.): Human Mental Workload: Models and Applications, H-WORKLOAD 2018. CCIS. Springer, Cham (2019). https://doi.org/10.1007/978-3-030-142 73-5
3. Longo, L., Leva, M.C. (eds.): Human Mental Workload: Models and Applications, H-WORKLOAD 2019. CCIS. Springer, Cham. (2019). https://doi.org/10.1007/978-3-030-324 23-0
4. Reid, G.B., Nygren, T.E.: The Subjective Workload Assessment Technique: A Scaling Procedure for Measuring Mental Workload, vol. 52. North-Holland, Amsterdam (1988)
5. Stassen, H.G., Johannsen, G., Moray, N.: Internal representation, internal model, human performance model and mental workload. Automatica **26**(4), 811–820 (1990)
6. De Waard, D.: The measurement of drivers' mental workload. The Traffic Research Centre VSC, University of Groningen (1996)
7. Hart, S.G.: NASA-task load index (NASA-TLX); 20 years later. In: Human Factors and Ergonomics Society Annual Meeting, vol. 50. Sage, Los Angeles (2006)
8. Smith, A.P., Smith, K.: Effects of workload and time of day on performance and mood. In: Megaw, E.D. (ed.) Contemporary Ergonomics, pp. 497–502. Taylor & Francis, London (1988)
9. Evans, M.S., Harborne, D., Smith, Andrew P.: Developing an objective indicator of fatigue: an alternative mobile version of the psychomotor vigilance task (m-PVT). In: Longo, L., Leva, M. (eds.) H-WORKLOAD 2018. CCIS, vol. 1012, pp. 49–71. Springer, Cham (2019). https://doi.org/10.1007/978-3-030-14273-5_4
10. Fan, J., Smith, A.P.: Mental workload and other causes of different types of fatigue in rail staff. In: Longo, L., Leva, M. (eds.) H-WORKLOAD 2018. CCIS, vol. 1012, pp. 147–159. Springer, Cham (2019). https://doi.org/10.1007/978-3-030-14273-5_9
11. Cortes Torres, C.C., Sampei, K., Sato, M., Raskar, R., Miki, N.: Workload assessment with eye movement monitoring aided by non-invasive and unobtrusive micro-fabricated optical sensors. In: Adjunct Proceedings of the 28th Annual ACM Symposium on User Interface Software & Technology, pp. 53–54 (2015)
12. Yoshida, Y., Ohwada, H., Mizoguchi, F., Iwasaki, H.: Classifying cognitive load and driving situation with machine learning. Int. J. Mach. Learn. Comput. **4**(3), 210–215 (2014)
13. Wilson, G.F., Eggemeier, T.F.: Mental workload measurement (chap. 167). In: Karwowski, W. (ed.) International Encyclopedia of Ergonomics and Human Factors, 2nd edn., vol. 1. Taylor & Francis, London (2006)
14. Young, M.S., Stanton, N.A.: Mental workload (chap. 39). In: Stanton, N.A., Hedge, A., Brookhuis, K., Salas, E., Hendrick, H.W. (eds.) Handbook of Human Factors and Ergonomics Methods, pp. 1–9. CRC Press, Boca Raton (2004)
15. Young, M.S., Stanton, N.A.: Mental workload: theory, measurement, and application. In: Karwowski, W. (ed.) International Encyclopedia of Ergonomics and Human Factors, 2nd edn., vol. 1, pp. 818–821. Taylor & Francis, London (2006)
16. Moustafa, K., Luz, S., Longo, L.: Assessment of mental workload: a comparison of machine learning methods and subjective assessment techniques. In: Longo, L., Leva, M. (eds.) H-WORKLOAD 2017. CCIS, vol. 726, pp. 30–50. Springer, Cham (2017). https://doi.org/10.1007/978-3-319-61061-0_3
17. Hart, S.G., Staveland, L.E.: Development of NASA-TLX (Task Load Index): results of empirical and theoretical research. Adv. Psychol. **52**(C), 139–183 (1988)

18. Tsang, P.S., Velazquez, V.L.: Diagnosticity and multidimensional subjective workload ratings. Ergonomics **39**(3), 358–381 (1996)
19. Karasek Jr, R.A.: Job demands, job decision latitude, and mental strain: implications for job redesign. Adm. Sci. Q. **24**, 285–308 (1979)
20. Smith, A.P.: A review of the effects of noise on human performance. Scand. J. Psychol. **30**, 185–206 (1989)
21. Smith, A.P., Jones, D.M.: Noise and performance. In: Smith, A.P., Jones, D.M. (eds.) Handbook of Human Performance, Vol. 1: The Physical Environment, pp. 1–28. Academic Press, London (1992)
22. McNeer, R., Bennett, C., Dudaryk, R.: Intraoperative noise increases perceived task load and fatigue in anesthesiology residents: a simulation based study. Anesth. Analg. **122**(2), 512–525 (2016)
23. Rosen, M., et al.: Sensor-based measurement of critical care nursing workload: Unobtrusive measures of nursing activity complement traditional task and patient level indicators of workload to predict perceived exertion. PLoS One **13**(10), e0204819 (2018)
24. Jahncke, H., Bjorkeholm, P., Marsh, J., Odelius, J., Sorqvist, P.: Office noise: can headphones and masking sound attenuate distraction by background speech? Work **55**(3), 505–513 (2016)
25. Gao, J., et al.: Quantitative evaluations of the effects of noise on mental workloads based on pupil dilation during laparoscopic surgery. Am. Surg. **84**(12), 1951–1956 (2018)
26. Becker, A., Warm, J., Dember, W., Hancock, P.: Effects of jet engine noise and performance feedback on perceived workload in a monitoring task. Int. J. Aviat. Psychol. **5**(1), 49–62 (1995)
27. Rousseau, D.M.: Psychological and implied contract in organisations. Empl. Responsib. Rights J. **2**(2), 121–139 (1989). https://doi.org/10.1007/BF01384942
28. Rousseau, D.M.: Psychological Contract in Organisations: Understanding Written and Unwritten Agreements. Sage, Thousand Oaks (1995)
29. Guest, D., Conway, R.: Communicating the psychological contract: an employer perspective. Hum. Resour. Manag. J. **12**(2), 22–38 (2002)
30. Dabos, G.E., Rousseau, D.M.: Mutuality and reciprocity in the psychological contract of employees and employers. J. Appl. Psychol. **89**(1), 52–72 (2004)
31. Marks, A.: Developing a multiple foci conceptualization of the psychological contract. Empl. Relat. **23**(5), 454–469 (2001)
32. Millward, L.J., Hopkins, L.J.: Psychological contracts, organizational and job commitment. J. Appl. Soc. Psychol. **28**(16), 1530–1556 (1998)
33. Bal, M.P., De Cooman, R., Mol, T.S.: Dynamics of psychological contracts with work engagement and turnover intention: the influence of organizational tenure. Eur. J. Work Organ. Psychol. **22**(1), 107–122 (2003)
34. Zhao, H., Wayne, S.J., Glibkowski, B.C., Bravo, J.: The impact of psychological contract breach on work-related outcomes: a meta-analysis. Pers. Psychol. **60**(3), 647–680 (2007)
35. Lee, K., Allen, N.J.: Organizational citizenship behavior and workplace deviance: the role of affect and cognitions. J. Appl. Psychol. **87**(1), 131–142 (2002)
36. Turnley, W.H., Bolino, M.C., Lester, S.W., Bloodgood, J.M.: The impact of psychological contract fulfilment on the performance of in-role and organizational citizenship behaviors. J. Manag. **29**(2), 187–206 (2003)
37. Robinson, S.L., Kraatz, M., Rousseau, D.M.: Changing obligations and the psychological contract: a longitudinal study. Acad. Manag. J. **37**(1), 137–152 (1994)
38. Guest, D.E.: Is the psychological contract worth taking seriously? J. Organ. Behav. **19**(1), 649–664 (1989)
39. Ilgen, D.R., Klein, H.J.: Organizational behavior. In: Rosenzweig, M.R., Porter, L.W. (eds.) Annual Review of Psychology, vol. 40, pp. 327–351 (1989)

40. Bandura, A., Cervone, D.: Differential engagement of self-reactive influences in cognitive motivation. Organ. Behav. Hum. Decis. Process. **38**(1), 92–113 (1986)
41. Ahmad, M.I., Firman, K., Smith, H., Smith, A.P.: Short measures of organisational commitment. Citizensh. Behav. Other Empl. Attitudes Behav.: Assoc. Well-Being BMIJ **6**(3), 516–550 (2018)
42. Ahmad, M.I., Firman, K., Smith, H., Smith, A.P.: Psychological contract fulfilment and wellbeing. Adv. Soc. Sci. Res. J. **5**(12), 90–101 (2018)
43. Smith, A.P., Smith, H.N.: A short questionnaire to measure wellbeing at work (Short-SWELL) and to examine the interaction between the employee and organisation. In: Charles, R., Wilkinson, J. (eds.) Contemporary Ergonomics and Human Factors 2017. Chartered Institute of Ergonomics and Human Factors, pp. 200–205 (2017)
44. Smith, A.P.: Noise, performance efficiency and safety. Int. Arch. Occup. Environ. Health **62**, 1–5 (1990). https://doi.org/10.1007/BF00397841
45. Meyer, J.P., Allen, N.J.: A three component conceptualization of organizational commitment. Hum. Resour. Manag. Rev. **1**(1), 61–89 (1991)
46. De Cooman, R., De Gieter, S., Pepermans, R., Jegers, M., Van Acker, F.: Development and validation of the work effort scale. Eur. J. Psychol. Assess. **25**(4), 266–273 (2009)
47. Kuvaas, B.: Performance appraisal satisfaction and employee outcomes: mediating and moderating roles of work motivation. Int. J. Hum. Resour. Manag. **17**(3), 504–522 (2006)
48. Smith, A.P.: Effects of noise on errors, injuries and subjective health of nursing staff. In: ICBEN 2017 (2017)

Influence of Complexity and Noise on Mental Workload During a Manual Assembly Task

Dominic Bläsing[(✉)] and Manfred Bornewasser

Institute of Psychology, University Greifswald, Franz-Mehring-Str. 47,
17489 Greifswald, Germany
{Dominic.Blaesing,Bornewas}@uni-greifswald.de

Abstract. Mass customization implies an increase of product variants, complexity, and information processing of operators. Generally it is supposed that this leads to an increase of mental workload. Using a real-work-like laboratory setting, subjects should complete tasks of increasing complexity while mental workload is obtained using various parameters (subjective, performance related, and physiological). Additionally subjects are confronted with two levels of industrial noise which will increase mental workload on top of complexity. Results indicate that there is a significant influence of complexity and the interaction of complexity and noise on mental workload. Further physiological reaction patterns (electrocardiographic and eye tracking data) to process parts with higher informational load are investigated and concurrent patterns for pupillary response, fixation duration, and heart rate variability can be shown.

Keywords: Mental workload · Manual assembly · Noise · ECG · Eye tracking

1 Complexity as a Part of Modern Assembly

Modern versions of mixed-model-assembly systems are characterized by mass customization, small batch sizes, rapidly varying product demand, high product variety, and frequently introduction of new products. This implies the processing of huge amounts of data at a high pace and makes assembly a process of high complexity.

Complexity can be defined as something difficult to understand, describe, predict or control [1]. Based on variety, McDuffie et al. [2] described a product-mix-complexity and found negative correlation between complexity and manufacturing performance. Frizelle and Woodcock [3] defined complexity as the variety and uncertainty associated with the sequence of assembly. They differentiated between structural complexity which is connected to the variety in the static system and operational complexity which is associated with the uncertainty of the dynamic system. Both are quantified by an information-theoretic entropy measure. Finally, Zhu et al. [4] proposed operator choice complexity which describes a sequence of choices throughout the work process concerning e.g. proper parts or tools. It is defined as the average uncertainty or randomness in a choice process. Thus manual assembly in the era of mass customization has lost its predictable and repetitive character.

© Springer Nature Switzerland AG 2020
L. Longo and M. C. Leva (Eds.): H-WORKLOAD 2020, CCIS 1318, pp. 147–174, 2020.
https://doi.org/10.1007/978-3-030-62302-9_10

Zhu et al. [4] describe choice processes with respect to time. Choices imply different cognitive functions of information processing, ranging from perception to the automatic or cognitively controlled selection of a motor response [5]. A central element in this process is the working memory which is seen as a storage unit with the functionality of comparing incoming and already existing information as well as the initiation of a behavioral response. Empirical investigations of human choice making show that humans are restricted in their ability to make choices in response to a given number of stimuli. Hick's law [6] says that the choice reaction time depends on the number of stimulus alternatives if all the alternatives are equal. Additionally a negative correlation was shown between response time and errors. With increasing information (represented through varying stimuli) completion time and number of errors increase too. Transferred to manual assembly this indicates that the number of possible parts and tools to choose from leads to potentially longer decision times and an increased chance for assembly failures. Thus, there is a strong connection between variety of stimulus alternatives, working memory, and quality of performance.

1.1 Relation of Complexity and Mental Workload

Even in the era of digitization, manual assembly is an important part of work in small and medium sized production companies. However, physical activities like grasping, lifting, or fixing parts are supplemented more and more by mental activities like information acquisition, choosing, or deciding. Thus, manual assembly becomes a rapid sequence of cognitive and motor activities. Operators are forced to constantly gain and retain information from different sources, make choices between varying parts, tools, mounting options, and product variations and finally decide between different physical activities, altogether leading to the final product. As a consequence, a constant transition between physical and mental workload becomes more and more characteristic for modern manual, assembly [4].

Manual Assembly (and work in general) is always an interactive process between a given task (in a specific set) and individual characteristics of the operator. To solve the task a specific amount of activation or arousal is needed. To describe this relationship from a cognitive perspective the terms mental workload, mental effort, mental strain or many more are used.

Mental workload is a hypothetical construct which can be described as a relation between external demands and available resources of an operator. It is often expressed by a demand-resources-, a task-resources- or a demand-supply ratio [7, 8] and neither the task nor the individual characteristics alone can predict it [9]. Quite similar, Chen et al. [10] define cognitive load as a multi-dimensional construct representing "the load imposed on the working memory during performance of a cognitive task" (p. 4). Working memory is the central entity, where cognitive or mental workload exerts its main influence. At the same time working memory is the known bottleneck of information processing (what induced Miller [11] to propose his famous 7 plus/minus 2 bit-rule of information).

The human ability to process a certain amount of information at the same time is restricted. However, there is consensus that cognitive capacities can be augmented by operator skills and knowledge [12]. In general two ways of information processing and decision making in dependency to prior experience are possible: automatic processing and reasoning. While automatic processing is fast, unconscious, widely liberated from attentional resource constraints, and mostly used for well-known situations, during new and unfamiliar situations reasoning requires a lot more attention and cognitive resources [13, 14]. Endsley [15] describes the fast, automatic reactions as intuition which is defined as recognizing informational patterns already stored in the long-term memory, while reasoning is connected to effort, motivation, and concentration.

There is the assumption of an optimal state between demands and resources. Workload is optimal when there is equality (defined as comfort zone by Hancock and Warm [7] and as flow by Thomas [16]), it becomes suboptimal if there is imbalance between demand and resources. Such imbalances are gradually associated with attentional deficits, reduced alertness, performance degradation, and errors [17]. Suboptimal workload can mean either overload or underload. In both cases operators can try to adapt and to compensate deficiencies, otherwise performance necessarily degrades. The Redlines-Model [18] and the Model of Maximal Adaptability [7] describe the relationship between demand, resources, and capacity. Excessive overload can affect selective attention dramatically leading to narrowed sampling and different kinds of errors [19].

Variety implies an increase of information processing and at the same time a decrease of automatic processing. That is the reason why Hollnagel [20] in his cognitive ergonomic approach proposed to optimize information management and instructions to increase the fit to the operator's cognitive conditions. This could be realized by technological means like digital assistance systems [21], by better presentation of information [22], or by explicitly using different modalities of information processing and resource pools (visual, auditory [8]). Modern cognitive and even neurocognitive ergonomics [23, 24] not only offer a lot of inspirations for a better design of assembly tasks, but also for a better human-machine interaction. A favoured solution are adaptive and context-dependent human-computer systems which allow flexible task allocations and an adaptation to the workload of the individual operator. However, accomplishing such workload-matched adaption is dependent on the ability to measure mental workload changes in real time.

1.2 Noise as a Distractor

Information might be functional (like instructions) or dysfunctional (like noise). Both have their influence on cognitive processing. Noise is one of the main environmental sources of discomfort at the workplace beside temperature, light, or dust and can lead to an increase of physical and mental workload [25]. Information-theoretically, noise can be conceptualized as a configuration of signals which are of no relevance for task completion. However, such signals gradually stimulate different attentional reactions which lead for example to a short term distraction of cognitive processes or to a complete loss of concentration.

A meta-analysis by Szalma and Hancock [26] confirmed that noise has a significant influence on human performance. Additionally they showed which kind of noise configurations are most distracting. The influence of noise is higher for accuracy than for task speed. Speech noise has a higher overall effect size than nonspeech noise and there is a significant difference between intermitted and constant noise as well as an influence of short- and long term exposure. The effect of noise on performance is larger for cognitive than for psychomotor tasks.

The underlying mechanism of the relationship between noise and mental workload is a widely discussed topic. There are different approaches which have one thing in common: Noise is interfering the capability to adapt to a given task by increasing the general arousal of a person and reducing the amount of incoming information. This can be the case by masking inner speech [27], minimizing working memory by disrupting the rehearsal processes in the articulatory loop [28] or an attentional narrowing mechanism or attentional shift due to the new cue [29]. This effect will be maximized using impact noises, i.e. short bursts of infrequent noise [30]. All approaches focus on capacity problems and overlapping resource pools. These can be integrated into the general workload approach of Wickens [8] or the maximal adaptability theory of Hancock and Warm [7].

1.3 Mental Workload Measurement

There are several possible ways to assess mental workload using subjective rating scales, performance and behavior related parameters, or physiological measures [17]. In the last years there is an observable tendency to use physiological measurements as a more objective and less manipulable approach to get a deeper insight into mental workload levels and changes during a task [10].

Subjective rating scales, like the NASA Task Load Index (NASA TLX), are a fast and easy way to get an overview of the momentary load of a person and are the most used measurement technique for mental workload [31]. There are two disadvantages in this method: It is a retrospective snapshot that requires the ability of introspection and it is nearly impossible to track mental workload in real time during the whole assembly process. Each question will disrupt the task and increase the mental workload due to the additional resources required to give an answer.

Most prominently used performance features are speed and accuracy. Transferred to an assembly task this means assembly time and assembly failures. In addition, the usage of behavioral data like object handling at the working place, interactions with assistance systems or work interruptions can be tracked through direct or (better) technically supported observations. Although performance and behavioral data often have the character of objective parameters, it is not always possible to assess them real time during a process. Assembly time normally is expressed only in a single value and can only be used for a comparisons of different persons or models. Similarly, failures can be the result of mental overload but give no reference to the point on which the overload occurred.

Physiological measurements offer a chance to circumvent these disadvantages. When facing changing conditions, the organism is striving for a state of balance or homeostasis through the process of allostasis [32]. Activation of the autonomous nervous system (ANS) or the hypothalamic-pituitary-adrenal axis (HPA axis) will lead to an increase of supplied energy. The process of supplying energy is usually connected to an increased activity of the sympathetic part of the ANS which leads to measurable changes in different physiological parameters. Most applied measurement techniques are electroencephalography (EEG), electrocardiography (ECG), eye related measurements, galvanic skin response (GSR), and functional near-infrared spectroscopy (fNIRS), used either alone or in combination. Following the given circumstances in manual assembly, the used systems should be non-intrusive, lightweight, and mobile.

From the raw ECG it is necessary to detect R-Peaks (the most prominent feature of an ECG, indicating a distinct heart beat). Further calculations of either heart rate (HR) or heart rate variability (HRV) are based on inter-beat-intervals (RR-intervals). HRV is a general term for a class of parameters that can be clustered in either time-domain, frequency-domain, or non-linear measurements (for further details see [33]). HRV indicates for the balance of the ANS and shows to be sensitive for changes in both directions, relaxation due to increased parasympathetic activity and arousal or even stress in connection with increased sympathetic activity [34]. During stressful events HR should increase while HRV parameters will decrease to represent an overall change in load.

For this experiment we will focus on time-domain HRV parameters because they are less sensitive to missing beats and can be calculated even for ultra-short timeframes (below two minutes). The most commonly used time-domain HRV parameters SDNN (Standard Deviation of NN intervals – distance between normal R peaks without artifacts or arrhythmic beats) [35], RMSSD (Root Mean Square of Successive Differences) [36, 37], and pNN50 (Percentage of consecutive RR-intervals with a difference of more than 50 ms) [37] showed to be sensitive for changes in mental workload and even differentiate between load levels. One of the main problems for HRV measurement is the relationship between higher basal HR and lower HRV known as cycle length dependency [38]. We addressed this issue by additionally using the more robust HRV parameter rrHRV (Mean Euclidian distance between consecutive RR-intervals and a common center point) [39].

While the heart needs some time to adapt to changes in workload the eye reacts with a shorter latency [23]. The most common used eye feature is pupillary response or the dilation of the pupil which is not only correlated to illumination and distance of the fixated object but also to the momentary emotional and cognitive arousal of a person [40–42]. This neurophysiological reaction is presumed to be based in a neuron cluster called Locus Coeruleus which is part of the noradrenergic system [43]. During phases of increased arousal the pupil dilates and it constricts when arousal declines. Using pupillary response as an indicator for mental workload changes in less than a second are detectable [44].

Pupillary response is not the only relevant mental workload associated parameter using eye and gaze related features. Simplified there are two different types of eye movements: fixations (to percept and process information) and saccades (short rapid movements to switch between two fixation points). Both are in close relation to mental workload. For fixations the normally used parameter is the average fixation duration during a specific task. As a result of increasing cognitive demands and concentration fixation duration can increase [45–47]. This increase is connected to longer times of information intake or higher processing load [48]. Profiles or distributions of fixation durations during different task solving phases are also used as indicators for mental workload [49].

Saccadic movements can be analyzed using either the duration, amplitude (spatial distance between two fixations in degrees of visual angle°), or combined factors like saccadic peak/mean velocity (°/s). All three parameters show a direct relationship to mental workload [50–54]. Increasing Saccadic Peak Velocity (SPV) seems to be the most promising parameter to detect increases in mental workload and is even able to signal differences between workload levels [55, 56]. Especially for longer cognitive demanding periods SPV can decrease as a result of increasing mental fatigue or tiredness [54, 57].

1.4   Aim of the Present Investigation and Main Hypothesis

Empirical findings for the relationship of mental workload and physiological parameters are ambiguous. While there are several studies showing clear correlations between workload and assumed changes in the physiology, other studies cannot show those effects. In addition less is known about the potential of combining different parameters to overcome the individual weaknesses. We used a broad range of parameters to further discuss the possibility, chances, and obstacles of combining them for a better understanding of mental workload.

Central for our investigation is the influence of complexity of an assembly task and additional noise on mental workload during manual assembly. Supplementary, our investigation will try to give some insights into the dynamics of physiological data representing mental workload during process parts with mainly mental components in the phases of instruction. In order to get an impression of these fluctuations a pattern analysis of the physiological data will be run. The following hypotheses should be investigated:

H1: With increasing complexity mental workload will increase too.
H2: Task complexity in combination with noise level will lead to an interaction effect which increases the overall extent of mental workload.
H3: Situations with increased informational content will lead to specific short-time changes of mental workload.

Pattern analysis will be run for three different set ups: an overall analysis (H3) for all instruction phases at one, an analysis based on the complexity level (H3a), and a final analysis based on the different instructional steps (H3b).

Hypotheses 1 and 2 will be tested for all aspects of mental workload: subjective ratings, performance data, and physiological parameters while hypotheses 3 can only be answered using real-time and therefore physiological data.

2   Methodology

2.1   Experimental Design

To investigate the relationship between complexity, loudness, and mental workload a nested repeated measure design was chosen with 3 levels for complexity and 2 levels for noise. During the low complexity level no noise was presented. Subjects were randomly assigned to one of two groups and were confronted with noise of different loudness during medium and high complexity models. Group 1 got the intense condition for the two models with medium complexity while group 2 got a quieter version of the same noise. During the high complexity models noise presentation was reversed (Table 1).

Table 1. Experimental design complexity and loudness

Complexity	Low	Medium	High
Group 1	♩ (no sound)	*f* (forte-loud)	*p* (piano-quiet)
Group 2	♩ (no sound)	*p* (piano-quiet)	*f* (forte-loud)

2.2 Stimulus Material

The noise conditions subjects are exposed to during the experiment were live recorded in the truck bodywork support frame construction department of our partner company. With an unpattern fluctuation between low and high noise (as a result of mechanic screw mounting) it can be classified as an intermittent noise schedule with irregular occurring peaks of loud noise. The detected sound pressure level during original manufacturing at peaks was 127 dB(A) and ambient noise around 85 dB(A). During the experiment all noise levels were equally adjusted due to health protection reasons. Two different levels of loudness were used: an unmuted version with peaks of 95 dB(A) and ambient noise around 65.5 dB(A) and a subdued version with peaks at 76.1 dB(A) and 46.7 dB(A) ambient noise. This combination represents noise exposure when ear protection is used.

Two miniaturized assembly stations for truck bodyworks support frame construction were set up at our laboratory. The task was designed to be solved only in one way and the manual component was tried to cut short. To reduce assembly parts, tools, and the knowledge gap between unlearned subjects and skilled workers the laboratory task was adjusted. Crossbeams and screws in different colors were used instead of different crossbeam lengths and reinforcements. Distance and orientation stayed identical to real cases. For an easier assembly subjects only had to connect longitudinal and cross beams by using screws as simple plug connectors. Further adjustments and bolting was not necessary. This should neglect potential effects of manual learning during the experiment.

The assembly station was divided in two parts: a storage part (crossbeams and screws) and a mounting part. Using a monitor above the storage part instructions were given in three steps (Fig. 1):

1. Crossbeam color
2. Orientation and distance between crossbeams (no color information available)
3. Screw color (no information about crossbeam color, orientation and distance available)

Following the complexity conceptualization of Zhu et al. [4] we only manipulated operator choice complexity defined as "the average uncertainty or randomness in a choice process" ([4] p. 2). Assembly complexity therefore was controlled through choosing a number of different crossbeam colors (two to five), distances (regular pattern to random distances), orientations (easy pattern to chaotic non observable pattern), and screw colors (number of different colors and pattern). Through a systematic manipulation of those features six models out of over 1.1 sixillion possible solutions ($1.1*10^{21}$) were chosen (Table 2). This number also represents the possible amount of failures, models that can be assembled with the given material but in a wrong manner. Color or orientation

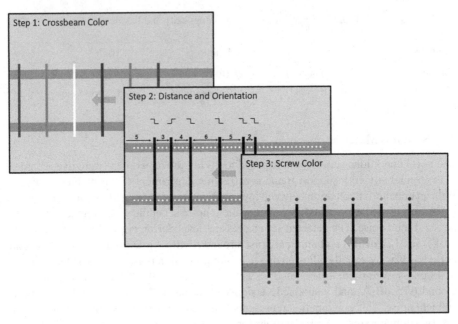

Fig. 1. Assembly instruction (example using high complexity) (Color figure online)

patterns can support subjects to remember information easier through chunking them and reduce the amount of unique information [11, 22]. Over all models predictability is getting lower with more chaotic patterns of color, orientation, and distances. The unique amount of information needed to assemble the models is increasing from roughly 10 bits for model 1 to 46 bits for model 5 and 6.

Table 2. Complexity manipulation

Complexity	Low		Middle		High	
Model	1	2	3	4	5	6
Crossbeam colors	2 (pattern)	2 (pattern)	3 (pattern)	3 (pattern)	5 (chaotic)	5 (chaotic)
Orientation	1	1	2 (pattern)	2 (pattern)	2 (chaotic)	2 (chaotic)
Distance	1	1	4 (pattern)	4 (pattern)	5 (chaotic)	5 (chaotic)
Screw colors	2 (paired)	3 (paired)	5 (paired)	5 (paired)	5 (chaotic)	5 (chaotic)
Information quantity	10	15	31	31	46	46

As a special reward manipulation subjects were able to influence the money they get for being part of the study by avoiding instructional check backs (each time they used the button would lead to a loss of 1.00€) and thus taking risk to make more mistakes (−0.50€ for each mistake).

2.3 Methods and Apparatus for Mental Workload Assessment

Mental workload assessment was based on subjective rating scales, performance parameters, ECG measurement, and eye tracking.

2.3.1 Subjective Measurement (NASA TLX)

For the assessment of subjective workload the NASA Task Load Index (NASA TLX) is used. The NASA TLX is a widely used six dimensional questionnaire with a 20 point Likert scale (for analysis transferred to the original 100 point scale) with items for mental, physical, and temporal demand, effort, performance, and frustration level. All scales beside performance are on a low to high scale, for performance a good to poor scale is used [31]. In deviation to the original weighted averaging approach the raw TLX score was used as an overall estimate of workload.

2.3.2 Performance

Performance parameters were either gathered using automatically generated time stamps or a manually generated failure protocol. As an additionally parameter the number of automatically recorded instructional check backs was used.

2.3.3 ECG

Following the guidelines for HR and HRV measurement in occupational science [36] a Faros eMotion 180° 1-channel Holter ECG device with a sampling frequency of 1000 Hz was used. Foam hydrogel Ag/AgCl electrodes were placed as advised by the manufacturer below the left collarbone and with a slight left shift below the left rips. The Holter ECG device was attached to an additional electrode below the right collarbone.

2.3.4 Eye Tracking

SensoMotoric Instruments (SMI) Eye Tracking Glasses 2 Wireless were used to gather data for pupillary response and eye events. The eye tracking device had a binocular sampling rate of 60 Hz and gathered data for pupillary response using integrated infrared sensors.

2.4 Subjects

Data from 46 subjects was gathered. Due to technical difficulties and terminations during the study only 39 subjects could be analyzed. From the remaining subjects 21 were part of group 1. Subjects were mainly female students (n = 30) of the University of Greifswald with a mean age of 24.03 years (SD = 2.6). All subjects declared that they had no known cardiovascular disease, diabetes, or epilepsy. Most subjects had normal (n = 26) or corrected to normal (n = 8) sight. For the remaining subjects no sight correction was necessary during the experiment. The mean reward was 20.15€ (SD = 4.46).

2.5 Procedure

After online registration for the study subjects were informed about procedure, measurement techniques (ECG and Eye tracking and their application), rewards, and exclusion criteria. Written consent was signed by each subject before the experiment started. First ECG, eye tracker, and headphones were applied, the eye tracker calibrated and subjects had to put on safety gloves to handle the cross beams. Subjects were guided to the next room where the two assembly stations were situated. After some demographic and health related questionnaires a 2-back task with a one minute learning and five minute testing phase was performed. Stimuli for this task (numbers 1 to 6) were of equal length (500 ms) with 2000 ms between stimuli [58].

The main part of the experiment was the assembly of seven different support frames. The first frame was preassembled and subjects had only to add two more beams. The experimenter was constantly available at this point and helped to understand the instructions for the rest of the study. The main six support frames were organized with increasing complexity and had to be assembled on alternating assembly stations to give some time to disassemble the finished frame.

For each support frame three different instructional steps were shown on a monitor in front of the assembly station for 10 s each. Subjects were allowed to show the last instruction again but could not go backwards. After every two frames subjective workload and complexity rating were performed.

Starting with support frame three a sound file with industrial noise was presented. Noise level changed for all subjects after support frame four. Assessment of noise loudness was performed after support frame six.

At the end of the experiment a five minute resting baseline in a seated position was performed followed by a short post interview to assess used strategies and the noise perception. Subjects were unequipped and got paid for their attendance.

2.6 Data Analysis

Eye tracking data was prepared using SMIs BeGaze solution for data analysis. Raw and event data export was performed for each subject and imported to Mathworks Matlab 2019a for further analysis. Pupillary response data was filtered for outliners and missing data and finally interpolated using a combination of data from the second eye and linear interpolation. For further analysis pupillary response was averaged using data from both eyes. Event related data (fixation and saccades) were adjusted using a plausibility check for physiological unlikely data (fixation durations less than 50 ms and more than 3.5 standard deviations above the mean, saccadic duration shorter than 10 ms and longer than 90 ms and saccadic velocity with more than 900°/s were excluded).

Fixation duration, saccadic duration, amplitude, and velocity were taken from the SMI BeGaze solution. Saccadic velocity is analyzed separately for the peak and mean velocity. Due to the irregular acceleration pattern during the saccade the mean velocity is taken as an alternative approach adjusted for outliers.

ECG data was prepared using the Matlab based HRVTool by Vollmer [59]. After automatic R-peak detection a manual correction was performed.

For further analysis mean values for all physiological parameters over the whole assembly time were calculated. For HR and HRV this was done in deviation to the recommended standards of ECG analysis from Sammito et al. [36] who propose a minimum duration of 300 s for HRV measurements. To guarantee the validity of our measurement no frequency domain related HRV parameters were chosen. Furthermore the mean assembly time for most frames was below 300 s, so again, an adaptation of the measurement length instead of using a fixed size should increase the validity of our measurement. The chosen HRV parameters are: rrHRV, SDNN, RMSSD, and pNN50.

3   Results

3.1   Manipulation Check

To prove that subjects experienced the different groups of support frames as drivers of complexity a complexity rating was performed. Using a slide controller subjects had to rate the last two support frames on a scale from 1 to 100 (no complexity to high complexity) after models 2, 4, and 6 as well as a direct comparison between complexity levels starting after frame 4 (Table 3).

Table 3. Complexity rating

	Low	Medium	High	Delta-LM	Delta-MH
Group 1	23.90 (17.9)	54.62 (24.2)	70.67 (21.4)	75.62 (23.4)	70.33 (24.0)
Group 2	30.72 (18.1)	53.83 (16.7)	78.17 (17.7)	71.50 (17.3)	80.44 (22.0)
Overall	27.05 (18.1)	54.26 (20.8)	74.13 (19.9)	73.72 (20.7)	75.00 (23.4)

Significant differences between complexity levels can be found using a general linear model for repeated measurements $(F(1.73, 66.10) = 132.5, p < .001)$. No significant differences can be found between the two experimental groups. There seems to be no effect of loudness-order on perceived assembly complexity itself. But a tendency can be spotted for the silent-loud group (group 2) to rate the increase from medium to high bigger than before (71.50 to 80.44) while group 1 experience an opposite effect (75.62 to 70.33).

When asked how they perceived the noise (1 = not noticeable to 10 = unbearable) a significant difference for loudness perception between both groups can be observed $(t(37) = -3.02$ p $= .005$ (Group 1 mean $= 5.76$, SD $= 1.58$; Group 2 mean $= 7.39$, SD $= 1.79$). Data from post interviews reveals that subjects from group 1 showed a tendency to think that through concentration the noise was getting into the background. Only some of them verbalized that they noticed the difference between both conditions.

In group 2 more people recognized the difference and said that the silent condition had a motivational and atmospheric character while during the loud condition more concentration was needed to fulfill the task.

For a better classification of the mental workload aspect during the manual assembly tasks different complexity levels were compared with the 2-back task as a pure mental workload task. Using data from the mental load scale of the NASA TLX it can be seen that the models with the highest complexity reach equally high scores as the 2-back task (high complexity = 76.67 and 2-back = 79.23).

3.2 Performance Indicators

The used performance indicators of mental workload are assembly time, assembly failures, and number of check backs. Performance parameters were analyzed using combined values for the two frames of each complexity level. Assembly time increases from 554.1 s for low complexity to 735.4 s during high complexity (Table 4, Fig. 2). The differences between assembly times for all complexity levels is significant ($F(1.79, 67.60) = 39.49$, $p < .001$, partial $\eta^2 = .533$). The used planned comparison showed significant differences between all three levels of complexity.

Table 4. Assembly time, failures, and instruction repetition for different complexity levels

(mean/SD)	Assembly time			Assembly failure			Check backs		
	Low	Med	High	Low	Med	High	Low	Med	High
Group 1	542.8/104.2	634.2/124.9	787.6/204.7	2.76/4.8	4.67/7.4	7.86/10.4	0.24/0.5	0.81/1.1	4.19/2.2
Group 2	567.4/92.8	583.2/89.6	674.6/73.8	5.67/7.9	2.94/4.1	7.94/5.6	0.22/0.5	0.17/0.4	2.83/1.8
Overall	554.1/98.6	610.7/111.6	735.4/166.6	4.10/6.5	3.87/6.1	7.90/8.4	0.23/0.5	0.51/0.9	3.56/2.1

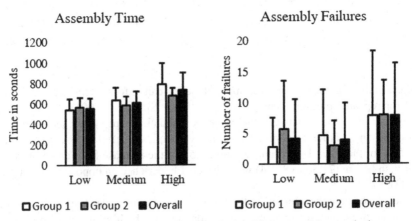

Fig. 2. Assembly time and failure in relationship to assembly complexity

The number of assembly failures and check backs show similar effects. Overall there is a significant effect of complexity on assembly failures ($F(2,74) = 5.248$, p =

.007, partial $\eta^2 = .124$). The standard deviation for failures is relative high. An outlier correction was not performed because subjects were obliged to decide if they'll risk the chance to make failures and loss money for those failures or if they would invest money and see the instruction again. Therefore high failure values can be the result of the subject's chosen strategy.

Using the number of check backs as a mental workload indicator an overall effect of complexity can be shown with numbers increasing from .23 repetitions for low complexity models to 3.56 for high complexity ones (Table 4). A repeated measures ANOVA analysis showed that those differences were significant (F(2,74) = 102.995, p < .001, partial $\eta^2 = .736$).

The influence of noise on performance was tested for the medium and high complexity models where noise was systematically manipulated. There is a significant effect for group membership on assembly time (F(1, 37) = 4.633, p = .038, partial $\eta^2 = .111$), but no interaction between complexity and group membership can be shown. During both conditions group 1 showed longer assembly times than group 2 (Table 4, Fig. 2).

An effect of sequence of noise exposition on assembly failures cannot be shown (F(1, 37) = .188, p = .667). And there is no interaction between loudness and complexity on assembly failures (F(1, 37) = .380, p = .541). Similar to assembly time, for check backs there is an overall effect of group membership on number of repetitions (F(1,37) = 6.130, p = .018, partial $\eta^2 = .142$) but no interaction effect. Both groups need for instructional repetition increases for the high complexity models with a stronger increase for group 1 (3.3) than group 2 (2.8).

3.3 Subjective Workload Ratings

Beside the interpretation of the Raw TLX Score (which considers all six subscales) the mental workload scale was additionally analyzed. For both scores significant differences between the three complexity levels can be observed (Raw Score: F(1.836,67.942) = 173.181, p < .001, partial $\eta^2 = .824$, Mental Workload: F(1.749,64.720) = 135.807, p < .001, partial $\eta^2 = .786$, see Fig. 3). An expanded analysis using the rating for the 2-back task (pairwise comparison from repeated measures ANOVA with all four measure points) shows that there is no significant difference between the support frames with high complexity and the mental workload during the 2-back task.

The influence of loudness sequence can only be shown for Raw TLX scores. A significant interaction concerning sequence condition and complexity level indicates different increases for both groups from medium to high complexity with a total difference of 9 points between the groups ($F_{interact}$(1,37) = 5.165, p = .029, partial $\eta^2 = .122$).

3.4 Physiological Data

For analysis of physiological data concerning the relationship of mental workload and complexity repeated measures ANOVAs were performed for each physiological parameter. For a better comparison to the subjective data only the support frames two, four, and six where chosen for the analysis.

Table 5 shows descriptive data for each phase (low, medium, high complexity, additionally for the 2-back task) as well as effect sizes for the repeated measures ANOVA.

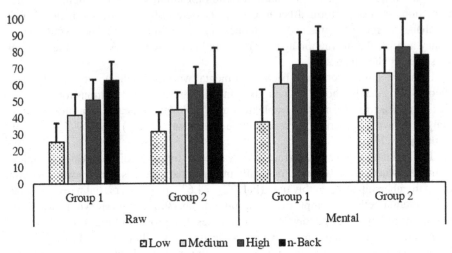

Fig. 3. Subjective workload ratings for different complexity and groups (2-back as a pure mental workload task in comparison)

There is no significant difference for HR, SDNN, RMSSD, pNN50, and Saccadic Amplitude for an overall comparison of all four phases. The largest effect sizes result for SPV (partial $\eta^2 = .452$), Pupillary Response (partial $\eta^2 = .397$), Fixation Duration (partial $\eta^2 = .391$), and rrHRV (partial $\eta^2 = .275$). While most of those parameters are able to detect differences between the pure mental workload task and the different assembly complexities a differentiation between medium and high complexity using planed comparison shows no significant differences.

All effect sizes decrease when the repeated measures ANOVA is conducted using only the three complexity levels. For pNN50, Saccadic Duration, Saccadic Mean and Peak Velocity no longer significant differences can be observed. For rrHRV (partial $\eta^2 = .185$), Pupillary Response (partial $\eta^2 = .303$), and Fixation Duration significant differences between the three complexity levels can be seen.

To test the influence of noise level on mental workload the means of both support frames of medium and high complexity were calculated for different physiological parameters. Using those values the interaction of complexity and noise level was tested using a repeated measures ANOVA (Fig. 4).

A significant interaction effect was found for HR ($F_{interact}(1,37) = 9.246$, p = .004, partial $\eta^2 = .200$), rrHRV ($F_{interact}(1,37) = 4.852$, p = .034, partial $\eta^2 = .116$), and Pupillary Response ($F_{interact}(1,37) = 37.798$, p < .001, partial $\eta^2 = .505$), while interactions for RMSSD ($F_{interact}(1,37) = 4.084$, p = .051) and pNN50 ($F_{interact}(1,37) = 3.782$, p = .059) are only close to significance. From a mental workload perspective all interaction patterns for HR, rrHRV, pNN50, and RMSSD indicate the same result: while group 1 experiences less mental workload from medium to high complexity workload for group 2 increases or at least stays on the same level (HR). Pupillary Response shows a similar interaction term. However it shows a much stronger form. Group 1 and group

Table 5. Physiological parameters during assembly of models with low, medium, and high‘ complexity (2-back as a pure mental workload task for comparison)

Complexity	Low	Medium	High	2-back	η^2 partial
Heart Rate	98.10 (15.49)	99.43 (14.90)	98.01 (15.01)	98.56 (15.48)	.025/ .073
rrHRV	3.15 (1.35)	2.93 (1.18)	2.85 (1.05)	2.52 (1.00)	**.275***/ **.185***
SDNN	48.65 (17.20)	48.58 (14.69)	49.62 (20.28)	48.27 (17.86)	.004/ .005
RMSSD	23.88 (11.83)	23.02 (9.73)	22.24 (15.11)	19.78 (9.30)	.061/ .017
pNN50	4.86 (5.78)	4.34 (4.74)	3.91 (5.38)	3.25 (4.47)	**.093*/** .056
Pupillary Response	3.39 (.40)	3.47 (.40)	3.44 (.41)	3.17 (.41)	**.397***/ **.303***
Fixation Duration	228.13 (20.21)	232.49 (21.41)	234.62 (24.60)	267.45 (45.46)	**.391***/ **.162***
Saccadic Duration	66.22 (3.23)	66.16 (2.92)	66.29 (3.45)	64.54 (5.16)	**.078*/** .002
Saccadic Amplitude	5.89 (1.18)	5.93 (1.29)	6.13 (1.45)	5.43 (1.67)	.059/ .036
Saccadic Mean Velocity	85.60 (10.76)	85.80 (12.67)	87.28 (14.14)	75.78 (17.56)	**.303***/ .026
SPV	178.59 (24.12)	179.38 (24.96)	181.23 (26.44)	151.54 (33.19)	**.452***/ .012

*$\alpha < .05$ **$\alpha < .01$ ***$\alpha < .001$

2 nearly change their exact position. While group 1 had a greater pupil dilation during the medium complex support frames group 2 showed a greater dilation during the high complexity models and vice versa.

3.5 Pattern Analysis

Beside the comparison of the three complexity levels a pattern analysis of the main mental workload events is conducted. These events concern the first information intake of each instructional step. Informational load can be classified in two ways: a) in accordance to the complexity levels low, medium, high and b) following the different instructional steps (1 crossbeam color, 2 distance and orientation, 3 screw color). Due to the high correlation and physiological/mathematical connection of Saccadic Amplitude (degrees of visual angle), Saccadic Duration (ms), SPV (°/ms), and Saccadic Mean Velocity only Saccadic Duration and SPV are taken into account for this analysis.

The first pattern analysis is conducted for the different complexity levels. Most prominent changes can be seen for Pupillary Response and Fixation Duration (Fig. 5). While

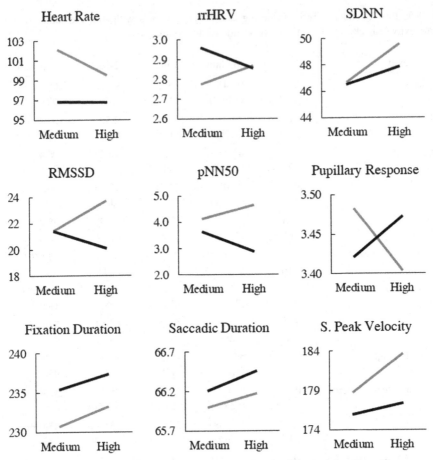

Fig. 4. Overview interaction loudness and complexity for physiological data (grey line = group 1 - forte-piano, black line = group 2 - piano-forte)

Fixation Duration keeps increasing after the instructional presentation, pupil dilation tends to decrease first and then rapidly increases. While Saccadic Duration and Peak Velocity tend to show decreases over time, ECG related parameters show nearly no striking patterns.

Beside model complexity the amount of information per step can influence mental workload and therefore physiological reaction patterns. With different amounts of information for each step (see Table 2) it is possible that there are significant differences between the three steps. The first step is always limited to a maximum of six bits of information – only the color and sequence of the cross beam is shown as a necessary component of this step. In step 2 and 3 twelve bits of information are presented, six orientations and six distances (step 2) as well as twelve screw colors (step 3). There are noticeable differences between the three steps with step 2 showing the biggest influence on physiological mental workload parameters (Fig. 6).

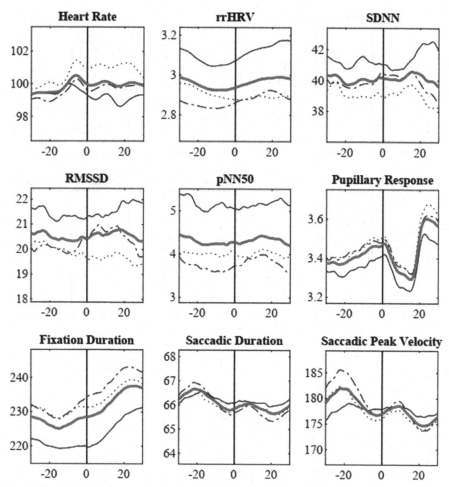

Fig. 5. Physiological parameter patterns during information processing (first encounter with new assembly instructions complexity level analysis (n = 234 per level – low = grey line, medium = grey dottet, high = grey dot and stroke; overall pattern = red line n = 702) (Color figure online)

To further investigate those patterns a repeated measures ANOVA for three consecutive 10 s time frames was conducted: pre-instruction (20–10 s before subjects pressed the button for a new instructional step), the instruction itself (10 s of instructional representation), and post-instruction (starting 10 s after the instructional presentation ended). During this time two things become evident: eye related parameters show significant changes for complexity levels as well as for step wise comparisons. However, heart related parameters are only showing significant changes during step 1 (HR partial η^2 = .124) and step 2 (partial η^2 = .0.96). Fixation Duration and Pupillary Response tend to be most sensitive for short-term changes in mental workload (overall Pupillary Response partial η^2 = .151; Fixation Duration partial η^2 = .135). The largest effect sizes were

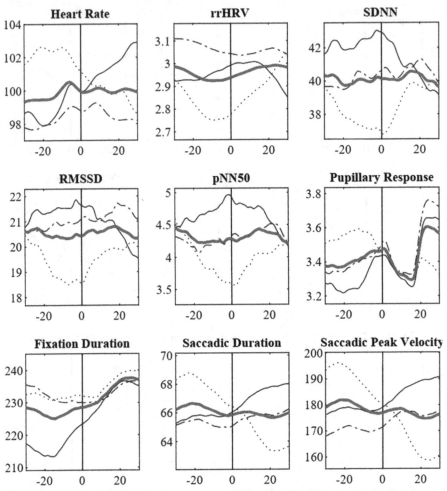

Fig. 6. Physiological parameter patterns during information processing (first encounter with new assembly instructions stepwise analysis (n = 234 per step – step 1 = grey line, step 2 = grey dottet, step 3 = grey dot and stroke; overall pattern = red line n = 702) (Color figure online)

observed for the changes during step 1 (Pupillary Response partial $\eta^2 = .453$ and Fixation Duration partial $\eta^2 = .371$).

Differences between the complexity levels and steps were examined using repeated measures ANOVAs for both cases (complexity levels and steps). For complexity levels rrHRV, pNN50, Fixation Duration, and Pupillary Response show significant differences with effect sizes between .122 for pNN50 and .517 for Fixation Duration (Table 6). Comparing all three steps there are significant differences for HR, SDNN, RMSSD, Fixation Duration, Saccadic Duration, and SPV, with the biggest effect size for SDNN (partial $\eta^2 = 123$). But it is also noticeable that subjects seemed to be more stressed before step 2 (rrHRV, SDNN, RMSSD, pNN50, and Saccadic Duration/SPV) than before step 1 and 3 but tend to relax during the instructional presentation. A possible explanation might be the necessary physical component of crossbeam placement during step 1.

Table 6. Physiological parameters after initial presentation of each instructional step (10 s presentation duration, sorted by complexity and stepwise)

	Low	Med	High	η^2 partial	Step 1	Step 2	Step 3	η^2 partial
HR	99.18 (15.27)	101.11 (15.17)	99.74 (15.82)	.074	100.43 (16.57)	100.57 (14.52)	99.03 (14.82)	**.083***
rrHRV	3.10 (1.36)	2.88 (1.15)	2.88 (1.09)	**.135****	3.00 (1.28)	2.82 (1.22)	3.04 (1.21)	.060
SDNN	40.80 (14.81)	39.11 (15.61)	40.33 (14.50)	.037	42.22 (15.74)	37.57 (14.20)	40.45 (16.23)	**.123****
RMSSD	21.34 (9.97)	19.63 (9.15)	20.75 (9.06)	.073	21.44 (9.78)	19.20 (9.66)	21.07 (9.27)	**.091***
pNN50	5.08 (6.29)	3.96 (5.01)	3.82 (4.20)	**.122****	4.82 (5.58)	3.71 (5.63)	4.33 (4.78)	.056
Pupillary Response	3.34 (.36)	3.43 (.37)	3.43 (.38)	**.313*****	3.37 (.39)	3.40 (.35)	3.42 (.40)	.032
Fixation Duration	220.80 (25.05)	232.07 (25.85)	235.47 (26.11)	**.517*****	226.16 (24.96)	231.92 (28.08)	230.25 (25.65)	**.081***
Saccadic Duration	66.14 (3.42)	65.97 (3.34)	65.86 (3.61)	.012	66.59 (3.72)	65.91 (3.58)	65.48 (3.37)	**.101***
SPV	178.25 (23.29)	177.22 (21.82)	178.49 (24.66)	.007	182.09 (23.22)	177.10 (25.97)	174.77 (23.59)	**.091***

$*\alpha < .05$ $**\alpha < .01$ $***\alpha < .001$

4 Discussion

The experiment showed some evidence that task complexity has an effect on mental workload. While subjective and performance measures reflect significant increases of mental workload physiological indicators do not thoroughly corroborate the assumptions. Table 7 gives an overview of effect sizes for all indicators.

Comparably, expected significant interaction effects of noise intensity and complexity on mental workload are selectively to be found for Pupillary Response, HR, and rrHRV as well as for the raw NASA TLX. Surprisingly there are no effects concerning performance indicators.

Finally, pattern analysis of physiological data revealed that changes of mental workload are better to be detected during short time windows than during longer ones. Using different physiological parameters, it is possible to differentiate between different levels of complexity (rrHRV, pNN50, Pupillary Response, Fixation Duration) as well as between different instructional steps (HR, SDNN, RMSSD, Fixation Duration, Saccadic

Table 7. Result overview (effect size partial $\eta^2 < .1 = +$; $<.25 = ++$; $\geq .25 = +++$)

	Speed	Failure	Check backs	NASA raw	NASA Ment.	HR	rrHRV	SDNN	RMSSD	pNN50	Pup Resp	Fix Dur	Sacc Dur	Sacc Amp	SMV	SPV
H1	+++	++	+++	+++	+++		++				+++	++				
H2				++		++	++				+++					
H3a							++					++	+++	+++		
H3b						+		++	+				+	++		+

Duration, SPV). This might indicate that different physiological parameters are more or less sensitive for specific reactions to mental workload.

In summary complexity and noise separately and in interaction do have some influence on mental workload, however, this influence is expressed over different indicator patterns. Complexity alone leads to more eye tracking activities, contrary to this effect, noise more to an increase of HR and HRV. As a side effect of the study we were able to show that there is no difference between the high complexity support frames and the 2-back task as a pure mental task (Fig. 3). For most physiological parameters (beside HR) effect sizes for repeated measures ANOVA are bigger when the 2-back tasks is involved in the analysis, for Saccadic Duration, Saccadic Mean and Peak Velocity, and pNN50 differences were no longer significant when the 2-back task was excluded from analysis (Table 5). So even when subjects were not able to subjectively differentiate between the highest complexity support frame and the pure mental workload task physiological reactions are able to show the difference.

4.1 General Discussion

There are three main points that need to be discussed: The missing differentiation between medium and high complexity for physiological data, the missing effects for noise on performance indicators and the effects of the physiological parameters during the primarily mentally based interactions with the informational system.

As Table 7 shows, task complexity had significant influence on several indicators of mental workload. Under conditions of medium and high complexity subjects needed more time and made more mistakes. At the same time they rated the more complex tasks as more mentally demanding. However, expected differences of physiological mental workload indicators were rare for conditions of medium and high complexity. Thus, results indicate some kind of dissociation [18]. While post hoc subjective estimations and behaviorally based measures show differences between medium and high complexity levels physiological measures do not indicate different extents of mental workload.

A first explanation for this non-confirming result could be that, in contrast to the subjective ratings, the medium and high complex task were objectively experienced as similar in cognitive demand. Both seemed to be rather easy and thus belonging to the comfort zone of mental load [7, 18]. In both cases task demand did not exceed resource supply, thus leading to a balanced state and not to some kind of overload. That means, even in the high complexity condition there were still resources at one's disposal to solve the task without any capacity problems [8]. This might imply that the used physiological parameters are of different sensitivity. Some of them might only detect greater differences, e.g. between zones or areas of workload, whereas others are able to reflect smaller differences even inside different zones of adaptation.

A second explanation could be that the stepwise presentation of the assembly instructions already reduces complexity. Thus, when subjects had objectively to process 46 or 31 bits of information during high or medium complexity tasks (see Table 2), the information was presented step by step in small units. This stepwise presentation over the course of assembly made it easy to handle even greater amounts of information. Probably this procedure resulted in reduced mental workload. The presentation of all necessary information in one instructional step would have made the task impossible.

A third explanation could rely on masking effects of physical load on mental workload. There are a lot of research findings which show that physical activities are associated with HR-changes. Usually these changes are much stronger than HR-changes caused by mental or cognitive activities [60]. Although we tried to reduce physical and motor activities as far as possible and to pronounce information processing activities, the resulting assembly task left a lot of possibilities for masking effects, e.g. when the subjects looked for further instructions or when they manipulated assembly parts or tools. Additionally, masking could also be the result of delayed appearance of HR-adaptations which get in overlap or even conflict with short-term changes of cognition-based activities. A consequence of these delay effects could be that short-term changes of HR based on cognitive activities are repeatedly masked by long-term-changes of physical activities.

The physiological pattern analysis additionally underlines this explanation. On the one hand HR and HRV show slower changes during the chosen 60 s window (Fig. 5 and 6) due to the slower adaptation of the heart to changing demands and the mathematical base of HRV computation which takes the last 30 beats into account. Especially for Step 1 a strong increase of HR is visible after the instruction was presented (Fig. 6). Video analysis showed that this increase is the result of the first assembly phase. During this phase the cross beams had to be placed on the assembly station requiring more physical work than the remaining steps.

Concerning noise manipulation there are no differences of performance related parameters. Neither speed, accuracy, nor instructional check backs showed some kind of systematic variation, although there are some significant differences concerning physiological parameters. A possible explanation is that subjects quickly adapted to the noise and used some defensive technique in order to prevent external impacts of noise. Some subject reported that they tried intensively to focus their concentration on the task and to actively prevent dysfunctional noise influences. Thus, subjects choose some kind of strategy to voluntarily avoid any kind of disruption of information processing or resource competition in working memory [8, 61]. This strategy on the one hand leads to some kind of suppression of noise influences and on the other hand to a better performance. Probably physiological indicators increase because of higher voluntary investments in concentration. Thus, mental workload in the case of complexity and noise is perhaps not caused by the task but by concentration.

These findings firstly show that the task constellation is of crucial importance. Secondly the physiological indicators are more or less well suited to depict mental and physical activities. Thirdly there are considerable differences between subjects. The central limitations of the present study concern these three aspects of our investigation.

4.2 Limitations

The chosen assembly task turned out to be multifaceted in terms of the sequence of informative and executive activities as well as the influence of the assembly steps to be carried out. This makes the ecological validity of the study questionable. A clear cut separation of cognitively and physically relevant work steps seems to be impossible. This may be due to the fact that many cognitive and physical activities were carried out simultaneously. Theoretically, perception, consolidation, and remembering can easily be identified in the work process but it is difficult to observe them distinctively even in laboratory settings. This is also the truth for physiological indicators. For further research and analysis it might be appropriate to break down complete tasks into different, distinct parts of work with more or less mental activities. However, this puts ecological validity even more into question.

Another limitation concerns the measuring instruments. Based on Chen et al. [10] and Longo [17] we included a plausible selection of different measuring instruments in the investigation, i.e. we operationalized the concept of mental workload differently. This included subjective assessments (mostly carried out post hoc), performative and behavioral measurements (e.g. of times or repeated use of an informational assistance system which, however, is also strongly influenced by motivation), as well as physiological procedures. Questions arise how well each individual instrument is able to record relevant changes of mental work load, which component of workload is recorded, and how much overlap consists between the parameters of mental workload.

As diverse as the instruments may be the question is what exactly each instrument captures, what aspect it stands for, and how the instruments are related. Chen et al. [10] assume that each parameter captures a part of mental workload that is difficult to specify and it is therefore important to combine different parameters. The weakness of one parameter should be compensated by the strength of another one. This idea is attractive but also difficult to implement because for a lot of parameters it is unclear what they exactly capture, how much they correlate with other parameters, and how to align them.

A final point concerns the sample. This applies in particular to the selection of subjects but also to the difficulty in recording the used strategies to approach such a practical task without special experience. While the task was adapted to fit the prerequisites of the subjects and keep the focus on the more mentally aspects they still had some (unexpected) degrees of freedom to use different strategies or made failures that a qualified specialist would not use or make. Using a healthy and young population in a laboratory setting can lead to effects that are not to be observed in field. For example HRV not only depends on smoking, eating behaviour, and fitness level but also on age and sex [62]. Those factors are not systematically to control in a field setting with a rather small number of assembly workers. Thus, for a systematic analysis laboratory as well as field research is needed but the question is how to manage an optimal fit between more theory-based and more case-based approaches. It cannot be excluded that both are even rather incompatible.

The first more nomothetic approach has a tendency to reduce the number of variables to be considered, while the second more ideographic one has to take into account a great number of variables which determine the character or the signature of the situation [7].

4.3 Future Work

In the near future advancements in theoretical assumptions and models of information processing are needed. There are a lot of exciting approaches in ergonomic research on mental workload. Nevertheless, central concepts of these approaches have intuitive appeal but remain difficult to define and to measure [18, 63, 64]. Theoretical terms like task demand, attentional resources, capacity, automatic or controlled processing, redline, and acceptability threshold do not find universal agreement. This makes theoretical as well as practical work in the field difficult because each kind of ergonomic application implies the identification of situations when workload is suboptimal leading to errors, health impairments, and accidents.

In order to determine whether there is a case of suboptimal workload ergonomists have to be able to measure workload directly and accurately. It seems to be relatively easy to further improve external objective measures that represent the stimulus or response side in the traditional behaviorist sense. Even eye tracking remains more attached to this external reality than, for example, the EEG which captures internal organismic processes in the brain and really shows with some delay "the brain at work" [24]. However, we are probably still a long way from being able to objectively and directly grasp recognition and selection processes on the neurophysiological level (which Parasuraman [24] wishes to). To measure the semantic content of brain processes by physiological procedures seems to be impossible [65]. That is the reason why neurophysiological data have to be combined with behavioral and subjective data. They increase the interpretability of physiological data.

Methodological demands for the near future lie in the improvement of existing and the creation of new mental workload indicators and measurement techniques. Even though we already used several techniques there are still much more that have already proven to react sensitively to changes in mental workload like galvanic skin response [10], different frequency domains in EEG measurements [66–68], or functional near infrared spectroscopy (fNIRS [69]). As a consequence of an enduring miniaturization trend of measurement technology it might be possible to integrate these approaches in field research too. For example using cEEGrid electrodes has shown to be a valid way to assess mental workload from EEG data in a less intrusive and more practicable way with less preparation time and discomfort for the subject [70].

But it is not only important to use large numbers of instruments and indicators but to select representative combinations of associated measures that illuminate various aspects of mental workload. Theoretical concepts and measuring instruments need to be tailored to one another, i.e. to determine which aspect of information processing can be captured by which method and indicator. Thus, we have to ask the question how valid a performance measures is which normally is influenced by a lot of dispositional variables. Similarly the question is how valid e.g. an HR measure is that reacts strongly to energetic movement aspects which systematically cover mental aspects of workload.

This is also the prerequisite for the determination of limits and limit crossings as they are described in the Redlines model [18].

For the distant future the task is to make it possible to detect mental workload changes from physiological data in real time during the assembly task. This implies to develop mathematical models and to define meaningful change points in those parameters directly from raw data. First mathematical approaches are already in place [71]. However, researchers have been working on this for 25 years without great success [15]. The core problem here is probably less modeling than measurement.

The usage of machine learning algorithms can probably help to improve measurement from a mathematical point of view and show the best possible solution if the sample size is big enough. However, for a successful integration of machine learning algorithms in ergonomic research a solid theoretical framework is needed and objective measurement techniques are mandatory to understand those algorithms and the solutions they offer.

4.4   Practical Relevance and Conclusion

The practical relevance of these developments lies in two areas of assembly that are currently receiving a lot of attention: Firstly, we need better objective data to determine task load and mental workload when more and more variants have to be assembled. This makes assembly a critical factor that is fundamentally important for any health management. The aim here is to get closer to information processing and no longer be satisfied with derived performance measures or even subjective impressions.

Secondly, we also need evidence on whether informational assistance helps to reduce workload. That would be a first step in deciding who needs which assistance and which support through digital assistance systems. Reliable knowledge is needed for when, how often, and for how long the comfort zone is left, where the limits of adaptation lie, how long the adaptation zone is left or redlines are exceeded and mental overload occurred. These information are necessary to predict how often and under which constellation assistance systems or changes of work organization are required.

In this context it is also important to further develop already existing approaches to cognitive ergonomics. Conventionally, this can happen if the requirements for different resource pools are better distributed [8], i.e. not only visual but also auditory or even tactile channels are used. Traditional information management in the sense of Hollnagel [20] also provides recommendations how to tailor information design to the cognitive skills of assembly workers. Finally, motivation, flow, and commitment can also be promoted as factors that influence attention, concentration, and effort and thus help to avoid crossing redlines in direction of cognitive overload [22].

Funding. The author acknowledge the financial support by the Federal Ministry of Education and Research of Germany in the project Montexas4.0 (FKZ 02L15A261).

References

1. Sivadasan, S., Efstathiou, J., Calinescu, A., Huatuco, L.H.: Advances on measuring the operational complexity of supplier–customer systems. Eur. J. Oper. Res. **171**, 208–226 (2006). https://doi.org/10.1016/j.ejor.2004.08.032

2. MacDuffie, J.P., Sethuraman, K., Fisher, M.L.: Product variety and manufacturing performance: evidence from the international automotive assembly plant study. Manag. Sci. **42**, 350–369 (1996)
3. Frizelle, G., Woodcock, E.: Measuring complexity as an aid to developing operational strategy. Int. J. Oper. Prod. Manag. **15**, 26–39 (1995). https://doi.org/10.1108/01443579510083640
4. Zhu, X., Hu, S.J., Koren, Y., Marin, S.P.: Modeling of manufacturing complexity in mixed-model assembly lines. J. Manuf. Sci. Eng. **130**, 051013 (2008). https://doi.org/10.1115/1.2953076
5. Wickens, C.D., Hollands, J.G., Banbury, S., Parasuraman, R.: Engineering Psychology and Human Performance. Pearson, Boston (2013)
6. Hick, W.E.: On the rate of gain of information. Q. J. Exp. Psychol. **4**, 11–26 (1952). https://doi.org/10.1080/17470215208416600
7. Hancock, P.A., Warm, J.S.: A dynamic model of stress and sustained attention. J. Hum. Perform. Extreme Environ. **7** (1989). https://doi.org/10.7771/2327-2937.1024
8. Wickens, C.D.: Multiple resources and mental workload. Hum. Factors: J. Hum. Factors Ergon. Soc. **50**, 449–455 (2008). https://doi.org/10.1518/001872008X288394
9. Recarte, M.A., Pérez, E., Conchillo, A., Nunes, L.M.: Mental workload and visual impairment: differences between pupil, blink, and subjective rating. Span. J. Psychol. **11**, 374–385 (2008)
10. Chen, F., et al.: Robust Multimodal Cognitive Load Measurement. Springer, Cham (2016). https://doi.org/10.1007/978-3-319-31700-7
11. Miller, G.A.: The magical number seven plus or minus two: some limits on our capacity for processing information. Psychol. Rev. **63**(2), 81–97 (1956)
12. Rasmussen, J.: Skills, rules, and knowledge; signals, signs, and symbols, and other distinctions in human performance models. IEEE Trans. Syst. Man Cybern. **SMC-13**, 257–266 (1983). https://doi.org/10.1109/TSMC.1983.6313160
13. Kahneman, D.: Attention and Effort. Prentice-Hall, Englewood Cliffs (1973)
14. Kahneman, D.: Thinking, Fast and Slow. Penguin Books, London (2012)
15. Endsley, M.R.: Toward a theory of situation awareness in dynamic systems. Hum. Factors: J. Hum. Factors Ergon. Soc. **37**, 32–64 (1995). https://doi.org/10.1518/001872095779049543
16. Thomas, H.R.: Schedule acceleration, work flow, and labor productivity. J. Constr. Eng. Manag. **126**, 261–267 (2000). https://doi.org/10.1061/(ASCE)0733-9364(2000)126:4(261)
17. Longo, L.: Experienced mental workload, perception of usability, their interaction and impact on task performance. PLoS One **13**, e0199661 (2018). https://doi.org/10.1371/journal.pone.0199661
18. Young, M.S., Brookhuis, K.A., Wickens, C.D., Hancock, P.A.: State of science: mental workload in ergonomics. Ergonomics **58**, 1–17 (2015). https://doi.org/10.1080/00140139.2014.956151
19. Wickens, C.D.: Multiple resources and performance prediction. Theor. Issues Ergon. Sci. **3**, 159–177 (2002). https://doi.org/10.1080/14639220210123806
20. Hollnagel, E.: Cognitive ergonomics: it's all in the mind. Ergonomics **40**, 1170–1182 (1997). https://doi.org/10.1080/001401397187685
21. Bornewasser, M., Bläsing, D., Hinrichsen, S.: Informatorische Assistenzsysteme in der manuellen Montage: Ein nützliches Werkzeug zur Reduktion mentaler Beanspruchung? Zeitschrift für Arbeitswissenschaft **72**, 264–275 (2018). https://doi.org/10.1007/s41449-018-0123-x
22. Mattsson, S., Fast-Berglund, Å.: How to support intuition in complex assembly? Proc. CIRP **50**, 624–628 (2016). https://doi.org/10.1016/j.procir.2016.05.014
23. Parasuraman, R., Rizzo, M. (eds.): Neuroergonomics: the Brain at Work. Oxford University Press, New York (2008)
24. Parasuraman, R., Christensen, J., Grafton, S.: Neuroergonomics: the brain in action and at work. NeuroImage. **59**, 1–3 (2012). https://doi.org/10.1016/j.neuroimage.2011.08.011

25. Loeb, M.: Noise and Human Efficiency. Wiley, Chichester (1986)
26. Szalma, J.L., Hancock, P.A.: Noise effects on human performance: a meta-analytic synthesis. Psychol. Bull. **137**, 682–707 (2011). https://doi.org/10.1037/a0023987
27. Poulton, E.C.: Masking, beneficial arousal and adaptation level: a reply to Hartley. Br. J. Psychol. **72**, 109–116 (1981). https://doi.org/10.1111/j.2044-8295.1981.tb02168.x
28. Baddeley, A.D., Hitch, G.: Working memory. In: Psychology of Learning and Motivation, pp. 47–89. Elsevier (1974). https://doi.org/10.1016/S0079-7421(08)60452-1
29. Broadbent, D.E.: The current state of noise research: reply to Poulton. Psychol. Bull. **85**, 1052–1067 (1978). https://doi.org/10.1037/0033-2909.85.5.1052
30. Casali, J., Robinson, G.: Noise in industry: auditory effects, measurement, regulations, and management. In: Karwowski, W., Marras, W. (eds.) Occupational Ergonomics, pp. 16-1–16-32. CRC Press (2003). https://doi.org/10.1201/9780203010457.pt2
31. Hart, S.G.: NASA-task load index (NASA-TLX); 20 years later. Proc. Hum. Factors Ergon. Soc. Ann. Meet. **50**, 904–908 (2006). https://doi.org/10.1177/154193120605000909
32. Ramsay, D.S., Woods, S.C.: Clarifying the roles of homeostasis and allostasis in physiological regulation. Psychol. Rev. **121**, 225–247 (2014). https://doi.org/10.1037/a0035942
33. Shaffer, F., Ginsberg, J.P.: An overview of heart rate variability metrics and norms. Front. Public Health **5** (2017). https://doi.org/10.3389/fpubh.2017.00258
34. Thayer, J.F., Åhs, F., Fredrikson, M., Sollers, J.J., Wager, T.D.: A meta-analysis of heart rate variability and neuroimaging studies: implications for heart rate variability as a marker of stress and health. Neurosci. Biobehav. Rev. **36**, 747–756 (2012). https://doi.org/10.1016/j.neubiorev.2011.11.009
35. Castaldo, R., Montesinos, L., Wan, T.S., Serban, A., Massaro, S., Pecchia, L.: Heart rate variability analysis and performance during a repeated mental workload task. In: Eskola, H., Väisänen, O., Viik, J., Hyttinen, J. (eds.) EMBEC/NBC -2017. IP, vol. 65, pp. 69–72. Springer, Singapore (2018). https://doi.org/10.1007/978-981-10-5122-7_18
36. Sammito, S., Thielmann, B., Seibt, R., Klussmann, A., Weippert, M., Böckelmann, I.: Guideline for the application of heart rate and heart rate variability in occupational medicine and occupational science. ASU Int. **2015** (2015). https://doi.org/10.17147/ASUI.2015-06-09-03
37. Cinaz, B., La Marca, R., Arnrich, B., Tröster, G.: Towards continuous monitoring of mental workload (2012). https://doi.org/10.5167/UZH-66801
38. McCraty, R., Shaffer, F.: Heart rate variability: new perspectives on physiological mechanisms, assessment of self-regulatory capacity, and health risk. Global Adv. Health Med. **4**, 46–61 (2015). https://doi.org/10.7453/gahmj.2014.073
39. Vollmer, M.: A robust, simple and reliable measure of heart rate variability using relative RR intervals. In: 2015 Computing in Cardiology Conference (CinC), pp. 609–612. IEEE, Nice (2015). https://doi.org/10.1109/CIC.2015.7410984
40. Iqbal, S.T., Zheng, X.S., Bailey, B.P.: Task-evoked pupillary response to mental workload in human-computer interaction. In: Extended abstracts of the 2004 conference on Human factors and computing systems - CHI 2004, p. 1477. ACM Press, Vienna (2004). https://doi.org/10.1145/985921.986094
41. Mathôt, S.: Pupillometry: psychology, physiology, and function. J. Cogn. **1** (2018). https://doi.org/10.5334/joc.18
42. Kosch, T., Hassib, M., Buschek, D., Schmidt, A.: Look into my eyes: using pupil dilation to estimate mental workload for task complexity adaptation. In: Extended Abstracts of the 2018 CHI Conference on Human Factors in Computing Systems - CHI 2018, pp. 1–6. ACM Press, Montreal (2018). https://doi.org/10.1145/3170427.3188643
43. Laeng, B., Sirois, S., Gredebäck, G.: Pupillometry: a window to the preconscious? Perspect. Psychol. Sci. **7**, 18–27 (2012). https://doi.org/10.1177/1745691611427305

44. Marquart, G., de Winter, J.: Workload assessment for mental arithmetic tasks using the task-evoked pupillary response. PeerJ Comput. Sci. 1, e16 (2015). https://doi.org/10.7717/peerj-cs.16

45. Marandi, R.Z., Madeleine, P., Omland, Ø., Vuillerme, N., Samani, A.: Eye movement characteristics reflected fatigue development in both young and elderly individuals. Sci. Rep. 8 (2018). https://doi.org/10.1038/s41598-018-31577-1

46. Marquart, G., Cabrall, C., de Winter, J.: Review of eye-related measures of drivers' mental workload. Proc. Manuf. 3, 2854–2861 (2015). https://doi.org/10.1016/j.promfg.2015.07.783

47. Luke, S.G., Darowski, E.S., Gale, S.D.: Predicting eye-movement characteristics across multiple tasks from working memory and executive control. Memory Cogn. 46(5), 826–839 (2018). https://doi.org/10.3758/s13421-018-0798-4

48. Underwood, G., Crundall, D., Chapman, P.: Driving simulator validation with hazard perception. Transp. Res. Part F: Traffic Psychol. Behav. 14, 435–446 (2011). https://doi.org/10.1016/j.trf.2011.04.008

49. Di Nocera, F., Camilli, M., Terenzi, M.: Using the distribution of eye fixations to assess pilots' mental workload. Proc. Hum. Factors Ergon. Soc. Ann. Meet. 50, 63–65 (2006). https://doi.org/10.1177/154193120605000114

50. May, J.G., Kennedy, R.S., Williams, M.C., Dunlap, W.P., Brannan, J.R.: Eye movement indices of mental workload. Acta Physiol. (Oxf) 75, 75–89 (1990). https://doi.org/10.1016/0001-6918(90)90067-P

51. Brookings, J.B., Wilson, G.F., Swain, C.R.: Psychophysiological responses to changes in workload during simulated air traffic control. Biol. Psychol. 42, 361–377 (1996). https://doi.org/10.1016/0301-0511(95)05167-8

52. Chen, S., Epps, J., Ruiz, N., Chen, F.: Eye activity as a measure of human mental effort in HCI. In: Proceedings of the 15th International Conference on Intelligent User Interfaces - IUI 2011, p. 315. ACM Press, Palo Alto (2011). https://doi.org/10.1145/1943403.1943454

53. Yang, Y., McDonald, M., Zheng, P.: Can drivers' eye movements be used to monitor their performance? A case study. IET Intell. Transp. Syst. 6, 444–452 (2012). https://doi.org/10.1049/iet-its.2012.0008

54. Manuel, V., et al.: AdELE: a framework for adaptive e-learning through eye tracking. In: Proceedings of IKNOW 2004. pp. 609–616 (2004)

55. He, X., Wang, L., Gao, X., Chen, Y.: The eye activity measurement of mental workload based on basic flight task. In: IEEE 10th International Conference on Industrial Informatics, pp. 502–507. IEEE, Beijing (2012). https://doi.org/10.1109/INDIN.2012.6301203

56. Zu, T., Hutson, J., Loschky, L.C., Rebello, N.S.: Use of eye-tracking technology to investigate cognitive load theory. In: 2017 Physics Education Research Conference Proceedings, pp. 472–475. American Association of Physics Teachers, Cincinnati (2018). https://doi.org/10.1119/perc.2017.pr.113

57. Di Stasi, L.L., et al.: Saccadic peak velocity sensitivity to variations in mental workload. Aviat. Space Environ. Med. 81, 413–417 (2010). https://doi.org/10.3357/ASEM.2579.2010

58. Fraser, S.A., Dupuy, O., Pouliot, P., Lesage, F., Bherer, L.: Comparable cerebral oxygenation patterns in younger and older adults during dual-task walking with increasing load. Front. Aging Neurosci. 08 (2016). https://doi.org/10.3389/fnagi.2016.00240

59. Vollmer, M.: HRVTool - an open-source matlab toolbox for analyzing heart rate variability. Presented at the 2019 Computing in Cardiology Conference, 30 December 2019 (2019). https://doi.org/10.22489/CinC.2019.032

60. DiDomenico, A., Nussbaum, M.A.: Effects of different physical workload parameters on mental workload and performance. Int. J. Ind. Ergon. 41, 255–260 (2011). https://doi.org/10.1016/j.ergon.2011.01.008

61. Macken, W., Tremblay, S., Alford, D., Jones, D.: Attentional selectivity in short-term memory: similarity of process, not similarity of content, determines disruption. Int. J. Psychol. **34**, 322–327 (1999). https://doi.org/10.1080/002075999399639

62. Sammito, S., Böckelmann, I.: Factors influencing heart rate variability. Int. Cardiovasc. Forum J. **6**, (2016). https://doi.org/10.17987/icfj.v6i0.242

63. Hancock, P.A.: Whither workload? Mapping a path for its future development. In: Longo, L., Leva, M.C. (eds.) H-WORKLOAD 2017. CCIS, vol. 726, pp. 3–17. Springer, Cham (2017). https://doi.org/10.1007/978-3-319-61061-0_1

64. Wickens, C.D.: Mental workload: assessment, prediction and consequences. In: Longo, L., Leva, M.C. (eds.) H-WORKLOAD 2017. CCIS, vol. 726, pp. 18–29. Springer, Cham (2017). https://doi.org/10.1007/978-3-319-61061-0_2

65. Hancock, P.A.: Neuroergonomics: where the cortex hits the concrete. Front. Hum. Neurosci. **13** (2019). https://doi.org/10.3389/fnhum.2019.00115

66. Lobo, J.L., Ser, J.D., De Simone, F., Presta, R., Collina, S., Moravek, Z.: Cognitive workload classification using eye-tracking and EEG data. In: Proceedings of the International Conference on Human-Computer Interaction in Aerospace - HCI-Aero 2016, pp. 1–8. ACM Press, Paris (2016). https://doi.org/10.1145/2950112.2964585

67. Tops, M., Boksem, M.A.S.: Absorbed in the task: personality measures predict engagement during task performance as tracked by error negativity and asymmetrical frontal activity. Cogn. Affect. Behav. Neurosci. **10**, 441–453 (2010). https://doi.org/10.3758/CABN.10.4.441

68. Wascher, E., Getzmann, S., Karthaus, M.: Driver state examination—Treading new paths. Accid. Anal. Prev. **91**, 157–165 (2016). https://doi.org/10.1016/j.aap.2016.02.029

69. Li, L., Liu, Z., Zhu, H., Zhu, L., Huang, Y.: Functional near-infrared spectroscopy in the evaluation of urban rail transit drivers' mental workload under simulated driving conditions. Ergonomics **62**, 406–419 (2019). https://doi.org/10.1080/00140139.2018.1535093

70. Wascher, E., et al.: Evaluating mental load during realistic driving simulations by means of round the ear electrodes. Front. Neurosci. **13** (2019). https://doi.org/10.3389/fnins.2019.00940

71. Hoover, A., Singh, A., Fishel-Brown, S., Muth, E.: Real-time detection of workload changes using heart rate variability. Biomed. Sig. Process. Control **7**, 333–341 (2012). https://doi.org/10.1016/j.bspc.2011.07.004

Human, Organizational Factors and Mental Workload for Tunnel Operators in Emergency Situations

Myrto Konstantinidou[1]([✉]), Kostis Kazaras[1], and Konstantinos Kirytopoulos[2]

[1] NCSR Demokritos, Systems Reliability and Industrial Safety Laboratory, Terma Patriarchou Grigoriou, 15310 Athens, Greece
myrto@ipta.demokritos.gr
[2] NTUA School of Mechanical Engineering, 15770 Athens, Greece

Abstract. Accident rates appear to be slightly lower in tunnels than on open road, however an accident in a tunnel may have much greater impact; especially in the event of fire, where the enclosed space hinders the dissipation of smoke and poses difficulty in ensuring safe escape route of the tunnel users. In order to assess the risk of such events that may cause heavy losses as well as serious damage to the tunnel infrastructure and facilities, it is crucial to focus on the key elements that constitute the road tunnel system. Taking into account that the road tunnel operator's performance is of utmost importance for the overall safety of these critical infrastructures, this paper examines the cognitive overload that may occur during emergency situations. The analysis reveals that the main factors that have a substantial effect on the mental effort of the tunnel operator are the level of information processing, the available time to complete the necessary tasks and the number of switches the operator has to make between different task-sets. In order to improve the operator's performance and reduce the mental workload in this safety critical domain of the transportation system, various performance shaping mechanisms are analyzed in a holistic and systemic perspective.

Keywords: Tunnel operators · Human factors · Organizational factors · Emergency situations · Mental workload · Fuzzy logic · QRA

Abbreviations

CCTV:	Close Circuit Television
CPCs:	Common Performance Conditions
CREAM:	Cognitive Reliability and Error Analysis Method
DG:	Dangerous Goods
LIP:	Level of Information Processing
NCSR:	National Center for Scientific Research
NTUA:	National Technical University of Athens
OECD:	Organization for Economic Co-operation and Development
QRA:	Quantitative Risk Assessment
PIARC:	World Roads Association

L. Longo and M. C. Leva (Eds.): H-WORKLOAD 2020, CCIS 1318, pp. 175–191, 2020.
https://doi.org/10.1007/978-3-030-62302-9_11

PSFs: Performance Shaping Factors
SCADA: Supervisory Control and Data Acquisition
TBRS: Time-Based Resource Sharing

1 Introduction

The tunnels are an important element in supporting an efficient and modern road network. There are several types of tunnels such as road, rail, pedestrian or bicycle tunnels. Due to the significant improvement of technology in the construction sector, in recent years the tunnels have become an economically viable solution for the development of new road networks. As a result, their numbers are growing steadily, as more and more tunnels are being developed, especially in Asian countries (due to economic growth), but also in Europe (as part of infrastructure strengthening), which in turn increases the number of people and the volume of goods transported through these critical infrastructures.

As a rule, tunnels are considered safe road infrastructures. There are many reasons for their increased level of safety, such as the fact that drivers are more careful when passing through them, but also their standard environment. For example, in extreme cases, driving in tunnels is not significantly affected by weather conditions, and there are usually no intersections, walkers, parked vehicles, cyclists or advertising stands, which are some of the most common causes of accidents on open roads. From this point of view, the tunnels are generally considered safer than the open road network in terms of accident rates. Undoubtedly, fire accidents are the greatest threat to road tunnel systems and destructive experiences such as the Mont Blanc fire in France (1999, 39 deaths, Fig. 1) or the fire in Yanhou, China (2014, 31 deaths) are indicative of the severity of such incidents. Indeed, numerous fire accidents in Europe over the past 20 years, resulting in many human and economic losses, have demonstrated safety in these infrastructures as a matter of paramount importance. The accidents in Mont Blanc (1999), Tauren (1999) and St. Gottard (2001) resulted in 58 deaths in just two years and forced the scientific and political community to begin a major review of the safety of these critical road infrastructures [1]. A detailed description of the accidents in Mont Blanc, Tauern and St. Gottard can be found in [2]. A much more extensive list of tunnel accidents is given by [3].

Beard and Cope [1] report: "Death, injuries and damage are due to the operation of the entire tunnel system. Risk assessment (and safety), therefore, should be as systemic as possible. The question is, how do we do that?" The answer to this question is crucial, not only for the process of assessing their overall level of risk (and therefore their safety), but also for determining the appropriate management actions for emergencies that may arise during their operation. Indeed, knowledge and deep understanding of precarious conditions and pathogenesis that may be subject to organizational and administrative/supervisory level, as well as dangerous/threatening events that may occur at the functional level may lead to a more effective response framework in case of emergencies. According to [4] the provision and the effective activation of technical safety measures such as the emergency ventilation systems is of utmost importance for saving lives in tunnels in case of a fire accident. However, before proceeding with the analysis of the

Fig. 1. The Mont Blanc accident (1999).

interaction of the elements that make up the system of road tunnels, it is necessary to record and understand the system of this critical road infrastructure.

The typical technical systems that consist the safety systems of a tunnel are depicted in Fig. 2 and are the following:

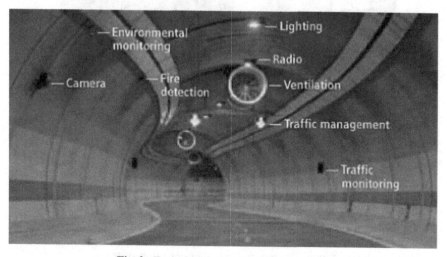

Fig. 2. Typical Technical Systems in a tunnel

- Fire detection system
- Traffic management system (visual signs)
- Traffic monitoring system
- Ventilation (fans)
- Radio system (acoustic messages)
- Lighting and emergency lighting
- Environmental monitoring system
- Cameras

Apart from the technical systems humans are a key element of the tunnel system. Indeed, people are intervening in all phases of an accident, from its inception (often responsible for the occurrence of events) to the controllers of the Control Center and the Emergency Services trying to control the incident. Therefore, in the field of road tunnels, with the term "human" we consider the tunnel user, the tunnel operator and the emergency/rescue team. In our paper we will focus on the tunnel operators as they are key players in the successful management of emergency situations (like fires) and whose mental workload is of utmost importance.

1.1 The Tunnel Operator

The tunnel operators (Fig. 3) play an important role in the safe operation of these critical infrastructures, having mainly the following responsibilities [5]:

Fig. 3. Tunnel operator

- Tracking traffic with cameras, sensors and other detection systems.
- Identifying dangerous situations that can escalate into accidents.
- Launch and implementation of planned action plans in the event of an incident.
- Provide information to the maintenance department regarding a malfunction of the technical equipment that may affect the safety of the tunnel.

- Provide information to tunnel users and emergency services in the event of an accident.
- Records and evaluation of learning from events.

In order to improve tunnel operators' performance, possible solutions can be found in improving aspects like recruitment, procedures and guidelines, training and exercise, task support and control room interface design [4]. A well-defined recruitment policy with appropriate selection criteria would lead to the acquisition of capable operators. Clear procedures and guidelines that follow best practices would minimize the chance of wrong reaction in case of an incident. Operators' training and exercise is also of utmost importance as it is the most reliable way of validating plans and evaluating the readiness of the system. Finally, improvement of task support and control room interface design will foster efficient actions when needed. However, the level of efficiency with regards to these aspects will differentiate among different tunnels. With a structured approach, these aspects that significantly affect the operators' performance, along with their case-specific efficiency level, can be included in the reaction and safety analysis, in the sense that they can be used in order to provide an educated guess of, basically, reaction times [6].

The aim of this paper is to analyze the factors that affect the performance of human operator in critical situations (such as fire) in tunnels and propose an easy-to-use tool based on fuzzy logic in order to take into account them when performing safety and Quantitative Risk Analysis (QRA). The paper is organized as following: after the short introduction the factors that affect tunnel operators' performance are presented in Sect. 2. Then in Sect. 3 a short description of QRA for tunnels is given, while in Sect. 4 the proposed fuzzy system for estimation of mental workload in operators is presented in detail. Section 5 finally concludes the paper.

2   Modeling the Performance of the Tunnel Operator

The operators of the road tunnels play an important role in their safe operation. However, their large contribution to the overall safety of the system is underestimated by current safety analyses, which expresses the variability of the tunnel operator's performance in input data, such as the time to close the tunnel in the event of an emergency and the time of activation of ventilation. It is noteworthy that the values of the parameters introduced are determined by the analyst either on the basis of the relevant literature or by arbitrary estimates. In this sense, the "work environment" and the various performance influencing factors are completely ignored by the analysis. It is important for safety analysis of road tunnels to take into account aspects such as:

1) The available systems for informing the tunnel operator about the operating status (e.g. cameras, CO sensors, smoke sensors, communication systems, alarms, etc.) and the systems used to manage events (e.g. x. ventilation), as it is the availability, reliability and efficiency of such systems that determine the performance of the tunnel operator and not the randomness.

2) Recruitment policy, training and organizational procedures: A Quantitative Risk Assessment (QRA) for road tunnel should look for organizational deficiencies that

may affect the operator's performance. For example, such deficiencies may include a poor recruitment policy that does not ensure the operator's ability to cope with emergencies, inappropriate work environment, inadequate supervision, inappropriate aids, lack of operating manuals, increased mental workload, etc.

2.1 Organizational Aspects

A significant part of the safety of road tunnels is affected by organizational factors and organizational aspects related to: (1) the maintenance and inspection of the tunnel, (2) the procedures for recruitment and training of operators, (3) the preparation of emergency plans, (4) cooperation with the emergency services and (5) the analysis of past events and from learning experiences. All of the above are undeniably critical, and the fact that they are rarely included in the safety analyses can hinder an accurate process of assessing the safety of these critical road infrastructures.

2.2 The Operation of the SCADA System

SCADA systems are widely used in modern road tunnels to monitor and control equipment. SCADA supports effective maintenance and proper response of the tunnel operator in the event of an emergency and usually monitors and controls the following:

- Power supply system
- Tunnel ventilation system
- Fire extinguishing systems
- Fire detection system
- Tunnel communication system
- Traffic management system

In order to ensure its safe operation, SCADA software is usually required to be designed and operated according to internationally recognized standards. It is noted that such a requirement ensures the reliability of the software but not necessarily its safe operation. Therefore, the safety critical issue is in the context that the SCADA may lead the tunnel operator based on its indications.

2.3 Human Reliability and Human Factors

The study of the human factor is extremely important for improving the safety of complex socio-technical systems. Unlike technical subsystems, which can be given a chance of failure, the reason why a human error can occur cannot be studied only through the analysis of a statistical distribution, as humans and equipment compose a single cognitive system (joint cognitive system).

Although various types of human errors are reported in the literature, most of them can be classified into three categories [7]:

- Skips and lapses. Such errors are related to the three stages of human information processing: perception, memory and attention. Skills errors can therefore be related to misunderstanding of messages, indications, objects, memory gaps (failure to retrieve information) and inappropriate habit patterns (routines) which may lead to reduced conscious attention.
- Rule based mistakes, which are related to deviations from rules, practices and established procedures. The two main behaviors that lead to such errors are: improper application of a good rule (unsuccessful application of good practice) and application of an incompatible rule, where a bad rule that is contraindicated is applied in a situation due to incorrect acceptance. These errors of empirical rules may be due to limited attention or due to the human tendency to adopt behaviors and practices that have been successful in the past.
- Knowledge based mistakes, which come from imperfections in the development and updating of mental models as well as from wrong reasoning in decision making. Mental models refer to the representation of the useful parts of a system, as, for example, an employee has stored them in his memory and uses them to perform his job duties. The more appropriate and reliable the mental model is for a particular task, the more correct and effective the execution of the task will be. Mental models therefore guide perception, action, and assist in predicting the course of events, as they describe various features of the system such as its structure, the relationships between its parts, their functions, and the potentially dangerous situations in which they may fall. The complexity of the system, the large volume of information, the narrow time margins, the lack of knowledge and the inability to reassess and adjust goals are some of the reasons that can lead to insufficient mental models and knowledge errors.

In addition to the above three categories of human errors, which refer to unintentional errors, there is also that category of errors which refers to errors that are made intentionally and relate mainly to [8]:

- Routine violations committed to avoid extra effort, faster work or bypassing processes that seem tedious or unnecessary.
- Occasional violations that must be committed by employees, as if the standard procedures are followed it is not possible to complete the work on time.

Every safety study of a system must identify those factors that can increase the mental difficulty of work and affect human performance. The study of the human factor has therefore to do with the study of the technical, labor, personal and organizational factors that can affect human performance and lead to accidents. The above factors are mentioned in the literature as Performance Shaping Factors (PSFs) of human performance and according to the systematic view of safety should be thoroughly examined in the safety study. It should be emphasized that human error can occur in a system even when PSFs are the best possible. When the only reason for the variability of human performance is the existence of random variations, then human behavior is under statistical control, so chances of specific errors can be attributed. The purpose of the safety analysis is to identify those non-random variations in human behavior that can be attributed to specific and explanatory causes (i.e. the corresponding PSFs) and cannot be adequately interpreted based on statistical distribution.

To assess the factors that may contribute to the occurrence of an accident PSFs can be classified into four categories [9]:

- Factors related to the technical and working environment. Factors related to the technical environment and determining human performance have to do with the complexity and frequency of work, the suddenness of events and the available scope for action. Respectively, the natural work environment (noise, temperature and atmospheric conditions, lighting), mental workload and working hours (shifts and rest breaks) significantly affect employee performance.
- Factors related to human-machine interaction (Human Machine Interface). The design of indicators and controls, the content and organization of information in the central control panel display and in the various electronic control screens, optical and audio alarms are all factors that significantly influence the performance of critical process operators.   .
- Factors related to the individual characteristics of the employee. Experience, age, fitness, and personality factors (such as risk-taking) clearly affect human performance.
- Organizational factors: It is the many administrative processes that affect human behavior not only on an individual level, but also on a group level. As modern facilities become more and more complex, with greater interdependencies of individual processes, work tasks often require group efforts and action coordination. It is therefore important to identify those PSFs that affect human behavior at the collective level.

2.4 Mental Workload

Mental workload is directly linked to the modal model working memory. From 1948, Tolman abandoned the idea that a mind simply connects stimuli and response and switched to the idea of a central control room elaborating incoming stimuli into cognitive maps of environment. In 1967, Posner declared that any information processing requires to keep tracking of incoming information and bringing it into contact with stored knowledge. The idea of the working memory has been formed afterwards and is still under great research nowadays [10]. Working memory develops through age, differs between individuals and has neural bases. The Time-Based Resource Sharing (TBRS) model [11] has been developed on the basis of working memory and takes into account the Cognitive Load (CL), as well as the number of distractions and the time during which attention is required to process each one of them. As expected, CL increases with the number of distractors to be processed in a fixed interval.

Regarding the mental workload, it is influenced by three main factors. The first is the time of work, the second is the degree to which mental work is required, and the third is the alternation of tasks and jobs [12]. For example, overtime is a working condition that creates conditions for fatigue and fatigue in employees increases the likelihood of human error, while when working methods are insufficient or the way to deal with problems is not known mental work has high demands on attention and memory. The problem of loss of skills due to the lack of practice that accompanies the excessive introduction of automation must be taken into account by the analysis of the safety of the system.

In any case, it should be noted that if an operator has taken on the role of supervising automation for more than 20 to 30 min without a break, there is a serious risk of losing his vigilance [13]. Other issues that may lead to insufficient control at this level are:

- Personnel handling automatic control systems do not understand or are not aware of possible automation failures.
- Control screens display only a small part of the information and are therefore very difficult for operators to recognize significant variable deviations on other screens.
- The display of the technological system on the control screens does not properly support the mental processes of attention, memory and decision making, thus leading to incorrect mental models.

Since elimination of human errors is extremely difficult to achieve, it is important to have mechanisms to intercept their effects. In this context, the safety study should examine the ways in which operators can recognize and correct their errors (or the effects of their errors) in order to keep the system running satisfactorily.

3 Tunnel Safety and Quantitative Risk Assessment (QRA)

QRA contribution has been an important factor to manage tunnels safety [14]; however, current risk assessment methods are also subject to many limitations. Kazaras et al. [15] present several aspects that might not be handled well by current road tunnel QRAs. Tunnel control center operator's performance variability is one of these factors not appropriately handled by the QRAs, thus forming a major challenge that the analyst must overcome. Tunnel operators play a significant role in the safety and operation of the tunnels [16], particularly in the detection and mitigation of critical events. Their fundamental role in the safe operation of road tunnels includes among others: a) the continuous monitoring of the traffic, b) the detection of critical events and c) the assistance of rescue services during evacuation operations. This considerable contribution to the overall tunnel safety is not adequately handled by current QRAs, which reflect tunnel operator's performance variability in modelling input parameters such as: time to close the tunnel in case of an emergency and time to activate emergency ventilation. The main issue is that such input parameters are usually determined by the analysts either on the basis of the relevant literature or they are just arbitrary estimations. In this sense, the "error-prompting context" and the performance shaping mechanisms are totally neglected from the analysis [15].

QRA models, such as the OECD/PIARC DG-QRA Model (Organization for Economic Co-operation and Development/World Roads Association Dangerous Goods-Quantitative Risk Assessment Model) [17], have been developed to assist decision making by providing objective estimates of risks. Nevertheless, current road tunnel QRAs are also subject to many limitations, as mentioned in [15, 18] and [19]. One of the most striking limitations is the fact that the performance variability of the tunnel operator is not taken into consideration by the analyst, despite the fact that it plays an extremely important role on the development of the accident. The term performance variability refers mainly to the time elapsing between the occurrence of an emergency situation (e.g. fire in tunnel) and the completion of the relevant corrective actions by the operator. Such actions may include time to close the tunnel, time to activate emergency ventilation, time to call the emergency services etc. The research problem raised here is to explore how the human factor can be incorporated in the analysis [15]. If this is done, the next question is whether there would be a significant difference in the risk analysis outcome or not. This paper aims at addressing the problem by exploring the utilization of fuzzy logic in order to provide more sophisticated estimations of the tunnel operator's performance in safety critical situations taking into account his mental workload. In fact, authors are proposing an easy to use fuzzy tool for the estimation of the mental workload of tunnel operator in critical operations. This tool has been developed based on the experience and knowledge of the authors and it constitutes only a suggestion as it does not produce validated results but it is on the orientation of taking into account factors such as the workload in QRAs. The proposed tool is presented in details in the following section.

4 Development of a Fuzzy Logic System for Tunnel Operator Mental Workload

Fuzzy logic addresses qualitative information perfectly as it resembles the way humans make inferences and take decisions. Fuzzy logic starts with the concept of a fuzzy set. A fuzzy set is a set without a crisp, clearly defined boundary [20]. The fundamental difference of fuzzy logic compared to conventional modeling techniques is on the definition of sets. Traditional set theory is based on bivalent logic where a number or object is either a member of a set or it is not. Contrary to that, fuzzy logic allows a number or object to be a member of more than one set and most importantly it introduces the notion of partial membership. According to Zadeh [21] who first introduced fuzzy logic theory, today fuzzy logic is far less controversial than it was in the past. There are over 50,000 papers and 5000 patents that represent a significant metric for its impact. Several fuzzy logic systems have been proposed for human reliability analysis to calculate not only the probability of erroneous actions [22] but also the dependence between human actions [23] as well as the estimation for the response time of the operator in the performance of a critical task [24]. In this paper authors are presenting the development of a fuzzy system for the estimation of tunnel's operator mental workload in critical situations (such as fires). The results of the developed fuzzy model can be further incorporated in QRA studies. The fuzzy system presented here under is a system developed by the authors according to their previous experience in developing such systems according to CREAM methodology [6, 22, 24, 25]. For the time being it has not been tested in real environment nor in simulator. It is in the intention of the authors to validate the system with data coming from VR simulators. This will be possible in the near future after the completion of the project currently the authors are working on. For the development of the fuzzy system the steps followed in previous models have been followed. These are:

1) Selection of the input parameters
2) Development of the fuzzy rules
3) Defuzzification and results

Those steps are described in detail in the following paragraphs.

4.1 Selection of the Input Parameters

In order to develop the fuzzy system for the estimation of the tunnel operator's mental workload in order to be able to activate the safety critical systems relevant methodologies for human reliability analysis such as CREAM methodology [25] have been studied. Taking into account that the tunnel operator's performance is a function of many factors, the selection of the input parameters has been made so that the most important influencing factors have been considered, while maintaining the system at a reasonable size. Moreover, the consideration of working memory (according to what has been mentioned in Sect. 2.4) has been taken into account. Based on the aforementioned criteria, three input parameters have been selected. These parameters are: the Level of Information Processing (LIP), the Available Time and the Number of Switches Between Tasks. The aforementioned criteria have been also mentioned as major performance shaping factors in the road tunnels safety related literature [4]. Finally, a unique output parameter has been defined and that is the 'Tunnel Operator's Mental Workload, meaning the mental workload of the tunnel operator in order to be able to activate the emergency equipment of the tunnel (i.e. emergency ventilation and systems to close safely the tunnel). At this step, in order to better depict the impact of each input parameter, the risk analyst should associate two or more fuzzy sets for the description of the parameter. For the development of the particular fuzzy sets it has been considered that design options and procedures may significantly differ from tunnel to tunnel. However, based on the relative literature [4] it can be deduced that typical characteristics of fuzzy sets for the input and the output parameter can be the following:

Level of Information Processing (LIP) Levels of Processing model, describes memory recall of stimuli as a function of the depth of mental processing. Deeper levels of analysis produce more elaborate, longer-lasting, and stronger memory traces than shallow levels of analysis.

In our case LIP refers to the capacity of the system for deeper levels of analysis by assisting the tunnel operators with relevant signals that would support them in recognizing the critical situation and act accordingly: Three fuzzy sets, namely 'Inadequate', 'Adequate' and 'Supportive' have been defined on the input space of this variable. The LIP is characterized as 'Inadequate' if the system does not produce any visual signs. It is characterized as 'Adequate' if the system produces alarms and visual signs when e.g. there is smoke in the tunnel and finally it is characterized as 'Supportive' if the system produces alarms (visual and sound signals) and also the tunnel is supervised by a Close Circuit Television (CCTV) that enables the visual location of the smoke point.

Available Time according to CREAM [25] pictures the time available to carry out a task: Three fuzzy sets with the names 'Continuously inadequate', 'Temporarily Inadequate' and 'Adequate' were defined for this input variable and range from 1 to 100. The first set 'Continuously inadequate', affects negatively the mental workload, while the third one 'Adequate' affects it positively. The second one 'Temporarily Inadequate' has not a significant effect on operators' mental workload.

Number of Switches Between Tasks as taken from CREAM also enumerates the number of tasks a person is required to pursue or attend to at the same time (i.e. evaluating the effects of actions, sampling new information, assessing multiple goals): Two fuzzy sets were defined for this input parameter, namely 'More than actual capacity' and 'Matching current capacity' The range is again from 1 to 100 and the first set has a negative effect on human mental workload and performance while the second one has a positive effect.

Mental Workload: Three fuzzy sets have been defined for the output variable namely "excessive", "normal" and "optimal". All fuzzy sets refer to the level of tunnel operators' mental workload in emergency situations.

The fuzzy sets defined for each variable are presented in Table 1 and 2 while a graphical representation of the input variable "Level of Information Processing" and the output variable "Mental Workload" are presented in Fig. 4 and 5.

Table 1. Number of fuzzy sets defined for each input and output variable.

	Contextual performance conditions [25]	Number of fuzzy sets
INPUT	Level of Information Processing	3
	Available Time	3
	Number of Switches Between Tasks	2
OUTPUT	Mental Workload	3

Table 2. Input variables and their relevant fuzzy sets

Level of Information Processing (LIP)		Available time		Number of switches between tasks	
Fuzzy set	Input space	Fuzzy set	Input space	Fuzzy set	Input space
Inadequate	$0 < x < 40$	Continuous inadequate	$0 < x < 40$	More than actual capacity	$0 < x < 30$
Adequate	$20 < x < 80$	Temporary inadequate	$20 < x < 80$	Matching current capacity	$0 < x < 100$
Supportive	$60 < x < 100$	Adequate	$60 < x < 100$		

4.2 Development of the Fuzzy Rules

Literature review [4] and expert judgment were the knowledge base for the development of the fuzzy rules. It should be noted that the development of fuzzy rules in every application is based on the knowledge and on the experience of the analyst regarding the specific application. The rules are constructed in simple linguistic terms and can be understood at a common sense level. These rules result in specific and reproducible results (same inputs give same output). The first rule of the system is: "if the LIP is inadequate, the available time is continuously inappropriate and the number of switches is more than the actual capacity of the operator then the tunnel operator's mental workload is excessive". The other rules have been defined accordingly as presented in Table 3.

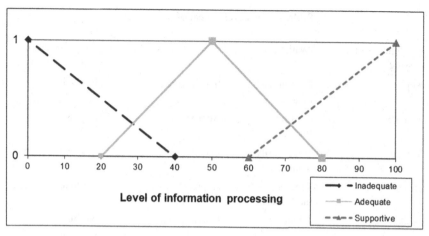

Fig. 4. Fuzzy sets representation for the "Level of Information Processing" input variable

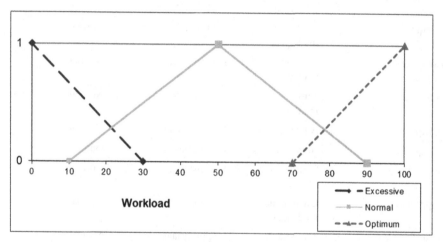

Fig. 5. Fuzzy sets representation for the "Mental Workload" output variable

4.3 Defuzzification and Results

The final step in the development of a fuzzy system is the deffuzification. This is the case when an actual crisp number is needed as an output of the model. In this case the mental workload of the operator does not have to be a crisp number. It can actually be a fuzzy set that would serve as an input to the estimation model of operators' response time.

As mentioned previously, the estimated mental workload affects directly the estimated operators' response time. According to the different estimated levels of mental workload the operators' response time may vary from 60 to 420 s. These different estimates may have a very important effect in the calculated evacuation time for tunnels in

Table 3. The development of fuzzy rules

Level of information processing	Available time	Number of switches	Tunnel operator mental workload
Inadequate	Continuously Inadequate	Inappropriate	Excessive
Inadequate	Continuously Inadequate	Appropriate	Excessive
Inadequate	Temporarily Inadequate	Inappropriate	Excessive
Inadequate	Temporarily Inadequate	Appropriate	Normal
Inadequate	Adequate	Inappropriate	Normal
Inadequate	Adequate	Appropriate	Normal
Adequate	Continuously Inadequate	Inappropriate	Excessive
Adequate	Continuously Inadequate	Appropriate	Normal
Adequate	Temporarily Inadequate	Inappropriate	Normal
Adequate	Temporarily Inadequate	Appropriate	Normal
Adequate	Adequate	Inappropriate	Normal
Adequate	Adequate	Appropriate	Optimum
Supportive	Continuously Inadequate	Inappropriate	Normal
Supportive	Continuously Inadequate	Appropriate	Normal
Supportive	Temporarily Inadequate	Inappropriate	Normal
Supportive	Temporarily Inadequate	Appropriate	Optimum
Supportive	Adequate	Inappropriate	Optimum
Supportive	Adequate	Appropriate	Optimum

case of a fire accident. For this purpose, a specific QRA should be conducted. Respectively the calculated response time with the developed fuzzy system that is described in [6], can be used as an input parameter in a conventional road tunnel QRA model, such as the OECD/PIARC DG-QRA. As far as the OECD/PIARC DG-QRA Model is concerned, the tunnel operator's response time affects two particular input variables of the model. The first one is the 'time taken to activate the emergency ventilation' and the other one is the 'time delay to stop approaching traffic'. Current road tunnel risk analysis methods, such as the OECD/PIARC DG-QRA Model, only request the operator's response time as an input parameter without considering the conditions that may affect this variable. Therefore, the proposed fuzzy logic system can be used in this step of the analysis so as to consider some basic human and organizational aspects. In order to examine the influence of the variance of the tunnel operator's response time on the overall risk level a sensitivity analysis with the OECD/PIARC DG-QRA Model has been conducted (for more details please refer to [6]).

4.4 Limitations and Further Research

It has to be pointed out one more time that the developed system is only a suggestion in order to include mental workload in safety studies and QRAs and has not be tested with experiments in simulators nor with real data from control centers. It is in the intention of the authors though, to collect data from the control rooms in order to validate the estimations. Moreover, in the current project authors are working on, VR experiments will be conducted that will include the parameter of mental workload as an influencing factor to human performance. Therefore, VR stations with different layouts will be designed in order to test tunnel operators' performance in critical situations. The results of these experiments will be published (hopefully) in a following paper.

5 Conclusions

The management of an emergency is a very critical area for mitigating the effects of a catastrophic event. During emergency management many staff members are called upon to assist. They may include technicians, engineers, firefighters, police, nurses along with special working conditions which make cooperation in these missions extremely difficult. Much of the challenge that arises in emergency management of road tunnels concerns the conflicting priorities and the plethora of dilemmas that may arise that are not always easy to identify and prioritize. The complexity that arises in the management of an emergency is due to:

- the number of activities to be performed simultaneously.
- the fact that many times the result of one activity is a prerequisite for starting another.
- the multiple tasks that need to be analyzed and implemented.
- the difficulty of understanding the relationships, the dependences and the interconnections of the parts that are comprised in the affected system.

In addition to the difficulties presented in business planning, great attention must also be paid to the processes of warning and informing the communities and users who are directly affected by the emergency situation on the road infrastructure. The challenges here are: choosing the warning time, designing the variable messages and dealing with gaps in the guidelines by the public. In an emergency, we expect the Tunnel Operator to be in charge of many tasks and responsibilities that need to be implemented at the operational level in a short period of time. Given that emergency management services are becoming increasingly dependent on technology, an information system that could gather information and support the implementation and coordination of the business plan will be an extremely supportive factor for the management of crises. However, in order to design such a system, it is necessary to determine the organizational structure of the group that will be called to manage the emergency and to deeply understand all the precarious conditions and pathogenesis that may be at organizational and administrative level, as well as the threatening events that may occur at the operational level in the road tunnel system.

Acknowledgment. This research has been co-financed by the European Union and Greek national funds through the Operational Program Competitiveness, Entrepreneurship and Innovation, under the call RESEARCH – CREATE – INNOVATE (project code: T1EDK-02374).

References

1. Beard, A.N., Cope, D.: Assessment of the Safety of Tunnels. Commissioned by the European Parliament; Report IP/A/STOA/FWC/2005–28/SC22/29. Published in February 2008 on the European Parliament web-site under the rubric 'Science and Technology Options Assessment' (STOA) (2008)
2. ITA: Updated survey of existing regulations and recognized recommendations (operation and safety of road tunnels) (2011). http://www.ita-aites.org/fileadmin/filemounts/general/pdf/ItaAssociation/ProductAndPublication/Commitees/ITA_COSUF/Updated_Survey_Road_Tunnel_Regulations_August_2011.pdf
3. Carvel, R., Marlair, G.: A history of fire incidents in tunnels. In: Beard, A., Carvel, R. (eds.) The Handbook of Tunnel Fire Safety, pp. 4–41. Thomas Telford, London (2005)
4. PIARC: Human factors and road tunnel safety regarding users. World Road Association, France (2008)
5. Papaioannou, P., Georgiou, G.: Human behaviour in tunnel accidents and incidents: end users, operators and response teams, Report of European Project UPTUN, No. GRD1-2001-40739 (2003)
6. Kirytopoulos, K., Konstandinidou, M., Nivolianitou, Z., Kazaras, K.: Embedding the human factor in road tunnel risk analysis. Process Saf. Environ. Prot. **92**(4), 329–337 (2014)
7. Reason, J.: The Human Contribution: Unsafe Acts, Accidents and Heroic Recoveries. Ashgate, Aldershot (2008)
8. Reason, J.: Human Error. Cambridge University Press, Cambridge (1990)
9. Kontogiannis, T.: Ergonomic approaches to safety management and organization, Greece (2019)
10. Barrouillet, P., Camos, V.: Working Memory: Loss and Reconstruction. Psychology Press, New York (2015)
11. Plancher, G., Barrouillet, P.: On some of the main criticisms of the modal model: reappraisal from a TBRS perspective. Mem. Cogn. **48**, 455–468 (2019). https://doi.org/10.3758/s13421-019-00982-w
12. Neerincx, M.: Cognitive task load design: model, methods and examples. In: Hollnagel, E. (ed.) Handbook of Cognitive Task Design, pp. 283–305. Lawrence Erlbaum Associates, Mahwah (2003)
13. Bainbridge, L: Ironies of automation. In: Rasmussen, J., Duncan, K., Leplat, J. (eds.) New Technology and Human Error, pp. 271–283. Wiley, Hoboken (1987)

14. PIARC: Risk Analysis for Road Tunnels. World Road Association, France (2008)
15. Kazaras, K., Kontogiannis, T., Kirytopoulos, K.: Proactive assessment of breaches of safety constraints and causal organizational breakdowns in complex systems. Saf. Sci. **62**, 233–247 (2013)
16. PIARC: Integrated Approach to Road Tunnel Safety. World Road Association, France (2007)
17. INERIS: Transport of Dangerous goods through road tunnels, Quantitative Risk Assessment Model (v. 3.60 and v. 3.61) Reference Manual. Verneuil-en-Halatte, France (2005)
18. Bjelland, H., Aven, T.: Treatment of uncertainty in risk assessments in the Rogfast road tunnel project. Saf. Sci. **55**, 34–44 (2013)
19. Kazaras, K., Kirytopoulos, K., Rentizelas, A.: Introducing the STAMP method in road tunnel safety assessment. Saf. Sci. **50**, 1806–1817 (2012)
20. Zadeh, L.A.: Fuzzy logic and the calculi of fuzzy rules and fuzzy graphs. Multiple-Valued Logic **1**, 1–38 (1996)
21. Zadeh, L.A.: Is there a need for fuzzy logic? Inf. Sci. **178**(13), 2751–2779 (2008)
22. Konstandinidou, M., Nivolianitou, Z., Kiranoudis, C., Markatos, N.: A fuzzy modeling application of CREAM methodology for human reliability analysis. Reliab. Eng. Syst. Saf. **91**, 706–716 (2006)
23. Zio, E., Baraldi, P., Librizzi, M., Podofillini, L., Dang, V.N.: A fuzzy set-based approach for modeling dependence among human errors. Fuzzy Sets Syst. **160**(13), 1947–1964 (2009)
24. Konstandinidou, M., Nivolianitou, Z., Kiranoudis, C., Markatos, N.: Fuzzy systems for the estimation of operators' response time in critical situations. In: 13th International Symposium on Loss Prevention, Bruges, Belgium, 6–9 June 2010 (2010)
25. Hollnagel, E.: Cognitive Reliability and Error Analysis Method (CREAM). Elsevier Science Ltd., Amsterdam (1998)

Proper Communication Style Promotes Team Workload Redistribution Through Backup Behavior Among Air Traffic Controllers

Han Qiao[1,2], Eh Xiaotian[1,2], and Jingyu Zhang[1,2(✉)]

[1] CAS Key Laboratory of Behavioral Sciences, Institute of Psychology, Beijing, China
zhangjingyu@psych.ac.cn
[2] University of Chinese Academy of Sciences, Beijing, China

Abstract. The volume of air traffic has increased considerably in recent years, and the task load of air traffic controllers (ATCos) is reaching a new high. Both researchers and practitioners are seeking novel methods to prevent overload. Backup behaviors are generally beneficial for team performance in air traffic control (ATC) by redistributing team mental workload. In this paper, we would like to focus on how communication styles influence backup behaviors. Based on interviews, we found controllers tend to use different communication styles when they need backup, but what kind of communication style can promote backup and in what situations such communication style can benefit backup are not clear. We recruited 20 licensed ATCos and carried out two experiments on ATC simulators. We found that presenting emotions and using explanations are in favor of backup, but only when these communication modes fit with the situations.

Keywords: Communication style · Team workload · Backup · Air traffic management

1 Introduction

Air Traffic Control (ATC) is the service provided to airlines, ensuring that aircraft fly safely from one place (departure) to another one (arrival). Air Traffic Controllers (ATCos) are subject to a strong workload in the work process. And the context is made more complicated by the increase in air traffic and personnel shortage. The resulting problem is the occurrence of security incidents and the decline of flight punctuality. With the development of technologies, Decision Support Tools (DST) were introduced to help reduce the ATCo workload by monitoring the environment and presenting effective visual displays to help from the conflict detection process to instruction implementation [1]. A few studies in human factors have devoted to figuring out obstacles of human-machine interaction and cooperation, such as trust [2], which have already been implemented in DST designs in ATC [3].

In the last twenty years, the emphasis has been shifted from ATC to Air Traffic Management (ATM). Consequently, it is underlined the active role of flow management and

© Springer Nature Switzerland AG 2020
L. Longo and M. C. Leva (Eds.): H-WORKLOAD 2020, CCIS 1318, pp. 192–206, 2020.
https://doi.org/10.1007/978-3-030-62302-9_12

traffic structuring, rather than 'simple' conflicts avoidance [4]. Hence, another solution to reduce the workload is promoting the rational redistribution of task load between units, and make more efficient use of existing resources. To better support the cooperation among people who worked together based on computers, one of the avenues researchers have been paying attention to is borrow proper communication modes from human to human cooperation to the field of human cooperation supported by computers. Research in the domain of interface design and AI has been exploring factors influencing the communication of people through computers. For example, Defence Advanced Research Projects Agency (DARPA) initiated an XAI (explainable AI, that means all the AI algorisms are able to explain their rationale) program which identified a number of different explanation user interface design techniques [5]. Moreover, in the computer-based communication process, how to present the information of seeking help is quite essential to gain others' trust about the information or empathy for the situation, which could further impact their decision to offer help or not. However, few studies have explored how specific communication styles of professional ATCos would influence the backup decision in the process of conducting ATC simulated tasks. In this paper, we focus on how the information was presented by asking for help during conducting ATC task would influence the backup decision of the other. The results could provide some insights and evidence for DST designs in ATC.

1.1 Typical Situations in Need of Backup in ATC

Backup behaviors (see Fig. 1) are generally defined as helping other team members to perform their roles [6, 7]. Since it can compensate and redistribute the unbalanced resources at the team level, backup has been considered as one of the essential aspects of teamwork [8]. Studies have found evidence that backup behavior can improve team effectiveness [9, 10]. However, few studies have investigated the backup behavior in Air Traffic Controllers (ATCos) (for an exception study which used survey method, see [11].

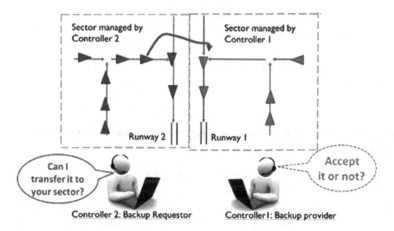

Fig. 1. Backup behavior in ATC

To know in what situations there was a need for help and what the communication styles ATCos used in their daily work in those situations, we did an interview of 5 professional controllers from the North China Air Traffic Management Bureau before our experiments. We found that there were mainly two kinds of situations when controllers request backup from their teammates during the approach control (there were three kinds of ATC, tower, approach, en-route, in this paper, we exclusively focus on approach control). One is when their task load is too high, and the other is the aircraft has close-landing demand. For ATCos, the main factor affecting the task load is the complexity of traffic in the airspace degree. Among the indicators that reflect the complexity of air traffic, the most intuitive one is widely used by researchers is the number of aircraft in the airspace [8, 12, 13]. For approach control, the more aircraft there are, the more operations the controller has to perform, and the higher the load. When the task load is beyond the controller's cognitive resource, he/she is likely to ask the ATCo from the other sector for help. Another factor is a specific situation in the parallel approach; if an aircraft can be transferred to another sector to reduce the distance to the ground, the aircraft is called "an aircraft with a need to land nearby". This is because every airline has its own relatively fixed drop-off area at the airport. For example, an airline's landing area is in the east, and one of its planes will approach from the west, land on the west runway as planned, and take a long taxi to the east landing area. If the aircraft is handed over to the east fifth approach sector corresponding to the east runway during the approach, it can land on the east runway closer to the east landing area, saving the crew and passengers' waiting time. See Fig. 2 for example.

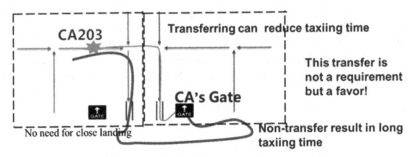

Fig. 2. Close-landing demand of to-be-handover aircraft

1.2 Requirement Does not Guarantee Backup: Communication Style May Influence it

In the independent parallel approach scenario that this study focuses on, one controller has no interaction with the independently operating neighborhood when there is no backup request, so it is not necessary to follow up on the task situation in the neighborhood at any time. Therefore, if the backup requester wishes to emphasize his or her needs, it must be reflected in the communication. Otherwise, the requester may not be aware of it.

1.2.1 Expressing Emotions

Through interviews, we learned that controllers use some special expressions to express special needs in their daily operations. For example, when a plane in its jurisdiction is in urgent need of help, the controller will mark "GQ" on the plane, which means "begging for help"; When the situation becomes more urgent, the note may be changed to "GQQQQQ" to further emphasize the need for backup. Although controllers' non-verbal clues limit emotional information convey [14], according to the Social Information Processing theory [15], text words can also be used to convey information about social relationships (e.g., emotional information). Empirical studies have also found that effective text-based emotional cues, such as exclamation marks, uppercase, repetition, boldface and stressed words (such as negative words), are all effective cues for high-arousal intense emotions [16, 17], these clues also overlap (e.g., repetition) with the clues adopted by the controller in the control practice. Therefore, we proposed Hypothesis 1:

H1: *Expressing urgency based on emotional cues would increase the intention of backup in the ATC task*

1.2.2 Providing Explanations

Academic research has linked the absence of adequate explanations to decreased levels of cooperation [18, 19]. Recent work has found that giving excuses can improve organizational justice and further promote cooperation. Much of this research measured or manipulated the variation in explanation adequacy, defined as the extent to which provided explanations are clear, reasonable, and detailed. In the field of human relations, there is also much literature in line with this point that explanations can benefit conflict management [38]. According to mechanisms underlying explanations and conflict management, conflict is mainly caused by the incompatibility of goals, values, and explanations can provide adequacy, sincerity, and multiplicity to reduce distrust, non-cooperation, complaints, and little attention to shared values [38]. Similarly, in ATC, providing appropriate excuses may offer rationality of the requirement and increase the probability of which the receiver accepts it. Also, through interviews with professional ATCos, we found that for the aircraft to be transferred having close landing demand, the requester often explained this requirement to the receiver: "receiving aircraft CA1000 can be convenient for the crew/passengers". Therefore, we proposed Hypothesis 2:

H2: *Providing explanation about current situations would increase the intention of backup in ATC tasks*

1.3 Consistent with Real Situations is Vital

When the requester emphasizes the need in the communication, the requested controller responds more positively to the actually more urgent request. That is to say, the match between the communication style and the actual situation determines the attitude and response of the controller who receives the communication request. When the communication style matches the actual task situation, the feedback of the backup request is more positive. When the communication style does not match the actual task situation, the backup request is likely to be rejected. This is because, in the ATC communication mode based on radio and computer multimedia communication, the information transmission mainly relies on the text-based clues, the non-verbal clues are relatively limited. In text-based communication, the information receiver is suspicious of the authenticity of the information [20]. After all, the sender can control the emotional cues they use in the text [21]. In face-to-face communication, emotional expression tends to be spontaneous and difficult to control, so it is authentic and credible [22, 23]. Whether the text cue matches the actual situation will affect the response of the message receiver to the message and the sender. The study found that when the original expression of the penny game was matched with the actual situation, the recipients rated the expresser more highly and had a stronger desire for cooperation [24]. Language expression and the actual situation does not match can lead to the receiver having negative emotional reactions [25, 26]. Similarly, the controller, faced with a backup request, will not accept all of the requestor's descriptions in the communication but is likely to perform active validation (the backup requested controller can be informed of the requester's situation). For the task level variable of requester task load (the task load of the requester remains unchanged), the high requester task load level reflects the urgency of the requester in the backup demand, so the corresponding communication style is the expression of the urgency of the requester in the communication. When the requester's communication style matches its task load, the requester's backup intention is higher than that when the requester's communication style was not consistent with his task load, and it is more likely to make a backup decision. Based on the emotional clues provided by the literature and mentioned by the controller in the interview, in combination with the characteristics of Chinese (no uppercase) and the limitation of ATC communication (the font cannot be changed), we chose exclamation points, repetition and emphasis words as the clues to convey the urgency of the backup request, for example, "request to take over the aircraft CA1000!! Request aircraft CA1000!!". Therefore, Hypothesis 3 is proposed:

H3:   *Expressing urgency could increase backup intention only when the task load of the requestor is high in ATC tasks*

For the close-landing demand of the to-be-handover aircraft, when the requestor explains this situation in text, the receiver has the motivation and condition (the requestor can see the aircraft's call sign and the position of its company's gate to figure out if the aircraft really has close landing demand) to check if the description of the requestor is consistent with the authentic situation. If the explanation of the requestor's saying is true, the receiver is more likely to backup to make it convenient for the crew and passengers. Otherwise, the receiver has more chances to refuse the backup. Therefore, we proposed Hypothesis 4:

H4:   *Providing explanation of current situations could increase backup intention only when the explanation is consistent with the reality in ATC tasks*

In sum, this paper focuses on the what kind of communication style influences the controller's backup intention and in what situations such communication style can benefit backup. We designed two within-subjects design on a medium-fidelity ATC simulator and recruited 20 licensed controllers to complete ATC tasks. Experiment 1 tested Hypothesis 1 and Hypothesis 3; Experiment 2 tested Hypothesis 2 and Hypothesis 4.

2   Method

2.1   Participants

Twenty licensed ATCos participated in the experiment, performing simulated parallel approach control tasks, and providing demographic data. All participants were volunteered and participated anonymously and were told that their data would be kept confidential and used only for scientific purposes. They were paid 100 yuan after completing the experiment. Finally, 19 valid data were obtained, ranging from 26 years old to 50 years old ($M = 34.05$, $SD = 6.54$). The minimum experience of them was one year; the maximum was 24 years ($M = 9.50$, $SD = 6.53$).

2.2   Task

ATC-Simulator, a medium-fidelity ATC simulation platform, was used to simulate the parallel runway operation. In each scenario, there were two final approach sectors, each of which contained a runway. All participants managed the sector on the right side of the screen, while the adjacent side on the left side was operated by another hypothetical ATCo performing the pre-planned operation. Each plane had a label showing its call sign, direction, altitude, course, and speed. Participants could use two supportive tools. One is a scale of 10 nm * 20 nm located in the lower-left corner of the screen. The other is a distance/time calculation tool to get the distance and angle from the former point to the latter point and the angle, time, and distance of aircraft flying from the current position to the point at current speed. The participants can see the conditions in both sectors, but they can only issue orders to aircraft in their own sectors.

At the beginning of each scenario, multiple aircraft appeared in both sectors, and the participants were required to constantly monitor and adjust the speed and altitude of the aircraft to fulfill the following three requirements: (1) do not violate the minimum separation standard (5 nautical miles level, 1000 ft vertical); (2) keep the speed of aircraft less than 200 knots and the altitude of aircraft less than 3000 ft when entering the Final; (3) keep a 5 min time interval between aircraft. This period lasted for 40 s, during which the participants were requested to make necessary interventions. After that, a series of dialog boxes popped up to collect the ratings of mental workload using the six items of NASA-TLX [27]. The average score of the six items was used as the mental workload ratings. After answering these questions, the task was frozen, and the participants were told that the colleague of the neighboring sector wanted to hand over an aircraft due to certain reasons, and asked how they would think and respond to this request. In this process, participants could see their current flight situation and the to-be-handed-over aircraft, but they could not make any interventions. Backup willingness was measured by an 8-point item, "How is your willingness to accept the handover aircraft" (One represents very low and eight represents very high). The backup decision was measured by a dichotomous force choice, "Do you accept or reject the aircraft?" (Zero represents rejection and one represents acceptance). When participants completed all the questions, they would enter the next scene. The interface about backup decisions can be seen in Fig. 3.

Fig. 3. The interface of backup decision making

2.3 Variables

2.3.1 Independent Variables

There were two independent variables in experiment 1: the communication style (urgent/not urgent) of the backup requester and the task load of the backup requester. Communication style was manipulated by changing the content representation of the backup request. Under the "urgent" condition, the requester communicates urgency to the requester through verbal cues (exclamation marks, repetition, and emphasis words), consisting of two statements, "urgent request to take over aircraft XXXXXX!!" And "request to take over the aircraft XXXXXX!! Request to take over the aircraft XXXXXX!!". Under the condition of "not urgent", the requester only makes a general statement, "request to take over the aircraft XXXXXX". The requestor's workload was manipulated by the number of aircraft in the requestor sector, with high, medium, and low levels corresponding to 9, 7, and 5 aircraft, respectively. Experiment 2 had two independent variables: the communication style of the backup requester (explain/not explain) and the close landing demand of the aircraft to be transferred. Communication style was manipulated by changing the content representation of the backup request. Under the "explain" condition, the requester would explain the convenience brought by the aircraft to the passengers/crew. There are two expressions, namely "request to take over the aircraft XXXXXX for the convenience of passengers" and "request to take over the aircraft XXXXXX for the convenience of the crew". Under the "not explain" condition, the requester only makes a general statement "request to take over the aircraft XXXXXX".

Close-landing demand was operated by changing the call signs of the aircraft to be transferred (the call signs correspond to the airline).

2.3.2 Controlled Variables

In Experiment 1 and Experiment 2, the task load of the backup requested controller was constant to seven aircraft, which was consistent with the task load of the requester at a medium level.

2.3.3 Measurement Variables

In each task scenario, the subjects reported their backup willingness and backup decision. Work experience was measured by the questionnaire.

2.4 Scene Design

The whole task consisted of 36 scenes. The first 6 were practice scenes, and the remaining 30 were formal scenes. Experiment 1 was 2 (communication style: urgent/not urgent) * 3 (requestor task load: high/medium/low) within-subjects design, and 6 different conditions were generated, each of which contained 3 differentiated scenarios, a total of 18 scenarios. Experiment 2 was 2 (communication style: explain/not explain) * 2 (close-landing demand: with/without) within-subjects design, generating four different conditions, each of which contained three differentiated scenarios, a total of 12 scenarios.

2.5 Experimental Procedure

When the subjects arrived, the experimenter gave them a brief description of the experimental process. They first signed an informed consent form and filled out a demographic questionnaire (gender, age, work experience). The subjects then completed a simulated ATC task on a 22-inch monitor. The task consisted of 6 practice scenarios and 30 formal scenarios, each lasting about an hour. Participants got paid when the task was completed.

3 Results

3.1 Results of Experiment 1

Taking willingness to backup as the dependent variable, we did 2 (communication style: urgent/not urgent) * 3 (requestor's task load: high/medium/low) repeated measurement analysis of variance (work experience as the covariable). The results showed that the main effect of communication style (urgent/not urgent) was significant, $F(1, 17) = 7.642$, $p < .05$, $\eta_p^2 = .310$; the main effect of the requester task load approached significant, $F(2, 34) = 2.567$, $p = .092$, $\eta_p^2 = .131$, the higher the requester's task load, the higher the requested controller's willingness to backup. The interaction between the two was significant (see Fig. 4 for details), $F(2, 34) = 3.904$, $p < .05$, $\eta_p^2 = .187$. When the requester's task load was high, expressing urgency corresponded to a significantly higher backup willingness than not expressing urgency ($p < .05$). When the task load of the requester was medium ($p = .937$) and low ($p = .714$), there was no significant difference whether the requester expressed urgency or not. The post hoc analysis also showed that when the requester expressed urgency, he/she was more likely to get backup under high task load compared with medium task load ($p < .05$) or low task load ($p = .077$), and there was no difference in the likelihood of the requester getting backup under medium task load and low task load ($p = 1.000$); In the case that the requester did not express urgency, there was no difference in the likelihood that the requester would get backup under different levels of task load ($p = 1.000$).

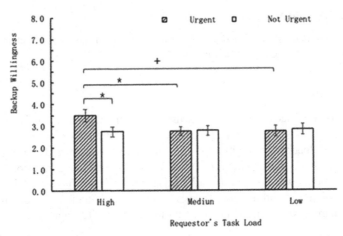

Fig. 4. The joint effect of communication style (expressing urgent or not expressing urgent) and requestor's task load on backup willingness

Taking backup possibility (the proportion of the support decision) as the dependent variable, we did 2 (communication style: urgent/not urgent) * 3 (the requester task load: high/medium/low) repeated measure analysis of variance (working experience as a covariate). Results showed that the main effect of communication style was significant, $F (1, 17) = 7.690$, $p < .05$, $\eta_p^2 = .311$; controllers expressing urgency were significantly more likely to receive backup than those not. The main effect of the requester's task load was significant, $F (2, 34) = 5.444$, $p < .01$, $\eta_p^2 = .243$; When the requester was under high task load, the probability of the requester's backup was higher than that of the requester under medium task load ($p < .01$) and low task load ($p < .01$), but there was no significant difference between the two ($p = 1.000$). No significant interaction (see Fig. 5 for details) was observed, $F (2, 34) = 1.286$, $p = . 289$, $\eta_p^2 = .07$. Whether the requester was under high task load (p = .108), medium task load (p = .537), or low task load ($p = .427$), there was no significant difference between expressing urgency and not expressing urgency. Post hoc test also showed that when the requester expressed urgency, the requester was more likely to get backup when the requester was under high task load than when the requester was under medium task load ($p < .01$) or low task load ($p < .01$), but there was no difference between medium and low task load in the likelihood of the requester getting backup ($p = 1.000$); While the requester did not express urgency, there was no difference in the likelihood of the requester receiving backup under different levels of task load ($p > . 10$).

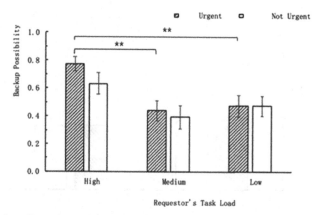

Fig. 5. The joint effect of communication style (expressing urgency or not expressing urgency) and requestor's task load on backup possibility

3.2 Results of Experiment 2

Taking willingness to backup as the dependent variable, we did 2 (communication style: explain or not explain) * 2 (close landing demand: with/without) repeated measure analysis of variance (working experience as a covariate). Results showed that the main effect of communication style (explain/not explain) was not significant, F (1, 17) = 2.220, $p = .155$, $\eta_p^2 = .005$; the main effect of close landing demand was not significant (see Fig. 6 for details), F (1, 17) = .087, $p = .772$, $\eta_p^2 = .116$. The interaction approached significant, F (1, 17) = 3.835, $p = .067$, $\eta_p^2 = .184$. When the aircraft to be handover had close landing demand, the willingness to backup was significantly higher when explaining it than not explaining it, $p < .05$. When there was no close landing demand for the aircraft to be handover, there was no significant difference in the willingness to backup when explaining it or not explaining it, $p = .920$.

Taking the possibility of backup as the dependent variable, we did 2 (communication style: explain or not explain) * 2 (close landing demand: with/without) repeated measure analysis of variance (working experience as a covariate. Results showed that the main effect of communication style was not significant, F (1, 17) = .187, $p = .671$, $\eta_p^2 = .011$; the main effect of close landing demand was not significant, F (1, 17) = .794, $p = .385$, $\eta_p^2 = .045$. The interaction was not significant (see Fig. 7 for details), F (1, 17) = 1.785, $p = .199$, $\eta_p^2 = .095$. Post hoc analysis showed that when the aircraft to be handover had close landing demand, and controllers were more likely to backup in explaining condition than not explaining condition ($p < .05$), but when the aircraft did not have close landing demand, there was no significant difference in explained or not explained the condition, $p = .434$.

4 Discussion

This paper focuses on what kind of communication style promotes backup decision in ATC and in what situations such communication style could benefit backup. The results

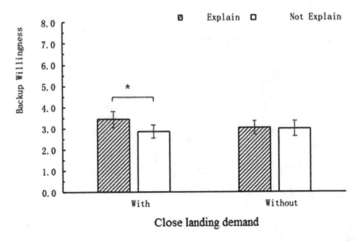

Fig. 6. The joint effect of communication style (explain or not explain) and close-landing demand of the to-be-handover aircraft on backup willingness

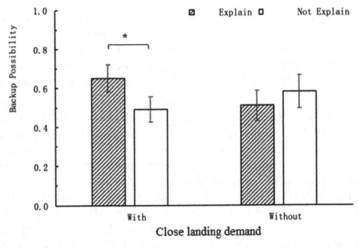

Fig. 7. The joint effect of communication style (explain or not explain) and the close-landing demand of the to-be-handover aircraft on backup possibility

of Experiment 1 showed that when the requester was under high task load, the "urgent" communication style condition had a higher backup intention than the "not urgent" communication style condition. Experiment 2 found that, when the aircraft to be transferred had a close-landing demand, the backup intention caused by "explanation" was higher than that caused by "no explanation". These results reflect a similar pattern, that is, if and only if the requester is really urgent or is about to transfer the aircraft with close-landing demand, the selection of a corresponding communication style (expressing "urgency" or "explaining" close-landing requirements) will positively facilitate the outcome of the backup request. In other words, improving the communication style will promote the occurrence of reasonable team backup, which is of great significance for improving the overall performance. Specifically, when the workload of one ATCo is higher than his/her capacity, it is high time that he need help from the other sector. Although this situation is urgent, there is less possibility of getting help based on physical statement monitoring due to immature technology. ATCos used more direct methods to express urgency such as repetition or adding exclamation marks. However, it is not always consistent between the expression and the real situation. It may be dependent on individual communication style; some prefer to use exaggerated signs, but others just tend to use pure words even for the same urgent situations. Besides, the explanation is quite necessary to receive backup. This result is parallel with the previous proposition in AI design [5].

However, for teamwork, it is not the case that the more backup happens, the better. Too much backup could lead to the inertia of the backup recipients and the neglect of their own tasks by the backup providers [28]. In this way, designers should consider this factor and try to normalize expression with different workload levels (indicated by real-time monitoring of behavioral and physical indexes) to reflect real situations when designing DST for communication between different ATCos. Admittedly, for the ATCo subject to high workload, one of the solutions to reduce his/her workload is seeking help from others. It is unknown whether the help-seeking behavior itself would increase the workload. The help-seeking behavior needs additional resources such as evaluating the possibility of getting help and how long it would take until getting a response from the other ATCo. To make correct decisions, the help-seeker should monitor the state of the other ATCo like how busy he/she is. Moreover, the ATCo should prepare well what to do if the help-seeking fails. Future research could explore this further.

There are also some limitations to this study. In Experiment 2, the close-landing demand of the aircraft to be transferred did not significantly affect the backup willingness and decision-making of the requested aircraft. The close-landing demand of the aircraft is a subtler and more complex factor than the task load (number of aircraft), and for the controller, whether or not to take this requirement into account can be influenced by many factors, such as relevant experience. The controller subjects in Experiment 1 and Experiment 2 came from a medium-sized airport and had little experience in parallel approach, so they were less familiar with the close landing demand of the aircraft than controllers from large airports [29]. Another possible reason is that the sample size is not large enough. The sample size has always been a common difficulty in the field with special industries such as ATC as the research object. In many studies, the sample size is less than 20 people when professional controllers are used as subjects [30–37]. Besides, we used only subjective measures to indicate the backup decision, which may weaken the evidence to some degree. Future research could use more objective indexes to test the replication of this study.

Acknowledgements. This research was supported by the National Key Research and Development Plan [grant number: 2016YFB1001203] and the Natural Scientific Foundation of China [31671148].

References

1. Debernard, S., Guiost, B., Poulain, T., Crevits, I., Annebicque, D., Millot, P.: Integrating human factors in the design of intelligent systems: an example in air traffic control. Int. J. Intell. Syst. Technol. Appl. **7**(2), 205–226 (2009)
2. Nothdurft, F., Heinroth, T., Minker, W.: The impact of explanation dialogues on human-computer trust. In: Kurosu, M. (ed.) HCI 2013. LNCS, vol. 8006, pp. 59–67. Springer, Heidelberg (2013). https://doi.org/10.1007/978-3-642-39265-8_7
3. Hoc, J.M., Debernard, S.: Respective demands of task and function allocation on human-machine cooperation design: a psychological approach. Connection Sci. **14**(4), 283–295 (2002)
4. Pasquini, A., Pozzi, S.: Evaluation of air traffic management procedures—safety assessment in an experimental environment. Reliab. Eng. Syst. Saf. **89**(1), 105–117 (2005)
5. Kistan, T., Gardi, A., Sabatini, R.: Machine learning and cognitive ergonomics in air traffic management: recent developments and considerations for certification. Aerospace **5**(4), 103 (2018)
6. Dickinson, T.L., McIntyre, R.M.: A conceptual framework for teamwork measurement. In: Brannick, M.T., Salas, E., Prince, C. (eds.) Team Performance Assessment and Measurement: Theory, Methods, and Applications, pp. 19–43. Erlbaum, Mahwah (1997)
7. Morgan Jr., B.B., Glickman, A.S., Woodard, E.A., Blaiwes, A., Salas, E.: Measurement of team behaviors in a Navy environment (NTSC Report No. 86-014). Naval Training System Center, Orlando (1986)
8. McIntyre, R.M., Salas, E.: Measuring and managing for team performance: lessons from complex environments. In: Guzzo, R.A., Salas, E. (eds.) Team Effectiveness and Decision Making in Organizations, pp. 9–45. Jossey-Bass, San Francisco (1995)
9. De Dreu, C.K.W.: Cooperative outcome interdependence, task reflexivity, and team effectiveness: a motivated information processing perspective. J. Appl. Psychol. **92**(3), 628–638 (2007)
10. Neuman, G.A., Wright, J.: Team effectiveness: beyond skills and cognitive ability. J. Appl. Psychol. **84**(3), 376–389 (1999)
11. Smith-Jentsch, K.A., Kraiger, K., Cannon-Bowers, J.A., Salas, E.: Do familiar teammates request and accept more backup? transactive memory in air traffic control. Hum. Factors **51**(2), 181–192 (2009)
12. Laudeman, I.V., Shelden, S. G., Branstrom, R., Brasil, C.L.: Dynamic density: an air traffic management metric. No. NASA-TM-1988-11226. Moffet Field, CA: NASA Ames Research Center (1998)
13. Gianazza, D.: Forecasting workload and airspace configuration with neural networks and tree search methods. Artif. Intell. **174**(7–8), 530–549 (2010)
14. Daft, R.L., Lengel, R.H.: Organizational information requirements, media richness, and structural design. Manage. Sci. **32**(5), 554–571 (1986)
15. Walther, J.B.: Interpersonal effects in computer-meditated interaction: a relational perspective. Commun. Res. **19**(1), 52–91 (1992)
16. Hancock, J.T., Landrigan, C., Silver, C.: Expressing emotion in text-based communication. In: Proceedings of the CHI 2007 Conference on Human Factors in Computing Systems, pp. 929–932. Association for Computing Machinery Press, New York (2007)
17. Byron, K., Baldridge, D.: Toward an understanding of nonverbal cues and emotion in email communication. In: Weaver, K.M. (ed.), Best paper proceedings of the Academy of Management annual meeting, Organizational Communication and Information Systems Division, pp. B1-B6. Pace University, Briarcliff Manor (2005)

18. Colquitt, J.A.: On the dimensionality of organizational justice: a construct validation of a measure. J. Appl. Psychol. **8**, 386–400 (2001)
19. Konovsky, M.A., Cropanzano, R.: Perceived fairness of employee drug testing as a predictor of employee attitudes and job performance. J. Appl. Psychol. **76**, 698–707 (1991)
20. Cheshin, A., Rafaeli, A., Bos, N.: Anger, and happiness in virtual teams: emotional influences of text and behavior on others' affect in the absence of non-verbal cues. Organ. Behav. Hum. Decis. Process. **116**(1), 2–16 (2011)
21. Byron, K.: Carrying too heavy a load? the communication and miscommunication of emotion by email. Acad. Manage. Rev. **33**(2), 309–327 (2008)
22. Ekman, P.: Telling Lies: Clues to Deceit in the Marketplace, Politics, and Marriage. W.W. Norton Press, New York (2009)
23. Ekman, P., Friesen, W.V., Scherer, K.: Body movement and voice pitch in deceptive interaction. Semiotica **16**, 23–27 (1976)
24. Stouten, J., Cremer, D.D.: Seeing is believing: the effects of facial expressions of emotion and verbal communication in social dilemmas. J. Behav. Deci. Making **23**(3), 271–287 (2010)
25. Newcombe, M.J., Ashkanasy, N.M.: The role of affect and affective congruence in perceptions of leaders: an experimental study. Leadersh. Quart. **13**(5), 601–614 (2002)
26. Cheshin, A., Rafaeli, A., Bos, N.: Anger, and happiness in virtual teams: emotional influences of text and behavior on others' affect in the absence of non-verbal cues. Organ. Behav. Hum. Decis. Process. **116**(1), 2–16 (2011)
27. Hart, S.G., Staveland, L.E.: Development of NASA-TLX (Task Load Index): results of empirical and theoretical research. In: Hancock, P.A., Meshkati, N. (eds.) Human Mental Workload, pp. 139–183. North Holland Press, Amsterdam (1988)
28. Barnes, C.M., Hollenbeck, J.R., Wagner, D.T., Derue, D.S., Nahrgang, J.D., Schwind, K.M.: Harmful help: the costs of backing-up behavior in teams. J. Appl. Psychol. **93**(3), 529–539 (2008)
29. Yu, S., Zhang, J., E, X.: How task level factors influence controllers' backup behavior: the mediating role of perceived legitimacy and anticipated workload. In: Harris, D. (ed.) HCII 2019. LNCS (LNAI), vol. 11571, pp. 150–164. Springer, Cham (2019). https://doi.org/10.1007/978-3-030-22507-0_12
30. Metzger, U., Parasuraman, R.: The role of the air traffic controller in future air traffic management: an empirical study of active control versus passive monitoring. Hum. Factors **43**(4), 519–528 (2001)
31. Boag, C., Neal, A., Loft, S., Halford, G.S.: An analysis of relational complexity in an air traffic control conflict detection task. Ergonomics **49**(14), 1508–1526 (2006)
32. Rantanen, E., Nunes, A.: Hierarchical conflict detection in air traffic control. Int. J. Aviat. Psychol. **15**(4), 339–362 (2005)
33. Sperandio, J.C.: Variation of operator's strategies and regulating effects on workload. Ergonomics **14**(5), 571–577 (1971)
34. Fothergill, S., Neal, A.: The effect of workload on conflict decision making strategies in air traffic control. Hum. Factors Ergon. Soc. Annu. Meet. Proc. **1**(1), 39–43 (2008)
35. Vuckovic, A., Kwantes, P., Neal, A.: A dynamic model of decision making in ATC: adaptation of criterion across angle and time. Hum. Factors Ergon. Soc. Annu. Meet. Proc. **55**(1), 330–334 (2011)
36. Stankovic, S., Loft, S., Rantanen, E., Ponomarenko, N.: Individual differences in the effect of vertical separation on conflict detection in air traffic control. Int. J. Aviat. Psychol. **21**(4), 325–342 (2011)

37. Zhang, J., Du, F.: Relational complexity network and air traffic controllers' workload and performance. In: Harris, D. (ed.) EPCE 2015. LNCS (LNAI), vol. 9174, pp. 513–522. Springer, Cham (2015). https://doi.org/10.1007/978-3-319-20373-7_49
38. Sitkin, S.B., Bies, R.J.: Social accounts in conflict situations: using explanations to manage conflict. Hum. Relat. **46**(3), 349370 (1993). https://doi.org/10.1177/001872679304600303

Task Demand Transition Peak Point Effects on Mental Workload Measures Divergence

Enrique Muñoz-de-Escalona[1(✉)], José Juan Cañas[1], Chiara Leva[2], and Luca Longo[3]

[1] Mind, Brain and Behaviour Research Centre, University of Granada, Granada, Spain
{enriquemef,delagado}@ugr.es
[2] School of Environmental Health, Technological University Dublin, Kevin Street, Dublin 2, Dublin, Republic of Ireland
mariachiara.leva@tudublin.ie
[3] School of Computer Science, Technological University Dublin, Dublin, Republic of Ireland
luca.longo@tudublin.ie

Abstract. The capacity to assess and manage mental workload is becoming more and more relevant in the current work environments as it helps to prevent work related accidents and achieve better efficiency and productivity. Mental workload is often measured indirectly by inferring its effects on performance, mental states, and psychophysiological indexes. Since these three main axes should reflect changes in task demands, convergence between measures is expected, however research has found that this convergence is not to be taken for granted as it is not often present. This study aims to explore how the task demand transition peak point may affect in mental workload divergence between measures during task-load changes: some measures might be more sensitive to abrupt changes in task demand than others and this could also be mediated by the task-load baseline. This was tested by manipulating task-load transitions and the point at which the change in the task load magnitude reaches its highest relative peak over time during a monitoring experiment, while psychophysiological (pupil size) and subjective perceptions were collected as indicators of subjects' workload alongside objective indicators of task performance from the simulation. The results showed that performance measure proved to be sensitive to abrupt increases in task demand in every condition whereas our physiological measure was only sensitive to a sudden increase in task-load during low mental workload baseline circumstances. Furthermore, contrary to what expected, subjective ratings of mental workload did not react to abrupt transitions in task-load in every condition but only to an absolute measure of the overall level of task demand.

Keywords: Mental workload · Workload measures · Convergence · Divergence · Dissociations · Insensitivities · Task demand transitions · Rates of change · Peak point

1 Introduction

Mental workload has been the subject of extensive research in many fields over the last several decades. Despite multiple efforts were made for reaching a consensus regarding

© Springer Nature Switzerland AG 2020
L. Longo and M. C. Leva (Eds.): H-WORKLOAD 2020, CCIS 1318, pp. 207–226, 2020.
https://doi.org/10.1007/978-3-030-62302-9_13

its definition, to date there is no solid agreement on defining a commonly accepted construct [1–4]. However, despite the difficulties in defining mental workload, the need to assess it in many safety critical workplaces is increasing, particularly in the workplace, for interaction [45, 46] and instructional design [47]. Mental workload is closely linked to mental fatigue and performance and so, with human error and work-related accidents [5–10]. On the one hand, a high mental workload situation sustained over time, which is defined as mental overload, increases the chance of making mistakes at work. But also, on the other hand, a very low mental workload can lead to the dangerous and unwanted phenomena defined as "out of the loop" [11, 12]. Hence, assessing mental workload could not only help to predict overload and underload situations and to prevent incidents and fatalities, but also having a good management of mental workload levels would also be advantageous to increase productivity at work [13–15]. There exist several different methodologies for measuring mental workload, but literature research has shown that not all those methodologies do necessarily coincide in providing the same results [16–20]. Empirical research has shown that divergences between measurements exist and, for that reason, the potential causes of these divergences has been the subject of intensive research in recent years [21–26]. There are several different explanations for this lack of convergence between measures. One of these explanations could be the differential effects of "task demand transitions" on mental workload measurements. While a person is performing a task, task demand may increase or decrease. This change in the magnitude of task demand over the duration of a task is what we call a "task demand transition", which could be smooth or abrupt.

The aim of this paper is to shed some light about mental workload divergences that might be produced by task demand transitions. Particularly, we want to explore how the task demand transition peak point (the moment in which the abrupt increase in task demand occurs) may affect in mental workload divergence between measures during task-load changes. In other words, it may be possible that task demand transition peak point may affect more and in different ways some mental workload measures than others so that it would facilitate the emergence of divergence between them. In Sect. 2 we will briefly review the most important explanations that have been suggested for this lack of convergence between measures, as well as certain key concepts about measuring mental workload. Then, in Sect. 3 we present the design and methodology used to undertake our study. In Sect. 4 we describe the results obtained from the data collection campaign, while in Sect. 5 we discuss our findings and suggest possible future directions in this research area. Finally, in Sect. 6 we provide an overview of the key conclusions derived from the study, as well as its major implications.

2   Related Work

2.1   Assessing Mental Workload

Assessing mental workload is not a simple task since it is not something that can be measured directly, and it has to be inferred from its different effects on behavior, mental states, and psychophysiological indexes. Mental workload has three well-established components, two of which are observable (performance and physiological) and one that is a non-observable subjective feeling of workload. In this sense there are three different categories of measures which are commonly used to assess mental workload:

1. **Performance measures:** this category is composed of primary task measures (n° of errors, reaction time) and secondary task measures (choice reaction-time tasks, time estimation, memory-search tasks). The goal is to measure objective task performance indexes with a view to assess the quantity and the quality of performed tasks.
2. **Physiological measures:** it includes physiological responses to mental activation (pupil diameter, heart rate variability (HRV), electroencephalogram (EEG)). The aim is to collect objective physiological data, which reacts to mental workload.
3. **Subjective measures:** comprises self-reported measures (NASA-TLX) which aim is to collect easy and low-cost subjective individual-related mental workload data.

Each different category has its own advantages and disadvantages. Performance measures, for example, have a high diagnostic value, which allows to investigate which cognitive process is mainly involved in performing certain tasks; but it comes with the disadvantage of a high level of intrusiveness, as operators have to perform simultaneous tasks and that can be dangerous in certain contexts [27]. Physiological measures, on the other hand, are very sensitive to mental workload phasic changes and have high internal validity but are also highly intrusive and require special equipment and specific expert knowledge [28]. Finally, subjective self-reporting measures are very low cost and easy to implement but are vulnerable to cognitive biases [29]. In general it is safe to say that the ideal way of assessing mental workload would involve a triangulation of at least one of each different type of measures, so as to obtain a performance measure, a physiological measure and a subjective measure in such a way that each would contribute extra information and reinforce the overall evaluation. In line with this assumption, we could expect that each different measure of mental workload should converge, but the literature shows multiple examples of situation where this assumption could not be verified [16–19, 21, 23].

2.2 Convergences and Divergences Between Mental Workload Measurements

Far from what could be expected, the different indexes of mental workload, gathered by using different categories of measures, do not necessarily coincide in providing the same results. Literature research has increasingly shown studies that offer evidence about this lack of correlation among measurements (divergences) [16–19, 21, 23], which could be due to the occurrence of dissociations and/or insensitivities in mental workload measures. Associations occur when mental workload measures tracks task-load change, dissociations take place when a mental workload reflection contradict a change in task demands whereas insensitivities occurs when that workload reflection does not change with a change in task demands. Research has shown that this lack of convergence among different measurements due to dissociations or insensitivities do not only occurs between the three different categories of methodologies, but also between different particular methods within each category. For example, numerous studies have shown proof of divergences among well-established physiological measures which are supposed to reflect the level mental workload experienced and its changes in the same way [20, 21]. For example, pupil size and blink rate have been proved to be ocular parameters sensitive to task demand changes, but sometimes both can be affected by certain non-workload factors (such as brightness and relative humidity), that would impact on the emergence of dissociations among measures. One can only wonder why do we find divergences between measurements that are supposed to be reflecting the same construct? Researchers have identified multiple possible causes about this phenomenon, which can be related to a lack of specificity or to a lack of diagnosticity. The former would explain divergences by the existence of non-workload factors affecting measurements, while the latter might point to the fact that different measures could be reflecting different aspects of mental workload. Mental workload is a multidimensional construct and these lack of specificity and diagnosticity would be consistent with multi-resources theories [30]. Hancock (2017) has offered many reasons about the occurrence of dissociations and insensitivities among mental workload measures, which he defined as the AID's of workload [22]. Timescale considered between measures is one of the possible causes: it may be possible that some measures reflect task demand changes within seconds while other may show a longer latency. Muñoz-de-Escalona & Cañas (2018) found that divergences among measures are more susceptible to appear after an abrupt change in task demands occurs, due to the emergence of higher latency differences between measurements. They found that the subjective measure of mental workload reacted sooner than pupil size (physiological response) to a high peak in task demands. In other words, divergences between subjective and physiological measures were higher because subjective measure may have reached its maximum value before the physiological measures did [23].

2.3 Sensitivity to Rates of Change and Peak Point During Task Demand Transitions

Hancock (2017) points out in his study that another possible factor underpinning dissociations and insensitivities among assessment methods is the differential sensitivity of mental workload measures to rates of change during task-load transitions [22]. In other words, some measures might be more sensitive to change in task demand than others, so that when abrupt shifts in task-load are experienced, divergences will also appear across different measures due to their different sensitivities towards the rate of change. That is precisely what was found in a previous study showing higher divergences between mental workload measures during variable rate of change conditions than during lineal rate of change conditions [23]. According to the study by Muñoz-de-Escalona & Cañas (2019) [23] dissociations in performance and pupil size (physiological measure) appeared after an abrupt change in task demands during increasing task-load conditions, while the subjective measure was not affected by the rate of change in the task-load but rather by the absolute level of task demand experienced. These interesting results revealed that divergences between measures might be higher during increasing variable rate of change conditions. However, this study did not addressed the possible effects that the task demand transition peak point may have in the emergence of divergence between mental workload measures: it may be possible that some measures are more sensitive to abrupt changes in task-load levels than others and, furthermore, it may also be possible that some measures might be more sensitive to task-load change under certain circumstances. Therefore, this motivated the purpose of this study, to explore the possible effects that the peak point during task demand transitions may have in mental workload divergences between measures.

3 Design and Methodology

The hypothesis of this research is that the effects on mental workload measures will be different depending on when the high shift in task-load arises. When task demands are low, there are many resources available to be used so, if there is a sudden shift in task-load, the amount of mental resources mobilized to cope with the task will be higher than if we depart from a higher task demand situation, since in this latter case, human resources are limited. Thus, in more detail, we hypothesized that we will find higher divergences between mental workload measurements when the high shift in task-load arises in a low task demand situation because physiological measures should react sooner than performance and subjective measures, as they reflect that extra activation needed to cope with the task. In this study we manipulated 2 variables: (1) task-load change and (2) task-load change peak point. This manipulation was tested in a task-battery experiment which participants performed for 20 min to collect (a) perceived mental workload, (b) task performance and (c) pupil size as our three types of complementary mental workload primary measures.

3.1 Materials and Instruments

The MATB-II Software. Measurements of task performance were collected through the use of the second version of the Multi-Attribute Task Battery (MATB-II), a computer program designed to evaluate operator performance and workload through means of different tasks similar to those carried out by flight crews, with a user-friendly interface as to allow non-pilot participants to utilize it [31]. MATB-II comes with default event files, which can easily be altered to adapt to the needs or objectives of an experiment. The program records events presented to participants, as well as participants' responses. The MATB-II contains the following four tasks: the system monitoring task (SYSMON), the tracking task (TRACK), the communications task (COMM), and the resource management task (RESMAN) (see Fig. 1).

1) The SYSMON task is divided into two sub-tasks: lights and scales. For the lights sub-task, participants are required to respond as fast as possible to a green light that turns off and a red light that turns on, and to turn them back on and off, respectively. For the scale sub-task, participants are required to detect when the lights on four moving scales deviate from their normal position and respond accordingly by clicking on the deviated scale.
2) In the TRACK task, during manual mode, participants are required to keep a circular target in the center of an inner box displayed on the program by using a joystick with their left hand (the dominant hand was needed for the use of the mouse). During automatic mode, the circular target will remain in the inner box by itself.
3) In the COMM task, an audio message is played with a specific call sign and the participant is required to respond by selecting the appropriate radio and adjusting

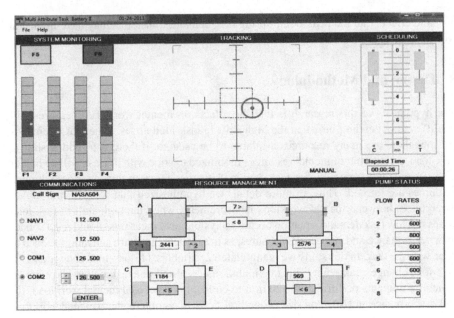

Fig. 1. MATB-II task display. Taken from https://matb.larc.nasa.gov/

for the correct frequency, but only if the call sign matches their own (call sign: "NASA504"). No response is required of the participant for messages from other call signs.

4) In the RESMAN task, participants are required to maintain the level of fuel in tanks A and B, within ±500 units of the initial condition of 2500 units each. In order to maintain this objective, participants must transfer fuel from supply tanks to A and B or transfer fuel between the two tanks.

The Use of Tobii T120 Eyetracker. Pupil diameter measurements were obtained using an infrared-based eye tracker system, the Tobii T120 model marketed by Tobii Video System (see Fig. 2). This system is characterized by its high sampling frequency (120 Hz). This equipment is completely non-intrusive, has no visible eye movement monitoring system, and provides high precision and an excellent head compensatory movement mechanism, which ensures high-quality data collection. In addition, a calibration procedure is completed within seconds, and the freedom of movement it offers participants allows them to act naturally in front of the screen, as though it were an ordinary computer display. Thus, the equipment allows for natural conditions in which to measure eye-tracking data [32].

The Use of the Instantaneous Self-assessment Scale. We employed an easy and intuitive instant subjective workload scale called instantaneous self-assessment (ISA), which provides momentary subjective ratings of perceived mental workload during task performance (see Fig. 3). ISA has been used extensively in numerous domains, including during ATC tasks. Participants write down how much mental workload they currently

Fig. 2. Tobii T120 Eyetracker system

experience on a scale ranging from 1 (no mental workload) to 9 (maximum mental workload), presented from left to right in ascending order of mental workload experienced. This broad range would help us to obtain a good granularity of collected data. Participants were taught to use the scale just before beginning the experimental stage. While the method is relatively obtrusive, it was considered the least intrusive of the available online workload assessment techniques [33, 34].

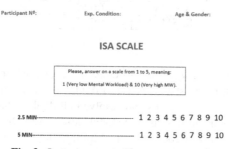

Fig. 3. Instantaneous self-assessment scale

3.2 Participants

The experiment was run with 45 undergraduate and postgraduate students from two Irish universities. Participants' ages ranged from 20 to 42, with an average of 23.4 and a standard deviation of 4.75. A total of 26 women and 19 men participated. Participation was voluntary and the participants were recruited by providing a seminar about mental workload and its measurements during normal lessons related to Human factors topics. The requirements for participation included (1) not being familiar with the MATB-II program, (2) English as a native language, and (3) visual acuity or correction of visual impairment with contact lenses, as glasses impair the utilized eye-tracking device from collecting data. The voluntary participation was rewarded with extra credit.

3.3 Procedure

Participants went through an experimental session consisting of two phases:

1. **Training stage:** a 30 min training session allowed each participant to familiarize themselves with the program so that they could carry out the tasks securely during the data collection stage. The procedure was conducted as follows: upon entering the lab and after filling out the informed consent form, the participant was asked to read the MATB-II instruction manual. The researcher then sat down with the participant to allow for questions and resolve any doubts on how to use the program. Afterward, on a computer monitor, participants were presented with each MATB-II task separately and were first given a demonstration as to how to execute the task. Following this they were given some time (3 min or more if needed) to try and perform the task themselves. Participants would then evaluate task difficulty on a scale ranging from 1 (very easy) to 9 (very difficult). The average difficulties evaluated by the participants for each task of the MATB-II are reported in Table 1.

Table 1. Task Difficulty Level Average Assessed by Participants.

Task	Difficulty Average
TRACK	4.16 (σ1.69)
SYSMON	2.71 (σ1.39)
COMM	3.33 (σ1.97)
RESMAN	5.11 (σ1.95)

The participants were always free to consult the manual and ask the researcher questions during the training stage in case of doubts or uncertainties. Once each participant had completed all four tasks and resolved all doubts, they were ready for the data collection stage, which followed immediately afterwards. During the training stage, participants could work in one room equipped for training with the MATB-II software, and no performance shaping factors was recorded in relation to the environmental conditions as we ensure to have similar average luminosity and comfort for temperature and seating arrangements.

2. **Data collection stage:** the data collection stage lasted a period of 20 min for each participant and it was divided into four intervals of 5 min. In each interval participants had to perform one combination of tasks according to the assigned experimental conditions, while task performance, perceived mental workload, and pupil diameter were recorded. The participants were instructed to fill in the ISA scale every 2,5 min when a scheduled alarm sounded. Prior to the start of the MATB-II tasks, the eye-tracker system was calibrated for each participant while he or she was instructed to keep head and body movements to a minimum. During the data collection stage ensuring conformity with standard room conditions was essential to avoid external performance shaping factors to interfere with the results of the experiment. Thus, the testing rooms were temperature controlled to 21 °C, and lighting conditions (the

main extraneous variable in pupil diameter measurement) were kept constant with artificial lighting; there was no natural light in the rooms. Moreover, participants always sat in the same place, a comfortable chair spaced 60 cm from the eye-tracker system.

This study was carried out in accordance with the recommendations of the local ethical guidelines of the committee of the University of Granada institution: Comité de Ética de Investigación Humana. The protocol was approved by the Comité de Ética de Investigación Humana under the code: 779/CEIH/2019. All subjects gave written informed consent in accordance with the Declaration of Helsinki.

3.4 Variables

Independent Variables - We manipulated 2 independent variables:

1. **Task-load change:** this variable describes how task demand changes over time. Experimental conditions followed an increasing task demand pattern with a variable rate of change over time.
2. **Task-load rate of change peak point:** this variable describes when the participants experienced the most abrupt change in task demands.

First, we manipulated task-load by modifying the number and the combination of MATB-II active tasks that participants had to perform over time. We created six combination of tasks. Each combination of task made up a condition of increasing difficulty. Table 2 reports the task combinations considered. Task-load increases as the number of active task increases, but also as the relative difficulty of active tasks increases as well. Therefore, since task-load in each individual task was different, the overall task-load in each task combination allowed us to manipulate the task-load change peak point during the experimental session. For example, task combinations 2 and 3 both include 2 tasks, but task-load is higher in task combination 3 as the RESMAN task is more difficult than SYSMON task. Similarly, this is also true for task combinations 4 and 5 (both includes three tasks but task combination 5 is more difficult because it included the RESMAN tasks instead of the COMM task).

Table 2. Possible Sets of Task Combinations.

Task Combination	MATB-II Active tasks
1	TRACK
2	TRACK + SYSMON
3	TRACK + RESMAN
4	TRACK + SYSMON + COMM
5	TRACK + SYSMON + RESMAN
6	TRACK + SYSMON + COMM + RESSMAN

Then, to increase the task-load along the four intervals of five minutes during the experimental session, we created three experimental conditions each one corresponding to a different choice for the temporary moment in which the magnitude of task-load changes reaching its highest relative peak over time:

- in combination (1) the steepest change in task load is given during early stages of the overall task-load condition
- in combination (2) the steepest change in task load is given during medium stages of the overall task-load condition
- in combination (3) the steepest change in task load is given during the later stages of the overall task-load condition.

The three experimental conditions were:

1. **Condition 1: Highest rate of change during early stages of overall task load.**
   Task-load increased every 5 min, with a variable rate of change. Participants had to perform the following task combination: 1, 3, 5, and 6. The initial task-load in the first interval (task combination 1) was followed by an abrupt increase in the second interval (task combination 3) and from there, there was a decrease in the rate of change from task combination 3 moving unto 5 and then 6.
2. **Condition 2: Highest rate of change during medium stages of overall task load.**
   Task-load increased every 5 min, with a variable rate of change. Participants had to perform the following task combination: 1, 2, 5, and 6. The initial task-load of the first interval (task set 1) is followed by a slight task-load increase in the second interval (task set 2), then we find an abrupt increase in task-load rate of change where the participants were moved to task combination 5 and finally a slight decrease in the rate of change for task combination 6.
3. **Condition 3: Highest rate of change during later stages of overall task load.**
   Task-load increased every 5 min, with a variable rate of change. Participants had to perform the following task combination: 1, 2, 4, and 6. The initial task-load of the first interval (task set 1) is followed by a slight task-load increase moving into task set 2, followed by another slight change (moving into task combination 4) and finally we find an abrupt increase in task-load rate of change moving into task combination 6 (Fig. 4).

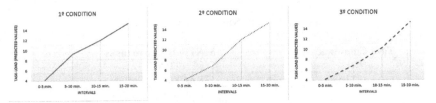

Fig. 4. Task-load rate of change evolution (current task-load) for the three experimental conditions.

By comparing these three conditions, we were able to measure the effect of task-load rate of change. A 3 × 4 mixed factorial experimental design was devised with

2 independent variables. One variable was task-load rate of change with 3 different levels that were manipulated between groups. The other variable was the interval when task-load changed, this variable had 4 levels and was manipulated within-subjects.

Dependent Variables

Performance. MATB-II records many indicators of participants' performance: root mean square deviation (RMSD) for the TRACK task, number of correct and incorrect responses for the SYSMON and COMM tasks, and the arithmetic mean of tanks "A-2500" and "B-2500" in absolute values for the RESMAN task. However, for the purposes of this experiment we will only consider the RMSD performance indicator, as it is the only task present during all task combinations in every experimental condition, allowing us to compare participants' performances through and between conditions. The SRMSD performance indicator reflects the distance of the circle to the target point, so that a higher score on this variable reflects a negative performance.

Pupil Size. Mental workload can be revealed by several physiological indexes such as EEG, HVR, and several ocular metrics. We decided to use pupil diameter as our physiological mental workload indicator, as it has been verified in the literature as an objective indicator for mental workload [35–43] and minimizes intrusiveness. While the eye-tracking system used allows a continuous sampling rate recording at 120 Hz, a total of 8 intervals lasting 2.5 min was set, so as to obtain 2 measures in each of the three intervals of different overall task-load levels. Since expressing pupil size in absolute values has the disadvantage of being affected by slow random fluctuations in pupil size (source of noise), we followed the recommendations provided by Sebastiaan Mathôt [44] regarding the baseline correction of pupil-size data. To do this, for every participant, we took his/her average pupil size during the session as a whole as a reference, which was then subtracted from the obtained value in each of the 8 intervals, thereby giving a differential standardized value that allowed us to reduce noise in the collected data. Analyses were carried out for the average of both the left and right pupils. A negative value meant that the pupil was contracting while a positive value meant that it was dilating.

Subjective Mental Workload. Traditional offline subjective workload assessment tools, such as the NASA Task load Index (NASA-TLX), do not allow researchers to obtain continuous subjective ratings from participants. In order to facilitate and establish comparisons between mental workload measures, it was necessary to obtain the subjective momentary ratings continuously throughout the experimental session. With this goal, we used the ISA, which is an online subjective workload scale created for this purpose. Ratings were obtained at 2.5-minute intervals throughout the 20 min of the experiment duration, obtaining a total of 8 subjective mental workload ratings (2 measures in each of the three intervals of different overall task-load levels).

Synchronization of Measures. Performance, pupil size, and subjective measures were obtained continuously throughout the experimental session. Synchronization between measures was simple, as the eyetracker and MATB-II performance log files began to record data simultaneously at the start of the experimental session. The scheduled alarm (every 2.5 min) was also synchronized by the experimenter, as it was simultaneously activated with the MATB-II software. This allowed the ISA scale to be synchronized with the performance and pupil size measures as well.

4   Results

To analyze collected results, we performed three one-way within-subjects ANOVA, one for each different workload measure. First, the ANOVA analysis for our performance measure revealed a significant task-load change main effect $F(3,126) = 42.53$, MSe $= 40.89$, $p < .01$, which means that participants' performance was impaired with the increase in task-load through intervals. On the other hand, although the main effect of the experimental condition was not significant $F(2,42) = 1.33$, MSe $= 427.5$, $p > .05$, the interaction effect task-load level by experimental condition was found to be significant $F(6,126) = 2.99$, MSe $= 40.89$, $p < .01$. This interaction was due to the different evolution of performance impairment through intervals depending on different experimental condition: in experimental condition 1, the greatest difficulties in performance normally occurred between intervals 1 to 2; in experimental condition 2 between intervals 2 to 3 and in experimental condition 3 between intervals 3 to 4. In order to confirm the above statements, we performed 3 mixed factorial ANOVAs, with experimental condition as between group factor, and a one pair of intervals (1 versus 2, 2 versus 3, and 3 versus 4) as the within-subject factor. The first partial ANOVA (int. 1 versus 2) showed a significant task-load change main effect $F(1,42) = 16.14$, MSe $= 41.87$, $p < .01$, a non-significant experimental condition main effect $F(2,42) = .65$, MSe $= 142.34$, $p > .05$, but also a significant interaction effect of task-load by experimental condition $F(2,42) = 3.87$, MSe $= 41.87$, $p < .05$. This interaction effect was explained by the abrupt impairment in task performance in experimental condition 1 that occurred in the second interval. This impairment evolved in a smoother way in experimental conditions 2 and 3. The second partial ANOVA (int. 2 versus 3), revealed a significant task-load main effect $F(1,42) = 16.19$, MSe $= 34.93$, $p < .01$, as well as a non-significant experimental condition main effect $F(2,42) = 1.70$, MSe $= 270.50$, $p > .05$, but a significant interaction effect task-load change by experimental condition $F(2,42) = 3.26$, MSe $= 34.93$, $p < .05$. These results were probably caused by the issues experienced by participants with performance recorded for experimental condition 2. Participants were better able to manage their performance in experimental conditions 1 and 3. In the third partial ANOVA (int. 3 versus 4), task-load change main effect was found to be significant $F(1,42) = 13.73$, MSe $= 24.13$, $p < .01$, experimental condition main effect was not found to be significant $F(2,42) = 3.10$, MSe $= 24.13$, $p > .05$, but again we found an interaction effect task-load change by experimental condition $F(2,42) = 3.10$, MSe $= 24.13$, $p = .05$. In this case participants experienced more difficulty with task load change within experimental condition 3, while in conditions 1 and 2 the impairment was smoother. Therefore, these data confirmed that the greatest performance impairment occurred when there was an abrupt increment in task-load (Fig. 5).

With respect to subjective perceptions, we found a linear increase in the subjective measure of mental workload in every experimental condition. ANOVAs' analysis revealed a significant main effect of task-load $F(3,126) = 242.5$; MSe $= .92$, $p < .01$.

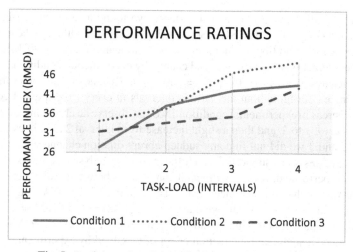

Fig. 5. Participants' performance during task development.

However, the overall task load effect of the experimental condition was not found to be significant $F_{(2,42)} = 3.19$; $MSe = 6.33$, $p > .05$, nor the interaction effect of task-load level by experimental condition, $F_{(6,126)} = 1.15$; $MSe = .92$, $p > .05$. Trend analysis confirmed this linear trend of task-load change effect $F_{(1,42)} = 339.26$; $MSe = 1.97$, $p < .01$ which means that there existed the same lineal increase in mental workload subjective perceptions through intervals in every experimental condition (Fig. 6).

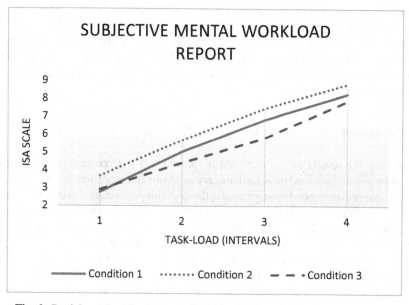

Fig. 6. Participants' subjective mental workload ratings during task development.

Finally, regarding our physiological variable, we found a significant effect for the overall task load $F(3,126) = 198.81$, $MSe = .007$, $p < .01$. And, although the main effect of the experimental condition was not found to be significant $F(2,42) = .90$, $MSe = .001$, $p > .05$, the interaction effect of task-load change by experimental condition was found to be significant, $F(6,126) = 3.09$, $MSe = .007$, $p < .01$. As we can see in the graph, pupil size increased throughout the various intervals in every experimental condition. However, whereas in experimental condition 1 we can observe an abrupt increase in pupil size from interval 1 to 2, and then a slight increase from interval 2 to 4, in experimental conditions 2 and 3 we did not find any sudden abrupt dilation change within intervals. These observations were supported by partial ANOVA analyses. A 3-mixed factorial ANOVAs was performed, with experimental condition as between group factor, and one pair of intervals as the within-subject factor. The first partial ANOVA (int. 1 versus 2) revealed a significant task-load change main effect $F(1,42) = 176.61$, $MSe = .005$, $p < .01$, a non-significant experimental condition main effect $F(2,42) = .19$, $MSe = .009$, $p > .05$, but also a significant interaction effect of task-load by experimental condition $F(2,42) = 11.77$, $MSe = .005$, $p < .01$. This interaction effect could be explained by the abrupt pupil size increase in experimental condition 1, while in the other groups, pupil size increased in a smoother and parallel way. In the second partial ANOVA (int. 2 versus 3), we found a significant task-load main effect $F(1,42) = 59.29$, $MSe = .007$, $p < .01$, a significant experimental condition main effect $F(2,42) = 3.46$, $MSe = .007$, $p < .05$ and a significant interaction effect task-load x experimental condition $F(2,42) = 3.46$, $MSe = .007$, $p < .05$. This interaction effect was due again to the different course of pupil size in experimental condition 1 with regard to experimental conditions 2 and 3, that is, pupil size increment is much slower in condition 1 than in conditions 2 and 3 which both follow a similar course again. Finally, the third partial ANOVA (int. 3 versus 4) showed a significant task-load change main effect $F(1,42) = 71.17$, $MSe = .002$, $p < .01$, a non-significant experimental condition main effect $F(2,42) = .55$, $MSe = .002$, $p > .05$, but in this case a non-significant interaction effect of task-load by experimental condition $F(2,42) = .55$, $MSe = .002$, $p > .05$. This non-significant interaction could be explained by the absence of significant differences between experimental conditions regarding pupil dilation (Fig. 7).

5 Discussion

In summary the results of the experiment showed that performance was negatively affected by overall task-load increased in every experimental condition, but we found that the participants experienced their greatest difficulty with performance in correspondence with the highest rate of change for the task load in each experimental condition. On the other hand, our physiological index, pupil size, also increased as task-load increased in every experimental condition but was not significantly affected by the rate of change in task load with the exception of the results recorded for experimental condition 1, where the highest dilation change matches the task-load change peak point. Finally, regarding subjective perception of mental workload, we did not find any differences between experimental conditions, as it increases linearly through intervals in every condition.

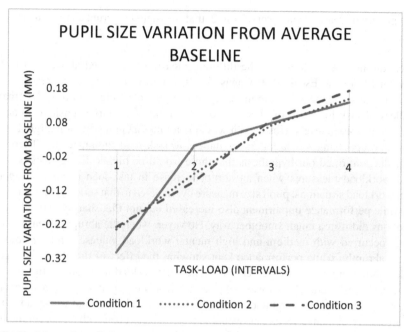

Fig. 7. Participants' pupil size variation ratings from the average baseline during task development.

Hence, considering our results, we found a triple association, which means that the three measures of mental workload reflected this construct successfully. However, it is also true that we found differences in the way each measure evolved through intervals:

- Our **performance index** reflected successfully task demand increase through intervals, but it also appeared to be sensitive to abrupt changes in task demands independently of the timing when this abrupt change took place. In other words, our performance measure seemed to be sensitive to abrupt changes at all times, that is, regardless of the current level of task demand.
- Our **subjective index**, on the other hand, seemed to be sensitive to task-load change, but was not sensitive to task-load rate of change regardless of the moment in which the abrupt change in task demand took place. We can appreciate in our results that subjective perceptions of mental workload increased linearly in every experimental condition with no abrupt changes through intervals. In other words, our subjective measure of mental workload seemed to be more sensitive to the absolute level of task demand than to task-load rate of change.
- Regarding our **physiological index**, our results showed that it was sensitive to task-load change as pupil size dilated through intervals. However, the key finding of this research is that pupil size index was also sensitive to abrupt changes in task demand but only when the abrupt change took place in a low task demand situation (experimental condition 1): we can see that during the "early task-load change peak condition" pupil

size greatly increased from interval 1 to 2, that is, when the abrupt change in task-load occurs.

Considering the evolution of the different measures explained above, and in line with what Muñoz-de-Escalona & Cañas (2019) found in their previous research, we have seen that some measures are more sensitive to the absolute level of task demands regardless of task-load rate of change and some others, are more sensitive to abrupt changes in task-load levels. However, it was also found that pupil dilation might be able to reflect abrupt changes in task demand under low task-load circumstances. Therefore, this results confirmed our hypothesis that there would be higher divergences between mental workload measures when an abrupt increase in task-load occurs during low mental workload situations: pupil size measure overreacted to that sudden change in task-load, while performance impairment also increased but not that sharply and subjective perceptions did it in a much smoother way. However, when the abrupt increase in task demand occurred with medium and high mental workload values, pupil size did not increase abruptly, while performance kept showing the effect of the abrupt change in task demands. And subjective perception of mental workload increased as the absolute value of task load increased but was not affected by any abrupt change in task demand. These results can be explained under resource theories. When mental workload is low, there are plenty of mental resources available to provide to cope with an abrupt increase of task demand. However, when workload level is higher, the absolute pool of mental resources could be running out and there would not be many more resources available to be assigned to the task to cope with the abrupt change in task demands. Therefore, human organism can mobilize much more resources in low task demand situations than in higher task demand situations in which the organism will try to save resources as they are more limited and can be depleted. This effect of the abrupt change in task demands is well reflected by the performance of the participants in the task. However, an additional factor we must consider is the fact that the pupil is a muscle and it has a dilation range, so that, when it approximates its limit it will not be able to continue increasing and that would also contribute to the way it is able or not to reflect changes in mental workload. Hence, this could be a contributing reason why pupil size only was able to reflect the abrupt change in task demand during low mental workload condition.

Finally, we again observed that the subjective feeling of mental workload is independent of some factors that affect performance and psychophysiological parameters of mental resources. People are more sensitive to absolute increases of task demand, as shown in other studies of mental workload and fatigue [24, 25]. This experiment however has some limitations that should be noted as the study was performed with a restricted number of students and we consider that this results should be validated with a more representative and numerous sample of the population in order to increase external validation. On the other hand, it has been repeatedly reported in the literature that divergences have been found not only between the different types of methodologies for measuring mental workload, but also within different measures of each methodology. It would have been interesting, for example, to register multiple physiological measures, which reflects mental activation, in order to analyze convergences and divergences within measures. In addition, it would have been interesting to gather more neurophysiological signals to support obtained findings about activation changes through conditions. Mental work-load divergence between measures is a problem which must be addressed with further research, as the factors affecting this phenomenon are multiple and difficult to interpret. Future research could also consider age effects in workload measure divergences which given the nature of the current sample was not significantly observed.

6 Conclusions

Mental workload assessment has been the subject of numerous studies in the last several years. Quantifying mental workload not only helps to prevent work-related accidents, but also increases productivity at work, so there is an increasing need in our modern society to measure a construct that even, to date, is very difficult to be defined. There exist three main axes for measuring mental workload: performance, physiological and subjective primary measures. Although it is natural to think that mental workload measures of the same person in the same situation should converge, previous studies have proven that divergences between mental workload measures are very frequent. This study aimed to shed some light about one possible cause for mental workload divergences. Particularly, we wanted to explore how abrupt increases in task demand would affect mental workload measures divergences, depending on the baseline task-load situation. Our findings suggest that although the three considered measures of mental workload were sensitive to the construct, there are differences that we must consider between the way each different measure reacts to sudden increases in mental workload. Firstly, performance measure proved to be sensitive to abrupt increases in task demand in every condition whereas our physiological measure (pupil size) was only sensitive to a sudden increase in task-load during low mental workload baseline circumstances. While subjective ratings of mental workload did not react to abrupt transitions in task-load in any experimental condition but only to the absolute increase in task load.

An important implication about this finding is that we must be cautious in selecting the methodology for assessing mental workload: the decision should be based on our particular goals, as each measure may be more suitable to represent different aspects of mental workload. For example, if we need to detect sudden changes in mental workload in every condition, it could be a better idea to trust performance index, however, if the goal is to detect sudden increases in mental workload during low mental workload sustained situations (certain train drivers) it would be a better idea to trust pupil size, as it seems to be very sensitive to abrupt increase in task-load in this particular situation. Finally, subjective perceptions of mental workload is sufficiently accurate to give an overall idea about the state in which the person finds himself/herself. In any case it is to be assumed that the best way to assess mental workload involves a triangulation of different types of measures, one for each different kind of methodologies, as every different index have its pros and cons and they all contribute relevant information. Last but not least we must be cautious about these findings, as it was obtained for a limited sample therefore further research is needed to continue clarifying the topic of mental workload assessment.

References

1. Babiloni, F.: Mental workload monitoring: new perspectives from neuroscience. In: Longo, L., Leva, M.C. (eds.) H-WORKLOAD 2019. CCIS, vol. 1107, pp. 3–19. Springer, Cham (2019). https://doi.org/10.1007/978-3-030-32423-0_1
2. Cain, B.: A review of the mental workload literature. Defence Research and Development Toronto (Canada) (2007)
3. Meshkati, N., Hancock, P.A. (eds.) Human mental workload, vol. 52. Elsevier (2013)
4. Moray, N. (ed.) Mental Workload: Its Theory and Measurement, vol. 8. Springer, New York (2011). http://doi.org/10.1007/978-1-4757-0884-4
5. Josten, E.J., Ng-A-Tham, J.E., Thierry, H.: The effects of extended workdays on fatigue, health, performance and satisfaction in nursing. J. Adv. Nursing **44**(6), 643–652 (2003). https://doi.org/10.1046/j.0309-2402.2003.02854.x
6. Taylor, A.H., Dorn, L.: Stress, fatigue, health, and risk of road traffic accidents among professional drivers: the contribution of physical inactivity. Annu. Rev. Public Health **27**, 371–391 (2006). https://doi.org/10.1146/annurev.publhealth.27.021405.102117
7. Lilley, R., Feyer, A.M., Kirk, P., Gander, P.: A survey of forest workers in New Zealand: do hours of work, rest, and recovery play a role in accidents and injury? J. Safety Res. **33**(1), 53–71 (2002)
8. Sarsangi, V., Salehiniya, H., Hannani, M., Marzaleh, M.A., Abadi, Y.S., Honarjoo, F., Derakhshanjazari, M.: Assessment of workload effect on nursing occupational accidents in hospitals of Kashan Iran. Biomed. Res. Therapy **4**(8), 1527–1540 (2017)
9. Rodgers, S.H.: An ergonomic approach to analyzing workplace accidents. Appl. occupat. Environ. Hygiene **15**(7), 529–534 (2000)
10. Kirschenbaum, A., Oigenblick, L., Goldberg, A.I.: Well being, work environment and work accidents. Soc. Sci. Med. **50**(5), 631–639 (2000)
11. Endsley, M.R., Kiris, E.O.: The out-of-the-loop performance problem and level of control in automation. Hum. Factors **37**(2), 381–394 (1995)
12. Young, M.S., Stanton, N.A.: Attention and automation: new perspectives on mental underload and performance. Theor. Issues Ergon. Sci. **3**(2), 178-194 (2002). https://doi.org.ezproxy.ub.unimaas.nl/10.1080/14639220210123789
13. Priya, D.S., Johnson, P., Padmavathi, R., Subhashini, A.S., Ayyappan, R., Ayyappan, M.: Evaluation of the relationship between workload and work capacity in petrochemical and tannery workers-a pilot study. Life Sci. Med. Res. **19**(1), 2–12 (2010)
14. Smith, A.P., Smith, H.N.: Workload, fatigue and performance in the rail industry. In: Longo, L., Leva, M.C. (eds.) H-WORKLOAD 2017. CCIS, vol. 726, pp. 251–263. Springer, Cham (2017). https://doi.org/10.1007/978-3-319-61061-0_17
15. Fan, J., Smith, Andrew P.: The impact of workload and fatigue on performance. In: Longo, L., Leva, M. (eds.) H-WORKLOAD 2017. CCIS, vol. 726, pp. 90–105. Springer, Cham (2017). https://doi.org/10.1007/978-3-319-61061-0_6
16. Yeh, Y.Y., Wickens, C.D.: Dissociation of performance and subjective measures of workload. Hum. Factors **30**(1), 111–120 (1988)
17. Yeh, Y.H., Wickens, C.D.: The dissociation of subjective measures of mental workload and performance (final report). (No. NASA-CR-176609; NAS 1.26:176609; EPL-84-2/NASA-84-2) (1984)
18. Casper, P.A. Dissociations among measures of mental workload: Effects of experimenter-induced inadequacy (1988)
19. Horrey, W.J., Lesch, M.F., Garabet, A.: Dissociation between driving performance and drivers' subjective estimates of performance and workload in dual-task conditions. J. Safety Res. **40**(1), 7–12 (2009)

20. Kamzanova, A.T., Kustubayeva, A.M., Matthews, G.: Use of EEG workload indices for diagnostic monitoring of vigilance decrement. Hum. Factors **56**(6), 1136–1149 (2014)
21. Matthews, G., Reinerman-Jones, L.E., Barber, D.J., Abich IV, J.: The psychometrics of mental workload: multiple measures are sensitive but divergent. Hum. Factors **57**(1), 125–143 (2015)
22. Hancock, P.A.: Whither workload? mapping a path for its future development. In: Longo, Luca, Leva, M.C. (eds.) H-WORKLOAD 2017. CCIS, vol. 726, pp. 3–17. Springer, Cham (2017). https://doi.org/10.1007/978-3-319-61061-0_1
23. Muñoz-de-Escalona, E., Cañas, J.J.: Latency differences between mental workload measures in detecting workload changes. In: Longo, Luca, Leva, M.C. (eds.) H-WORKLOAD 2018. CCIS, vol. 1012, pp. 131–146. Springer, Cham (2019). https://doi.org/10.1007/978-3-030-14273-5_8
24. Muñoz-de-Escalona, E., Cañas, J.J., van Nes, J.: Task demand transition rates of change effects on mental workload measures divergence. In: Longo, L., Leva, M.C. (eds.) H-WORKLOAD 2019. CCIS, vol. 1107, pp. 48–65. Springer, Cham (2019). https://doi.org/10.1007/978-3-030-32423-0_4
25. Muñoz-de-Escalona, E., Cañas, J.J., Noriega, P.: Inconsistencies between mental fatigue measures under compensatory control theories. Psicológica Journal, 1 (ahead-of-print) (2020)
26. Hancock, P.A., Matthews, G.: Workload and performance: associations, insensitivities, and dissociations. Hum. Factors **61**(3), 374–392 (2019)
27. Canas, J., Quesada, J., Antolí, A., Fajardo, I.: Cognitive flexibility and adaptability to environmental changes in dynamic complex problem-solving tasks. Ergonomics **46**(5), 482–501 (2003)
28. Ahlstrom, U., Friedman-Berg, F.J.: Using eye movement activity as a correlate of cognitive workload. Int. J. Ind. Ergonomics **36**(7), 623–636 (2006)
29. Bertrand, M., Mullainathan, S.: Do people mean what they say? Implications for subjective survey data. American Econ. Rev. **91**(2), 67–72 (2001)
30. Wickens, C.D.: Multiple resources and mental workload. Human Factors, **50**(3), 449–455 (2008). http://doi.org/10.1518%2F001872008X288394
31. Santiago-Espada, Y., Myer, R.R., Latorella, K.A., Comstock Jr, J.R.: The multi-attribute task battery ii (matb-ii) software for human performance and workload research: A user's guide (2011)
32. Lee, J., Ahn, J.H.: Attention to banner ads and their effectiveness: an eye-tracking approach. Int. J. Electron. Commerce **17**(1), 119–137 (2012). https://doi.org/10.2753/JEC1086-44151 70105
33. Brennan, S.D: An experimental report on rating scale descriptor sets for the instantaneous self assessment (ISA) recorder. DRA Technical Memorandum (CAD5) 92017, DRA Maritime Command and Control Division, Portsmouth (1992)
34. Jordan, C.S.: Experimental study of the effect of an instantaneous self assessment workload recorder on task performance. DRA Technical Memorandum (CAD5) 92011. DRA Maritime Command Control Division, Portsmouth (1992)
35. Matthews, G., Middleton, W., Gilmartin, B.Y., Bullimore, M.A.: Pupillary diameter and cognitive and cognitive load. J. Psychophysiol. **5**, 265–271 (1991)
36. Backs, R.W.Y., Walrath, L.C.: Eye movement and pupillary response indices of mental workload during visual search of symbolic displays. Appl. Ergon. **23**, 243–254 (1992). https://doi.org/10.1016/0003-6870(92)90152-l
37. Hyönä, J., Tommola, J., Alaja, A.: Pupil dilation as a measure of processing load in simultaneous interpreting and other language tasks. Q. J. Exp. Psychol. **48**, 598–612 (1995). https://doi.org/10.1080/14640749508401407
38. Granholm, E., Asarnow, R.F., Sarkin, A.J., Dykes, K.L.: Pupillary responses index cognitive resource limitations. Psychophysiology, **33**, 457–461 (1996). http://doi.org/10.1111/j.1469-8986.1996.tb01071.x

39. Iqbal, S.T., Zheng, X.S., Bailey, B.P.: Task evoked pupillary response to mental workload in human-computer interaction. In: Proceedings of the ACM Conference on Human Factors in Computing Systems, pp. 1477–1480. ACM, New York (2004). https://doi.org/10.1145/985 921.986094

40. Verney, S.P., Granholm, E., Marshall, S.P.: Pupillary responses on the visual backward masking task reflect general cognitive ability. Int. J. Psychophysiol. **52**, 23–36 (2004). https://doi.org/10.1016/j.ijpsycho.2003.12.003

41. Porter, G., Troscianko, T., Gilchrist, I.D.: Effort during visual search and counting: insights from pupillometry. Q. J. Exp. Psychol. **60**, 211–229 (2007). https://doi.org/10.1080/174702 10600673818

42. Privitera, C.M., Renninger, L.W., Carney, T., Klein, S., Aguilar, M.: Pupil dilation during visual target detection. J. Vis. **10**, 1–14 (2010). http://doi.org/10.1167/10.10.3

43. Reiner, M., Gelfeld, T.M.: Estimating mental workload through event-related fluctuations of pupil area during a task in a virtual world. Int. J. Psychophysiol. **93**(1), 38–44 (2014)

44. Mathôt, S., Fabius, J., Van Heusden, E., Van der Stigchel, S.: Safe and sensible preprocessing and baseline correction of pupil-size data. Behav. Res. Methods **50**(1), 94–106 (2018). https://doi.org/10.3758/s13428-017-1007-2

45. Longo, L.: Subjective usability, mental workload assessments and their impact on objective human performance. In: IFIP Conference on Human-Computer Interaction, pp. 202–223. Springer, Cham (2017)

46. Longo, L.: Experienced mental workload, perception of usability, their interaction and impact on task performance. PLoS ONE **13**(8), e0199661 (2018)

47. Longo, L.: On the reliability, validity and sensitivity of three mental workload assessment techniques for the evaluation of instructional designs: a case study in a third-level course. In: International Conference of Computer Supported Education CSEDU (2) 2018, pp. 166–178 (2018)

Causes of Rail Staff Fatigue: Results of Qualitative Analysis and a Diary Study

Jialin Fan[1]([⊠]) [iD] and Andrew P. Smith[2] [iD]

[1] School of Psychology, Shenzhen University, L3-1236, South Campus, 3688 Nanshan Road, Shenzhen 518000, China
FanJL@szu.edu.cn
[2] Centre for Occupational and Health Psychology, School of Psychology, Cardiff University, 63 Park Place, Cardiff CF10 3AS, UK
SmithAP@cardiff.ac.uk

Abstract. The purpose of this study was to investigate the causes of fatigue among rail staff by analysing qualitative data and conducting an online diary study. It had a closer look at the experience of fatigue among rail staff and brought a more detailed blueprint picture of fatigue and its causes in the rail staff's real-life. Study 1 analysed 133 responses of qualitative data from rail staff, and Study 2 was a diary study examining fatigue and its related risk factors before and after work, on the first and the last day of a working week in 19 rail staff. The findings from the two studies, using different methodologies, showed similar results that fatigue among rail staff was a result of heavy workload and a high workload would further increase fatigue. Fatigue before work mainly resulted from sleep quality, length of sleep, and the time spent on commute, while fatigue after work resulted from the perceived workload and shift type. Evidence has demonstrated that overtime work, specific shift patterns, insufficient rest days between opposed shifts, and poor timing of breaks during work were also associated with fatigue.

Keywords: Workload · Occupational fatigue · Rail staff · Qualitative analysis · Diary study

1 Introduction

Occupational fatigue is a daily experience among working people. It is also a well-established occupational hazard which has been identified as a contributing factor for incident and accident, for injuries and death, in a wide range of occupational settings (e.g., transport, hospital, construction), with implications on cognitive performance. Although the implications for fatigue in transport are well documented, the amount of research in rail fatigue was limited as this field was historically smaller than road and aviation fatigue [1, 2]. In the railway industry, fatigue is a risk for both train and human safety because the majority of jobs in this industry are safety-critical. Evidence for fatigue in rail staff has been found in many existing studies. Train drivers and signallers (i.e., railway controller) were the most investigated samples in fatigue studies [3], as fatigue-related human error in these roles could, obviously, result in serious safety consequences.

© Springer Nature Switzerland AG 2020
L. Longo and M. C. Leva (Eds.): H-WORKLOAD 2020, CCIS 1318, pp. 227–249, 2020.
https://doi.org/10.1007/978-3-030-62302-9_14

However, the other job roles in this industry were also safety-critical, including the conductor, engineer, and even station worker. Although some of these job roles do not involve the train operation, their duties are designed for ensuring the train, the rail track, the passenger, and the station are secured. An engineer, for example, working in the event of emergencies to resolve any faults that might occur in the railway infrastructure, was found to suffer from fatigue problems and the unpredictability of the call-out duties prevented relaxation which then further cumulated in fatigue [4]. A large-scale survey among UK train staff covering all the job roles [5] indicated that issues of fatigue were apparent in any job roles mentioned, even including the station workers who carry out the duties of selling and checking tickets, making sure that passengers get on and off the train safely, and signalling the conductors or driver to depart. Failure to manage rail staff fatigue would result in serious consequences. In general, the after-effect of fatigue includes impairments in attention, memory, information processing, decision-making, perception, and work performance [6, 7], as well as the decreased response of cells, tissues, or organs after excessive stress or activity [8]. It has also been found to have a negative association with mood, well-being, physical and mental health, and personal safety [9–12]. Fatigue and its impact on safety-critical performance increased the risk of human error and was suggested as a key issue in the rail industry [13]. In train accident and incident reports, staff fatigue is considered to be a causal factor [14–18]. By reviewing 98 rail investigation reports found in the SPARK, an organised library of researches and reports within the international rail community, Fan and Smith [3] found 23 of the reports identified fatigue as one of the contributory causes of the train incident or accident.

Rail staff fatigue is subject to general stressors of occupational fatigue (e.g., workload) and industry-specific factors (e.g., shift work). Smith [19] reviewed fatigue in different transport sectors and indicated that that the fatigue problem between sectors is similar, while the features between them are different. He suggested that the scientific approach to defining fatigue should apply to all of these sectors, but a "one size fits all" approach to regulating fatigue may be inappropriate to all. The amount of related fatigue studies in the rail industry, however, is very limited just as Anund et al. suggested [2], and the causes of rail staff fatigue required further studying. Section 1.1 and Sect. 1.2 review literature of the causes of fatigue in general, and in the railway industry. Then, the rationales and objectives of current studies are introduced in Sect. 1.3.

1.1 Causes of Occupational Fatigue in General

In general, the causes of occupational fatigue are varied, including generic causes not specific to the workplace (e.g., duration of the task, sleep loss), and work-related causes (e.g., workload, job support and control); it is also affected by individual differences and combined effects. Stress is the starting point of fatigue, and long-term stress results in fatigue. Cameron [20] stated that the term fatigue is synonymous with a generalised stress response over time, which suggests that the risk factors of occupational stress will also result in fatigue. The work-related causes of fatigue, therefore, could be the stressor of occupational stress, including work demands, lack of control and support, and individual differences. The causes could also be the working environment, shift work and the combined effects of these factors [5, 21]. The most prominent cause of fatigue is the time spent on tasks. Length of time-on-task leads to fatigue and a decrement in cognitive performance. Time-on-task refers to the length of time spent involved in a task. Cameron [20] pointed out that time is probably the most relevant variable which is uniquely associated with fatigue. In the course of prolonged tasks, it generally becomes increasingly difficult to maintain performance, which seems to reflect a cumulative increase in the effort required to deploy cognitive resources. In such cases, performance is impaired, and fatigue accumulates over time. The range of studies on the time on task effect involved periods of a few minutes in duration [22] to several weeks of 8-h days' continuous time [23]. The effect is particularly noticeable in tasks requiring sustained attention, with longer reaction times and/or greater numbers of errors [24]. Gilbertova and Glivicky [25] stated that this effect is amplified by monotony or boredom, while it may be suppressed in more interesting tasks. In addition, breaks (e.g. task switching) and rests provide fatigue recovery from such an effect [26].

Sleep loss is one of the main factors that can lead to fatigue. Many of the fatigue studies involve sleep-related risk factors, including sleep quality, duration, and deprivation [27–29]. Most people experience the feeling of fatigue after spending one or more nights without sleep. Technically, sleep loss is associated with significant declines in global metabolic activity within the brain, especially the pre-frontal inhibitory and thalamic information-processing system [30]. That is, alertness and attention decrease, and the probability of brief attentional lapses increases. Sleep deprivation also disrupts the normal functioning of the emotional-cognitive integration system, resulting in increased negative emotion [31] and impaired decision-making [32]. Additionally, May and Baldwin [33] noted that active and passive fatigue can impair the performance, either directly through task effects, or indirectly by worsening sleep-related fatigue.

In the workplace, job demands referring to physical or mental workload, were considered to result in occupational fatigue [34, 35]. Workload represents the cost of accomplishing mission requirements for the human operator and can be measured by using self-assessment (e.g., NASA-TLX). Frone and Tidwell [36] suggested that, other than physical or mental workload, there is emotional workload. Although workload (or job demands) are not necessarily negative, they may turn into stressors if meeting them requires high levels of effort. These stressors are, therefore, costly and are associated with negative responses such as depression, anxiety, and fatigue. Besides, Karasek [37] found that job control (i.e., the personal ability to control work activities) is a major moderator between high job demands and high strain. In the job demands-control model (JDC) he proposed, it is the combination of high job demands and low job control that is associated with high job strain. Results of the studies focusing on job control support its moderating effect on the relationship between high job demands and fatigue [38, 39]. Van Yperen and Hagedoorn [40] stated that as job demands increase, the high job control needed to limit fatigue also increases. In the 1980s, a social support dimension was added to the JDC model, resulting in the job demand-control social (JDCS) model [41]. The new element, social support at work, was defined as the overall levels of helpful social interaction available on the job from co-workers or supervisors [42]. This JDCS model indicated that high job demands combined with low control and low social support results in feelings of isolation and leads to higher levels of fatigue and strain.

Research on occupational fatigue has also focused on the effects of irregular hours of work (i.e., shift work). Humans have important physiological requirements for sleep and a stable biological clock, but in many industries, the jobs of humans are designed to operate on a 24/7 basis. When people lose sleep or have their internal clock disrupted, they usually begin to feel fatigued. Previous studies have identified the start time [43, 44], shift work, and its duration [45], as potential causes of fatigue. Shift work, especially the early morning shift and the night shift, disrupts the sleep-wake cycle [46] and deprives workers of sleep [47], which in turn reduces performance [48]. Shift workers may have little time to recover when working certain shift hours, which makes them more likely to suffer from chronic fatigue. When reviewing the literature on shift systems, Folkard, Lombardi, and Tucker [49] highlighted that the risk of an accident increases over a series of work shifts, especially at night, and also increases as the total shift length increases over 8 h (in any 24-h period).

Individual differences play a role in fatigue as well. Many individual factors have been studied, including personality [27, 50], coping type [51], health-related behaviours (e.g., smoking [52]; drinking excessive amounts of alcohol [53, 54]; eating habit [55]), and even clock genes [56]. The important role of individual differences (such as coping styles) on fatigue is indicated in the Demands, Resources, and Individual Effects model (DRIVE model) [57]. DRIVE model is an occupational fatigue model which demonstrates not only the effects of job demands and job resources (support and control), but also the impact of individual differences on work fatigue and health outcomes. Parkes [27, 50] stated that individual differences in personality and coping can play important roles in the processes by which work conditions influence fatigue and health outcomes. Karasek [37] noted that individuals can manage their job demands effectively in a controllable situation. In other words, the effect of job demands somehow depends on how individuals appraise stressors and act in response [35]. As for clock genes (also called clock circadian regulators), although the investigation of polymorphisms in occupational fatigue is in its infancy, some polymorphisms have already been identified, such as diurnal preference, an intrinsic period, responses to sleep deprivation and night shifts [56, 58–60]. Van Dongen and Belenky [61] suggested that the selection of individuals with a specific diurnal preference or those who are relatively little affected by sleep loss or circadian effects for specific tasks (e.g., night shifts or early morning shifts) can help to improve productivity, reduce errors, and decrease incidents and accidents. Although clock genes provide an interesting angle to understand the individual difference in perceived fatigue, the research presented in this paper does not study fatigue at the gene level yet.

1.2 Causes of Fatigue in Rail Industry

Just like the workers in any other industries, rail staff are subject to general stressors of occupational fatigue. Other than that, they are also exposed to industry-specific factors which could associate with fatigue, such as sustained vigilance works, shift-work, and harsh working environments [62, 63]. With systematically reviewing the causes of rail staff fatigue, Fan and Smith [3] summarised that the factors contributing to rail staff fatigue included long working hours, heavy workload, shift work, insufficient sleep, poor working environment, as well as individual differences. In particular, when separately measuring occupational fatigue in its three dimensions (i.e., physical, mental, and emotional fatigue) [36], workload plays an important role resulting in fatigue in all its three dimensions. Prolonged work and insufficient rest resulted in physical fatigue, while the poor shift pattern was more related to mental and emotional fatigue [64]. Darwent et al. [65] found that fatigue was generally associated with insufficient sleep obtained before shifts, but there were individual differences in fatigue resistance. Although the environmental factors were found to affect rail staff fatigue [66, 67], such effects seemed to appear in particular job roles. For example, noise and vibration were more influential in train drivers and conductors and associated with their fatigue, while fumes seemed to affect more engineers but were not found to contribute to fatigue [5].

1.3 Rationale of Present Research

Recent research has addressed the topic of work fatigue in the rail industry. Much of this has been concerned with the potential consequence and general causes of fatigue and there has been less research about the detailed causes of fatigue closely to rail staff members' real-life setting. There is limited evidence about cumulated fatigue in this industry and the understanding of the effect of current shift work on fatigue is not enough. Therefore, research is needed to explore the causes of rail staff fatigue in more detail using qualitative data. A diary study is also better for understanding cumulative fatigue. Diary studies have been used with fleet staff (i.e., engineer) in the railway industry [68], whereby fatigue and fatigue-related risk factors were assessed at the start and end of the first and the last day of their working week, with similar reliability and validity to an everyday diary. Considering the real-life setting, a simple measure and an "online" method is required so that the diary can be easily used in the workplace among rail staff. One reason is because an online single-item scale is as reliable as the offline version of it and longer scales [5, 64, 68]. The other is because such measures are able to measure fatigue without interrupting or changing staff members' work behaviour.

The main aim of the current research described in this paper is to investigate the causes of rail staff fatigue using two different methods including either qualitative data or a diary. The present research attempts to have a closer look at the fatigue experienced among rail staff and to have a more detailed blueprint picture of fatigue and its causes in the rail staff's real-life. Considering the effect of individual differences that has been mentioned in previous studies, the DRIVE model is used as the research framework in this paper as it has such elements and has been applied to workload and fatigue. The first study described in Sect. 2 uses qualitative data to investigate the causes of rail staff fatigue. The second study, a diary study, described in Sect. 3 assesses their fatigue and its risk factors in a real-life setting, at the start and end of the first and last day of a working week.

2 Study 1 - Qualitative Data

2.1 Methods

Participant. A total of 133 participants provided the qualitative data in the online survey. The majority of these participants were male (N = 104, 78.2%), with a mean age of 44.53 years (SD = 9.773, minimum 20.5yr, maximum 62.92yr). There were 63.9% of them who worked in South Wales, UK, while the rest worked in North Wales. The main occupations in the sample were train drivers (23.3%, N = 31), conductors (21.8%, N = 29), administrators (17.3%, N = 23), and engineers (15.8%, N = 21), followed by managers (15.0%, N = 20) and station workers (6.0%, N = 8). One participant had missing job type data. The School of Psychology Research Ethics Committee at Cardiff University reviewed and approved this online study.

Materials. This study uses qualitative data to investigate the causes of rail staff fatigue. The material used in this study was an online questionnaire investigating causes of rail staff fatigue. This questionnaire contains thirty-eight 10-point questions and one open-ended survey question, "Do you have any comments on your working hours? (e.g. how they could be improved)." The current paper mainly reports the results of the qualitative data of the survey (e.g., the responses of the open-end question), and the quantitative data was report in one of our previous paper [64].

Data analysis was carried out using SPSS 23. The thematic analysis strategy [69] was employed to analyse the qualitative data. The comments were read several times, and the themes listed above were identified and highlighted by coloured pens. Some text involved two or more theme.

2.2 Results - Thematic Analysis (Opening Question)

There were 133 responses to this question. The answers to this open-end question, "Do you have any comments on your working hours? (e.g. how they could be improved)", demonstrated that the factor of working hours is not the only risk factor of fatigue. The themes of these responses included job demands/overtime work, length of shift, timing to work, break/rest, flexibility of working pattern, and job support and control. Timing to work was the most popular theme, followed by length of shift, job demands/overtime work, break/rest, and flexibility of working pattern. The frequency of these themes is shown in Fig. 1

Theme 1. Timing of work. The first topic described was timing of work, the most popular theme being mentioned by 41 comments. Participants generally claimed that less shift-work would decrease the fatigue problem.

Participant 81 (engineer): "...*Shift-work and early shift start times affect me with fatigue.*"

Participant 115 (engineer): "*More day working, shorter night shifts.*"

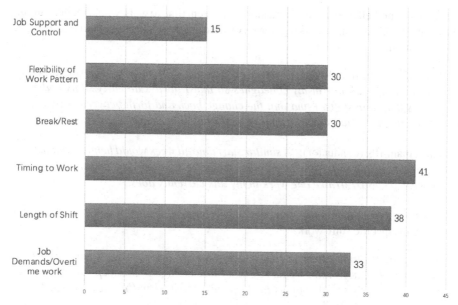

Fig. 1. Number of comments on each theme.

Participant 90 (train driver): *"If the shifts were better balanced instead of booking on at 03.27 in the morning and working through on night shift, I feel this would help."*

Participants described how the irregular hours of shift-work affected their work-life balance, and how difficult it was to recover from a series of night shifts when an early morning shift was scheduled immediately after.

Participant 94 (administrator): *"Too many late shifts, too many weekends, have no enough family time. Work/life balance heavily depends on work and changes on shifts always make things worse never better."*

Participant 28 (conductor): *"Spare shift which can be moved three hrs either way and it only advised 48 h before, messing up the healthy lifestyle, sleep and society activities. This should be reduced to an hour."*

Participant 69 (manager): *"We have to work during the nights. Sometimes working from the day shift on the previous day, then back to a morning start after minimal rest, which can be tiring."*

Participant 107 (conductor): *"Poor rostering is the main issue. One issue is finishing at 02.30 Sunday morning. Having Sunday off then in 03.43 starts Monday morning. How am I supposed to prepare my body for that?"*

Participants believed that having a more consistent time to work would reduce fatigue, especially within the same working week. A varied and too changeable start time resulted in their fatigue.

Participant 19 (train driver): *"I try to regulate my shift pattern by having a permanent swap with one of my colleagues so that I always do early shifts and he always does late shifts. I find that the change back and forth between early and late (shifts) is the largest contributory factor that influences my fatigue."*

Participant 109 (conductor): *"A similar start time all week would help enormously, e.g. if on earlies shifts starting around the same time all day, and not varying between 03.43-07.01 like one week in my link currently does."*

This participant mentioned that personal preference of time of day could help with coping with specific shift-work.

Participant 25 (train driver): *"I try to swap for the late turns as I find they suit me better. On early shift, I would say that I lose about a night sleep over the four shifts. I generally struggle to get to sleep early, even when I'm tired, though I do manage to get up OK."*

Theme 2. Length of Shift. The second theme highlighted the length of shift-work that the train crew took which was mentioned by 38 comments. Participants reported that current working hours were too long, that the length of each turn should be limited, and that the number of maximum working hours should be reduced.

Participant 9 (conductor): *"(Working hours) could bring in a maximum 9.5-h day with having a maximum of 4 h on a train at any given time."*

Participant 76 (engineer): *"Working hour should less 12 h and average 10-h shifts throughout the month."*

Participant 111 (engineer): *"I think 10 h should be maximum shift length when working on safety critical work."*

Participants also suggested a reduction in the length of early morning and night shifts.

Participant 75 (train driver): *"The jobs that start very early in the morning (before 6am) should not be allowed to be much longer than 6-7 h long in turn length."*

Participant 87 (engineer): *"Reduce 12 h to 10 h or even 8 h, especially on nights."*

Theme 3. Job Demands/Overtime Work. The third theme described the demands that were placed on the train crew and the overtime work that they take. With regards to job demands, participants described how the job demands were high.

Participant 40 (administrator): *"It's not the length of shifts that make me feel fatigued, but the constant questions, and the concentration needed to check tickets, make sure that people don't get stuck in the ticket barriers etc."*

Participant 85 (train driver): *"The commitment to covering on-call requirements and being called out in addition to normal daily hours, massively impinges on my fatigue and well-being."*

Participant 105 (train driver): *"... the problem comes with the intensity of work within the turn."*

More specifically, participants reported that the nature of their work can be mentally or emotionally demanding and that their fatigue is often more emotional or mental.

Participant 74 (train driver): *"Repetition of work, i.e. 4 h of constant driving over the same route multiple times, e.g. City line - mentally exhausting."*

Participant 128 (manager): *"I have a mentally challenging job."*

Participant 63 (station worker): *"...it's more emotional and mental fatigue that affect how I feel after a working day."*

Overtime work was frequently mentioned, and participants described how their overtime work had high demands.

Participant 84 (manager): *"I work 12 h shift. Every shift I work overtime for approximately 40 min (20 min at the start and 20 min after the shift finishes) to allow for a shift handover."*

Participant 50 (manager): *"The overtime mentioned is event working. It is expected in some departments that staff who volunteer for events complete their full shift before volunteering to work an event for payment. This can lead to staff working in excess of 12 h. A member of the resources team recently worked a 15-h shift; this is dangerous given that staff are managing large crowds and have to make safety decisions, which is difficult to do when tired. When finishing evening events, staff can finish as late as 01.30 but are expected to return to work for their normal shifts with very little rest."*

Participant 84 (manager): *"The commitment to covering on-call requirements and being called out in addition to normal daily hours, which massively impinges on my fatigue and well-being."*

Participants specifically pointed out that the reason for their high job demands and overtime work was insufficient staffing.

Participant 68 (conductor): *"There are not enough people to complete all the tasks that need completing. Many people within the function are doing two jobs and working in the evenings/weekends."*

Participant 56 (manager): *"Roster has insufficient staff for the number of hours required (i.e., the roster should have 7 to cover properly but only has 5). Overtime unavoidable at times as job mandatory to cover."*

Participant 106 (administrator): *"… the biggest issue is the amount of time we spend single manned (i.e. on our own with no backup or support at the station). This has increased in recent months due to staff cuts."*

Theme 4. Break/Rest. The fourth theme described was breaks during work and rest after work. Insufficient rest and break were reported to lead to fatigue, as well as increase risks to the safety.

Participant 105 (train driver): *"…the breaks are too infrequent and often too short. Too much time spent without a break leading to fatigue."*

Participant 122 (train driver): *"Breaks are very tight, and if we are late, we feel under pressure to take subsequent trains on time… (Break) sometimes was split into two rushed breaks. This means it is very difficult to eat a hot meal or to shut off for 5 min, which is not great in a safety critical environment."*

Participants mainly complained that the timing of rest during the shift was poorly placed, either too early or too late, and needed to be more thoughtful.

Participant 8 (conductor): *"The breaks are in the wrong place. Right at the start or right at the end."*

Participant 10 (conductor): *"…Could we please have breaks in the middle of a shift and not after 30 min of starting a ten-hour shift or at the end of one?"*

Participants also suggested to have more rest days and to arrange them more strategically, especially between opposing shifts.

Participant 37 (administrator): *"More recovery time. More occasions of consecutive rest days (1 occasion every six weeks at present)."*

Participant 54 (train driver): *"More rest between opposing shifts. Sometimes there is only 26 h between late afternoons and early mornings."*

Theme 5. Flexibility of Working Pattern. Flexibility of working pattern was frequently mentioned in the comments. Participants described how a flexible working pattern could benefit their work-life balance and suggested to increase flexibility of working time and working place.

Participant 5 (administrator): *"Flexible working would assist people to manage their day and improve work-life balance. For example, you can choose to come in at 7 knowing that you can leave at 3 and enjoy time with family or enjoy sunshine etc. Also, you can accrue flexible days."*

Participant 86 (manager): *"More flexible approach to start and finish times. I.e., if you work over one day, you should be able to finish early the next day for example. Come in later and go home later on some days or the other way around and more working from home where the job allows."*

Theme 6. Job Support and Control. Participants reported low levels of job support and control, mainly including lack of support from the manager or other colleagues and unfair arrangement of working time due to their younger age.

Participant 18 (manager): *"There is little concern from management or unions about the amount of work and length of turn for jobs starting during the late night. The reality of these shifts regardless of attempts to manage those means that almost all drivers working these shifts experience moments and incidents of micro-sleeps and concentration loss during them."*

Participant 36 (train driver): *"I am in the bottom link (rota) in work as I'm junior. We have ALL the very early starts and ALL the late starts. As you progress (10 years roughly), you move up the links and get easier start times. This should be spread out fairly and not left to the same 35 men."*

2.3 Summary

This study used qualitative data to investigate the causes of rail staff fatigue. The themes of the responses included job demands/overtime work, length of shift, timing to work, break/rest, flexibility of working pattern, and job support and control. In which, participants mainly reported that irregular timing of work and impaired work-life balance led to fatigue and that recovering from opposed shifts was extremely difficult. Participants also reported high job demands, especially mental and emotional demands, overtime work, and long length of shift-work. The amount of rest and break were reported as insufficient, while it was suggested that the timing of breaks during work could be better arranged. A flexible work pattern was believed to improve work-life balance. Participants also raised concerns about the lack of job support and control. These comments provided important insights into the nature of jobs in the railway industry and inspired the following diary study, described in Sect. 3.

3 Study 2 – A Diary Study

3.1 Overview (Links Between Study 1 and 2)

Study 1 showed that workload, overtime prolonged shift work, insufficient rest during work, and poorly arranged shift patterns were reported to be the essential causes of fatigue among rail staff. A diary study was the next logical step in this research in order to closely assess the rail staff's shift patterns and daily work lives. It would be useful to investigate occupational fatigue as it provided a record of subjective feelings and work experiences related to fatigue in context.

The present study is a diary study where individuals were required to record their fatigue before and after work, rest and breaks, their workload, and their shift pattern within one working week. The goal of this study was to demonstrate a relationship between fatigue workload, working hours and explore other risk factors mentioned in Study 1 described in Sect. 2, such as shift pattern, overtime work, sleep quality, and breaks during work. The experimental hypothesis for this study predicted that high workload, long working time, irregular shift time, and insufficient breaks will increase fatigue. Reported fatigue will be higher at the end of a workday and at the end of workweek due to the effect of workload.

3.2 Methods

Participant. Participants were recruited from volunteers from a train company in the UK (N = 19, mean (±SD) age = 41.86 ± 9.89 yr.; 74% male). The main job types reported were managers, conductors, drivers, station workers, engineers and administrators.

Materials. The diary consisted of 15 questions (shown in Table 1), including six questions to be answered before work and nine questions to be answered after work. It was designed based on the material used in Smith and Smith's [68] diary studies. The diary was completed immediately before starting work and immediately after finishing work on the first and the last day of a working week (4 days). The questions in the pre-work diary covered sleep duration and quality, time taken to travel to work, fatigue due to the commute, general health status, and alertness before starting work. The questions in the post-work diary recorded workload, effort, fatigue, stress, break duration, work duration, the time they finished work, and level of distraction during work. There were extra questions in the post-work diary on the last day which asked whether participants worked the same time every workday in the working week.

Procedure. An invitation e-mail attached with information about the study and an informed consent form was sent to potential participants. After participants signed and returned the forms, they were asked to provide the start date of their next working week. Then, the introduction of the diary and the links of the four test sections were sent to them. On the testing day(s), participants were asked to complete the online diary immediately before starting work and immediately after finishing work via a computer or mobile phone. Subjects were free to withdraw from the survey at any point. This study was reviewed and approved by the School of Psychology Research Ethics Committee at Cardiff University.

Analysis. Data analysis was carried out using SPSS 23. Data were analysed using a variety of tests, including Pearson correlation (one-tailed) and one-way ANOVA. The variables tested included subjective fatigue, workload, length of sleep, quality of sleep, time taken to travel to work, alertness, effort, stress, working hours, length of breaks, level of distraction, and time starting work (e.g., shift type).

Table 1. Questions in the diary.

Before-work Diary

1. How many hours sleep did you get last night?

This question asks about your recent sleep experience, no matter it was at daytime or at night.

_____ hours _____ minutes

2. How was the quality of your sleep?

Not at all good   Very good

| 1 | 2 | 3 | 4 | 5 | 6 | 7 | 8 | 9 | 10 |

3. How long did it take you to travel to work?

_____ hours _____ minutes

4. How fatigued did you feel from your commute?

Not at all   Very fatigue

| 1 | 2 | 3 | 4 | 5 | 6 | 7 | 8 | 9 | 10 |

5. How well are you feeling now?

Not at all well   Very well

| 1 | 2 | 3 | 4 | 5 | 6 | 7 | 8 | 9 | 10 |

6. How alert do you feel now?

Not at all   Very alert

| 1 | 2 | 3 | 4 | 5 | 6 | 7 | 8 | 9 | 10 |

After-work Diary

1. How was your workload today?

Very low   Very high

| 1 | 2 | 3 | 4 | 5 | 6 | 7 | 8 | 9 | 10 |

2. How much effort did you have to put into your job today?

Very little   A great deal

| 1 | 2 | 3 | 4 | 5 | 6 | 7 | 8 | 9 | 10 |

3. How fatigued do you feel now?

Not at all   Very fatigue

| 1 | 2 | 3 | 4 | 5 | 6 | 7 | 8 | 9 | 10 |

4. How stressed do you feel now?

Not at all   Very stressed

| 1 | 2 | 3 | 4 | 5 | 6 | 7 | 8 | 9 | 10 |

5. What was the total length of your breaks today?

_____ hours _____ minutes

6. What was the total length of your work today?

_____ hours _____ minutes

6.1. What time did you start work today?   (e.g. Hour: 23 Minute: 30)

_____ hours _____ minutes

(*continued*)

Table 1. (*continued*)

6.2. What time did you finish work today?

_____ hours _____ minutes

7. During your work today, to what extent were you thinking about other things rather than work?

Not at all   Very much so

1   2   3   4   5   6   7   8   9   10

8*. Did you work at the same time on other days of this week? (start time, end time, and length)

Yes   No

8.1* If no, which day(s) did you work at a different time? And what was the total length of your work on that day(s)?   (hours, minutes)

_____

8.2* What time did you start and finish work on each of those days? For example, Day 2 - 6.30 am

* The question only asked in the after-work diary on the last day.

3.3 Results

Descriptive. Overall, 19 participants fully completed the diary and 73.7% of them were male. The most common job types reported were managers (26.3%), followed by train drivers, conductors, engineers, station workers (all 15.8%), and administrators (10.5%). 31.6% of participants did night shifts or early morning shifts, while others did daytime shifts. During the testing week (4 working days), 43.1% of participants worked two or more different shift times. Table 2 below shows the difference in fatigue and other variables between the first and last workdays. As is shown, self-reported fatigue increased after work and over the workweek. Quality of sleep and alertness decreased during the week while work stress increased.

Table 2. Descriptive statistics for mean of variables.

	Variables	First Day		Last Day	
		Mean	S.D	Mean	S.D
Before Work	Length of Sleep (hour)	7.18	1.37	7.08	1.31
	Quality of Sleep	6.05	2.12	5.84	2.65
	Time Taken to Travel to Work (hour)	0.50	0.37	0.44	0.26
	Fatigue before Work	2.16	1.21	2.47	1.61

(*continued*)

Table 2. (*continued*)

	Variables	First Day		Last Day	
		Mean	S.D	Mean	S.D
	General Health Status (i.e., feeling well)	7.47	1.50	6.58	2.12
	Alertness	7.11	1.52	6.58	2.34
After Work	Subjective Workload	5.79	2.18	5.42	2.43
	Effort	7.16	2.01	6.37	2.63
	Fatigue after Work	6.42	2.12	7.11	2.00
	Stress	3.79	2.30	4.58	2.09
	Length of Breaks (hour)	0.90	0.69	0.87	0.51
	Working Hours (hour)	8.48	1.65	8.75	1.63
	Distraction during Work	5.11	2.58	5.32	2.65

The variable of time starting work was classified in to four shift type groups, including 1) the morning shift starting from 7:00 to 12:59, 2) the afternoon shift starting from 13:00 to 18:59, 3) the night shift starting from 19:00 to 00:59, and 4) the early morning shift starting from 1:00 to 6:59. In the first day, 47.4% of participant worked the morning shift, 15.8% of them worked the night shift, and 15.8% of them worked the early morning shift. In the last day, participants working morning shifts decreased to 36.8%, participants working night shifts slightly decreased to 10.5%, and those who worked early morning shifts slightly increased to 21.1%. The maximum working hours in both days was 12 h, and 21.1% of participants worked over 10 h every day during the week, this was mainly reported by engineers and drivers. The minimum working hours was 5.5 h on the first day and 5.75 h on the last day, reported from a station worker.

Analysis in Each Diary Session. A one-tailed Pearson correlation was run to investigate the association between fatigue and other risk factors in each diary. There were four diary sessions, before and after work on the first and last days of the work week.

In session 1, the first day before the work session, fatigue before work was associated with time spent travelling to work ($r (19) = .752$, $p < .01$), with more time spent on the commute being associated with higher fatigue ratings. Fatigue was also negatively correlated with general health status ($r (19) = -.469$, $p < .05$), and alertness ($r (19) = -.430$, $p < .05$) at a significant level. High sleep quality was significantly associated with longer length of sleep ($r (19) = .428$), better general health status ($r (19) = .601$), and more alertness ($r (19) = .462$), which were all $p < .05$.

In session 2, the first day after work session, high fatigue after work showed a considerable trend toward significance to correlate with higher distraction ($r (19) = .358$, $p = .066$). High workload was found to be associated with more effort ($r (19) = .606$), high stress ($r (19) = .491$) but lower distraction ($r (19) = -.471$) significantly, and high workload was also associated with shift type approaching conventional significance level (p = 0.056). High stress was found to be associated with less rest and breaks (r (19) = −.454), all p's < .05.

In session 3, the last day before work session, fatigue was significantly correlated with length of sleep (r (19) = .513), while the length of sleep was significant correlated with alertness (r (19) = .478), both p < .05. Alertness was also correlated with sleep quality (r (19) = .533, p < .01) and highly correlated with general health status (r (19) = .826, p < .001). In addition, sleep quality was correlated with general health status (r (19) = .750, p < .001) in this session.

In the session 4, the last day after work session, high fatigue after work was associated with high workload, more effort, and longer length of work, r from .400 to .550, all p < .05. Fatigue also on the very borderline of significance correlated with shift type (r (19) = .374, p = .057), stress (r (19) = .371, p = .059), and distraction (r (19) = .361, p = .064).

Analyses for Each Day. The before-after work difference scores for fatigue scores were calculated using the post-work scores minus the pre-work scores. The positive score of change in fatigue shows the participants were more fatigued after work. The one-way ANOVA was also run to analyse the effect of shift type on change of fatigue.

In the first day, change in fatigue shows the direction heading towards significance to be associated with break time during work (p = 0.10). Longer length of sleep was positively associated with a later time starting work (r (19) = .502) and negatively associated with a later time finishing work (r (19) = −.498), both p's < .05. Good sleep quality was significant associated with less distraction (r (19) = −.458, p < 0.05). No significant effect of shift type found on this day.

In the last day, greater change in fatigue showed a significant positive correlation with more distraction during work (r (19) = .485, p < .05). It was also close to the boundary of significance to correlate with the shorter length of sleep (p = .68), higher workload (p = .78), and worse quality of sleep (p = .85). A one-way analysis of variance showed that the effect of shift type was significant on fatigue changing, F(3,15) = 5.27, p = .011. Post hoc LSD test indicated that the average change on fatigue in morning shift (M = 3.29, S.D = 2.29) and night shift (M = 1.00, S.D = 2.83) groups were significantly different from either afternoon shift (M = 6.33, S.D = 1.37) or early morning shift (M = 6.25, S.D = 2.21) groups. These showed that the before-after fatigue for those who worked afternoon shift and early morning shift was change significantly greater than those who worked the morning shift and night shift. To be noticed that, there are only two participants in the night shift group on the last day thus the results about mean fatigue change of this group could be biased.

3.4 Summary

The present diary study aimed to examine the associations between fatigue, workload, working hours, and shift work in realistic situations, and also to explore the effects of other risk factors on fatigue mentioned in Study 1. It used the online diary to assess fatigue and fatigue-related risk factors before and after work, on the first day and the last day of a working week. The hypothesis for this study predicted that high workload, long working time, irregular shift time, and insufficient breaks would be associated with increased fatigue. It also predicted that reported fatigue would be higher at the end of the workday due to the workload effect. As expected, the effects of workload and working hours on fatigue were found in this study, with high workload or longer working hours leading to increased feelings of fatigue after work. Fatigue before work could be caused by commuting, poor quality or insufficient duration of sleep, while fatigue after work could result from workload, length of work, and shift type. The greater increased fatigue was found in the afternoon and early morning shift than in the normal morning shift. It was also found to be associated with less alertness and more distraction at work which would bring risk to work. Due to the limited sample size, the effects of insufficient breaks on fatigue were not found clearly in this study. Overall, this hypothesis was partially accepted.

4 Discussion

This research investigated the causes of rail staff fatigue using qualitative data (Study 1) and a diary (Study 2). The findings from these two studies, using different methodologies, showed similar results. In both studies, fatigue was found to be due to a heavy workload, long working time, shift-work, and insufficient rest and sleep, which was in line with previous studies [3, 5, 62, 70]. In Study 1, mental and emotional job demands were mentioned to be one of the causes of fatigue, which was consistent with previous research [64, 71] that reported workload in the modern railway industry to impose more cognitive demands rather than physical demands. The effect of workload on rail staff fatigue was found in both studies and a high workload would further increase fatigue as previous study suggested [5]. It was found that staff members who regularly started work in the morning were less fatigued than those who took the irregular shift work, especially the late afternoon or early morning shift. Poor sleep quality, insufficient length of sleep resulted in greater fatigue feeling, which was in line with previous studies either in the general fatigue field [27] or in the occupational fatigue field [70]. In addition, fatigue cumulated and increased the end of the week, suggesting an effect of cumulative work fatigue on the outcomes during a working week. It was very similar to fatigue among seafarers, that the occupational fatigue increased day by day, and cumulated at work and on leave [72].

It was found that fatigue before work was mainly associated with sleep quality, length of sleep, and the time spent on commute, while fatigue after work was associated with the workload and shift type. The effect of sleep on fatigue have been studied in previous papers which report that sleep loss results in the subjective feeling of fatigue, resulting in increased negative emotion and impaired decision-making [27, 29, 31, 32]. Meanwhile, sleep deprivation could be influenced by shift-work, resulting in fatigue at work [73]. Such effect of sleep was found in current research, additionally, the buffering effect of rest and breaks during work on fatigue as reported in Study 1. It was reported that insufficient rest and break lead to fatigue, as well as increased risks to safety, and vice versa. Participants suggested having more rest time or days allowed them to recover from fatigue. The length of breaks during work, however, was not clearly associated with change in fatigue in the diary study, which might be because of the poorly placed timing of rest during the shift. It was reported that the breaks during work were placed at the very beginning of the shift or nearly at the end of it. The arrangement of breaks needed to be more thoughtful, otherwise the buffering effect of it on fatigue was wasted.

As for time spent on commute, it reflected the time spend on the commute task. According to Cameron [20], time is one of the most relevant variables which is associated with fatigue. Overtime work was frequently mentioned to result in fatigue, and prolonged time of the work task usually came with high job demands and resulted in fatigue. The maximum working hours found in Study 2 was 12 h and the engineer (i.e., fleet) and train driver were the main job role that worked over 10 h. These two job types were indicated to be the high fatigue risk job in a large-scale study [5], and had been focused on in previous studies [3]. Although the result of the diary study showed the workload mainly resulted in fatigue rather than the length of work, the high workload and long working hours were associated with each other. The influences of working hours and job demands (i.e., workload) on fatigue were found and consistent with previous research [35]. As suggested by previous studies [45, 70], shift work and its duration were contributed to fatigue and impaired worker's wellbeing. Participants in Study 1 described how the irregular hours of shift-work affected their work-life balance, and how difficult it was to recover from a series of night shifts when an early morning shift was scheduled immediately after. Then in Study 2, shift work, especially early morning shift work was found to result in greater increases in fatigue. Although it was also commented in Study 1 that recovering from opposed shifts was extremely difficult, the shift pattern and its effect was not observed in the diary study due to the limited sample size.

The influence of individual differences was mentioned in Study 1, that personal preference of time of day could help with coping with specific shift-work. Such personal preference of time of day could be explained by the clock circadian regulator. As reviewed earlier in this paper, some polymorphisms of this regulator have already been identified, such as diurnal preference, an intrinsic period, responses to sleep deprivation and night shifts [56, 58–60]. Van Dongen and Belenky [61] suggested that the selection of individuals with a specific diurnal preference (e.g., night preference) to take specific shifts, especially night shift of early morning shift, can help to improve productivity, reduce errors, and decrease incidents and accidents. Such selections, however, should be done judiciously within ethically and legally acceptable boundaries and avoid discriminating based on genetic information.

4.1 Limitations

In the present diary study (Study 2), only one working week per staff was analysed, which might not comprehensively reflect the complete shift patterns in each individual or a single job role. The aim of our research was to investigate the causes of fatigue among rail staff, and the current literature covering different types of job that all may be susceptible to fatigue. The nature of different job roles varied to the extent that a few job roles were in highly sedentary working conditions (e.g., train driver) or in on-call work status (e.g., engineer), while others were not. Indeed, the results show that the occupational fatigue of our participants was influenced by workload, length of work, and shift type, and the subjective measurement of workload and the recording of start/end of work time were fair among all staff, reducing confounding effects. It is also important to consider that; the online diary study is less controlled than laboratory experiments. While the online diary is an advanced method for assessing fatigue closely in the context of daily work life, reminder texts or e-mails are needed to ensure that participants fill in each diary on time.

4.2 Implication for Future Research

Anund et al. [2] suggested that the amount of related fatigue studies in the rail industry is very limited. This research, therefore, enhances the knowledge of the causes of rail staff fatigue by analysing qualitative data and conducting an online diary study. It had a closer look at the fatigue experience among rail staff and brought a more detailed blueprint picture of fatigue and its causes in the rail staff's real-life. Similar results were found from these two studies using different methodologies, that fatigue among rail staff was a result of heavy workload, long working hours, shift-work, and insufficient rest and sleep. Besides, the qualitative data provide new angles for future study. In the future, the relationships between breaks, shift pattern, fatigue can be further studied, as well as the diurnal preference and strategies of sleep and rest between opposed shifts. Future research could investigate the timing of rest and breaks during work. This was frequently mentioned and complained about in Study 1 but was not assessed in Study 2 due to the limited sample. As part of the shift pattern, the record of duration and timing of breaks would be complex, and the required amount of data could be overwhelming. Therefore, to measure and analyse this factor, further data and a larger sample will be needed.

5   Conclusion

This research investigated the causes of fatigue among rail staff using qualitative data and diary. The findings from the two studies, using different methodologies, showed similar results that fatigue among rail staff was a result of heavy workload, long working hours, shift-work, and insufficient rest and sleep. Fatigue before work was mainly a result of sleep quality, length of sleep, and the time spent on commute, while fatigue after work resulted from the workload and shift type. Evidence has been provided that demonstrates how overtime work, specific shift pattern, insufficient rest day between opposed shifts, poor timing of breaks during work were also associated with fatigue, which could be further studied in the future.

Acknowledgments. The main content of this paper was part of JF's PhD thesis. JF would like to thank Prof. AS for his supervision and invaluable guidance in her PhD journey. Both authors are thankful to the anonymous reviewers for the comments which have helped in improving the article.

References

1. Phillips, R.O.: An assessment of studies of human fatigue in land and sea transport. TØI Report (2014). https://www.toi.no/getfile.php/Publikasjoner/T%C3%98I%20rapporter/2014/1354-2014/1354-2014-elektronisk.pdf

2. Anund, A., Fors, C., Kecklund, G., Leeuwen, W.V., Akerstedt, T.: Countermeasures for Fatigue in Transportation: A Review of Existing Methods for Drivers on Road, Rail, Sea and in Aviation. VTI Report 852A (2015)
3. Fan, J., Smith, A.P.: A preliminary review of fatigue among rail staff. Front. Psychol. **9**, 634 (2018)
4. Cebola, N., Golightly, D., Wilson, J.R., Lowe, E.: Fatigue, anxiety, performance for on-call safety critical decision makers in rail maintenance: a diary study. In: Dadashi, N., Scott, A., Wilson, J.R., Mills, A. (eds.) Rail Human Factors: Supporting Reliability, Safety and Cost Reduction, pp. 328–336. Taylor and Francis Group, Boca Raton (2013)
5. Fan, J., Smith, A.P.: The impact of workload and fatigue on performance. In: Longo, L., Leva, M.C. (eds.) H-WORKLOAD 2017. CCIS, vol. 726, pp. 90–105. Springer, Cham (2017). https://doi.org/10.1007/978-3-319-61061-0_6
6. Craig, A., Cooper, R.E.: Symptoms of acute and chronic fatigue. Handbook of Human Performance **3**, 289–339 (1992)
7. Cercarelli, L.R., Ryan, G.A.: Long distance driving behaviour of Western Australian drivers. In: Hartley, L.R. (ed.) Proceedings of the Second International Conference on Fatigue and Transportation: Engineering, Enforcement and Education Solutions, pp. 35–45. Canning ridge, Australia: Promaco (1996)
8. Hirshkowitz, M.: Fatigue, sleepiness, and safety: definitions, assessment, methodology. Sleep Med. Clinics **8**(2), 183–189 (2013)
9. Gander, P.H., Merry, A., Millar, M.M., Weller, J.: Hours of work and fatigue-related error: a survey of New Zealand anaesthetists. Anaesth. Intensive Care **28**(2), 178–183 (2000)
10. Horne, J., Reyner, L.: Vehicle accidents related to sleep: a review. Occupat. Environ. Med. **56**(5), 289–294 (1999)
11. Leonard, C., Fanning, N., Attwood, J., Buckley, M.: The effect of fatigue, sleep deprivation and onerous working hours on the physical and mental wellbeing of pre-registration house officers. Irish J. Med. Sci. **167**(1), 22 (1998)
12. Nicol, A.M., Botterill, J.S.: On-call work and health: a review. Environ. Health **3**(1), 15 (2004)
13. Bowler, N., Gibbon, W.H.: Fatigue and its contribution to railway incidents. British Rail Accident Investigation Branch (RAIB) (2015). https://www.rssb.co.uk/Library/risk-analysis-and-safety-reporting/2015-02-str-fatigue-contribution-to-railway-incidents.pdf
14. Kogi, K., Ohta, T.: Incidence of near accidental drowsing in locomotive driving during a period of rotation. J. Human Ergol. **4**(1), 65–76 (1975). https://doi.org/10.11183/jhe1972. 4.65
15. Ugajin, H.: Human factors approach to railway safety. Quarterly Report of RTRI **40**(1), 5–8 (1999). https://doi.org/10.2219/rtriqr.40.5
16. British Rail Safety and Standards Board T059 Main Report: Guidelines for the Management and Reduction of Fatigue in Train Drivers (2005). https://www.rssb.co.uk/research-development-and-innovation/research-project-catalogue/t059
17. British Rail Accident Investigation Branch.: Derailment of Two Locomotives at East Somerset Junction (2008). http://www.raib.gov.uk/publications/investigation_reports/reports_2009/report282009.cfm
18. British Rail Accident Investigation Branch.: Uncontrolled Freight Train Run-back between Shap and Tebay, Cumbria. https://www.gov.uk/raib-reports/uncontrolled-freight-train-run-back-between-shap-and-tebay-cumbria (2010)
19. Smith, A.P.: Adequate Crewing and Seafarers' Fatigue: The International Perspective. Centre for Occupational and Health Psychology, Cardiff University (2007). http://www.itfseafarers.org/files/seealsodocs/3193/ITF%20FATIGUE%20REPORT%20final.pdf
20. Cameron, C.: A theory of fatigue. Ergonomics **16**(5), 633–648 (1973). https://doi.org/10.1080/00140137308924554

21. Smith, A.P., McNamara, R.L., Wellens, B.T.: Combined effects of occupational health hazards. HSE Books, Sudbury (2004)
22. Gates, A.J.: Variations in efficiency during the day, together with practise effects, sex differences, and correlations. University of California Press, Berkeley (1916)
23. Huxtable, Z.L., White, M.H., McCartor, M.A.: A re-performance and re-interpretation of the Arai experiment in mental fatigue with three subjects. Psychological Monographs **59**(5), 1 (1945)
24. Davies, D.R., Parasuraman, R.: The Psychology of Vigilance. Academic Press (1982)
25. Gilbertova, S., Glivicky, V.: Monotony at work. Studia Psychologica **9**(4), 232–240 (1967)
26. Bergum, B.O., Lehr, D.J.: Vigilance performance as a function of interpolated rest. J. Appl. Psychol. **46**(6), 425 (1962)
27. Parkes, K.R.: Sleep patterns, shiftwork, and individual differences: a comparison of onshore and offshore control-room operators. Ergonomics **37**(5), 827–844 (1994)
28. Wadsworth, E.J., Allen, P.H., Wellens, B.T., McNamara, R.L., Smith, A.P.: Patterns of fatigue among seafarers during a tour of duty. Am. J. Ind. Med. **49**(10), 836–844 (2006)
29. Wadsworth, E.J., Allen, P.H., McNamara, R.L., Smith, A.P.: Fatigue and health in a seafaring population. Occup. Med. **58**(3), 198–204 (2008)
30. Thomas, M., et al.: Neural basis of alertness and cognitive performance impairments during sleepiness. I. Effects of 24 h of sleep deprivation on waking human regional brain activity. J. Sleep Res. **9**(4), 335–352 (2000)
31. Dinges, D.F., et al.: Cumulative sleepiness, mood disturbance and psychomotor vigilance performance decrements during a week of sleep restricted to 4–5 hours per night. Sleep: J. Sleep Res. Sleep Med. **20**, 267–277 (1997)
32. Killgore, W.D., Balkin, T.J., Wesensten, N.J.: Impaired decision making following 49 hours of sleep deprivation. J. Sleep Res. **15**(1), 7–13 (2006)
33. May, J.F., Baldwin, C.L.: Driver fatigue: The importance of identifying causal factors of fatigue when considering detection and countermeasure technologies. Transp. Res. Part F: Traffic Psychol. Behav. **12**(3), 218–224 (2009)
34. Moos, R.H.: Psychosocial factors in the workplace. In: Fisher, S., Reason, J. (eds.) Handbook of Life Stress, pp. 193–209. Wiley, Chichester (1988)
35. Hockey, G.R.J., Wiethoff, M.: Assessing patterns of adjustment to the demands of work. In: Puglisi-Allegra, S., Oliverio, A. (eds.) The Psychobiology of Stress, pp. 231–240. Kluwer, Dordrecht (1990)
36. Frone, M.R., Tidwell, M.C.O.: The meaning and measurement of work fatigue: Development and evaluation of the Three-Dimensional Work Fatigue Inventory (3D-WFI). J. Occupational Health Psychol. **20**(3), 273 (2015)
37. Karasek Jr., R.A.: Job demands, job decision latitude, and mental strain: Implications for job redesign. Administrative Sci. Quarterly **24**(2), 285–308 (1979)
38. Marshall, N.L., Barnett, R.C., Sayer, A.: The changing workforce, job stress, and psychological distress. J. Occupational Health Psychol. **2**(2), 99 (1997)
39. Van Yperen, N.W., Snijders, T.A.: A multilevel analysis of the demands–control model: is stress at work determined by factors at the group level or the individual level? J. Occupational Health Psychol. **5**(1), 182 (2000)
40. Van Yperen, N.W., Hagedoorn, M.: Do high job demands increase intrinsic motivation or fatigue or both? The role of job control and job social support. Acad. Manage. J. **46**(3), 339–348 (2003)
41. Johnson, J.V., Hall, E.M.: Job strain, work place social support, and cardiovascular disease: a cross-sectional study of a random sample of the Swedish working population. Am. J. Public Health **78**(10), 1336–1342 (1988)
42. Karasek, R.A., Theorell, T.: Healthy Work: Stress, Productivity and the Reconstruction of Working Life. Basic Books, New York (1990)

43. Smith, L., Folkard, S., Tucker, P., Macdonald, I.: Work shift duration: a review comparing eight hour and 12 hour shift systems. Occup. Environ. Med. **55**(4), 217–229 (1998)
44. Folkard, S., Tucker, P.: Shift work, safety and productivity. Occup. Med. **53**(2), 95–101 (2003)
45. Duchon, J.C., Keran, C.M., Smith, T.J.: Extended workdays in an underground mine: a work performance analysis. Human Factors: J. Human Factors Ergon. Soc. **36**(2), 258–268 (1994)
46. Ferguson, S.A., Lamond, N., Kandelaars, K., Jay, S.M., Dawson, D.: The impact of short, irregular sleep opportunities at sea on the alertness of marine pilots working extended hours. Chronobiol. Int. **25**(2–3), 399–411 (2008)
47. Akerstedt, T.: Sleepiness at work: Effects of irregular work hours. In: Monk, T. (ed.) Sleep, Sleepiness and Performance, pp. 129–152. Wiley, Oxford (1991)
48. Kjellberg, A.: Sleep deprivation and some aspects of performance. Wak. Sleep. **1**(2), 139–143 (1977)
49. Folkard, S., Lombardi, D.A., Tucker, P.T.: Shiftwork: safety, sleepiness and sleep. Ind. Health **43**(1), 20–23 (2005)
50. Parkes, K.R.: Personality and coping as moderators of work stress processes: models, methods and measures. Work Stress **8**(2), 110–129 (1994)
51. Cox, T., Ferguson, E.: Individual Differences, Stress and Coping. Wiley, Hoboken (1991)
52. Laaksonen, M., Piha, K., Martikainen, P., Rahkonen, O., Lahelma, E.: Health-related behaviours and sickness absence from work. Occup. Environ. Med. **66**(12), 840–847 (2009)
53. Dawson, D., Reid, K.: Fatigue, alcohol and performance impairment. Nature **388**(6639), 235 (1997)
54. Wiese, J.G., Shlipak, M.G., Browner, W.S.: The alcohol hangover. Ann. Internal Med. **132**, 897–902 (2000)
55. Yamazaki, S., Fukuhara, S., Suzukamo, Y., Morita, S., Okamura, T., Tanaka, T., Ueshima, H.: Lifestyle and work predictors of fatigue in Japanese manufacturing workers. Occup. Med. **57**(4), 262–269 (2007)
56. Arendt, J.: Shift work: coping with the biological clock. Occupational Med. **60**(1), 10–20 (2010)
57. Mark, G.M., Smith, A.P.: Stress models: A review and suggested new direction. In: Houdmont, J., Leka, S. (eds.) Occupational Health Psychology: European Perspectives on Research, Education and Practice, pp. 111–144. Nottingham University Press, Nottingham (2008)
58. Archer, S.N., Robilliard, D.L., Skene, D.J., Smits, M., Williams, A., Arendt, J., von Schantz, M.: A length polymorphism in the circadian clock gene Per3 is linked to delayed sleep phase syndrome and extreme diurnal preference. Sleep **26**(4), 413–415 (2003)
59. Von Schantz, M.: Phenotypic effects of genetic variability in human clock genes on circadian and sleep parameters. J. Genetics **87**(5), 513–519 (2008)
60. Landgraf, D., Shostak, A., Oster, H.: Clock genes and sleep. Pflügers Archiv-European J. Physiol. **463**(1), 3–14 (2012)
61. Van Dongen, H.P., Belenky, G.: Individual differences in vulnerability to sleep loss in the work environment. Ind. Health **47**(5), 518–526 (2009)
62. Lal, S.K., Craig, A.: A critical review of the psychophysiology of driver fatigue. Biol. Psychol. **55**(3), 173–194 (2001)
63. British Office of Rail Regulation,: Managing Rail Staff Fatigue (2012). http://orr.gov.uk/__ data/assets/pdf_file/0005/2867/managing_rail_fatigue.pdf
64. Fan, J., Smith, A.P.: Mental workload and other causes of different types of fatigue in rail staff. In: Longo, L., Leva, M. (eds.) Human Mental Workload: Models and Applications. Communications in Computer and Information Science, vol. 1012, pp. 147–159. Springer, Cham (2019)
65. Darwent, D., Dawson, D., Paterson, J.L., Roach, G.D., Ferguson, S.A.: Managing fatigue: it really is about sleep. Accident Anal. Prevention **82**, 20–26 (2015). https://doi.org/10.1016/j. aap.2015.05.009

66. Prakash, S., Khapre, P., Laha, S.K., Saran, N.: Study to assess the level of stress and identification of significant stressors among the railway engine pilots. Indian J. Occup. Environ. Med. **15**, 113–119 (2011). https://doi.org/10.4103/0019-5278.93201

67. Härmä, M., Kavousi, A., Zaheri, S., Hamadani, A., Mirkazemi, R.: Assessment of the noise annoyance among subway train conductors in Tehran. Iran. Noise and Health. **16**, 177–182 (2014). https://doi.org/10.4103/1463-1741.134918

68. Smith, A.P., Smith, H.N.: Workload, fatigue and performance in the rail industry. In: Longo, L., Leva, M.C. (eds.) H-WORKLOAD 2017. CCIS, vol. 726, pp. 251–263. Springer, Cham (2017). https://doi.org/10.1007/978-3-319-61061-0_17

69. Braun, V., Clarke, V.: Using thematic analysis in psychology. Qualitative Res. Psychol. **3**(2), 77–101 (2006)

70. Dorrian, J., Baulk, S.D., Dawson, D.: Work hours, workload, sleep and fatigue in Australian Rail Industry employees. Appl. Ergon. **42**, 202–209 (2011). https://doi.org/10.1016/j.apergo.2010.06.009

71. Young, M.S., Brookhuis, K.A., Wickens, C.D., Hancock, P.A.: State of science: mental workload in ergonomics. Ergonomics **58**, 1–17 (2015). https://doi.org/10.1080/00140139.2014.956151

72. Bal, E., Arslan, O., Tavacioglu, L.: Prioritization of the causal factors of fatigue in seafarers and measurement of fatigue with the application of the Lactate Test. Safety Sci. **72**, 46–54 (2015)

73. Cabonl, P., Lancelle, V., Mollard, R., Grau, J.Y., Blatter, C., Kaplan, M., et al.: Sleep, fatigue and hours of work of French train drivers. In: Wilson, J.R., Mills, A., Clarke, T., Rajan, J., Dadashi, N. (eds.) Rail Human Factors around the World, pp. 783–791. CRC Press, London (2012)

Author Index

Printed in the United States
By Bookmasters